Rurouni Kenshin

RESTORATION

Story and Art by
Nobuhiro Watsuki

2

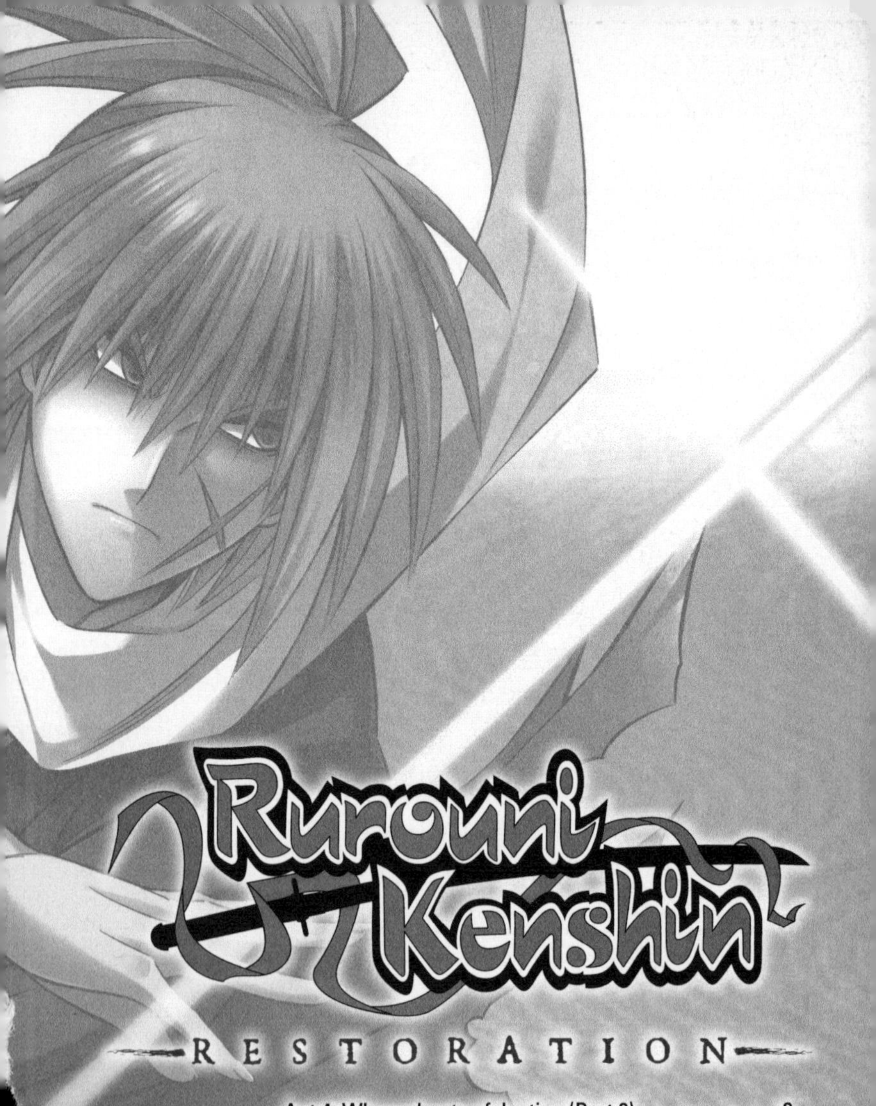
Rurouni Kenshin
RESTORATION

Calligraphy by Keita Amamiya.

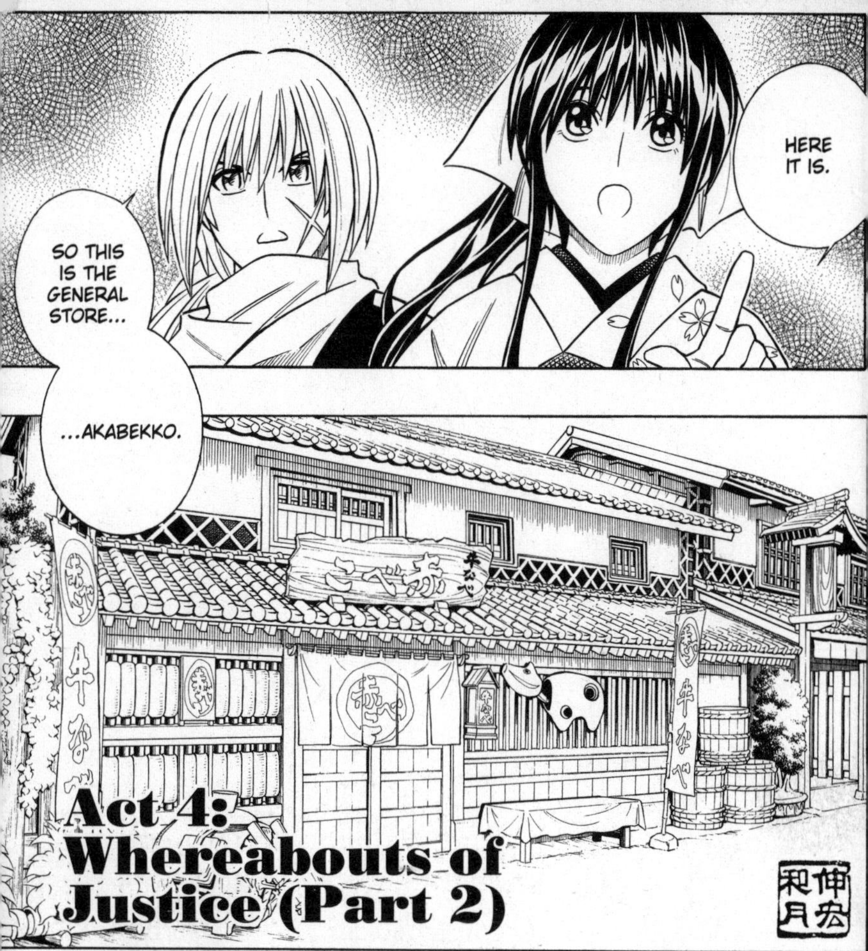
HERE IT IS.
SO THIS IS THE GENERAL STORE...
...AKABEKKO.
Act 4: Whereabouts of Justice (Part 2)

*SIGN: AKABEKO GYUNABE

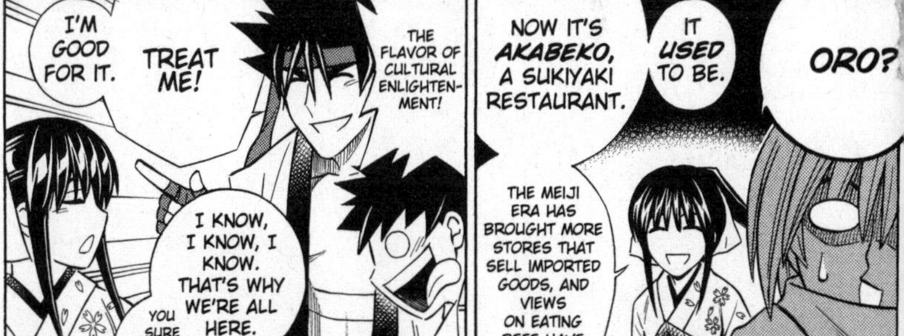
ORO?
IT USED TO BE.
NOW IT'S AKABEKO, A SUKIYAKI RESTAURANT.
THE MEIJI ERA HAS BROUGHT MORE STORES THAT SELL IMPORTED GOODS, AND VIEWS ON EATING BEEF HAVE CHANGED.
THE FLAVOR OF CULTURAL ENLIGHTENMENT!
TREAT ME!
I'M GOOD FOR IT.
I KNOW, I KNOW, I KNOW. THAT'S WHY WE'RE ALL HERE.
YOU SURE YOU'RE GOOD FOR IT?

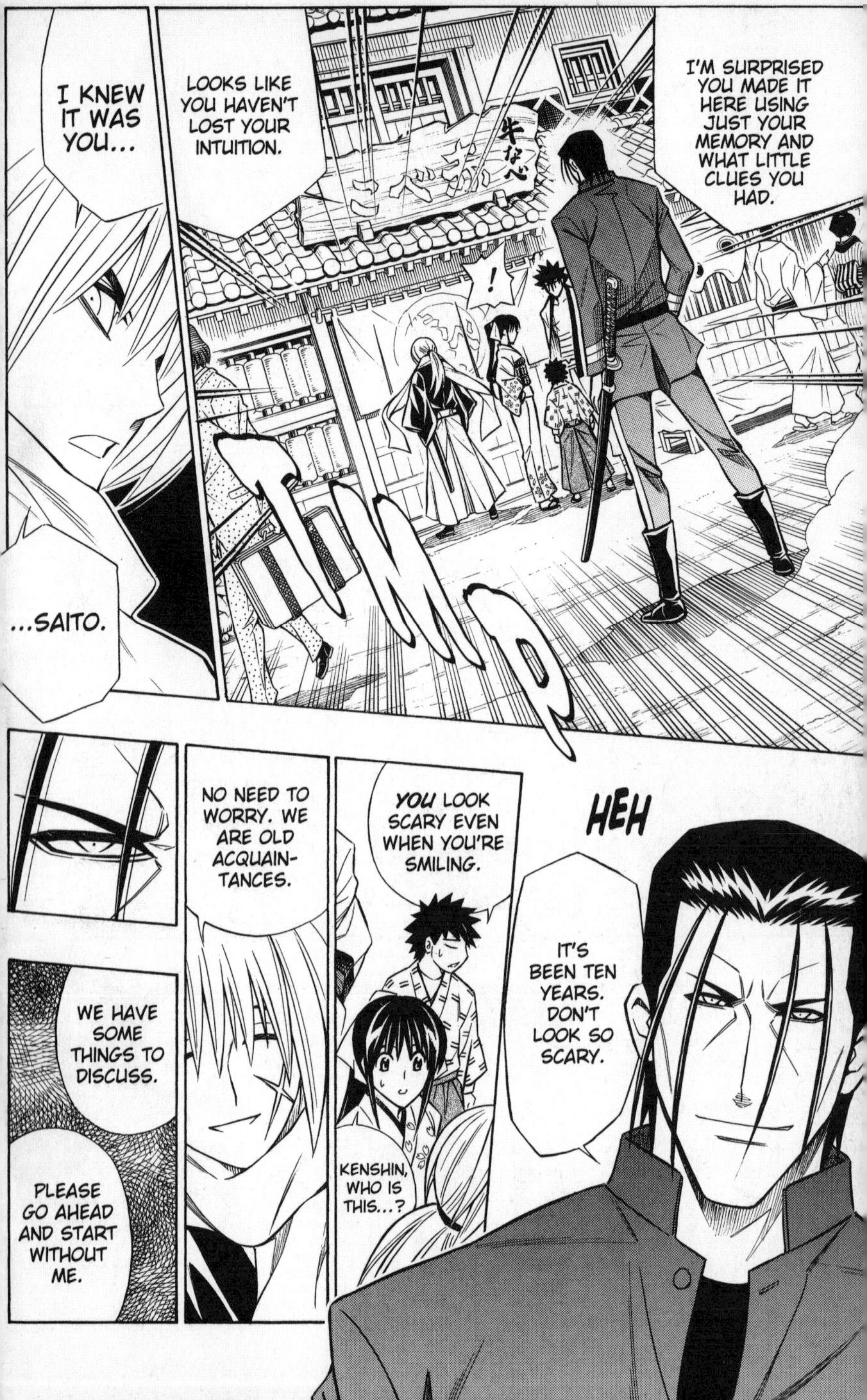
I'M SURPRISED YOU MADE IT HERE USING JUST YOUR MEMORY AND WHAT LITTLE CLUES YOU HAD.
牛なべ
LOOKS LIKE YOU HAVEN'T LOST YOUR INTUITION.
!
TMP
I KNEW IT WAS YOU...
...SAITO.
HEH
IT'S BEEN TEN YEARS. DON'T LOOK SO SCARY.
YOU LOOK SCARY EVEN WHEN YOU'RE SMILING.
KENSHIN, WHO IS THIS...?
NO NEED TO WORRY. WE ARE OLD ACQUAINTANCES.
WE HAVE SOME THINGS TO DISCUSS.
PLEASE GO AHEAD AND START WITHOUT ME.

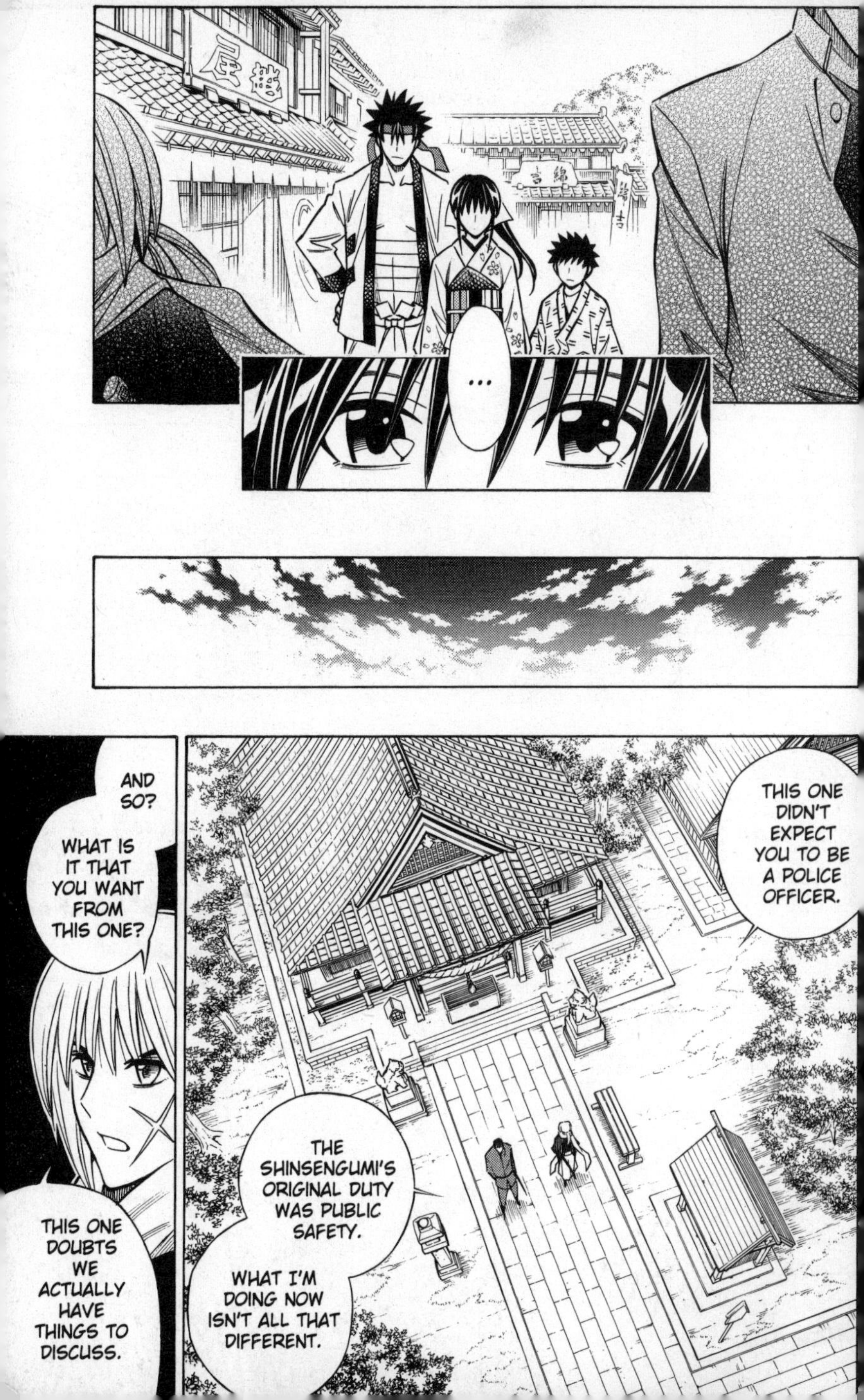
...
THIS ONE DIDN'T EXPECT YOU TO BE A POLICE OFFICER.
THE SHINSENGUMI'S ORIGINAL DUTY WAS PUBLIC SAFETY.
WHAT I'M DOING NOW ISN'T ALL THAT DIFFERENT.
AND SO?
WHAT IS IT THAT YOU WANT FROM THIS ONE?
THIS ONE DOUBTS WE ACTUALLY HAVE THINGS TO DISCUSS.

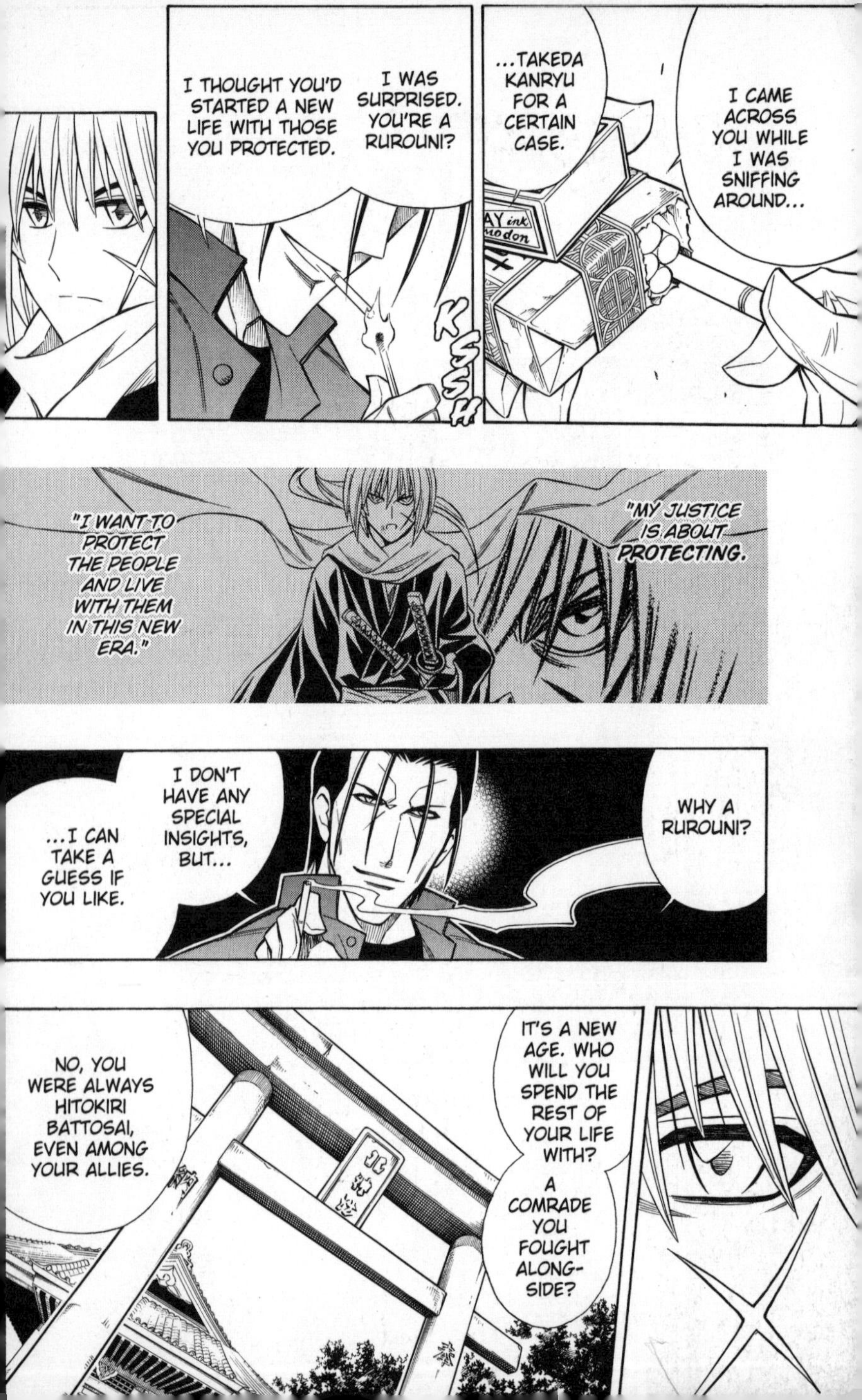
I CAME ACROSS YOU WHILE I WAS SNIFFING AROUND...
...TAKEDA KANRYU FOR A CERTAIN CASE.
KSSH
I WAS SURPRISED. YOU'RE A RUROUNI?
I THOUGHT YOU'D STARTED A NEW LIFE WITH THOSE YOU PROTECTED.
"MY JUSTICE IS ABOUT PROTECTING.
"I WANT TO PROTECT THE PEOPLE AND LIVE WITH THEM IN THIS NEW ERA."
WHY A RUROUNI?
I DON'T HAVE ANY SPECIAL INSIGHTS, BUT...
...I CAN TAKE A GUESS IF YOU LIKE.
IT'S A NEW AGE. WHO WILL YOU SPEND THE REST OF YOUR LIFE WITH?
A COMRADE YOU FOUGHT ALONG-SIDE?
NO, YOU WERE ALWAYS HITOKIRI BATTOSAI, EVEN AMONG YOUR ALLIES.

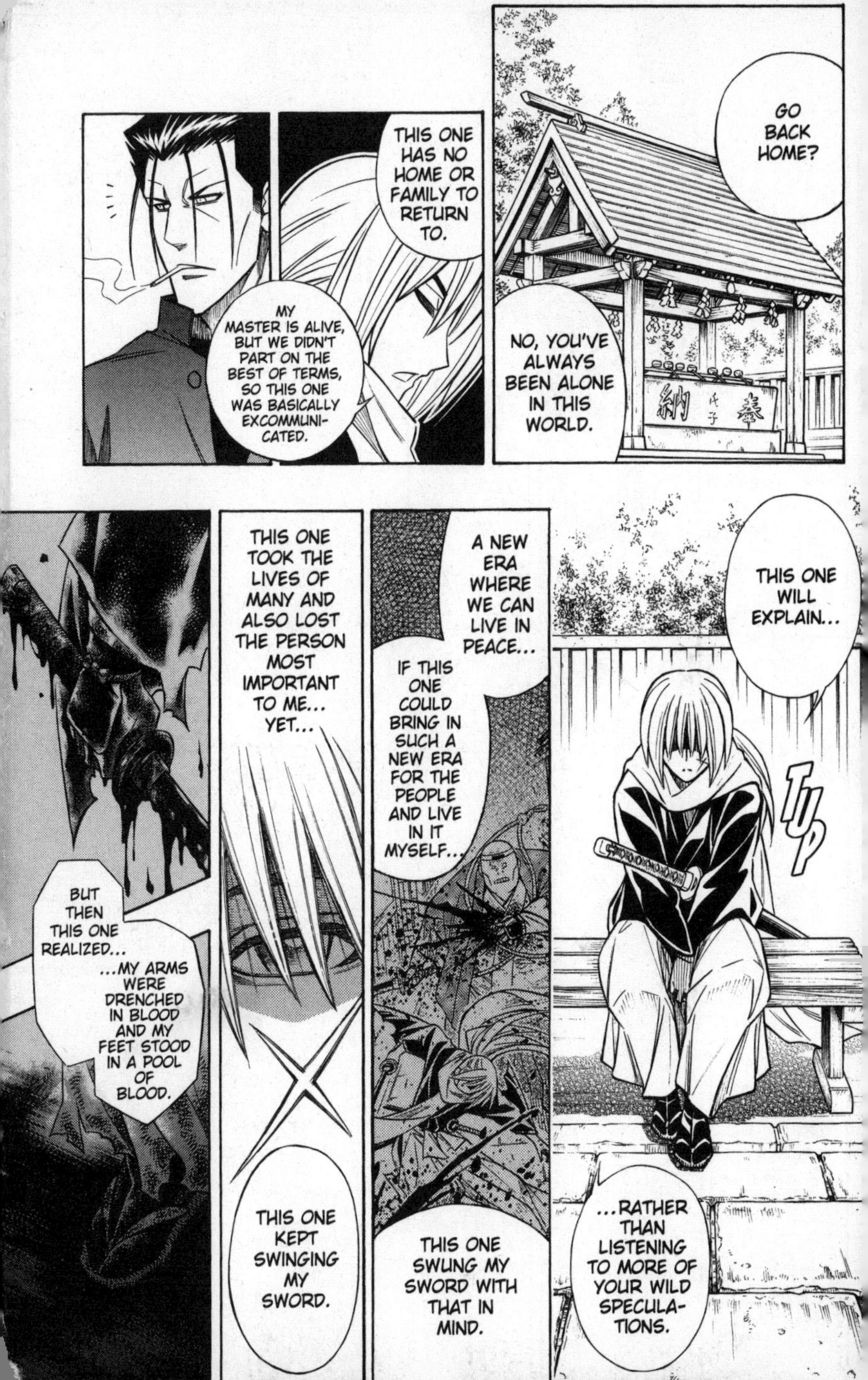
GO BACK HOME?
NO, YOU'VE ALWAYS BEEN ALONE IN THIS WORLD.
THIS ONE HAS NO HOME OR FAMILY TO RETURN TO.
MY MASTER IS ALIVE, BUT WE DIDN'T PART ON THE BEST OF TERMS, SO THIS ONE WAS BASICALLY EXCOMMUNICATED.
THIS ONE WILL EXPLAIN...
TUP
...RATHER THAN LISTENING TO MORE OF YOUR WILD SPECULATIONS.
A NEW ERA WHERE WE CAN LIVE IN PEACE...
IF THIS ONE COULD BRING IN SUCH A NEW ERA FOR THE PEOPLE AND LIVE IN IT MYSELF...
THIS ONE SWUNG MY SWORD WITH THAT IN MIND.
THIS ONE TOOK THE LIVES OF MANY AND ALSO LOST THE PERSON MOST IMPORTANT TO ME... YET...
THIS ONE KEPT SWINGING MY SWORD.
BUT THEN THIS ONE REALIZED...
...MY ARMS WERE DRENCHED IN BLOOD AND MY FEET STOOD IN A POOL OF BLOOD.

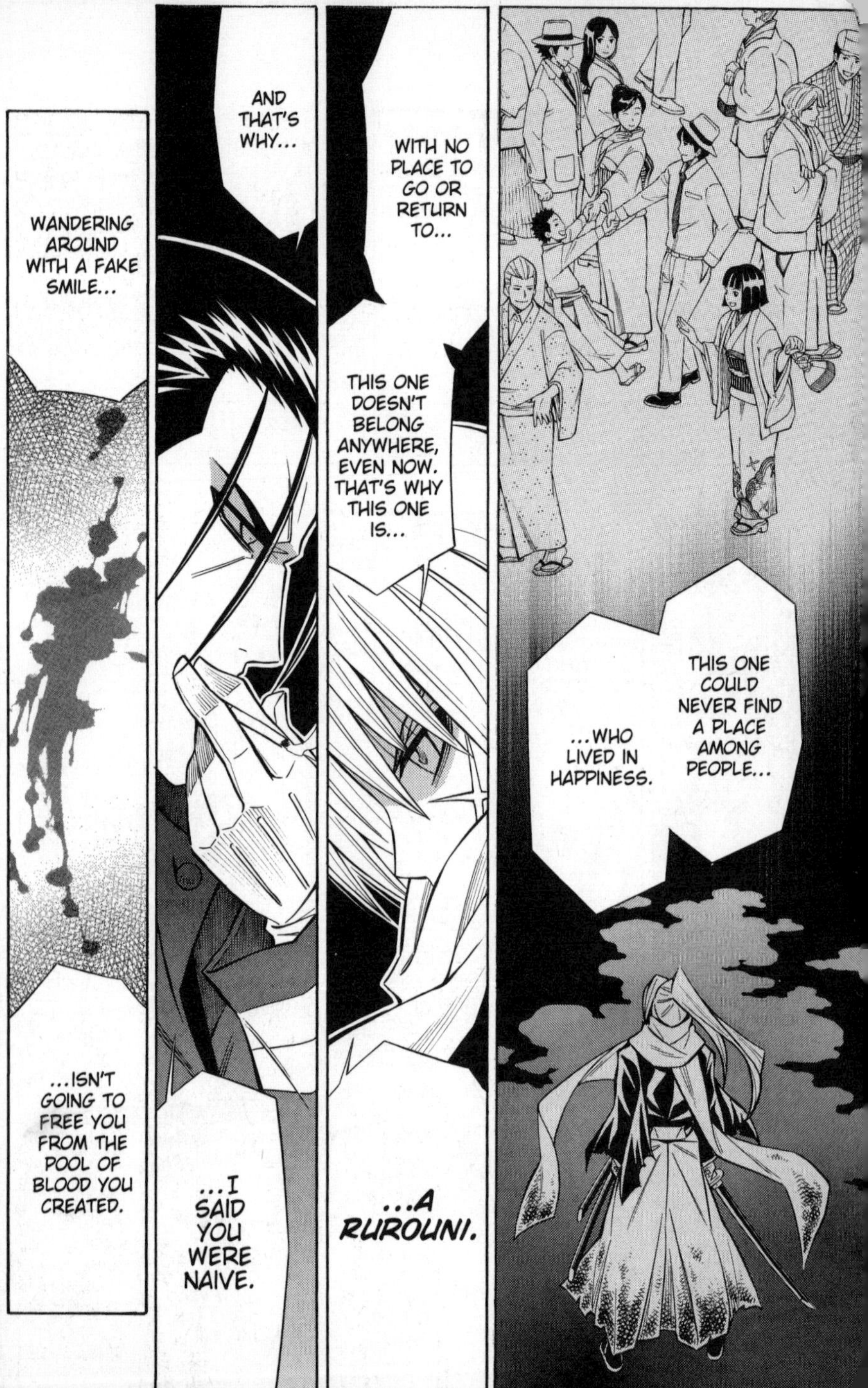
THIS ONE COULD NEVER FIND A PLACE AMONG PEOPLE...
...WHO LIVED IN HAPPINESS.
WITH NO PLACE TO GO OR RETURN TO...
THIS ONE DOESN'T BELONG ANYWHERE, EVEN NOW. THAT'S WHY THIS ONE IS...
...A RUROUNI.
AND THAT'S WHY...
...I SAID YOU WERE NAIVE.
WANDERING AROUND WITH A FAKE SMILE...
...ISN'T GOING TO FREE YOU FROM THE POOL OF BLOOD YOU CREATED.

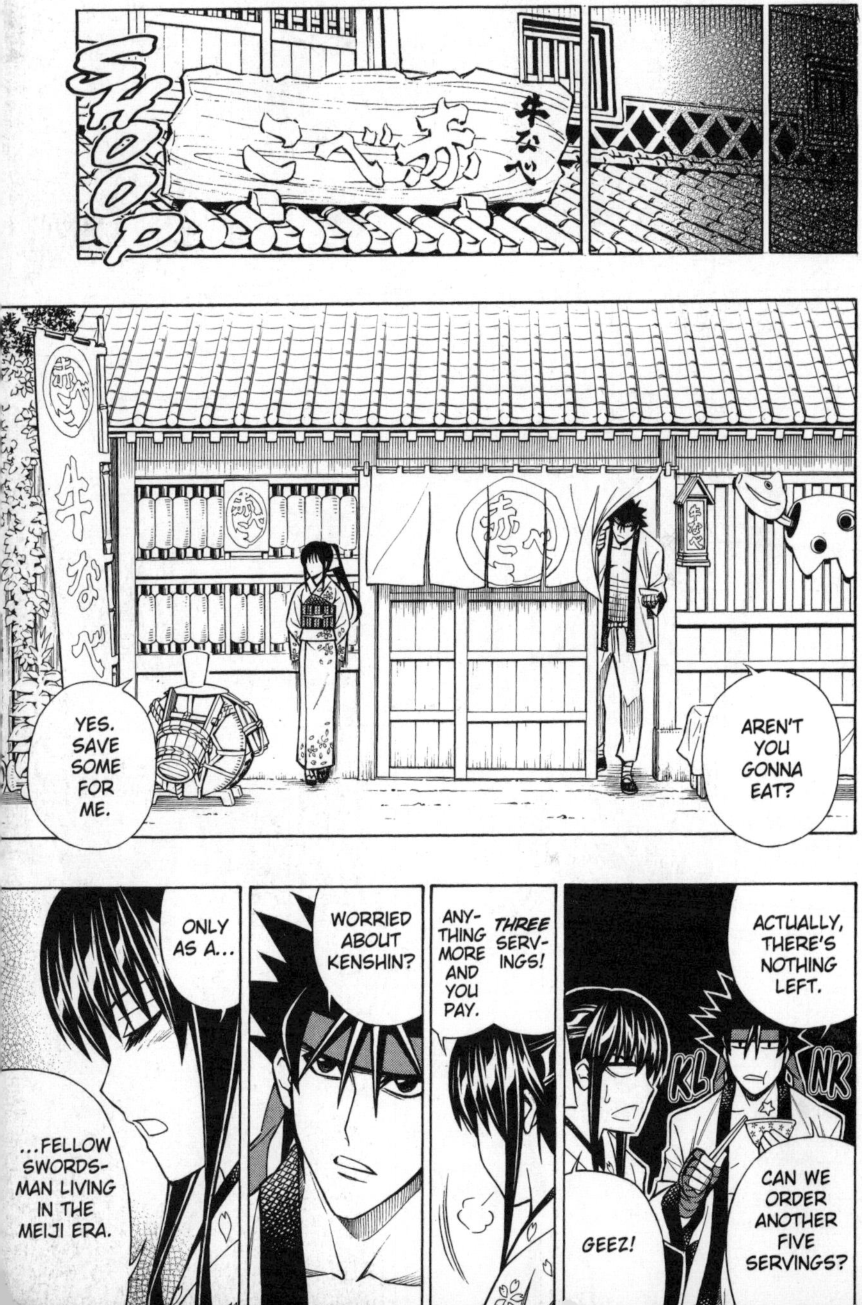

SHOOP
AREN'T YOU GONNA EAT?
YES. SAVE SOME FOR ME.
ACTUALLY, THERE'S NOTHING LEFT.
KLNK
CAN WE ORDER ANOTHER FIVE SERVINGS?
GEEZ!
THREE SERVINGS!
ANYTHING MORE AND YOU PAY.
WORRIED ABOUT KENSHIN?
ONLY AS A...
...FELLOW SWORDSMAN LIVING IN THE MEIJI ERA.

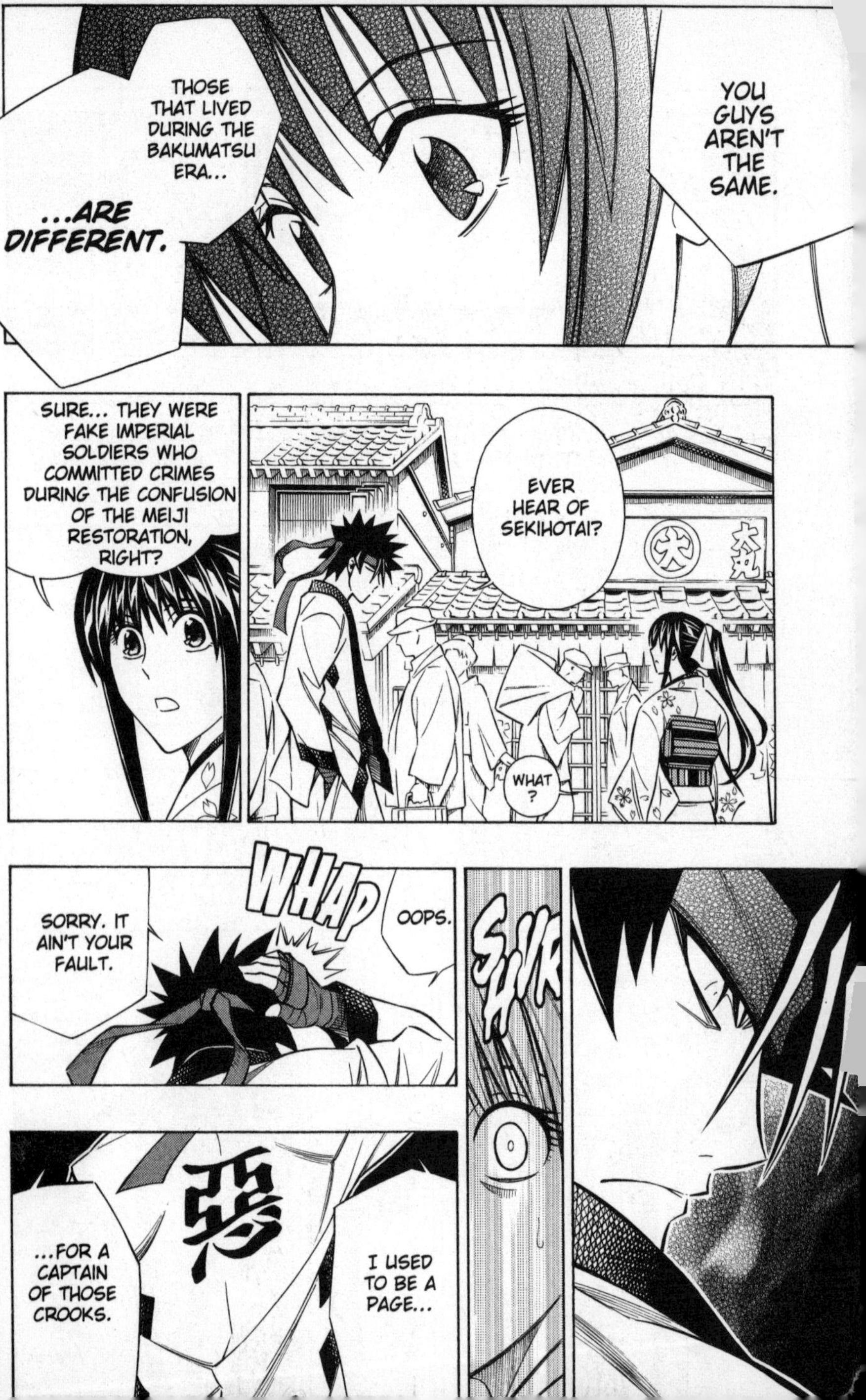
YOU GUYS AREN'T THE SAME.
THOSE THAT LIVED DURING THE BAKUMATSU ERA...
...ARE DIFFERENT.
EVER HEAR OF SEKIHOTAI?
WHAT?
SURE... THEY WERE FAKE IMPERIAL SOLDIERS WHO COMMITTED CRIMES DURING THE CONFUSION OF THE MEIJI RESTORATION, RIGHT?
SHIK
WHAP
OOPS.
SORRY. IT AIN'T YOUR FAULT.
I USED TO BE A PAGE...
...FOR A CAPTAIN OF THOSE CROOKS.

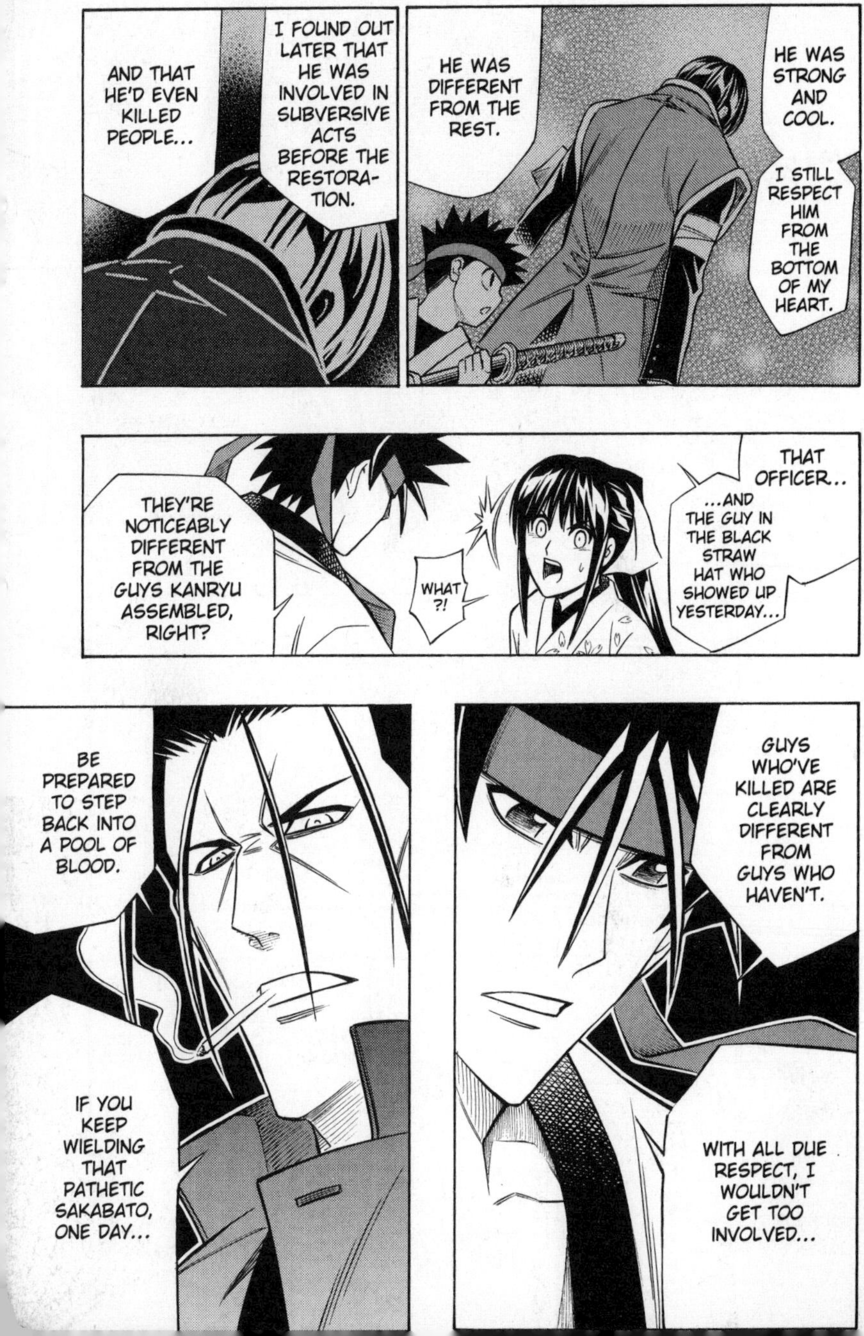
HE WAS STRONG AND COOL.
I STILL RESPECT HIM FROM THE BOTTOM OF MY HEART.
HE WAS DIFFERENT FROM THE REST.
I FOUND OUT LATER THAT HE WAS INVOLVED IN SUBVERSIVE ACTS BEFORE THE RESTORATION.
AND THAT HE'D EVEN KILLED PEOPLE...
THAT OFFICER...
...AND THE GUY IN THE BLACK STRAW HAT WHO SHOWED UP YESTERDAY...
WHAT?!
THEY'RE NOTICEABLY DIFFERENT FROM THE GUYS KANRYU ASSEMBLED, RIGHT?
GUYS WHO'VE KILLED ARE CLEARLY DIFFERENT FROM GUYS WHO HAVEN'T.
WITH ALL DUE RESPECT, I WOULDN'T GET TOO INVOLVED...
BE PREPARED TO STEP BACK INTO A POOL OF BLOOD.
IF YOU KEEP WIELDING THAT PATHETIC SAKABATO, ONE DAY...

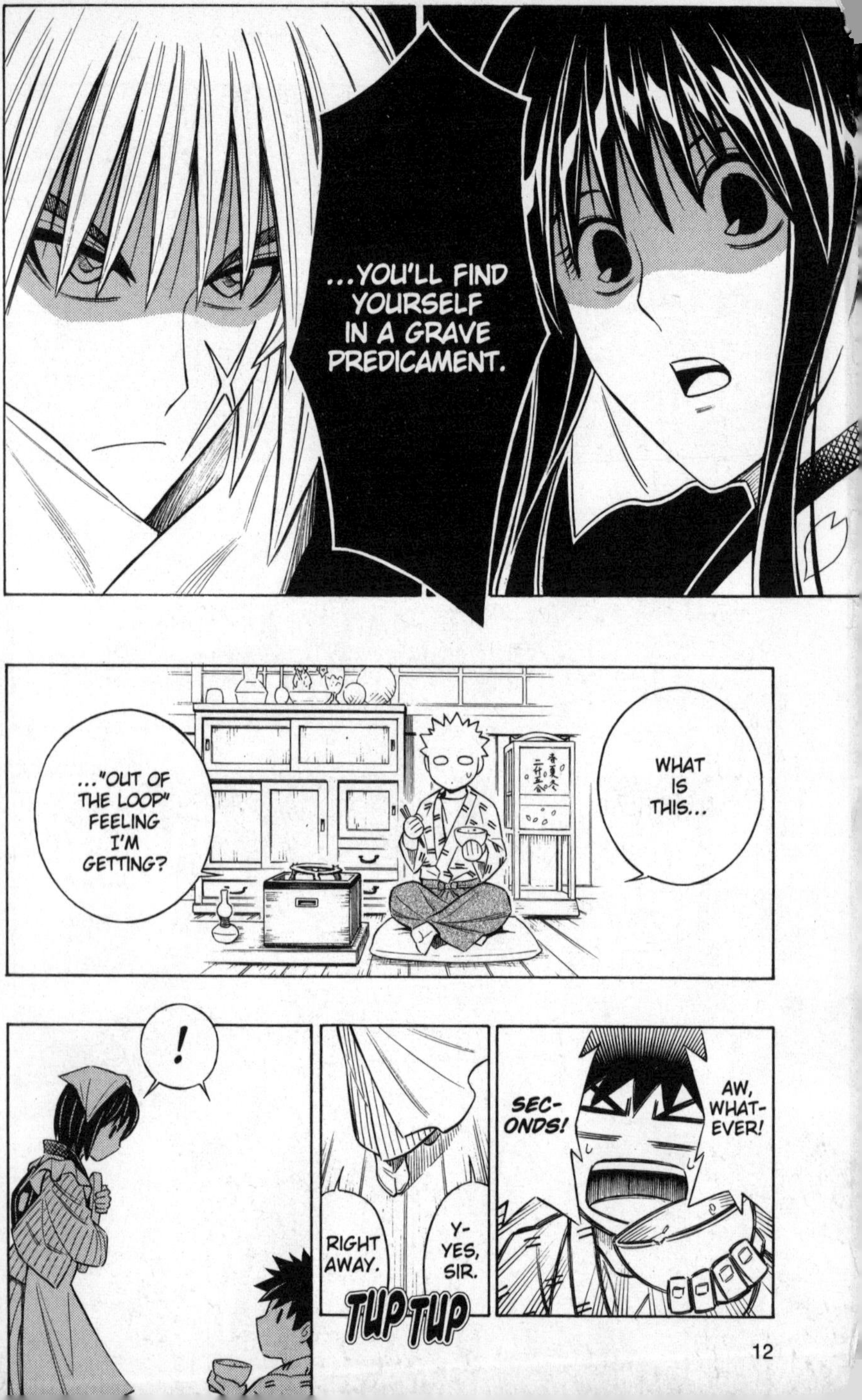
...YOU'LL FIND YOURSELF IN A GRAVE PREDICAMENT.
WHAT IS THIS...
..."OUT OF THE LOOP" FEELING I'M GETTING?
AW, WHAT-EVER!
SEC-ONDS!
Y- YES, SIR.
RIGHT AWAY.
TUP TUP
!

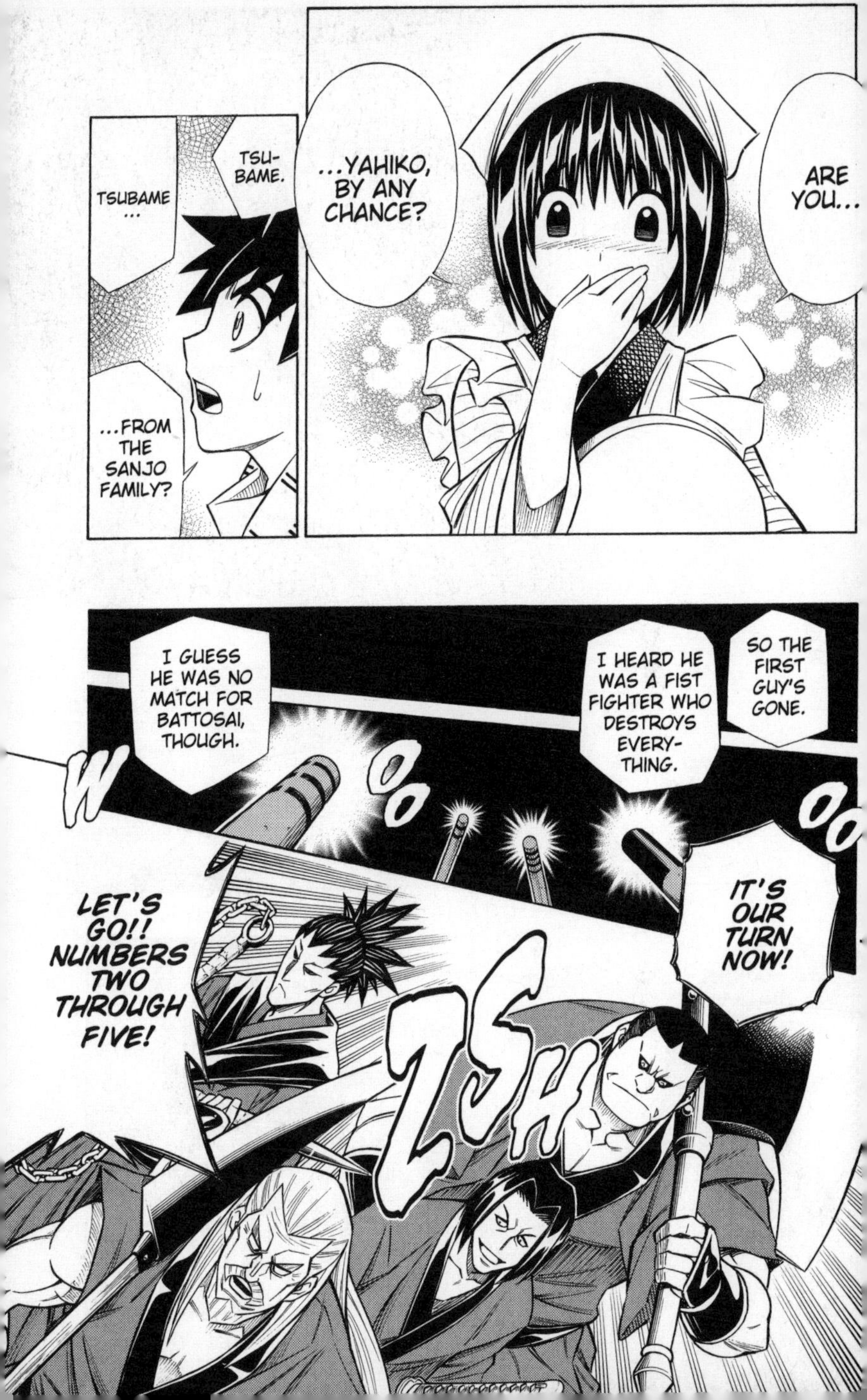
ARE YOU...
...YAHIKO, BY ANY CHANCE?
TSU-BAME.
TSUBAME ...
...FROM THE SANJO FAMILY?
SO THE FIRST GUY'S GONE.
I HEARD HE WAS A FIST FIGHTER WHO DESTROYS EVERY-THING.
I GUESS HE WAS NO MATCH FOR BATTOSAI, THOUGH.
WOOOO
IT'S OUR TURN NOW!
LET'S GO!! NUMBERS TWO THROUGH FIVE!
ZSH

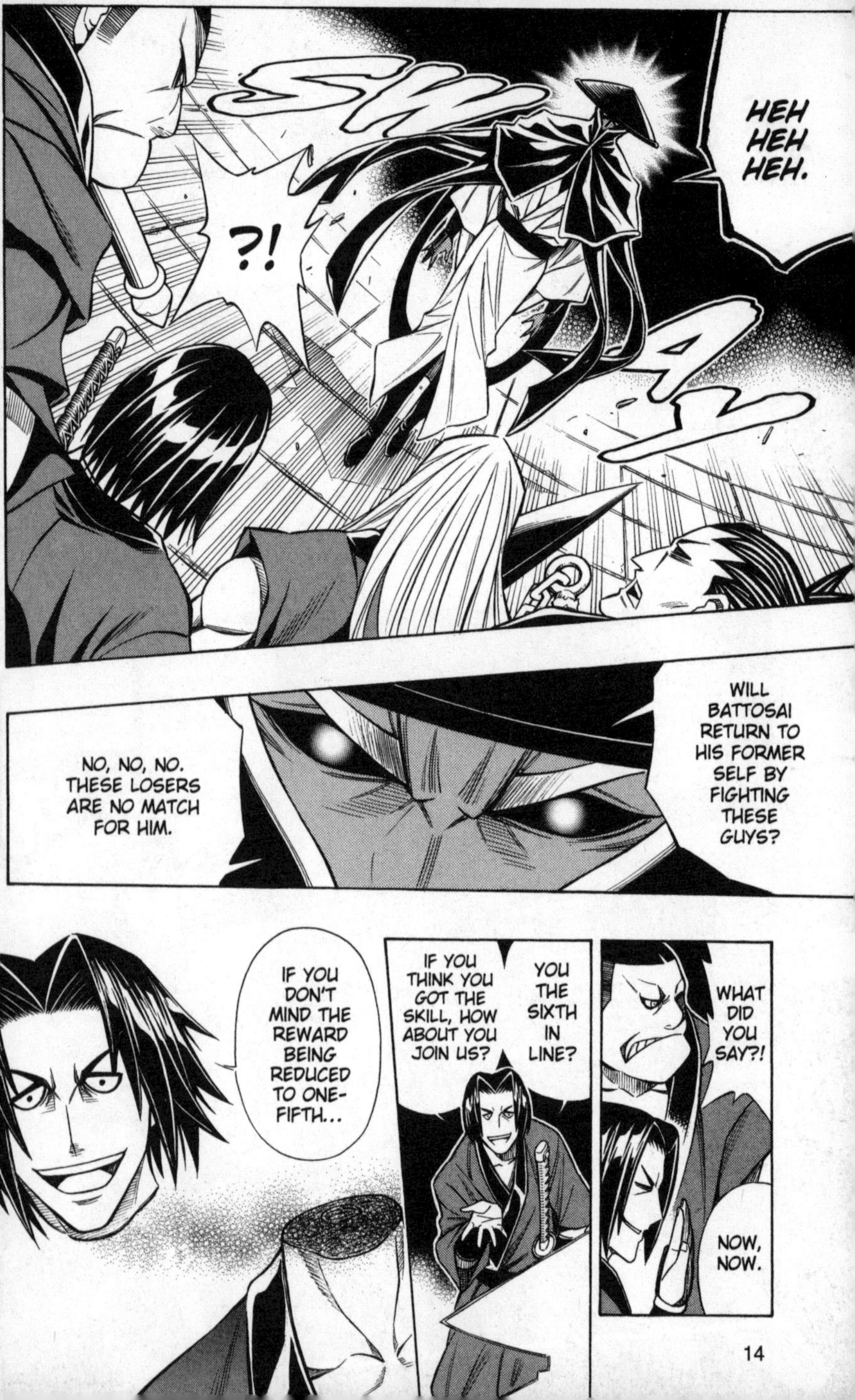
HEH HEH HEH.
?!
WILL BATTOSAI RETURN TO HIS FORMER SELF BY FIGHTING THESE GUYS?
NO, NO, NO. THESE LOSERS ARE NO MATCH FOR HIM.
WHAT DID YOU SAY?!
NOW, NOW.
YOU THE SIXTH IN LINE?
IF YOU THINK YOU GOT THE SKILL, HOW ABOUT YOU JOIN US?
IF YOU DON'T MIND THE REWARD BEING REDUCED TO ONE-FIFTH...

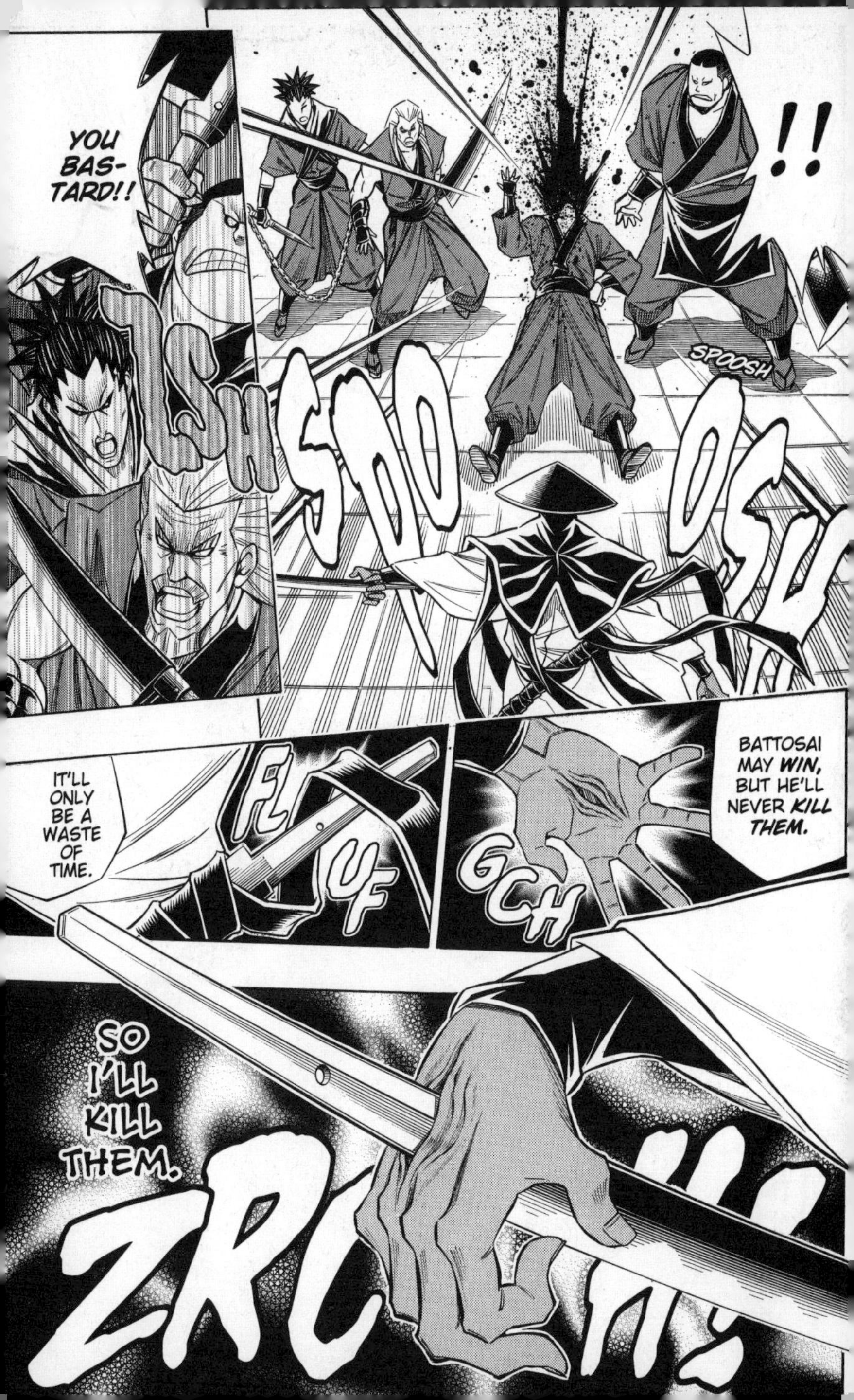
!!
SPOOSH
SDOOOSH
YOU BAS-TARD!!
TSCH
BATTOSAI MAY *WIN*, BUT HE'LL NEVER *KILL* *THEM.*
GCH
IT'LL ONLY BE A WASTE OF TIME.
FLUF
SO I'LL KILL THEM.
ZRC

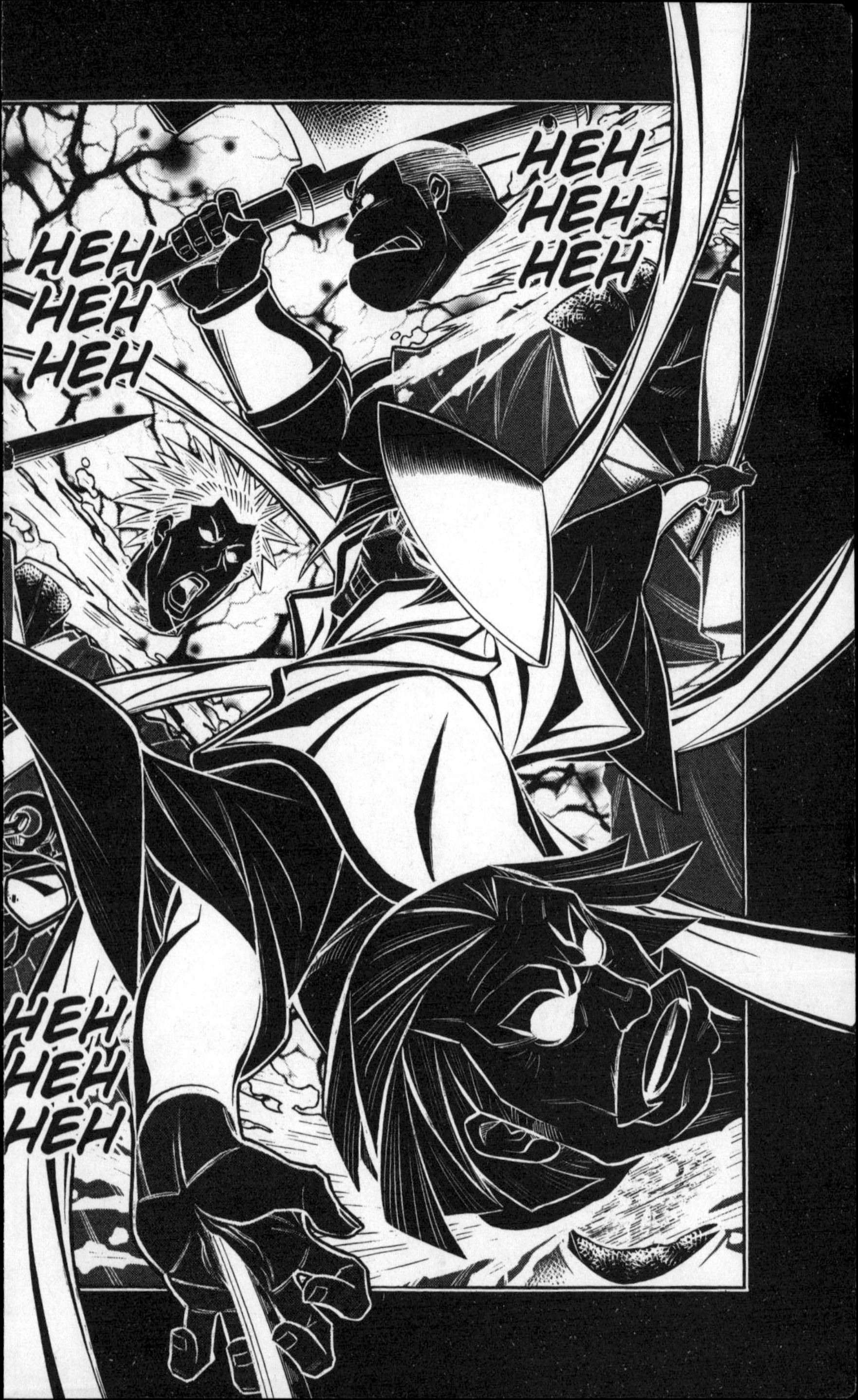
HEH HEH HEH
HEH HEH HEH
HEH HEH HEH

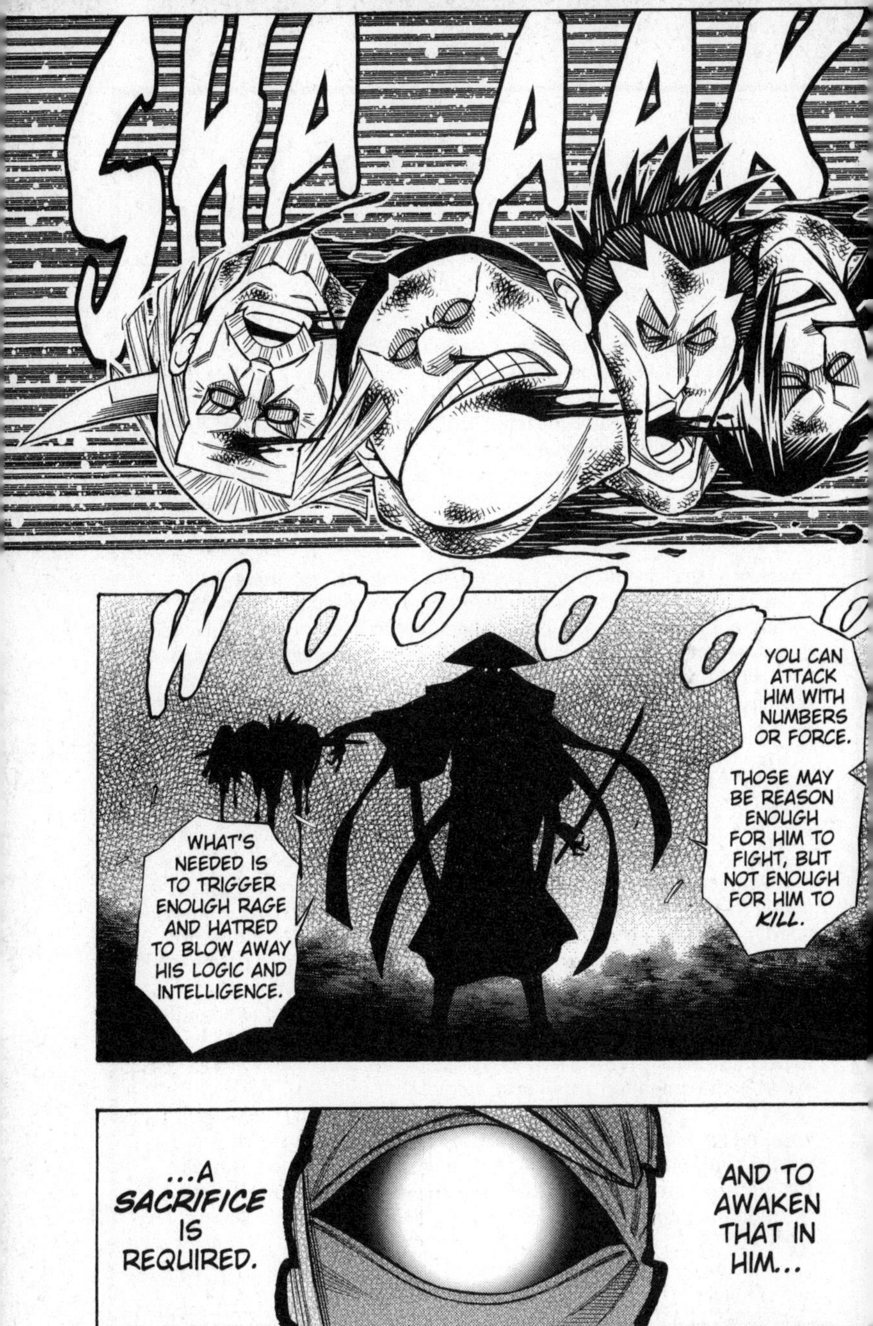
SHAAAK
WOOOOO
YOU CAN ATTACK HIM WITH NUMBERS OR FORCE.
THOSE MAY BE REASON ENOUGH FOR HIM TO FIGHT, BUT NOT ENOUGH FOR HIM TO KILL.
WHAT'S NEEDED IS TO TRIGGER ENOUGH RAGE AND HATRED TO BLOW AWAY HIS LOGIC AND INTELLIGENCE.
AND TO AWAKEN THAT IN HIM...
...A SACRIFICE IS REQUIRED.

FREE TALK 1

It's been a while. Watsuki here.

It's been almost a year since the first volume came out. The obvious difference in thickness between volume 1 and volume 2, as I wrote in another comment for this volume, is completely my fault. Nonetheless, this is the conclusion of *Rurouni Kenshin: Restoration*. Allow me to remind you that my comments here are merely a bonus. They have no bearing on the story, so to readers who feel they are unnecessary or are upset by them, please feel free to skip this section. Please.

Thankfully, the film *Rurouni Kenshin* has been well received. As I wrote in the first volume, a film belongs to the director. If I had to compare it to a family, it's like a child adopted by another family. So there's no need for Watsuki to be too worried. However, of course I can't say I have no attachment to it. Listening to people telling me they've watched it over and over on DVD and Blu-ray makes me feel glad that is has become a story loved by many.

One thing I felt vividly with the film adaptation is the difference in global recognition between comics and films. Watsuki is a hopeless manga artist who grew up reading manga and makes a living writing manga. In a world where the adult values are the standard, it seems that live-action films get greater recognition. Since my "manga fever" has always been too high, I didn't realize this. I knew it in my head, but I hadn't truly felt it. I was surprised to receive an offer to speak in my hometown. (Honestly, I don't like speaking in public, so I accepted the offer with the condition that it would be the only time. That may seem contradictory, but now I can freely turn down similar offers in the future. I purposely stepped in front of a bullet so I could then return back to my faraway base and barricade myself. It's a rather self-tormenting survival strategy.)

I am not saying film is better because of its higher degree of recognition. My biggest concern in adapting the story to film was letting down those who experienced the world of *Rurouni Kenshin* through the manga first.

Act 5: At Akabeko

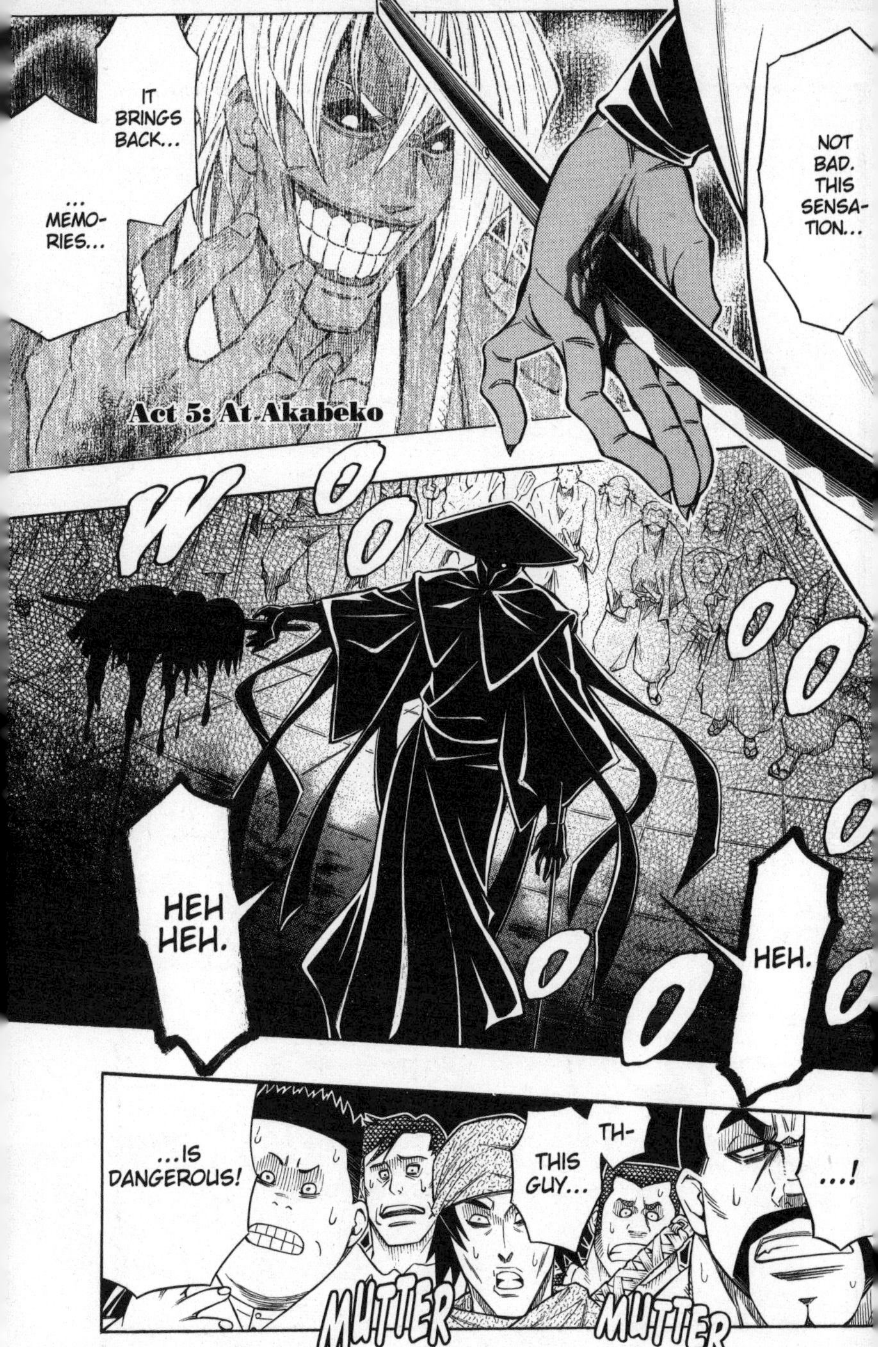
NOT BAD. THIS SENSATION...
IT BRINGS BACK...
...MEMORIES...
WOOOOOOOOOO
HEH.
HEH HEH.
...!
TH- THIS GUY...
...IS DANGEROUS!
MUTTER
MUTTER

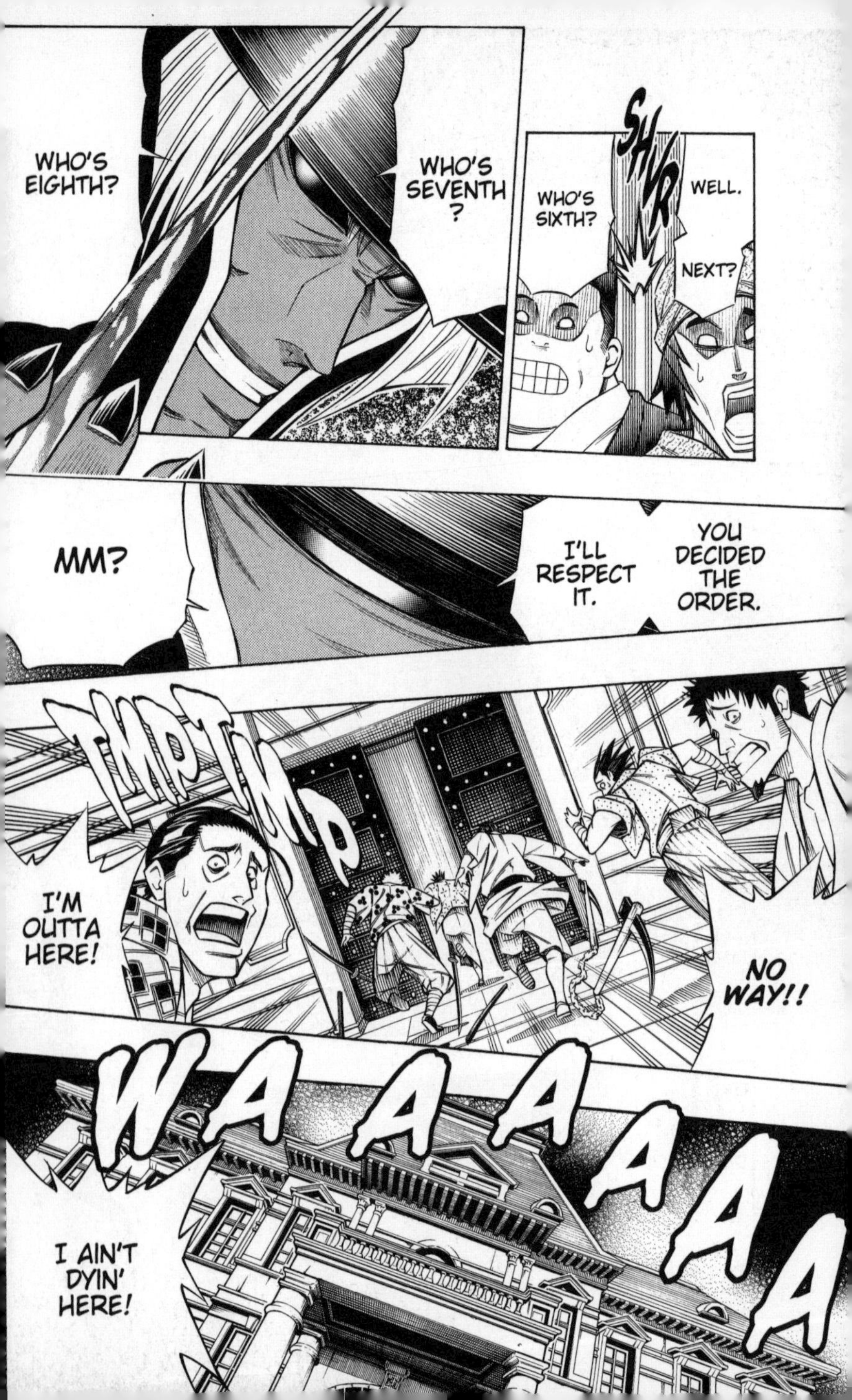
WELL.
SHVR
NEXT?
WHO'S SIXTH?
WHO'S SEVENTH?
WHO'S EIGHTH?
YOU DECIDED THE ORDER.
I'LL RESPECT IT.
MM?
TMP TMP
NO WAY!!
I'M OUTTA HERE!
WAAAAAAA
I AIN'T DYIN' HERE!

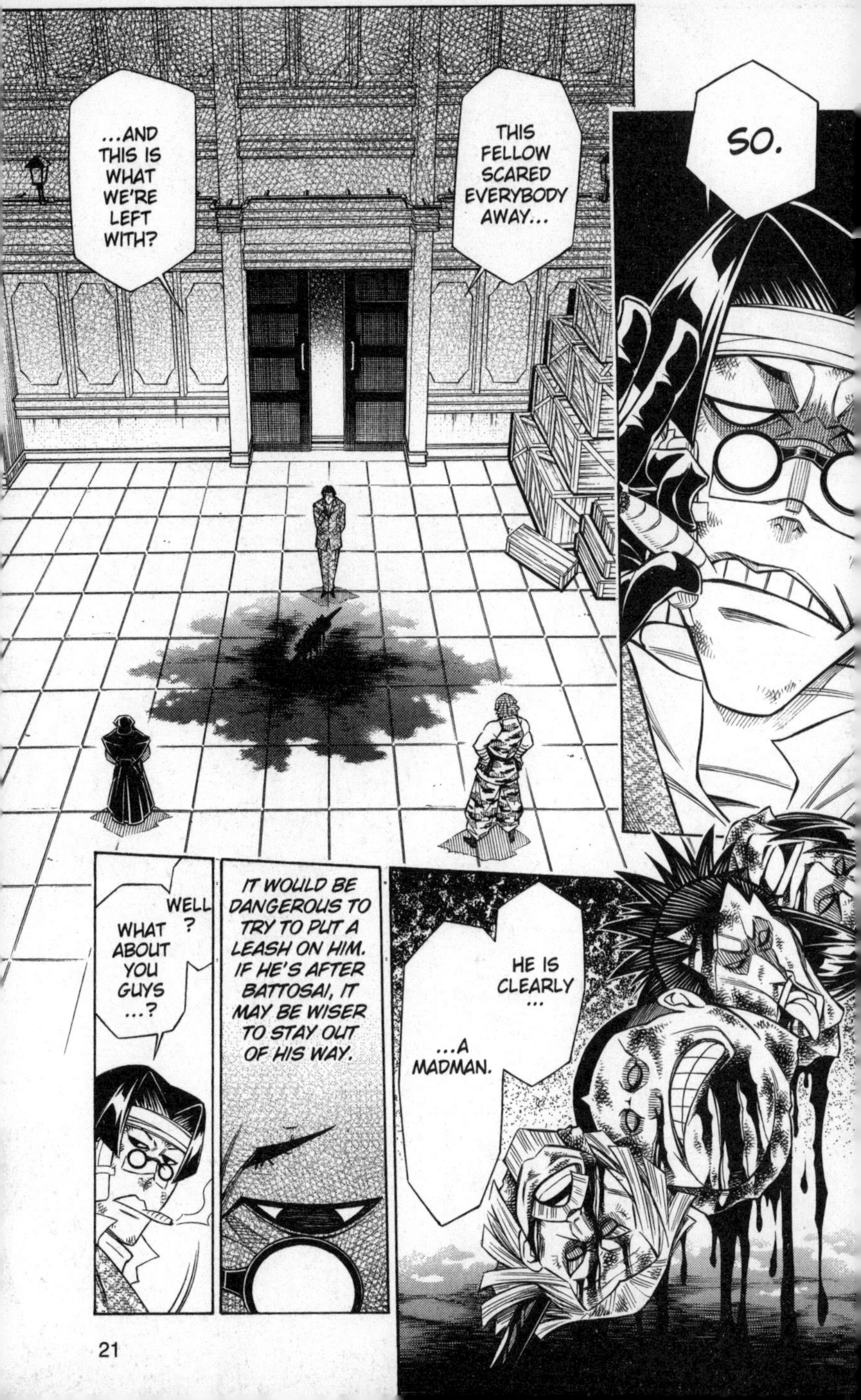
SO.
THIS FELLOW SCARED EVERYBODY AWAY...
...AND THIS IS WHAT WE'RE LEFT WITH?
HE IS CLEARLY ...
...A MADMAN.
IT WOULD BE DANGEROUS TO TRY TO PUT A LEASH ON HIM. IF HE'S AFTER BATTOSAI, IT MAY BE WISER TO STAY OUT OF HIS WAY.
WELL?
WHAT ABOUT YOU GUYS ...?

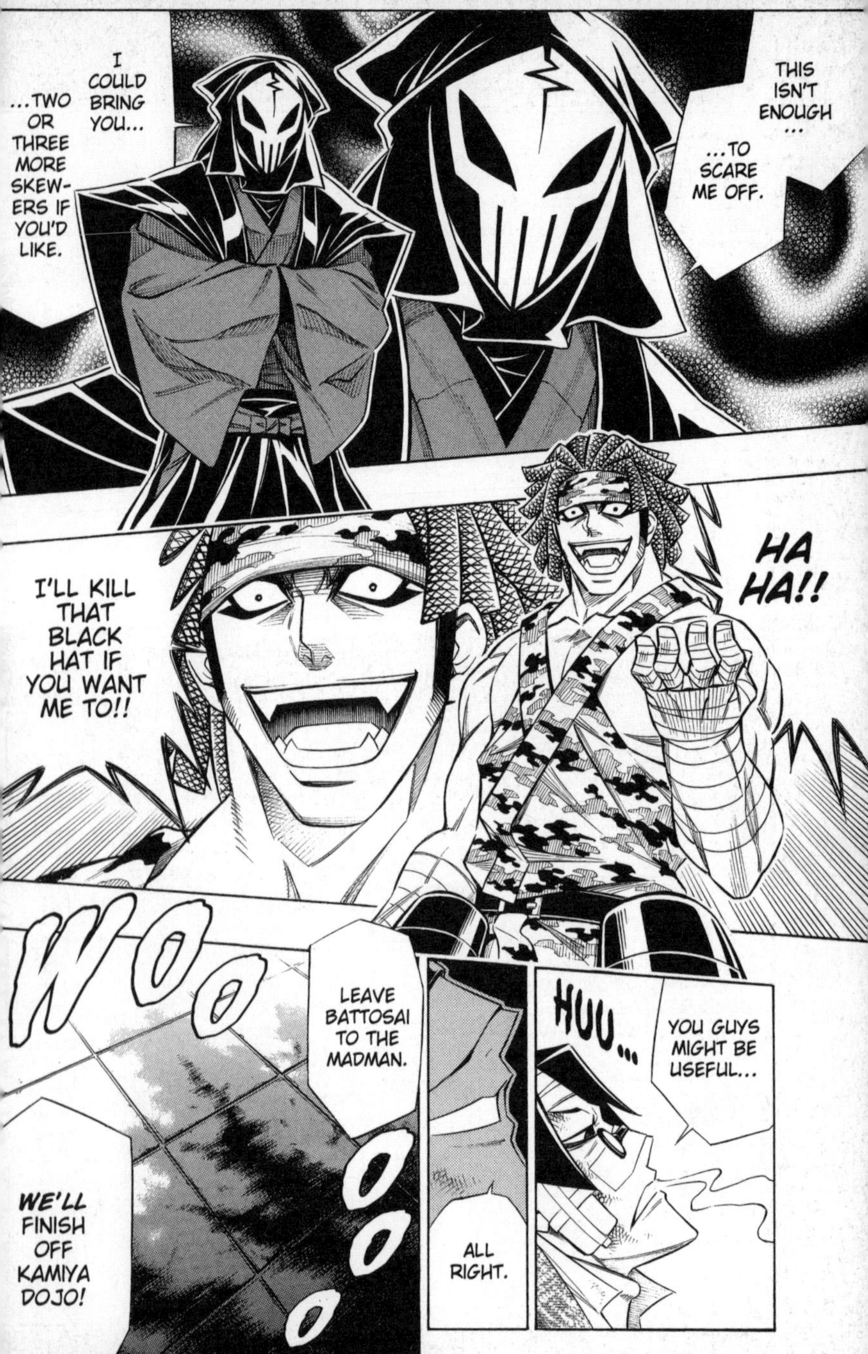
THIS ISN'T ENOUGH...
...TO SCARE ME OFF.
I COULD BRING YOU...
...TWO OR THREE MORE SKEWERS IF YOU'D LIKE.
HA HA!!
I'LL KILL THAT BLACK HAT IF YOU WANT ME TO!!
HUU...
YOU GUYS MIGHT BE USEFUL...
ALL RIGHT.
LEAVE BATTOSAI TO THE MADMAN.
WOOOOOOO
WE'LL FINISH OFF KAMIYA DOJO!

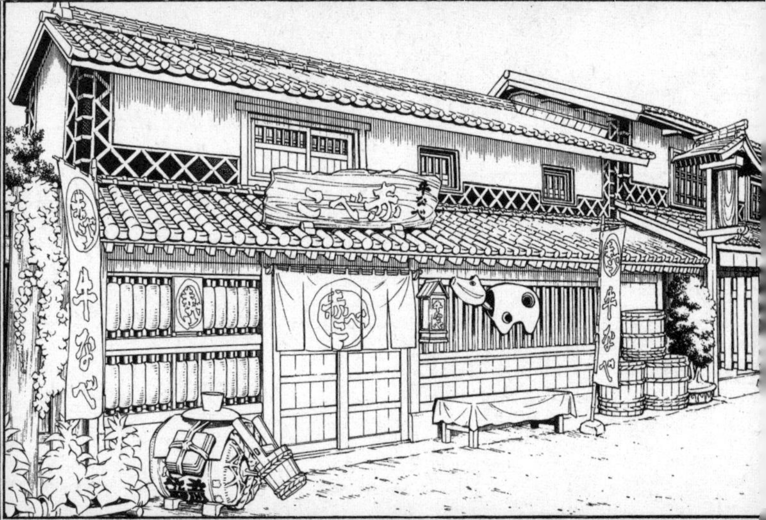
赤べこ
牛なべ
牛なべ

Act 5: At Akabeko

伸宏 和月

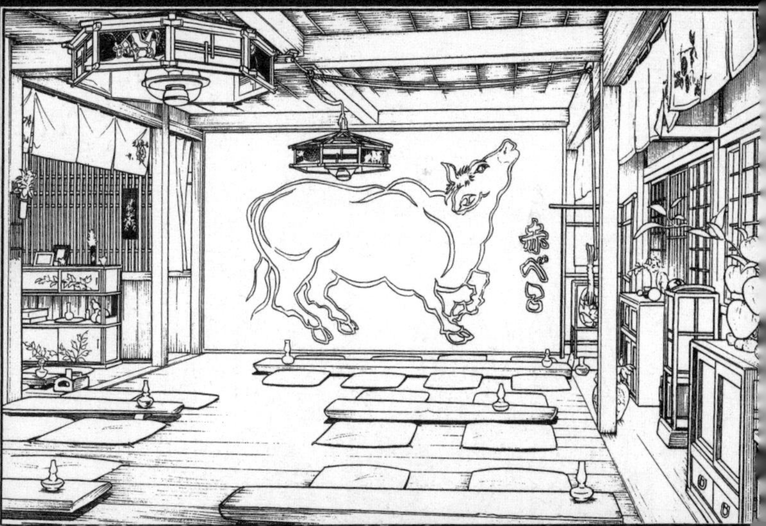
赤べこ

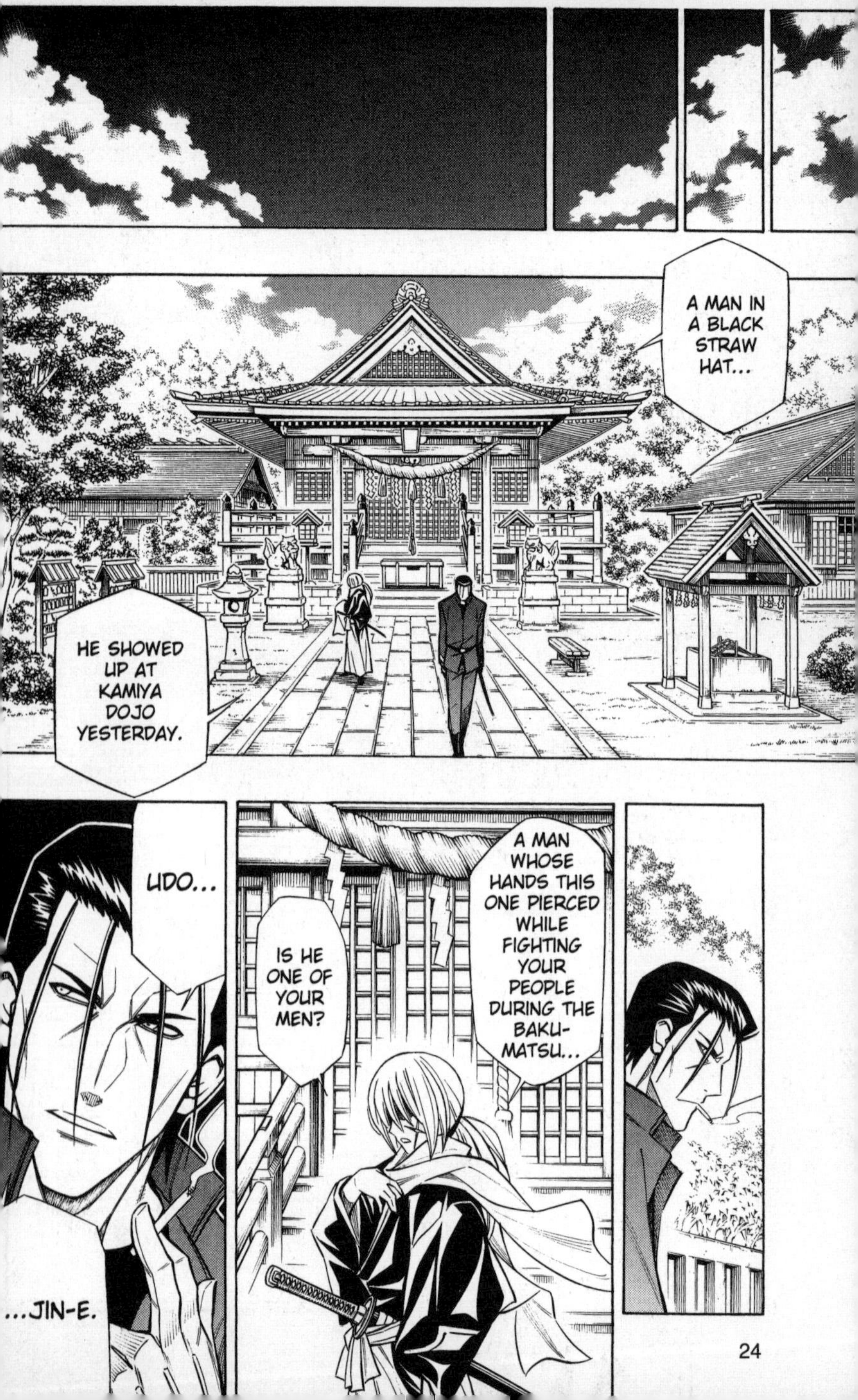
A MAN IN A BLACK STRAW HAT...
HE SHOWED UP AT KAMIYA DOJO YESTERDAY.
A MAN WHOSE HANDS THIS ONE PIERCED WHILE FIGHTING YOUR PEOPLE DURING THE BAKU-MATSU...
IS HE ONE OF YOUR MEN?
UDO...
...JIN-E.

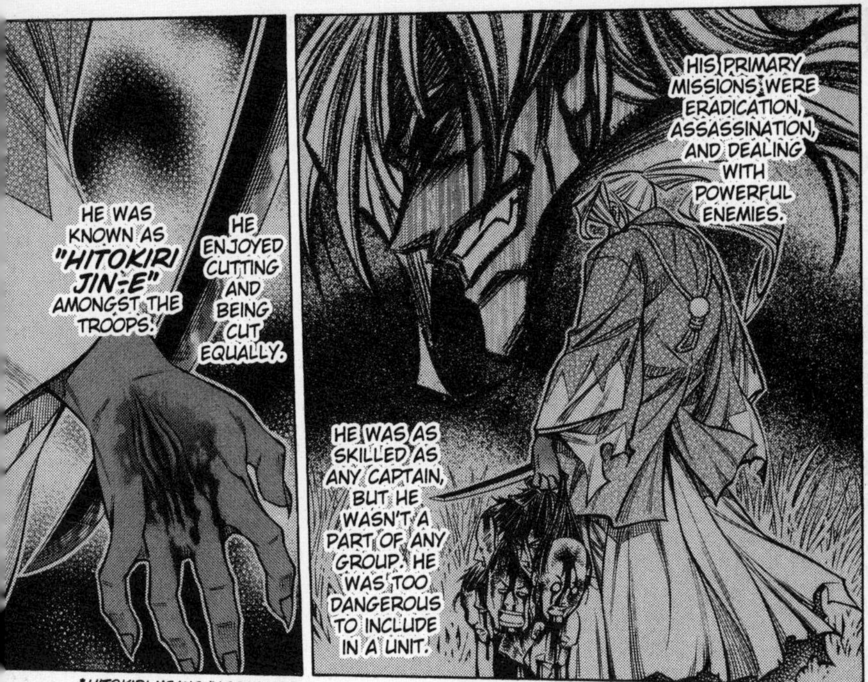
HIS PRIMARY MISSIONS WERE ERADICATION, ASSASSINATION, AND DEALING WITH POWERFUL ENEMIES.
HE WAS AS SKILLED AS ANY CAPTAIN, BUT HE WASN'T A PART OF ANY GROUP. HE WAS TOO DANGEROUS TO INCLUDE IN A UNIT.
HE ENJOYED CUTTING AND BEING CUT EQUALLY.
HE WAS KNOWN AS "HITOKIRI JIN-E" AMONGST THE TROOPS.

*HITOKIRI MEANS "ASSASSIN."

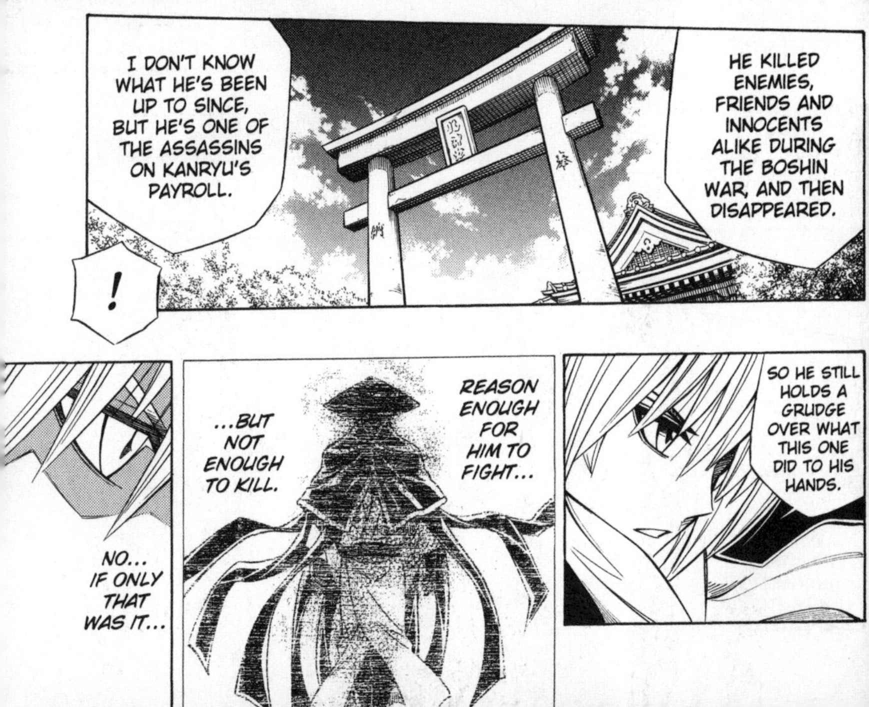
HE KILLED ENEMIES, FRIENDS AND INNOCENTS ALIKE DURING THE BOSHIN WAR, AND THEN DISAPPEARED.
I DON'T KNOW WHAT HE'S BEEN UP TO SINCE, BUT HE'S ONE OF THE ASSASSINS ON KANRYU'S PAYROLL.
!
SO HE STILL HOLDS A GRUDGE OVER WHAT THIS ONE DID TO HIS HANDS.
REASON ENOUGH FOR HIM TO FIGHT...
...BUT NOT ENOUGH TO KILL.
NO... IF ONLY THAT WAS IT...

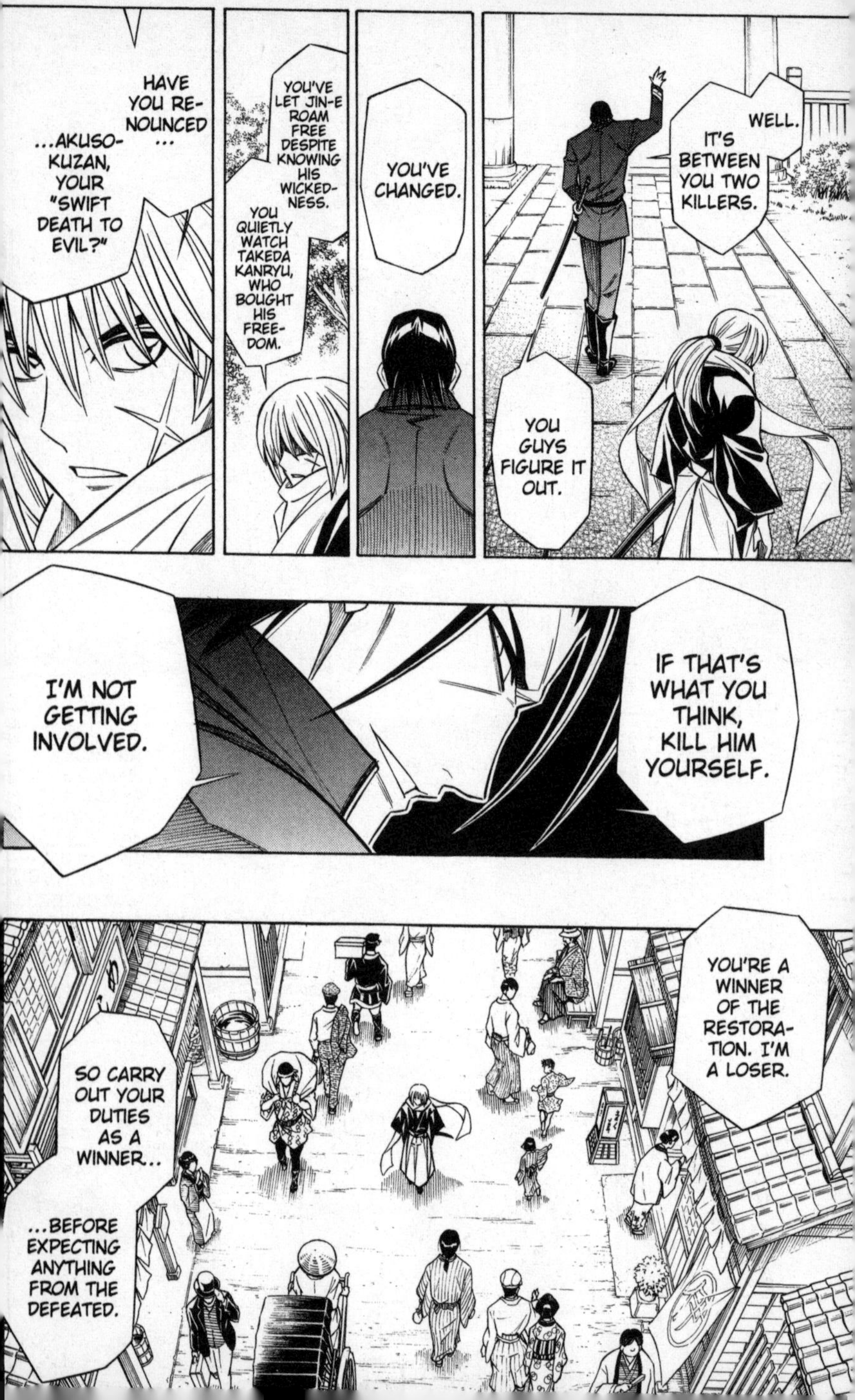
WELL. IT'S BETWEEN YOU TWO KILLERS.
YOU GUYS FIGURE IT OUT.
YOU'VE CHANGED.
YOU'VE LET JIN-E ROAM FREE DESPITE KNOWING HIS WICKED-NESS.
YOU QUIETLY WATCH TAKEDA KANRYU, WHO BOUGHT HIS FREE-DOM.
HAVE YOU RE-NOUNCED...
...AKUSO-KUZAN, YOUR "SWIFT DEATH TO EVIL?"
IF THAT'S WHAT YOU THINK, KILL HIM YOURSELF.
I'M NOT GETTING INVOLVED.
YOU'RE A WINNER OF THE RESTORA-TION. I'M A LOSER.
SO CARRY OUT YOUR DUTIES AS A WINNER...
...BEFORE EXPECTING ANYTHING FROM THE DEFEATED.

CHTIR

CHTIR

CHTIR CHTIR

CHTIR

CHTIR

KENSHIN! OVER HERE!

BOW

ORO?

WELCOME.

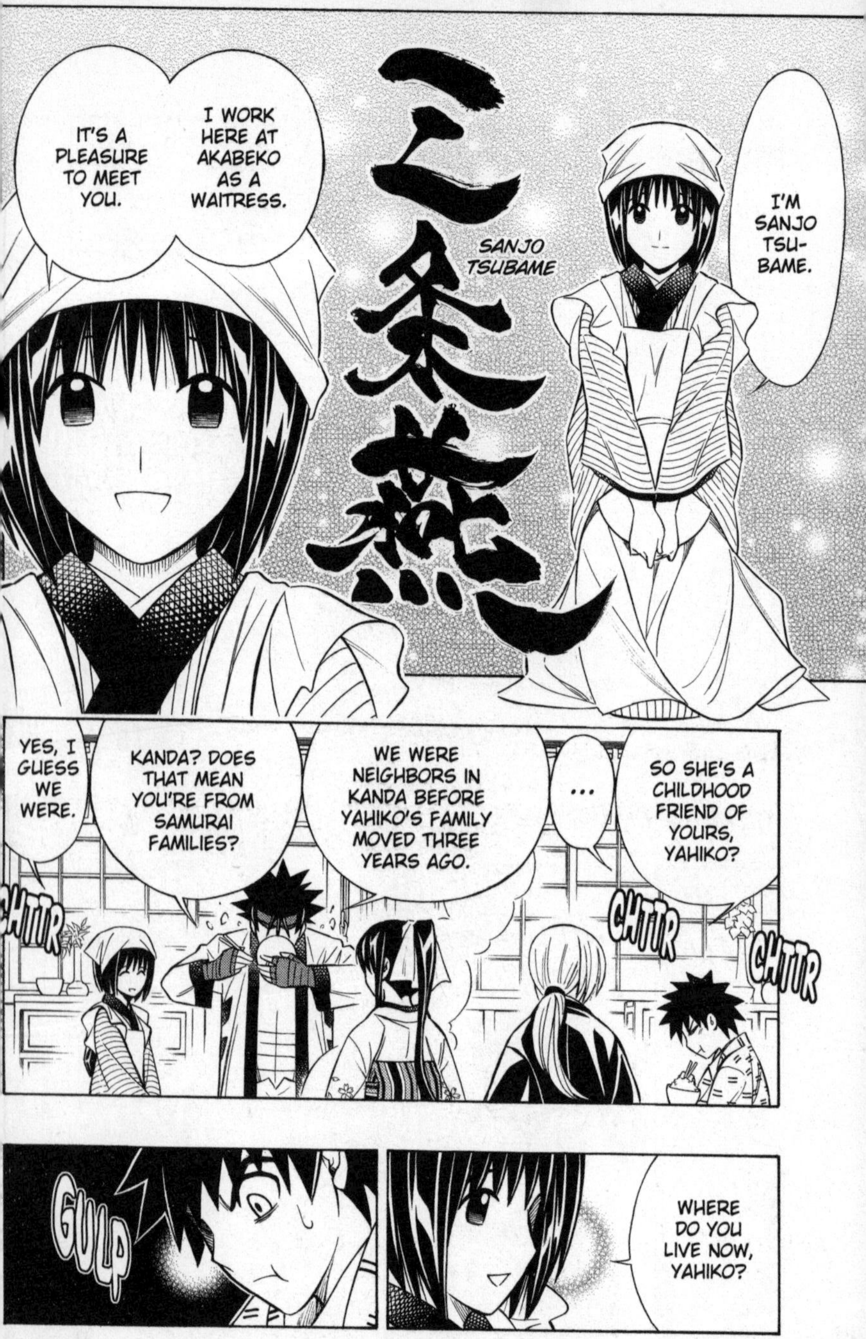
I'M SANJO TSU- BAME.
三条燕
SANJO TSUBAME
I WORK HERE AT AKABEKO AS A WAITRESS.
IT'S A PLEASURE TO MEET YOU.
SO SHE'S A CHILDHOOD FRIEND OF YOURS, YAHIKO?
CHTTTR
...
WE WERE NEIGHBORS IN KANDA BEFORE YAHIKO'S FAMILY MOVED THREE YEARS AGO.
CHTTTR
KANDA? DOES THAT MEAN YOU'RE FROM SAMURAI FAMILIES?
YES, I GUESS WE WERE.
WHERE DO YOU LIVE NOW, YAHIKO?
GULP

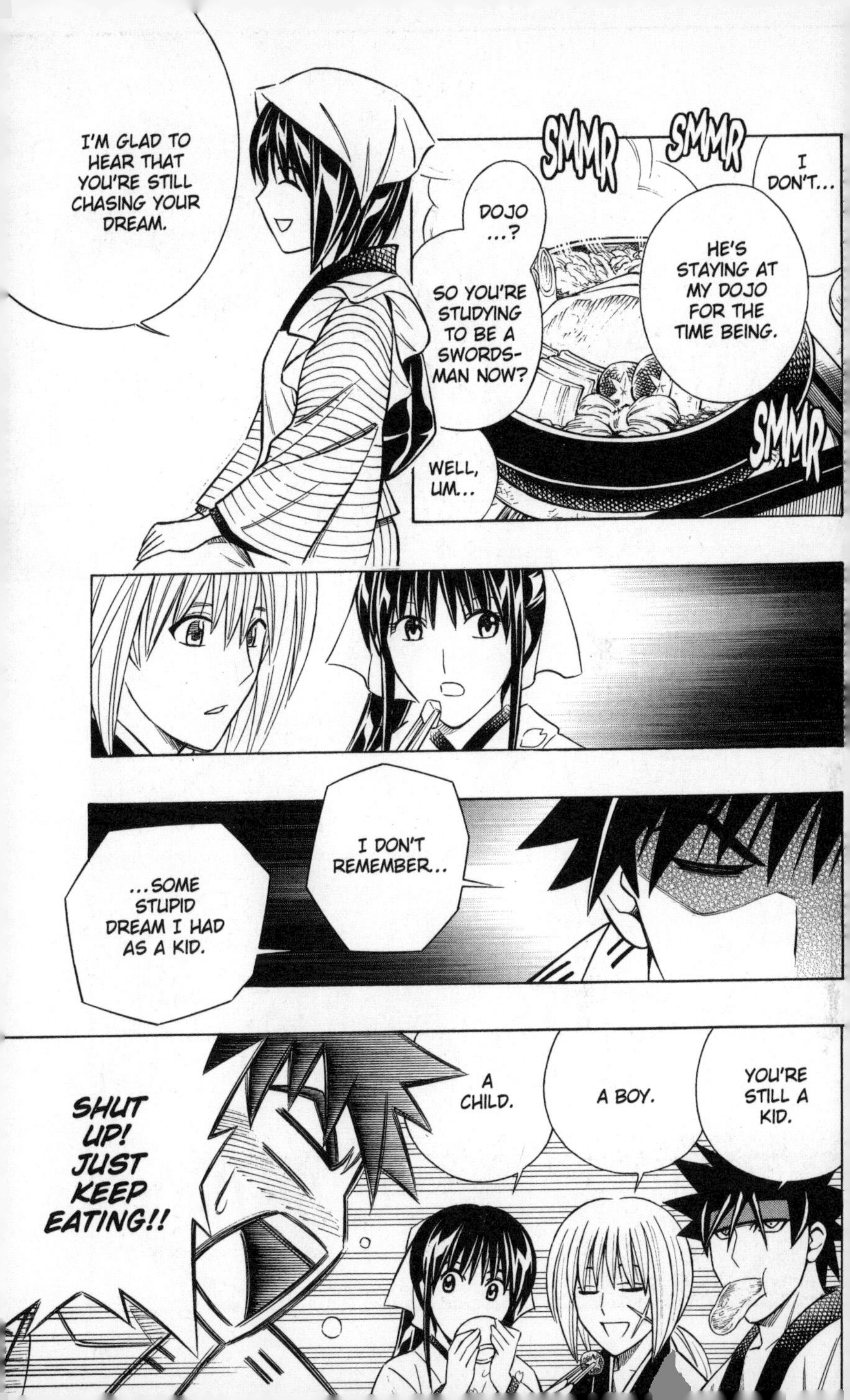

SMMR
SMMR
I DON'T...
HE'S STAYING AT MY DOJO FOR THE TIME BEING.
DOJO ...?
SO YOU'RE STUDYING TO BE A SWORDS-MAN NOW?
SMMR
WELL, UM...
I'M GLAD TO HEAR THAT YOU'RE STILL CHASING YOUR DREAM.
I DON'T REMEMBER...
...SOME STUPID DREAM I HAD AS A KID.
YOU'RE STILL A KID.
A BOY.
A CHILD.
SHUT UP! JUST KEEP EATING!!

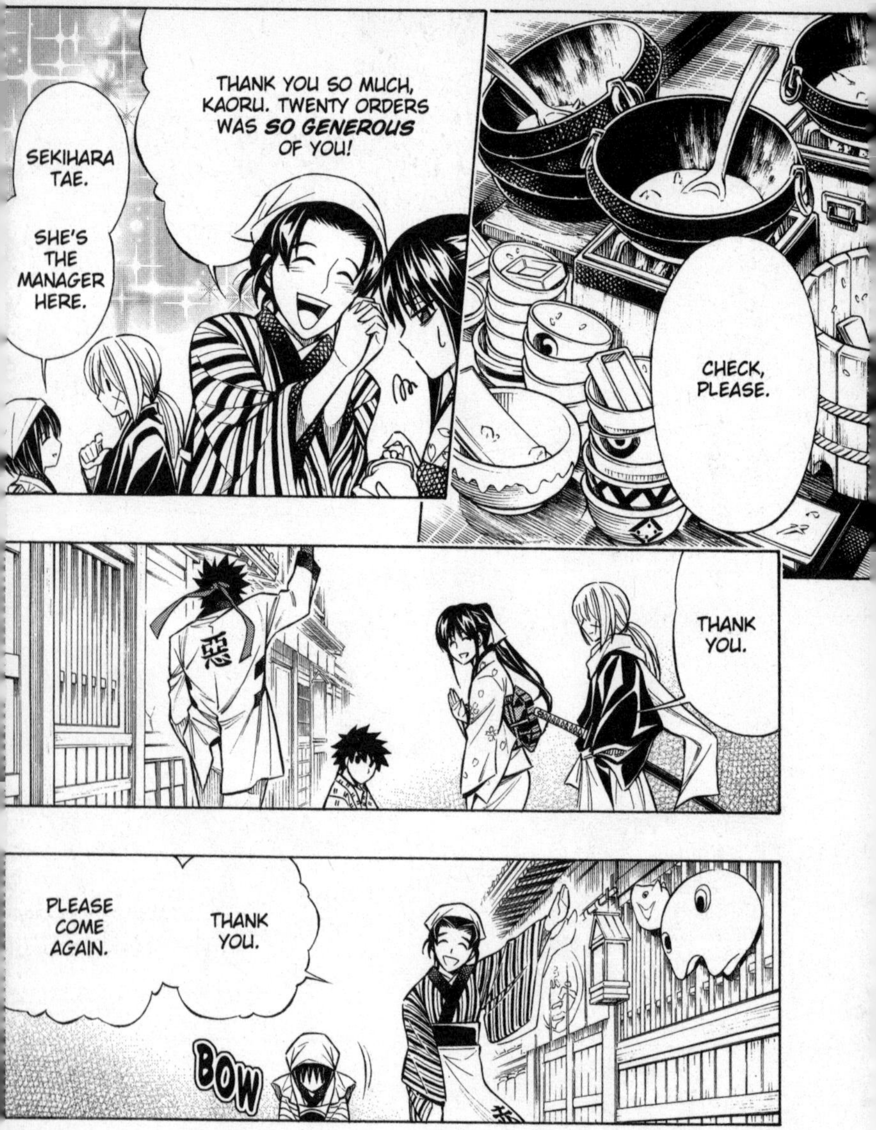
CHECK, PLEASE.
THANK YOU SO MUCH, KAORU. TWENTY ORDERS WAS *SO GENEROUS* OF YOU!
SEKIHARA TAE.
SHE'S THE MANAGER HERE.
THANK YOU.
THANK YOU.
PLEASE COME AGAIN.
BOW

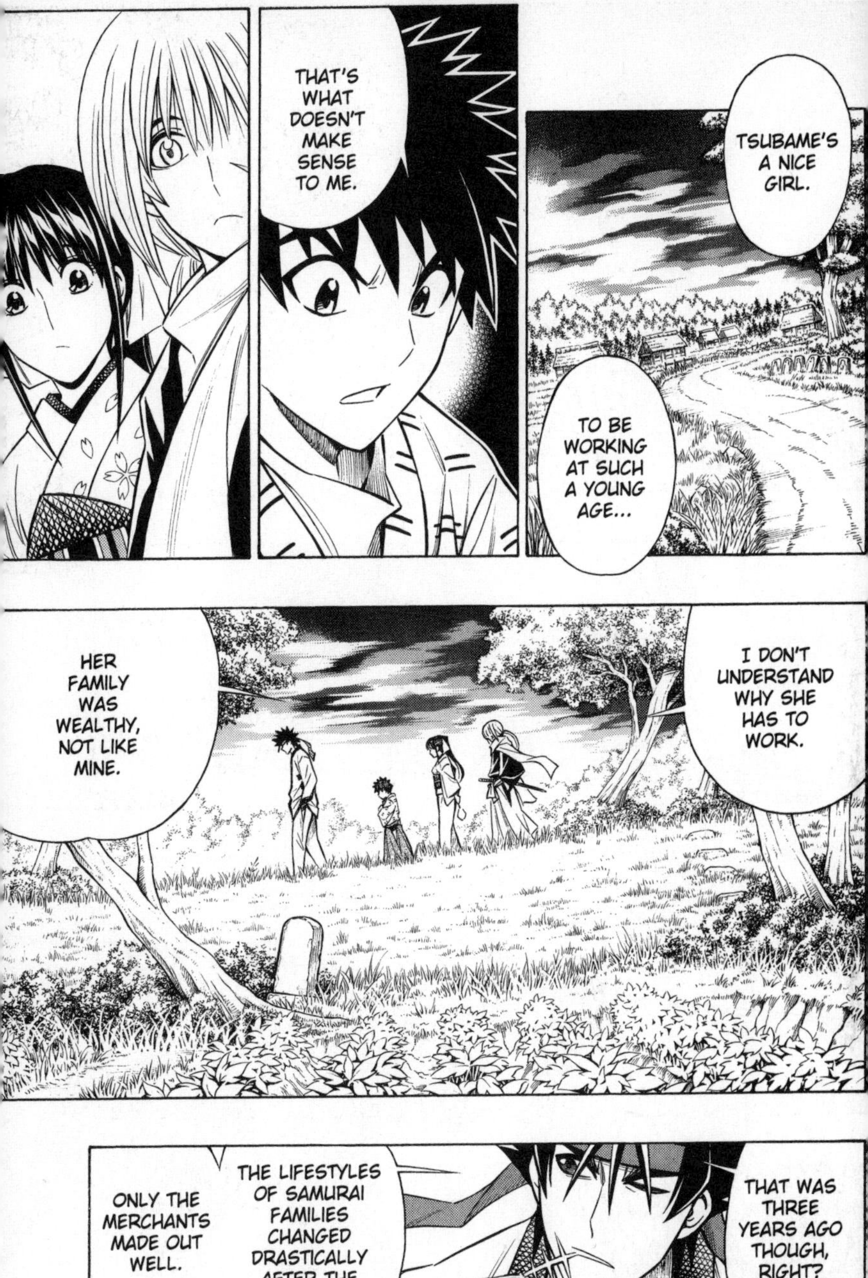
TSUBAME'S A NICE GIRL.
TO BE WORKING AT SUCH A YOUNG AGE...
THAT'S WHAT DOESN'T MAKE SENSE TO ME.
I DON'T UNDERSTAND WHY SHE HAS TO WORK.
HER FAMILY WAS WEALTHY, NOT LIKE MINE.
THAT WAS THREE YEARS AGO THOUGH, RIGHT?
THE LIFESTYLES OF SAMURAI FAMILIES CHANGED DRASTICALLY AFTER THE RESTORATION.
ONLY THE MERCHANTS MADE OUT WELL.

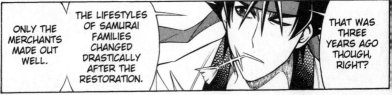

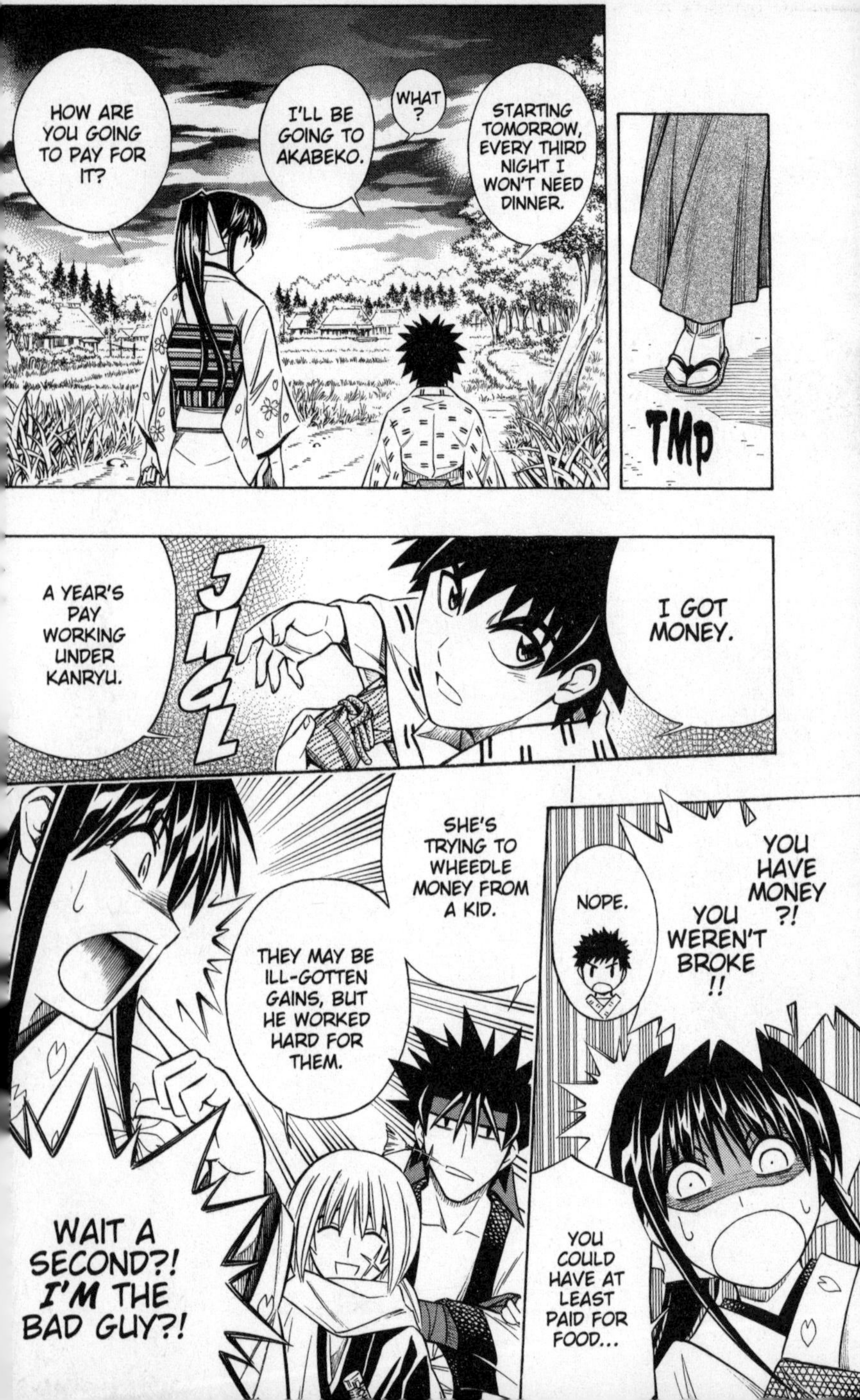
TMP
STARTING TOMORROW, EVERY THIRD NIGHT I WON'T NEED DINNER.
WHAT?
I'LL BE GOING TO AKABEKO.
HOW ARE YOU GOING TO PAY FOR IT?
I GOT MONEY.
JINGL
A YEAR'S PAY WORKING UNDER KANRYU.
YOU HAVE MONEY?!
YOU WEREN'T BROKE!!
NOPE.
YOU COULD HAVE AT LEAST PAID FOR FOOD...
SHE'S TRYING TO WHEEDLE MONEY FROM A KID.
THEY MAY BE ILL-GOTTEN GAINS, BUT HE WORKED HARD FOR THEM.
WAIT A SECOND?! *I'M* THE BAD GUY?!

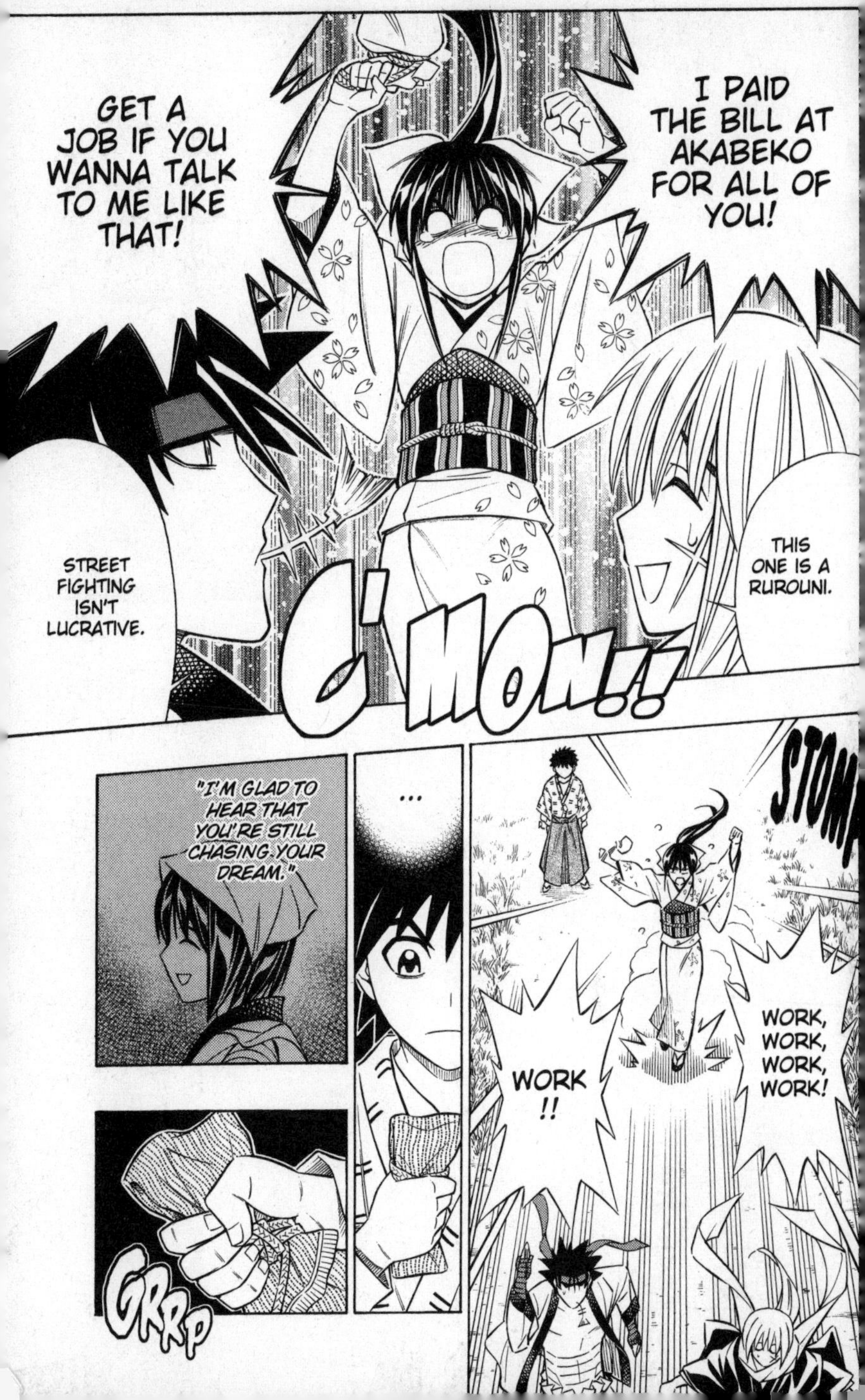
I PAID THE BILL AT AKABEKO FOR ALL OF YOU!
GET A JOB IF YOU WANNA TALK TO ME LIKE THAT!
THIS ONE IS A RUROUNI.
STREET FIGHTING ISN'T LUCRATIVE.
C'MON..!
STOMP
WORK, WORK, WORK, WORK!
WORK !!
...
"I'M GLAD TO HEAR THAT YOU'RE STILL CHASING YOUR DREAM."
GRRP

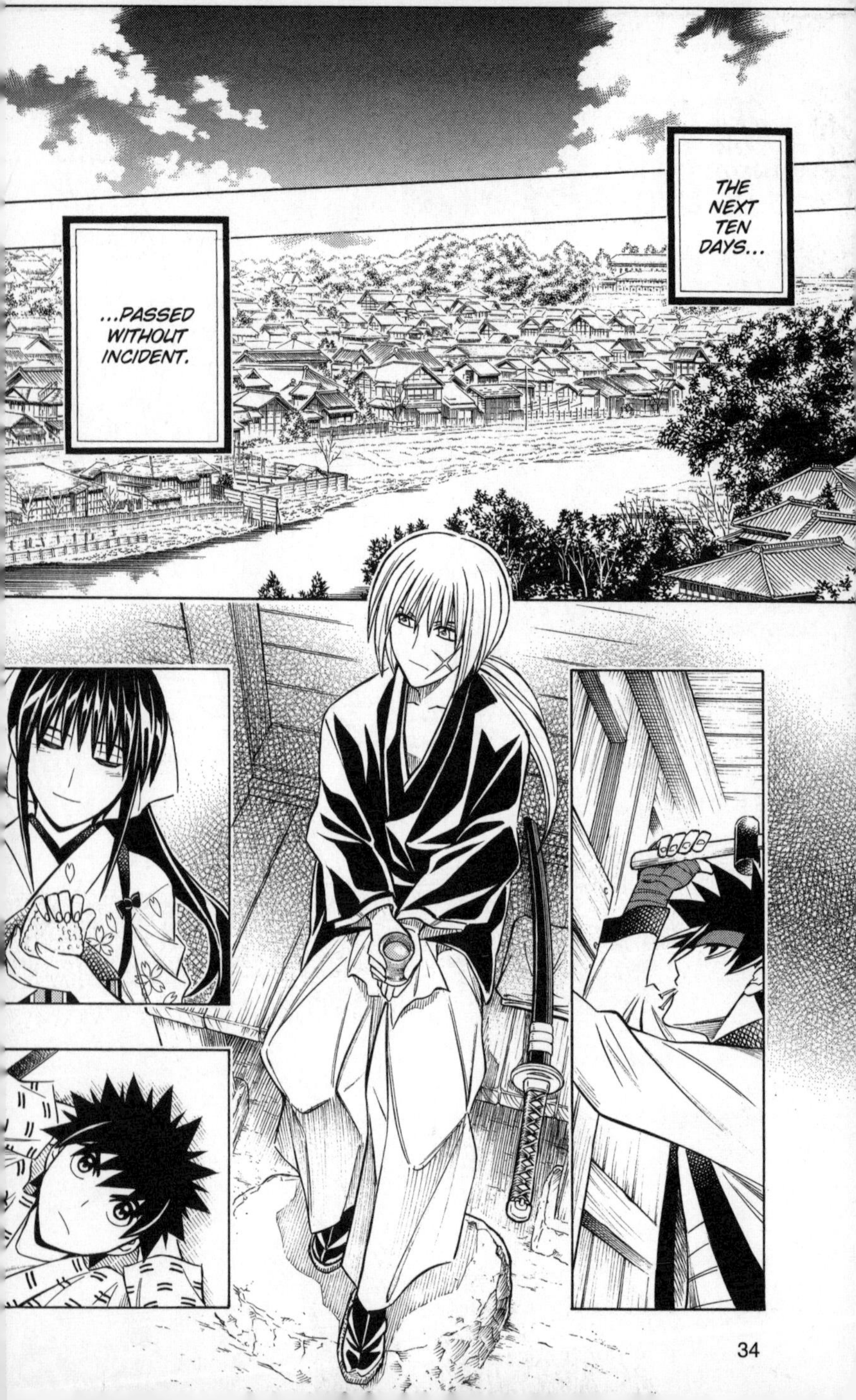
THE NEXT TEN DAYS...
...PASSED WITHOUT INCIDENT.

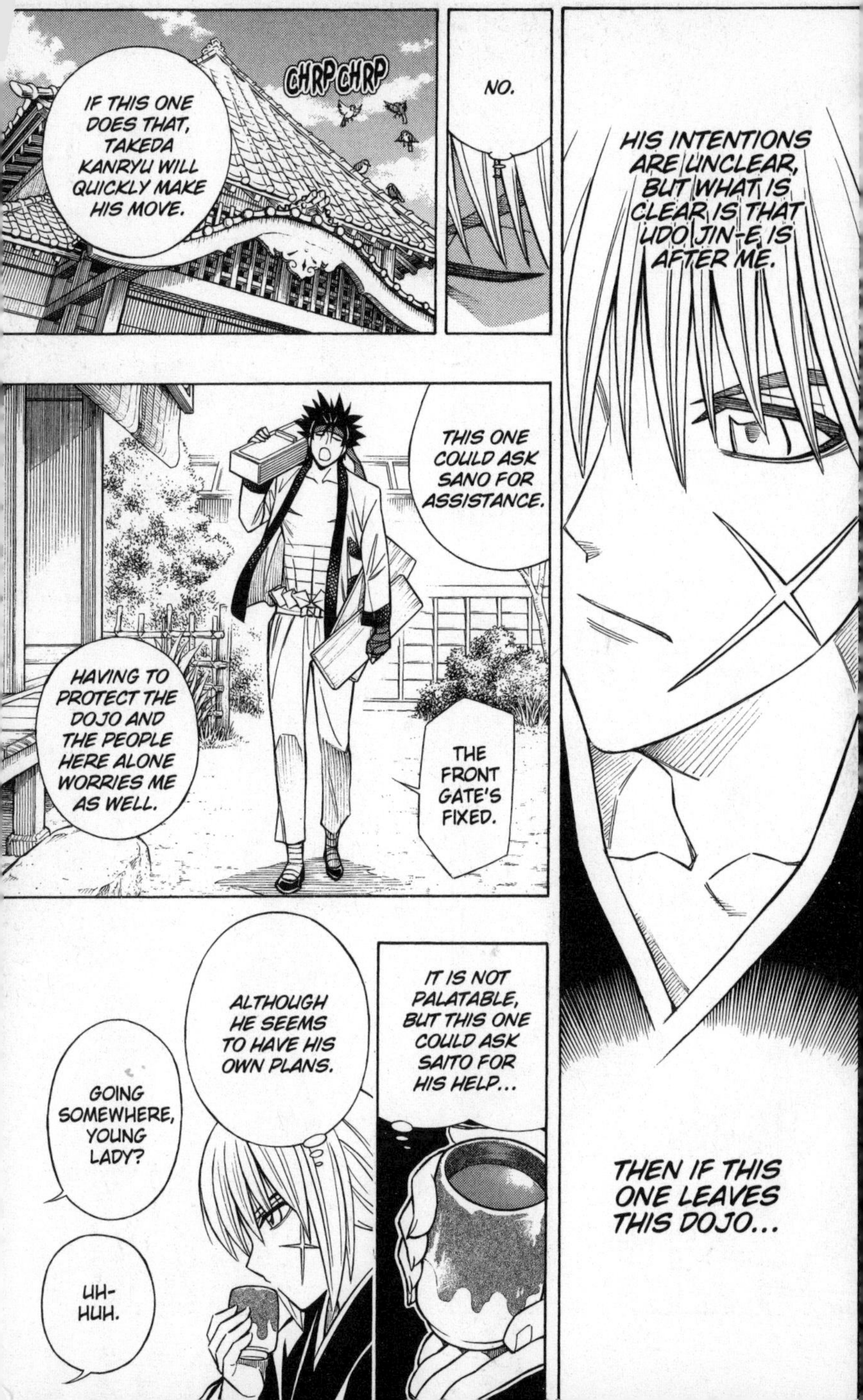
HIS INTENTIONS ARE UNCLEAR, BUT WHAT IS CLEAR IS THAT UDO JIN-E IS AFTER ME.
THEN IF THIS ONE LEAVES THIS DOJO...
NO.
CHRP CHRP
IF THIS ONE DOES THAT, TAKEDA KANRYU WILL QUICKLY MAKE HIS MOVE.
THIS ONE COULD ASK SANO FOR ASSISTANCE.
THE FRONT GATE'S FIXED.
HAVING TO PROTECT THE DOJO AND THE PEOPLE HERE ALONE WORRIES ME AS WELL.
IT IS NOT PALATABLE, BUT THIS ONE COULD ASK SAITO FOR HIS HELP...
ALTHOUGH HE SEEMS TO HAVE HIS OWN PLANS.
GOING SOMEWHERE, YOUNG LADY?
UH-HUH.

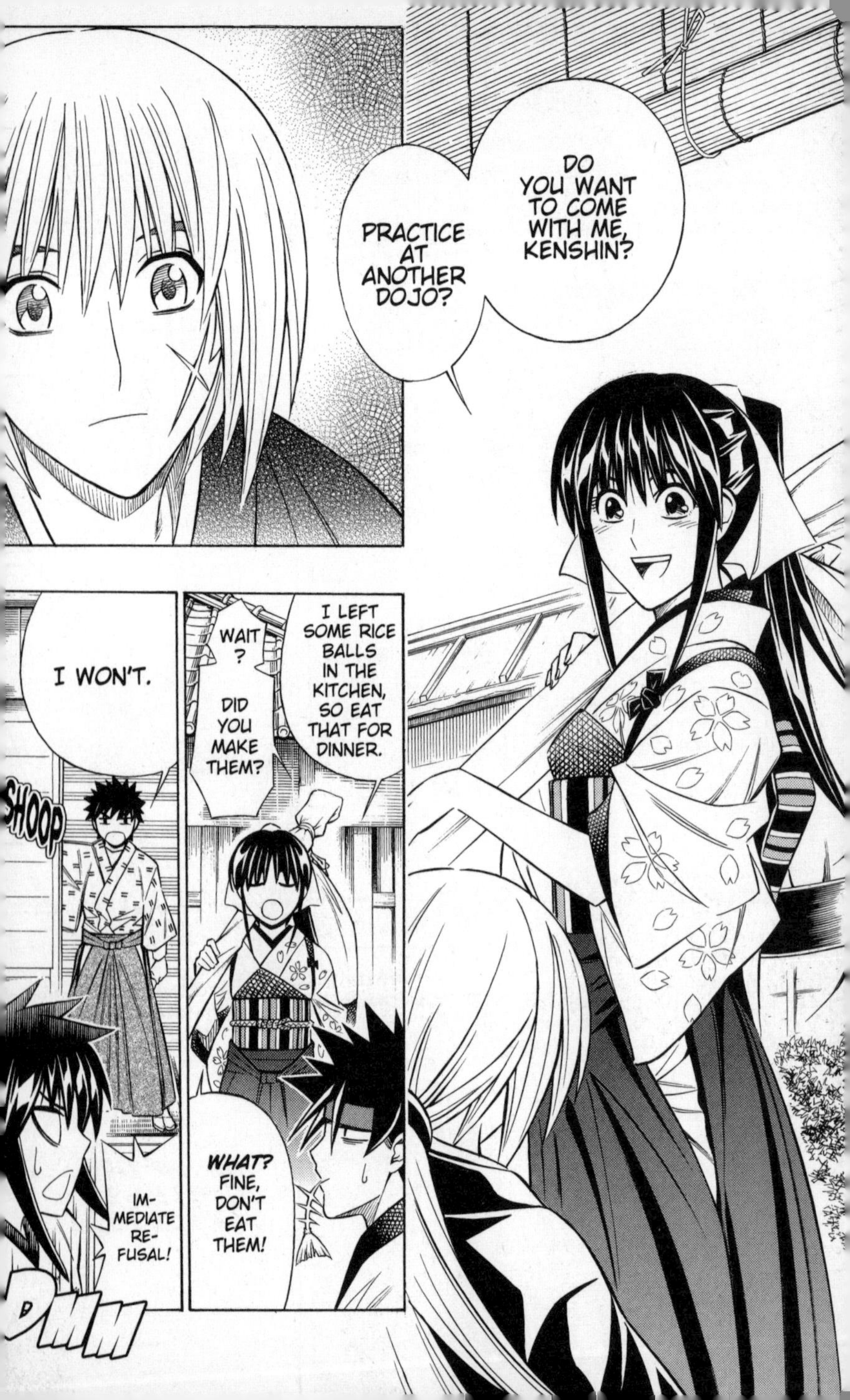
DO YOU WANT TO COME WITH ME, KENSHIN?
PRACTICE AT ANOTHER DOJO?
I LEFT SOME RICE BALLS IN THE KITCHEN, SO EAT THAT FOR DINNER.
WAIT? DID YOU MAKE THEM?
WHAT? FINE, DON'T EAT THEM!
I WON'T.
SHOOP
IM-MEDIATE RE-FUSAL!
DMM

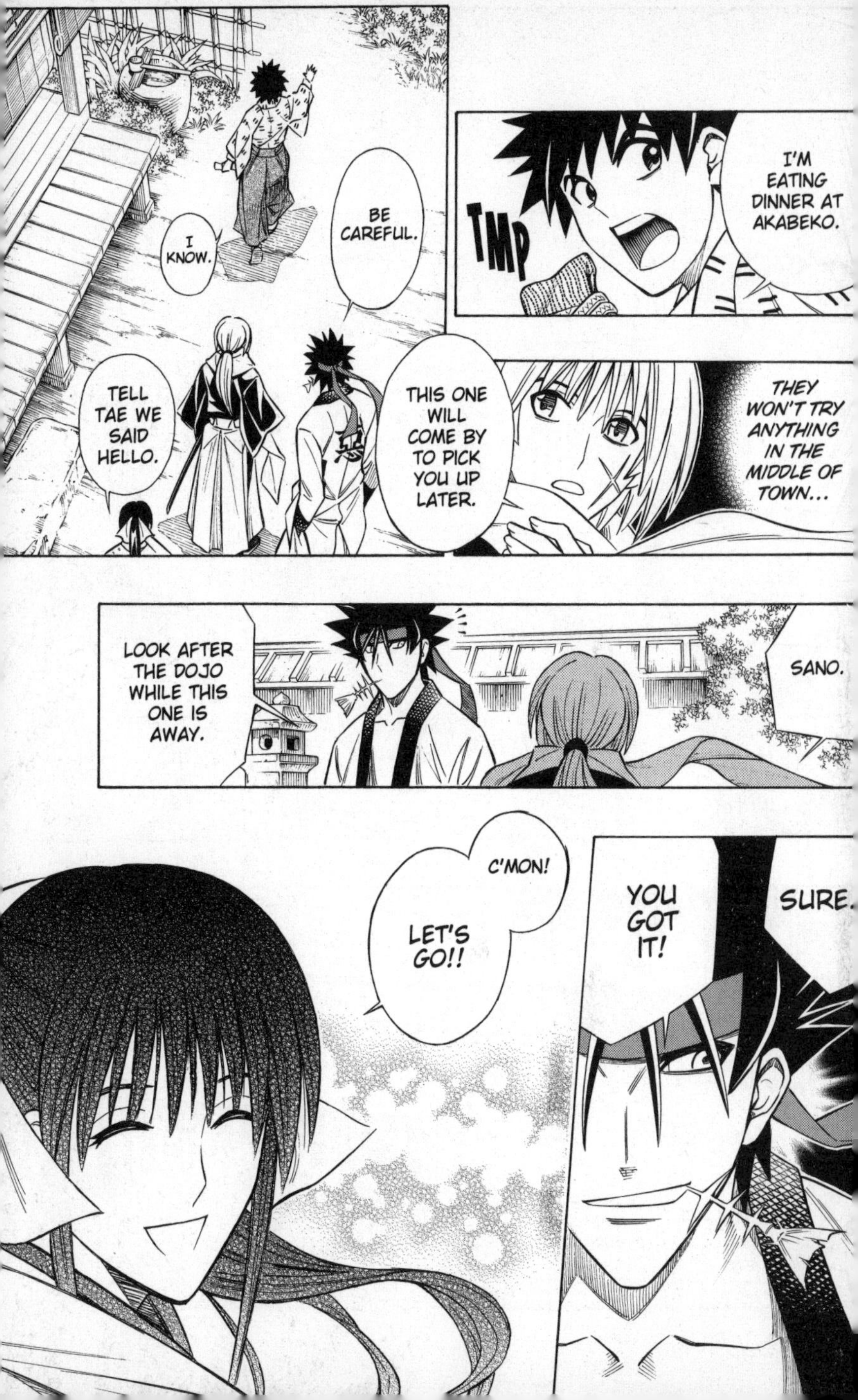
I'M EATING DINNER AT AKABEKO.
TMP
THEY WON'T TRY ANYTHING IN THE MIDDLE OF TOWN...
THIS ONE WILL COME BY TO PICK YOU UP LATER.
BE CAREFUL.
I KNOW.
TELL TAE WE SAID HELLO.
SANO.
LOOK AFTER THE DOJO WHILE THIS ONE IS AWAY.
SURE.
YOU GOT IT!
C'MON!
LET'S GO!!

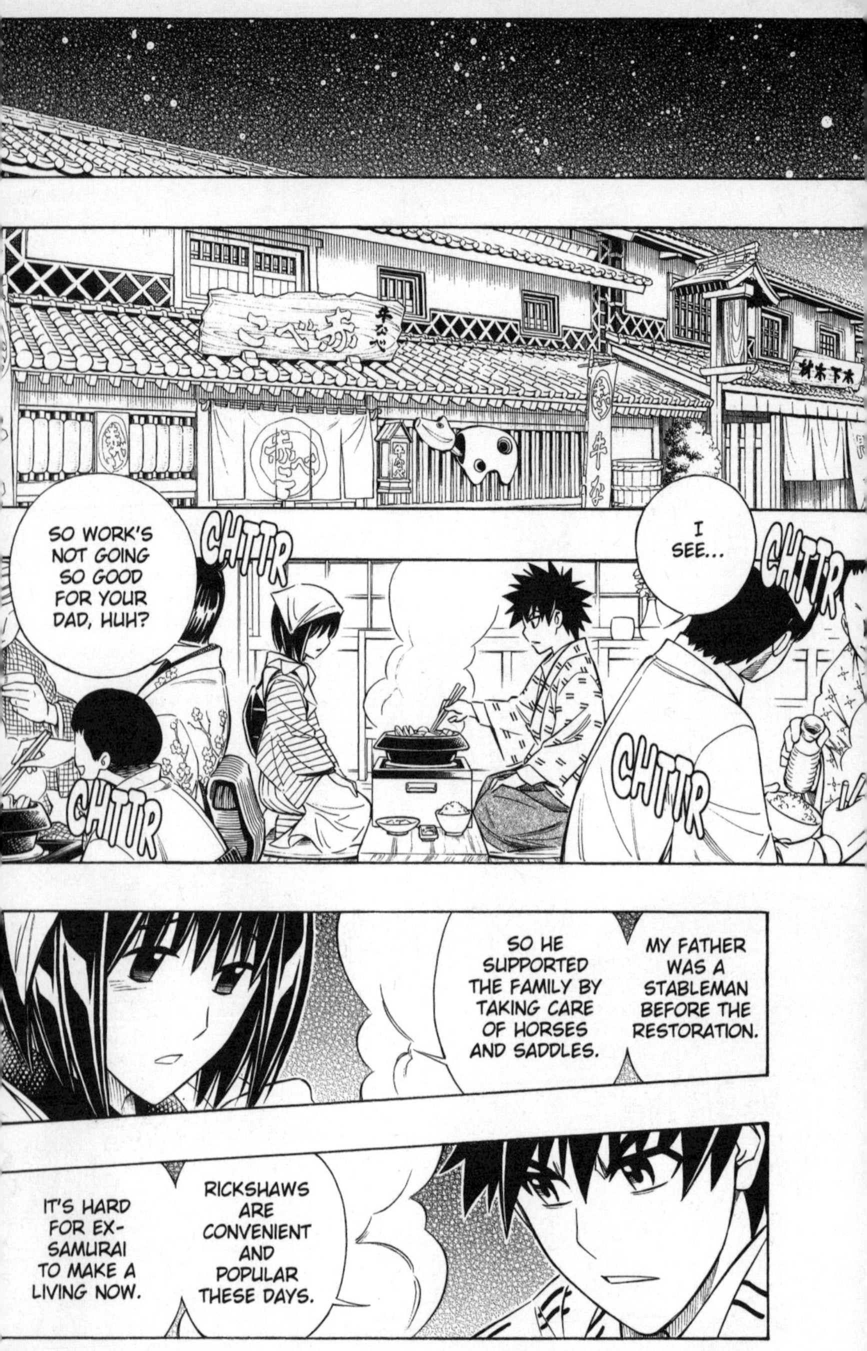
I SEE...
CHTTR
SO WORK'S NOT GOING SO GOOD FOR YOUR DAD, HUH?
CHTTR
CHTTR
CHTTR
MY FATHER WAS A STABLEMAN BEFORE THE RESTORATION.
SO HE SUPPORTED THE FAMILY BY TAKING CARE OF HORSES AND SADDLES.
RICKSHAWS ARE CONVENIENT AND POPULAR THESE DAYS.
IT'S HARD FOR EX-SAMURAI TO MAKE A LIVING NOW.

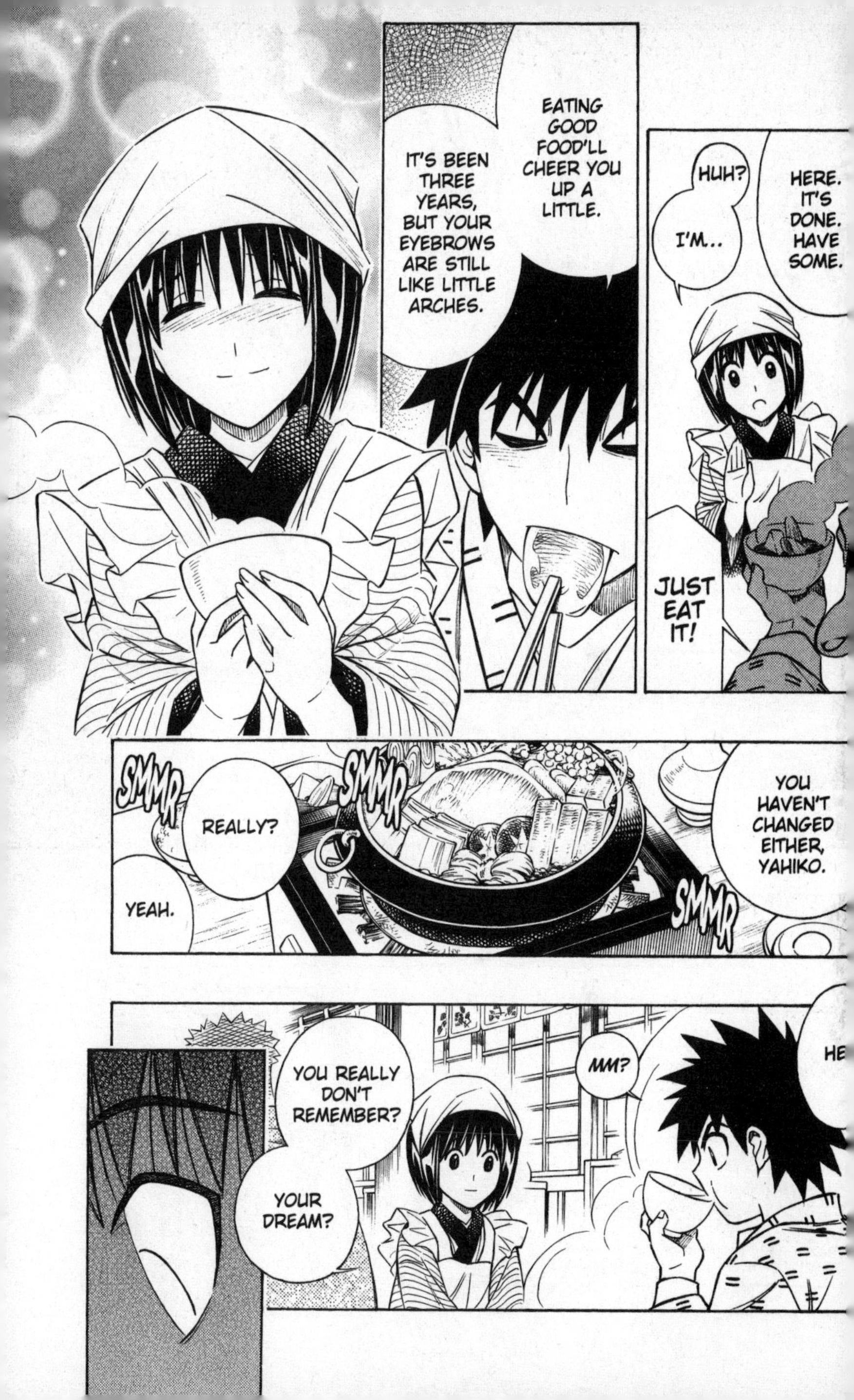

HERE. IT'S DONE. HAVE SOME.
HUH?
I'M...
JUST EAT IT!
EATING GOOD FOOD'LL CHEER YOU UP A LITTLE.
IT'S BEEN THREE YEARS, BUT YOUR EYEBROWS ARE STILL LIKE LITTLE ARCHES.
YOU HAVEN'T CHANGED EITHER, YAHIKO.
SMMR
SMMR
REALLY?
SMMR
YEAH.
MM?
YOU REALLY DON'T REMEMBER?
YOUR DREAM?

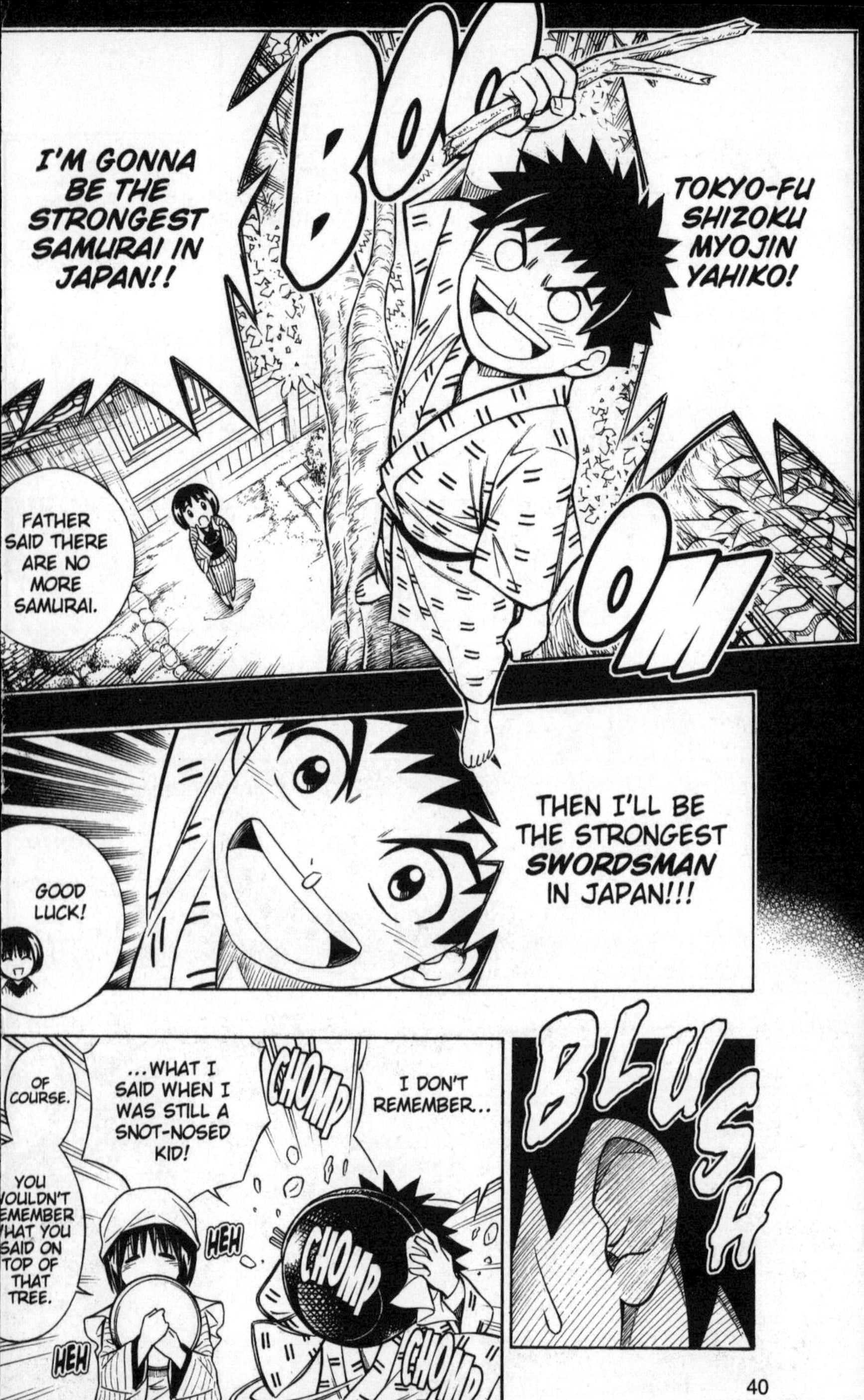
TOKYO-FU SHIZOKU MYOJIN YAHIKO!
I'M GONNA BE THE STRONGEST SAMURAI IN JAPAN!!
BOOOM
FATHER SAID THERE ARE NO MORE SAMURAI.
THEN I'LL BE THE STRONGEST SWORDSMAN IN JAPAN!!!
GOOD LUCK!
BLUSH
I DON'T REMEMBER...
CHOMP
...WHAT I SAID WHEN I WAS STILL A SNOT-NOSED KID!
OF COURSE.
YOU OULDN'T EMEMBER HAT YOU SAID ON TOP OF THAT TREE.
HEH
CHOMP
HEH
CHOMP

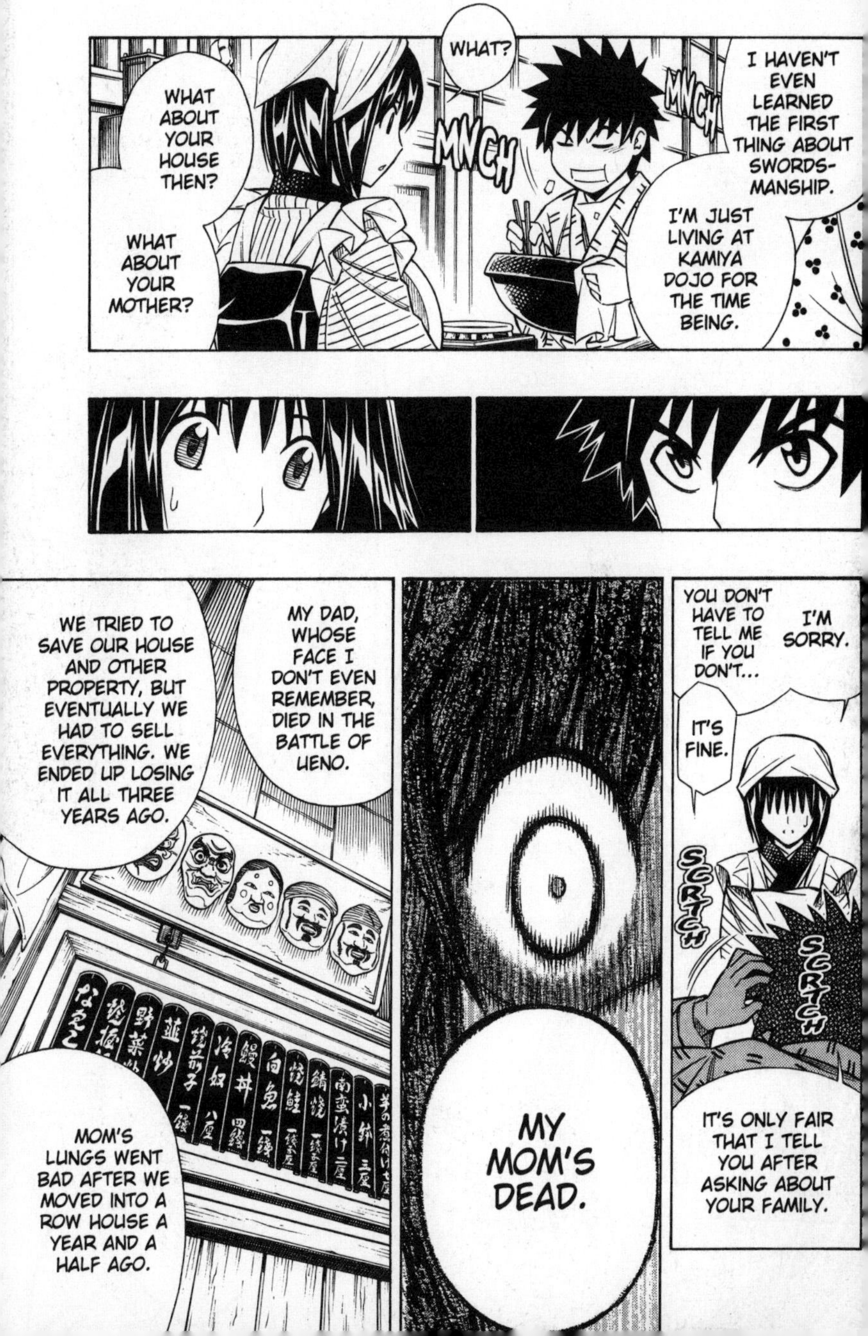
I HAVEN'T EVEN LEARNED THE FIRST THING ABOUT SWORDS-MANSHIP.
I'M JUST LIVING AT KAMIYA DOJO FOR THE TIME BEING.
MNCH
MNCH
WHAT?
WHAT ABOUT YOUR HOUSE THEN?
WHAT ABOUT YOUR MOTHER?
I'M SORRY.
YOU DON'T HAVE TO TELL ME IF YOU DON'T...
IT'S FINE.
SCRTCH
SCRTCH
IT'S ONLY FAIR THAT I TELL YOU AFTER ASKING ABOUT YOUR FAMILY.
MY MOM'S DEAD.
MY DAD, WHOSE FACE I DON'T EVEN REMEMBER, DIED IN THE BATTLE OF UENO.
WE TRIED TO SAVE OUR HOUSE AND OTHER PROPERTY, BUT EVENTUALLY WE HAD TO SELL EVERYTHING. WE ENDED UP LOSING IT ALL THREE YEARS AGO.
MOM'S LUNGS WENT BAD AFTER WE MOVED INTO A ROW HOUSE A YEAR AND A HALF AGO.

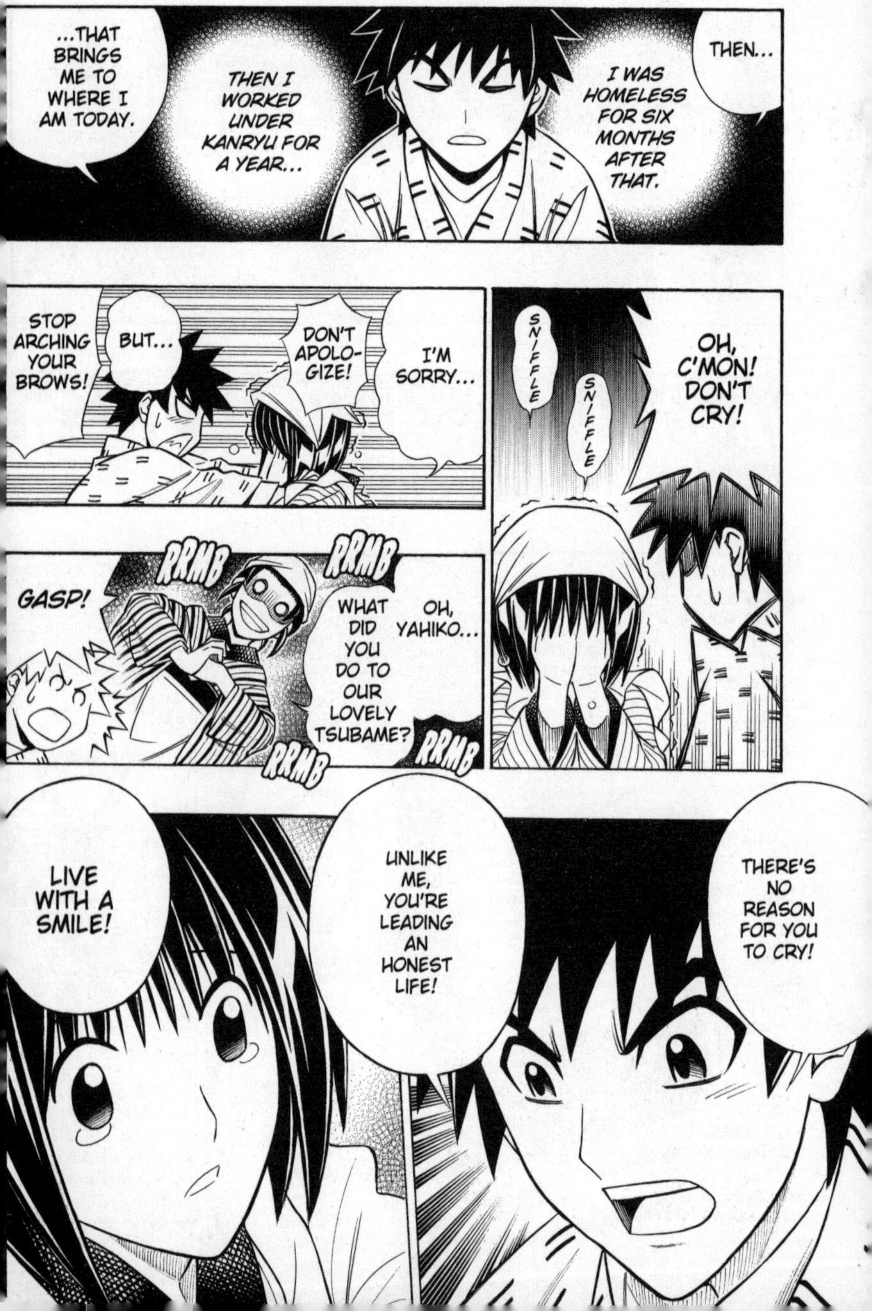
THEN...
I WAS HOMELESS FOR SIX MONTHS AFTER THAT.
THEN I WORKED UNDER KANRYU FOR A YEAR...
...THAT BRINGS ME TO WHERE I AM TODAY.
SNIFFLE
SNIFFLE
OH, C'MON! DON'T CRY!
I'M SORRY...
DON'T APOLOGIZE!
BUT...
STOP ARCHING YOUR BROWS!
RRMB
OH, YAHIKO...
WHAT DID YOU DO TO OUR LOVELY TSUBAME?
RRMB
RRMB
RRMB
GASP!
THERE'S NO REASON FOR YOU TO CRY!
UNLIKE ME, YOU'RE LEADING AN HONEST LIFE!
LIVE WITH A SMILE!

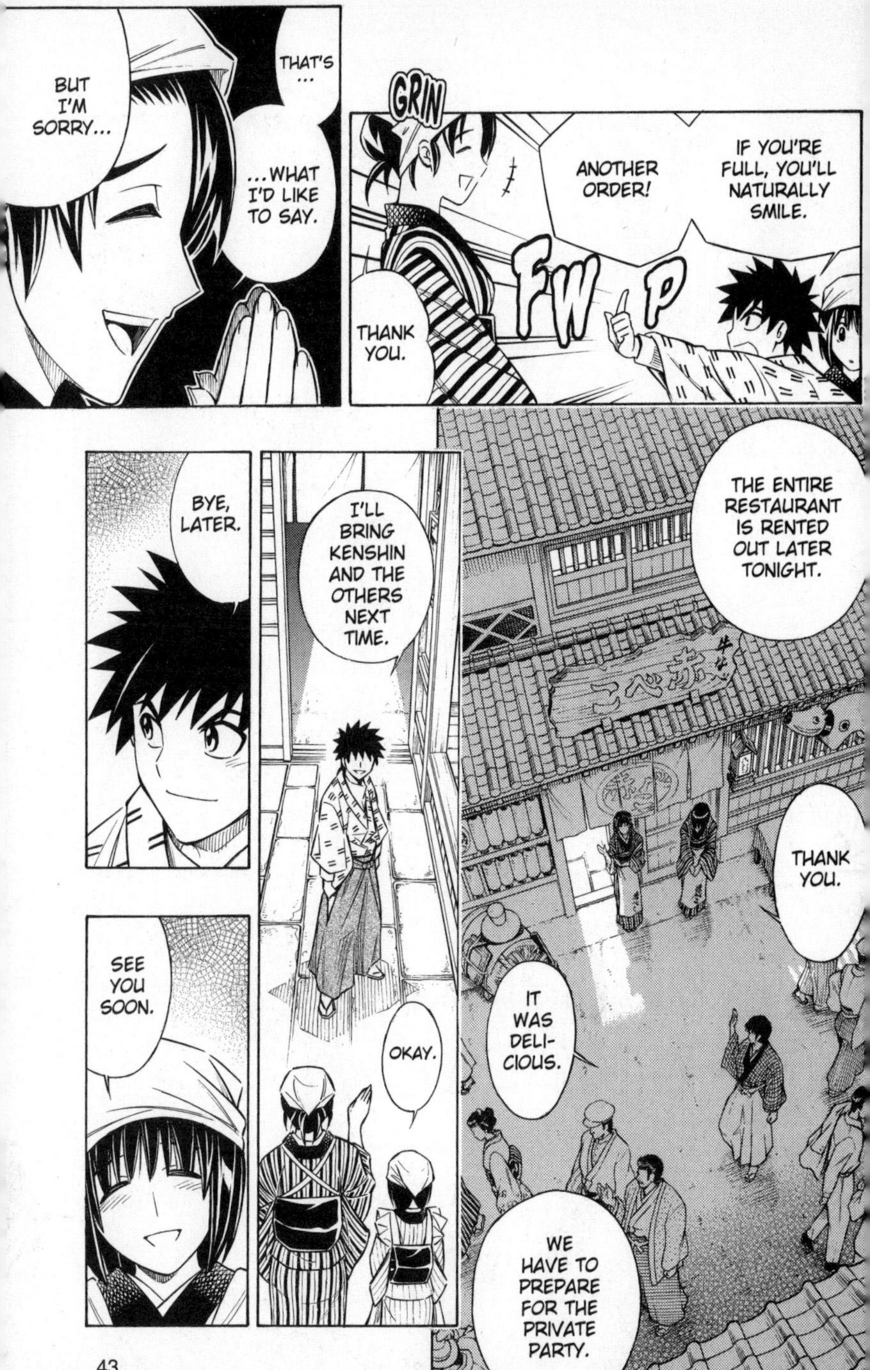
GRIN
IF YOU'RE FULL, YOU'LL NATURALLY SMILE.
ANOTHER ORDER!
FWP
THANK YOU.
THAT'S...
...WHAT I'D LIKE TO SAY.
BUT I'M SORRY...
THE ENTIRE RESTAURANT IS RENTED OUT LATER TONIGHT.
THANK YOU.
IT WAS DELICIOUS.
WE HAVE TO PREPARE FOR THE PRIVATE PARTY.
I'LL BRING KENSHIN AND THE OTHERS NEXT TIME.
OKAY.
BYE, LATER.
SEE YOU SOON.

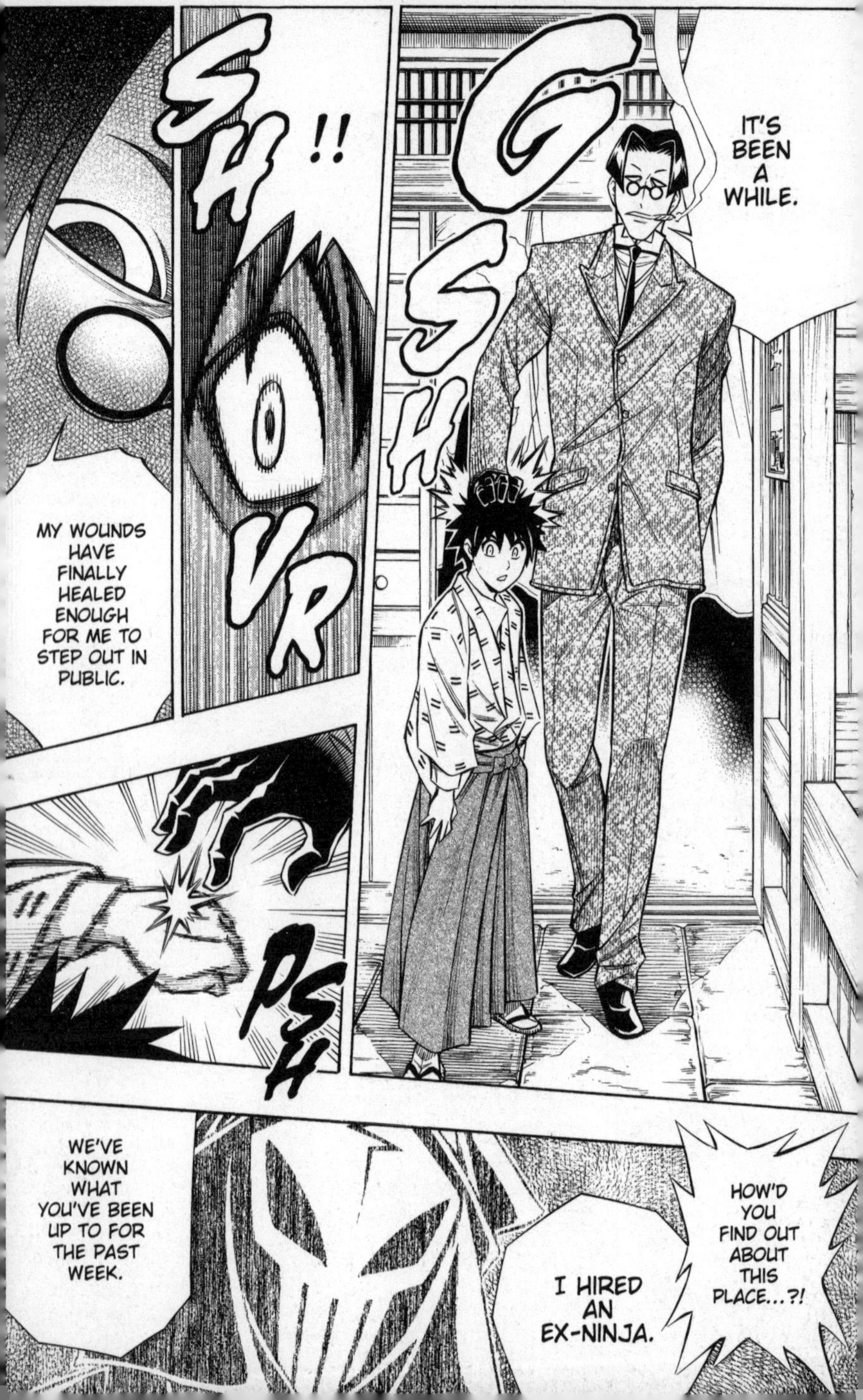
IT'S BEEN A WHILE.
GSH
SH!!
VR
MY WOUNDS HAVE FINALLY HEALED ENOUGH FOR ME TO STEP OUT IN PUBLIC.
PSH
HOW'D YOU FIND OUT ABOUT THIS PLACE...?!
I HIRED AN EX-NINJA.
WE'VE KNOWN WHAT YOU'VE BEEN UP TO FOR THE PAST WEEK.

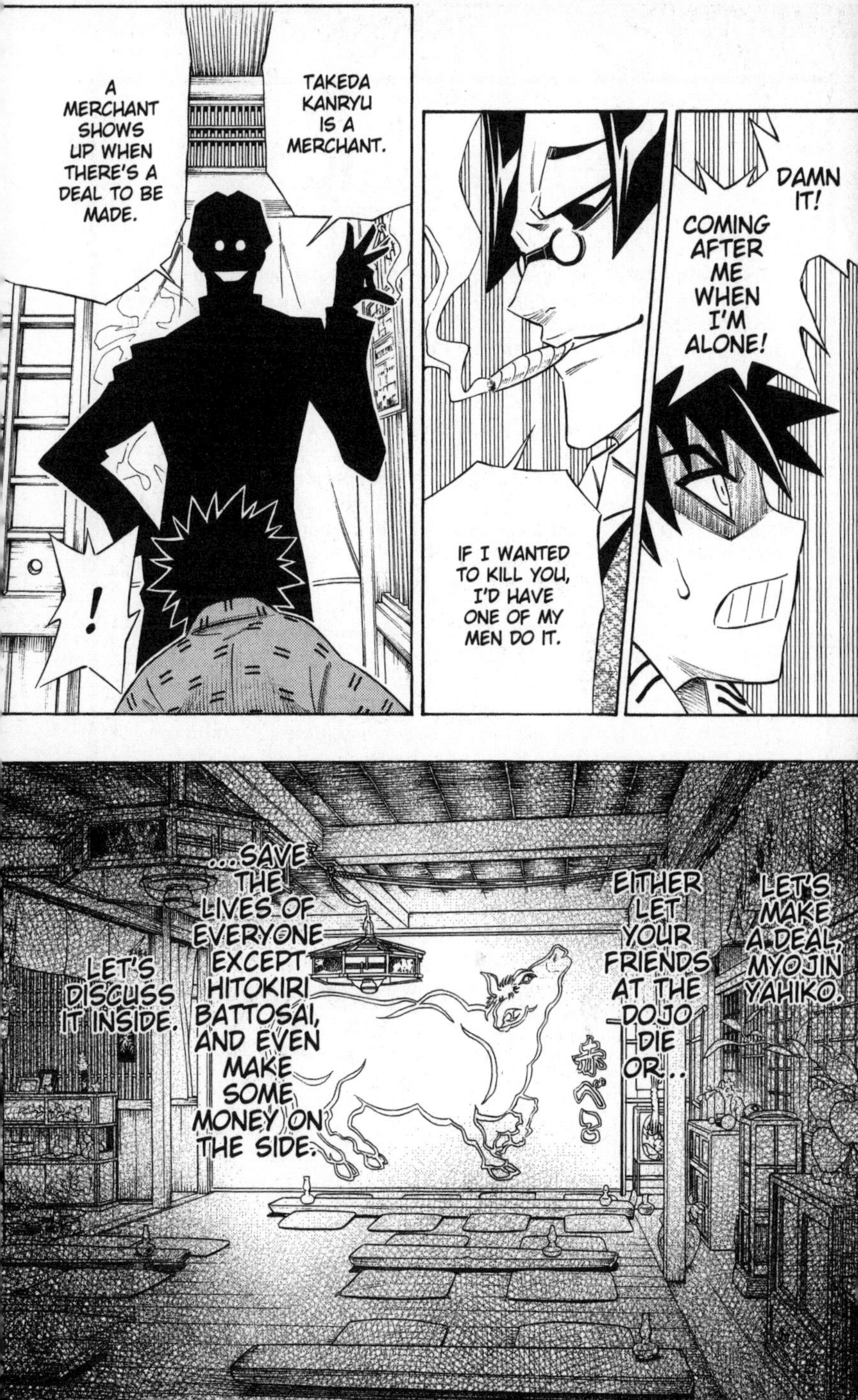
DAMN IT!
COMING AFTER ME WHEN I'M ALONE!
IF I WANTED TO KILL YOU, I'D HAVE ONE OF MY MEN DO IT.
TAKEDA KANRYU IS A MERCHANT.
A MERCHANT SHOWS UP WHEN THERE'S A DEAL TO BE MADE.
!
LET'S MAKE A DEAL, MYOJIN YAHIKO.
EITHER LET YOUR FRIENDS AT THE DOJO DIE OR...
...SAVE THE LIVES OF EVERYONE EXCEPT HITOKIRI BATTOSAI, AND EVEN MAKE SOME MONEY ON THE SIDE.
赤べこ
LET'S DISCUSS IT INSIDE.

FREE TALK 2

On the other hand, there are those who have experienced the world of *Rurouni Kenshin* through the film first. There were more of those people than I expected. Because there were so many of you, the success of the film was significant. The world of *Rurouni Kenshin* has spread because of it.

There are many works I fell in love with as a child and still like as an adult. Works that have continued in sequels, works that have continued as spinoffs, works that have been remade or refined, works that have continued in different mediums, and works that have concluded and remained permanently romanticized in our memories.

Continuance and completion: it's difficult to say which is better. Although *Rurouni Kenshin* concluded once ten-plus years ago, there are many requests for its continuation both from the creator and the audience. Then why not continue expanding its world for a little while longer? That's how I feel at the moment. Of course, I'll follow the definition of parallelism I wrote about in volume 1. I intend to work hard to not let down those who "experienced the world of *Rurouni Kenshin* through the film." (Although I haven't decided whether I'll write *Kenshin* as a manga again at this point...)

Thanks to the favorable reception of the film adaptation of *Rurouni Kenshin,* a sequel is going to be made. Parts 2 and 3, actually. It will revolve around the Kyoto arc. How will the very manga-esque parts be adapted? I'll be relying even more on the director and the film crew this time around. (Because I'm a manga artist, I intend to put more effort into manga). I am looking forward to the next celebration more from the readers' perspective.

Act 6: The Light of Meiji

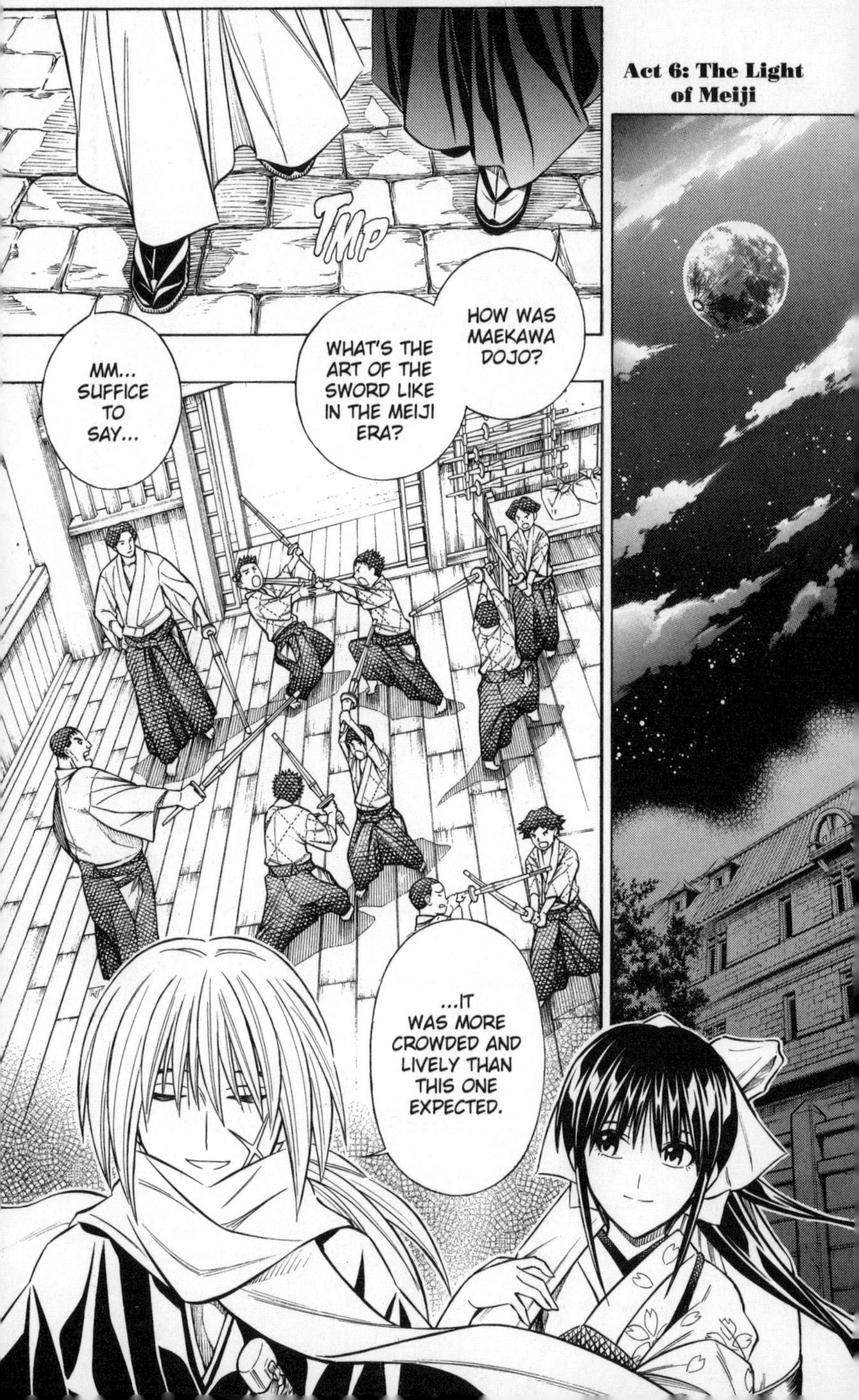
TMP
HOW WAS MAEKAWA DOJO?
WHAT'S THE ART OF THE SWORD LIKE IN THE MEIJI ERA?
MM... SUFFICE TO SAY...
...IT WAS MORE CROWDED AND LIVELY THAN THIS ONE EXPECTED.

BUT...

MY FATHER PASSED AWAY, SO NOW IT'S JUST ME...

WE USED TO BE BUSY TOO.

URGH.

THIS ONE EXPECTED IT TO BE A LITTLE MORE DESOLATE, LIKE KAMIYA DOJO.

...LIVELY AGAIN.

...IT'S GETTING...

SORRY.

IT'S IRRITATING TO HEAR THAT FROM AN ACTUAL FREE-LOADER, BUT I CAN'T SAY ANYTHING BACK.

RRGH.

IT'S FUNNY THAT NONE OF US ARE STUDENTS, BUT RATHER FREELOADERS THERE.

YEAH!

POMPH

OH.

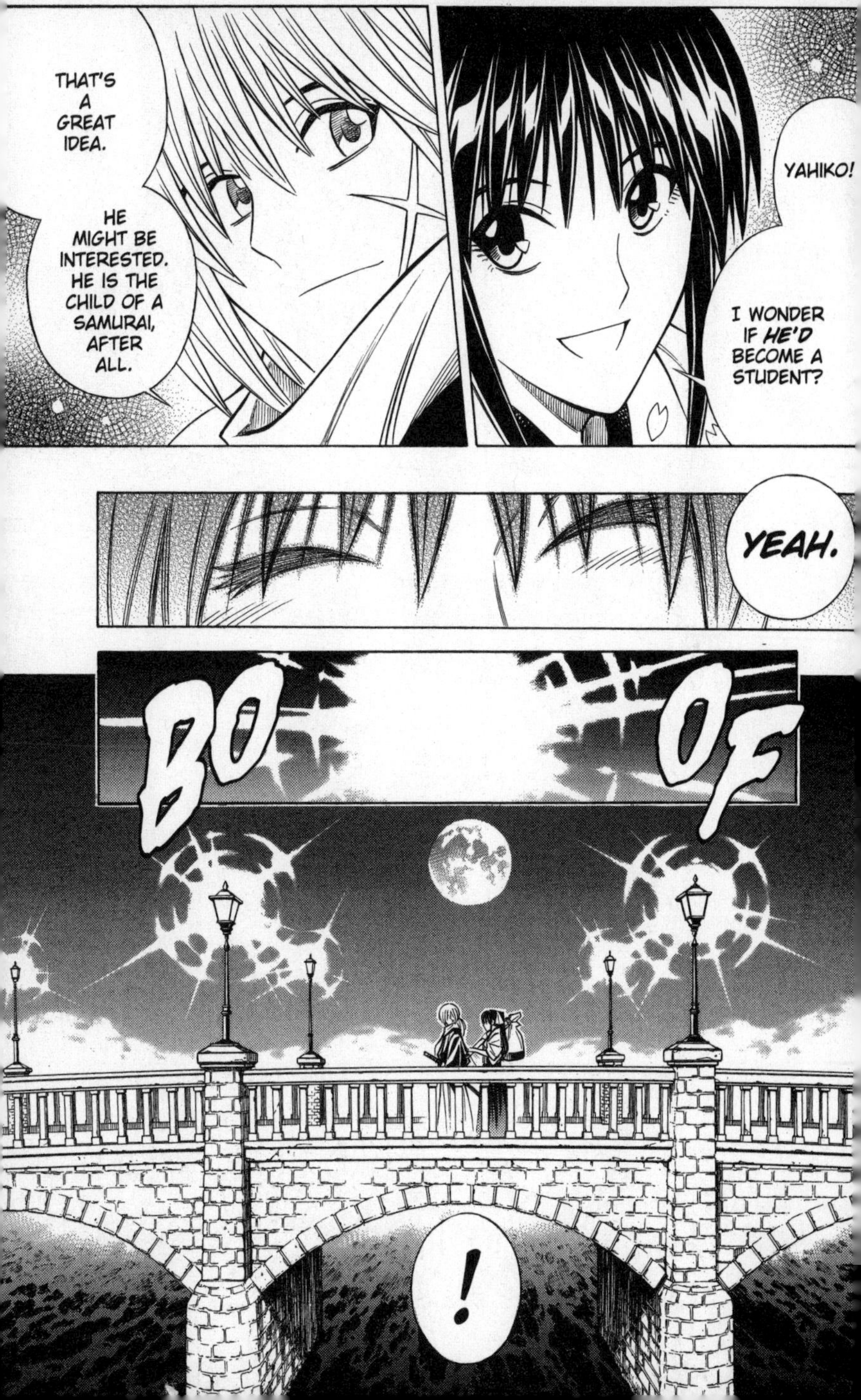
YAHIKO!
I WONDER IF HE'D BECOME A STUDENT?
THAT'S A GREAT IDEA.
HE MIGHT BE INTERESTED. HE IS THE CHILD OF A SAMURAI, AFTER ALL.
YEAH.
BOOF
!

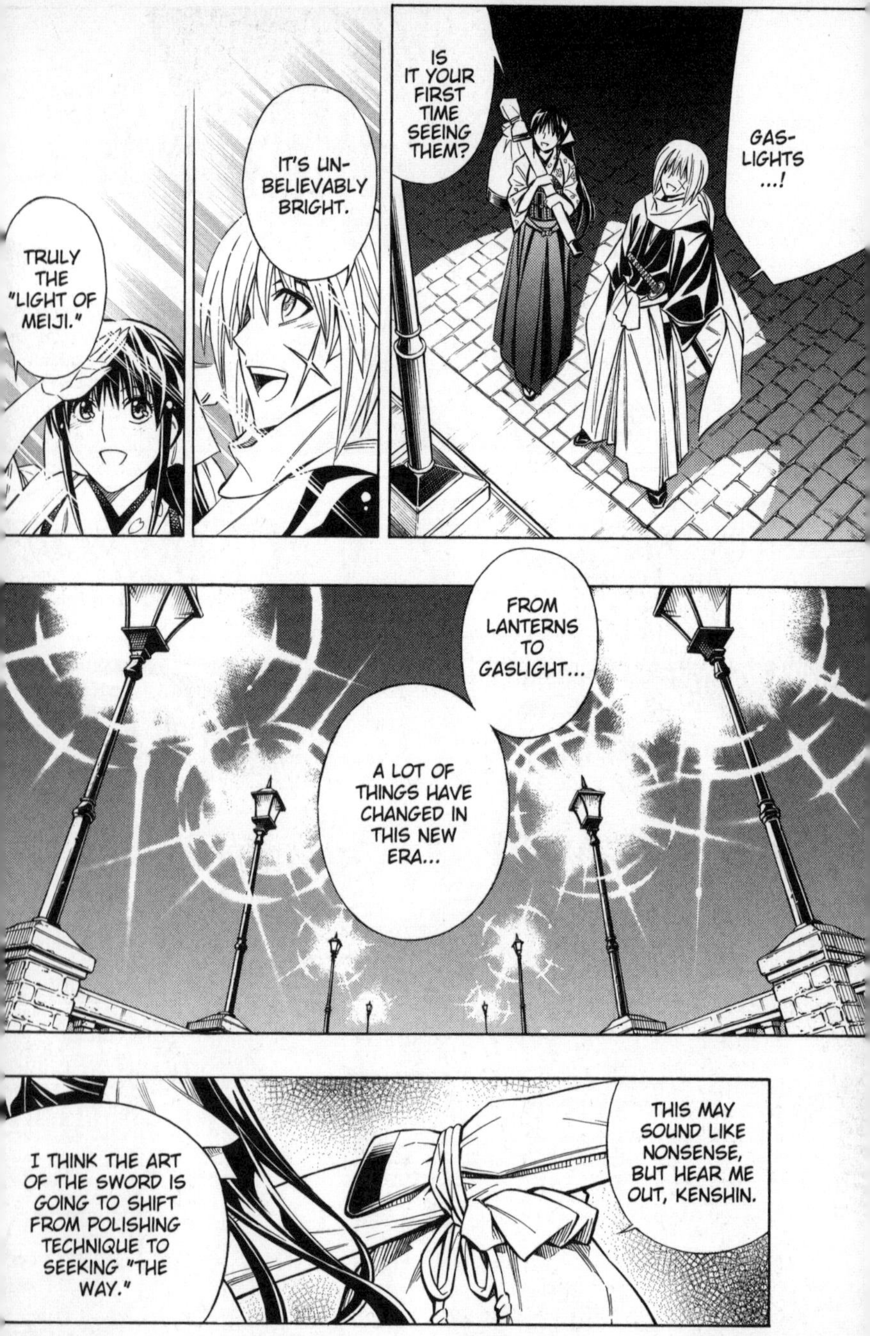
GAS-LIGHTS ...!
IS IT YOUR FIRST TIME SEEING THEM?
IT'S UN-BELIEVABLY BRIGHT.
TRULY THE "LIGHT OF MEIJI."
FROM LANTERNS TO GASLIGHT...
A LOT OF THINGS HAVE CHANGED IN THIS NEW ERA...
THIS MAY SOUND LIKE NONSENSE, BUT HEAR ME OUT, KENSHIN.
I THINK THE ART OF THE SWORD IS GOING TO SHIFT FROM POLISHING TECHNIQUE TO SEEKING "THE WAY."

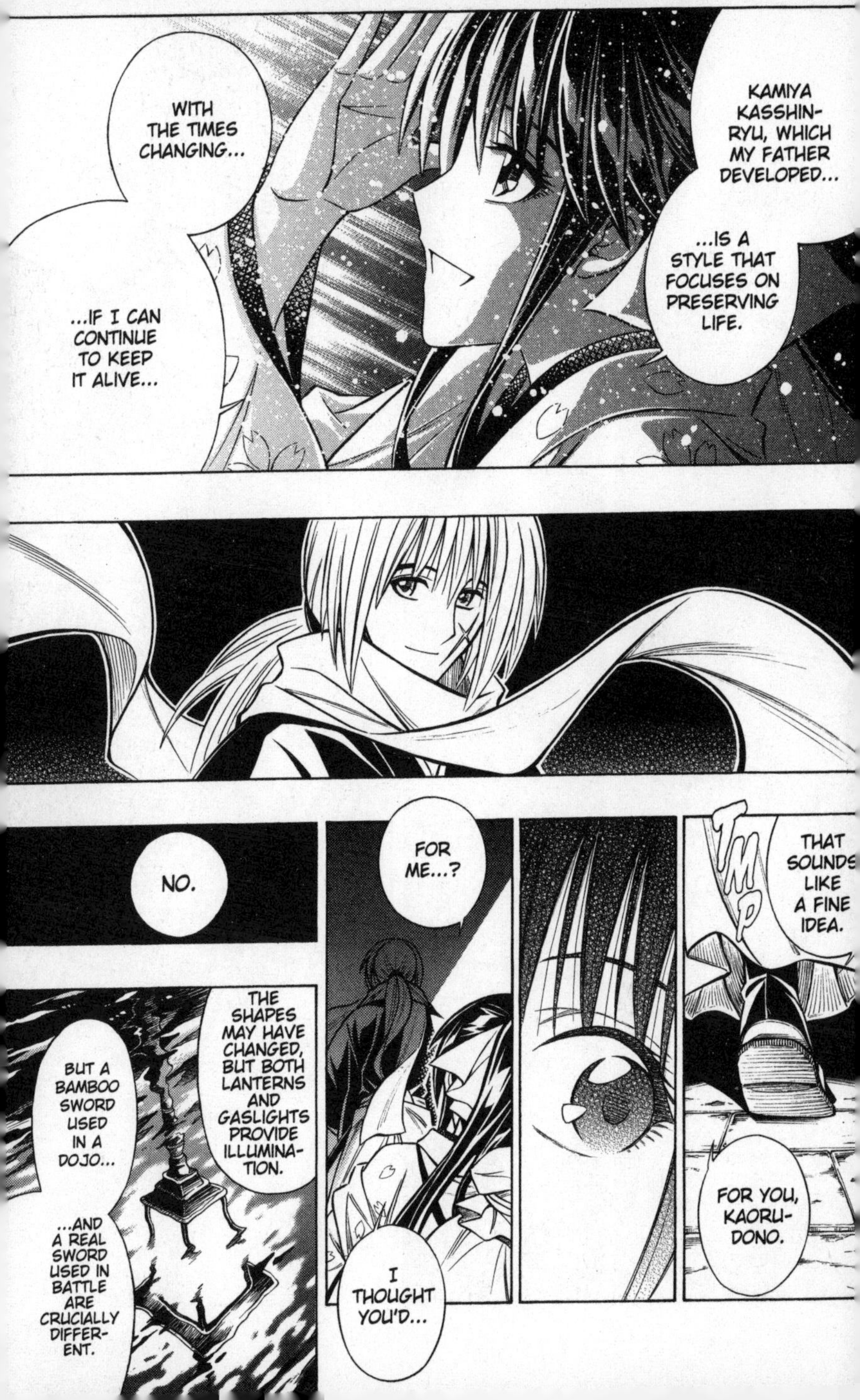
KAMIYA KASSHIN-RYU, WHICH MY FATHER DEVELOPED...
...IS A STYLE THAT FOCUSES ON PRESERVING LIFE.
WITH THE TIMES CHANGING...
...IF I CAN CONTINUE TO KEEP IT ALIVE...
TMP
THAT SOUNDS LIKE A FINE IDEA.
FOR YOU, KAORU-DONO.
FOR ME...?
I THOUGHT YOU'D...
NO.
THE SHAPES MAY HAVE CHANGED, BUT BOTH LANTERNS AND GASLIGHTS PROVIDE ILLUMINATION.
BUT A BAMBOO SWORD USED IN A DOJO...
...AND A REAL SWORD USED IN BATTLE ARE CRUCIALLY DIFFERENT.

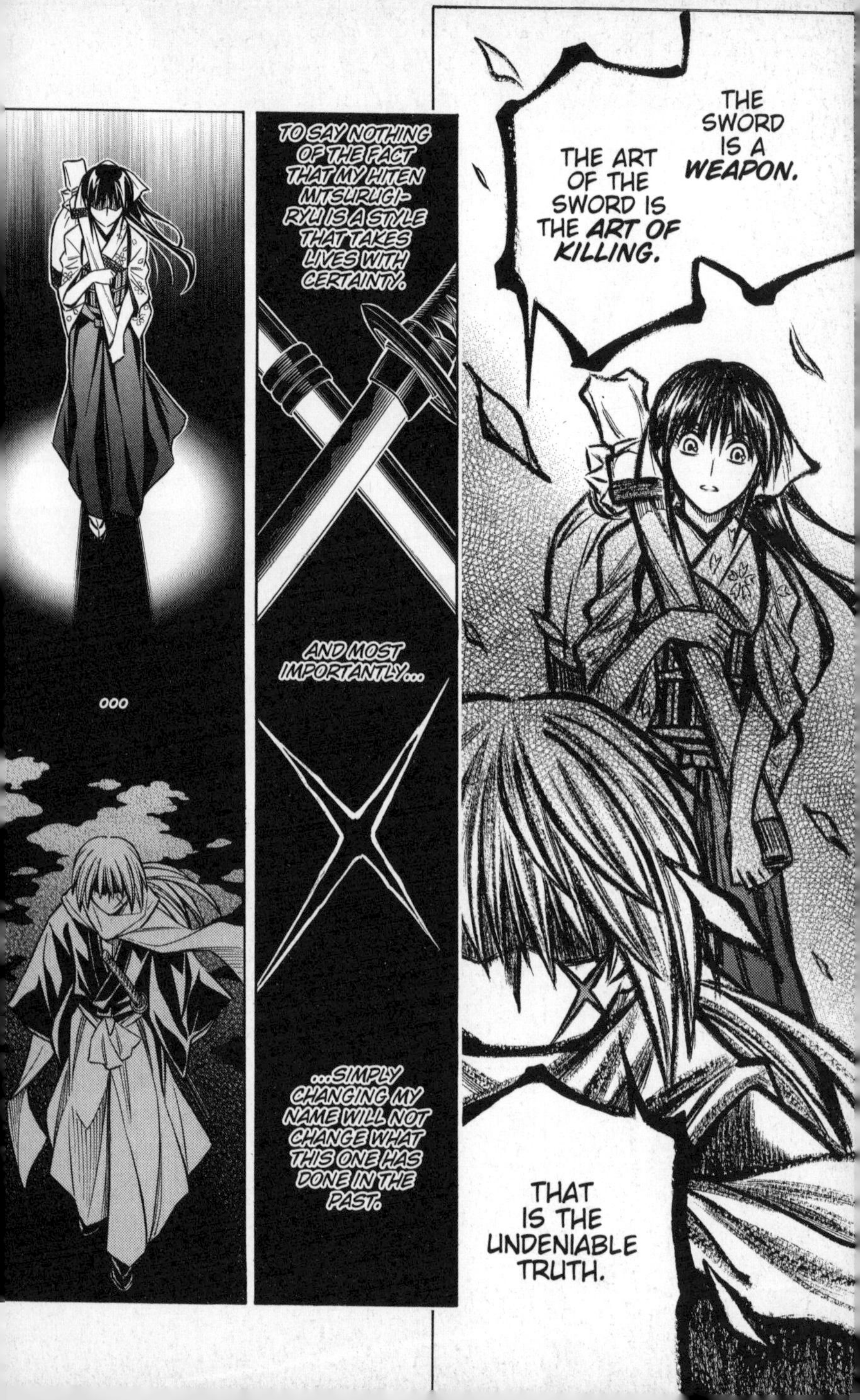
THE SWORD IS A WEAPON.
THE ART OF THE SWORD IS THE ART OF KILLING.
THAT IS THE UNDENIABLE TRUTH.
TO SAY NOTHING OF THE FACT THAT MY HITEN MITSURUGI-RYU IS A STYLE THAT TAKES LIVES WITH CERTAINTY.
AND MOST IMPORTANTLY...
...SIMPLY CHANGING MY NAME WILL NOT CHANGE WHAT THIS ONE HAS DONE IN THE PAST.
...

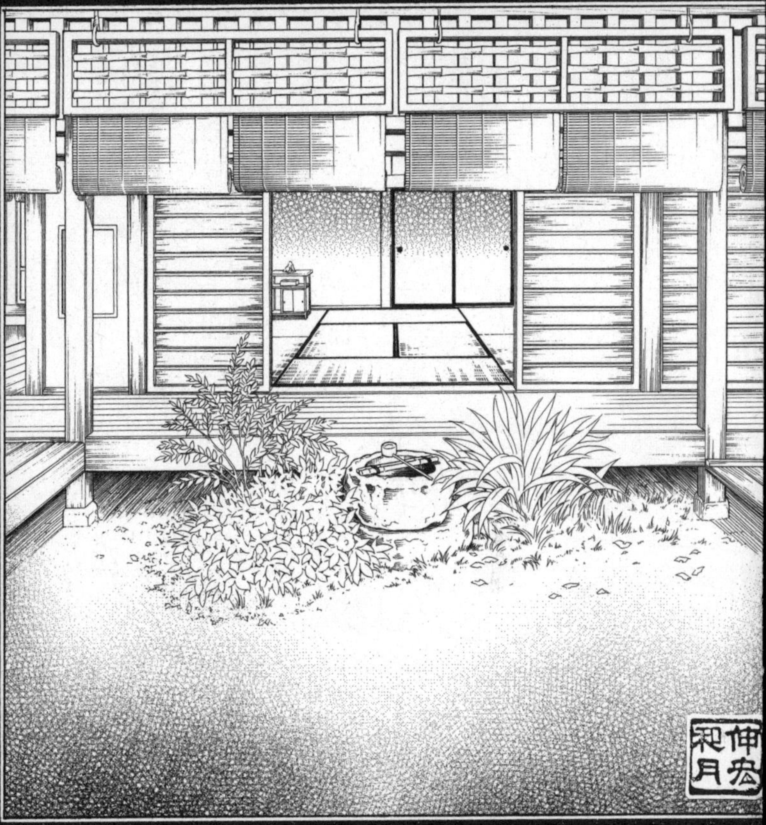
伸宏
和月

Act 6: The Light of Meiji

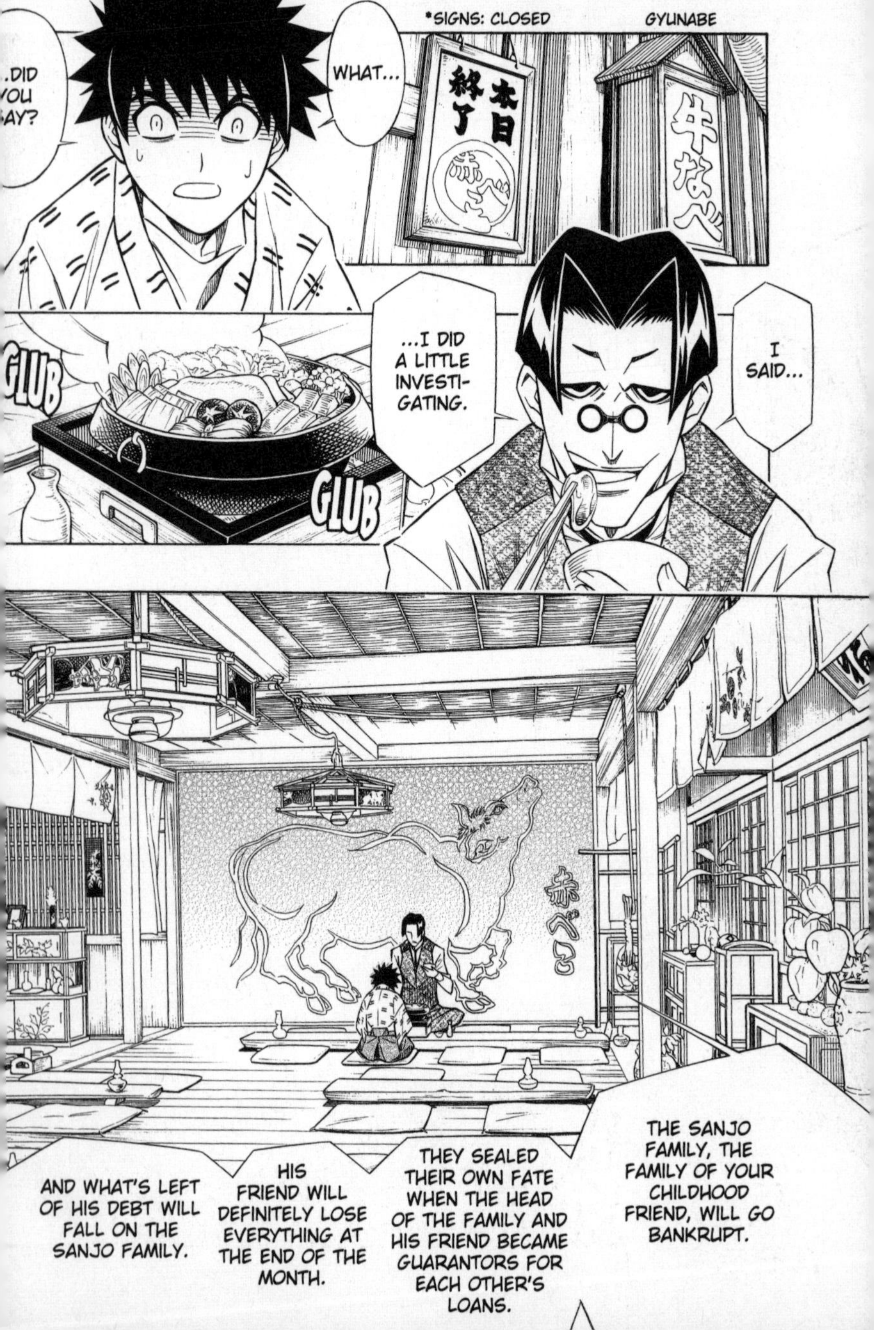
*SIGNS: CLOSED
GYUNABE
WHAT...
.DID YOU SAY?
I SAID...
...I DID A LITTLE INVESTI-GATING.
GLUB
GLUB
THE SANJO FAMILY, THE FAMILY OF YOUR CHILDHOOD FRIEND, WILL GO BANKRUPT.
THEY SEALED THEIR OWN FATE WHEN THE HEAD OF THE FAMILY AND HIS FRIEND BECAME GUARANTORS FOR EACH OTHER'S LOANS.
HIS FRIEND WILL DEFINITELY LOSE EVERYTHING AT THE END OF THE MONTH.
AND WHAT'S LEFT OF HIS DEBT WILL FALL ON THE SANJO FAMILY.

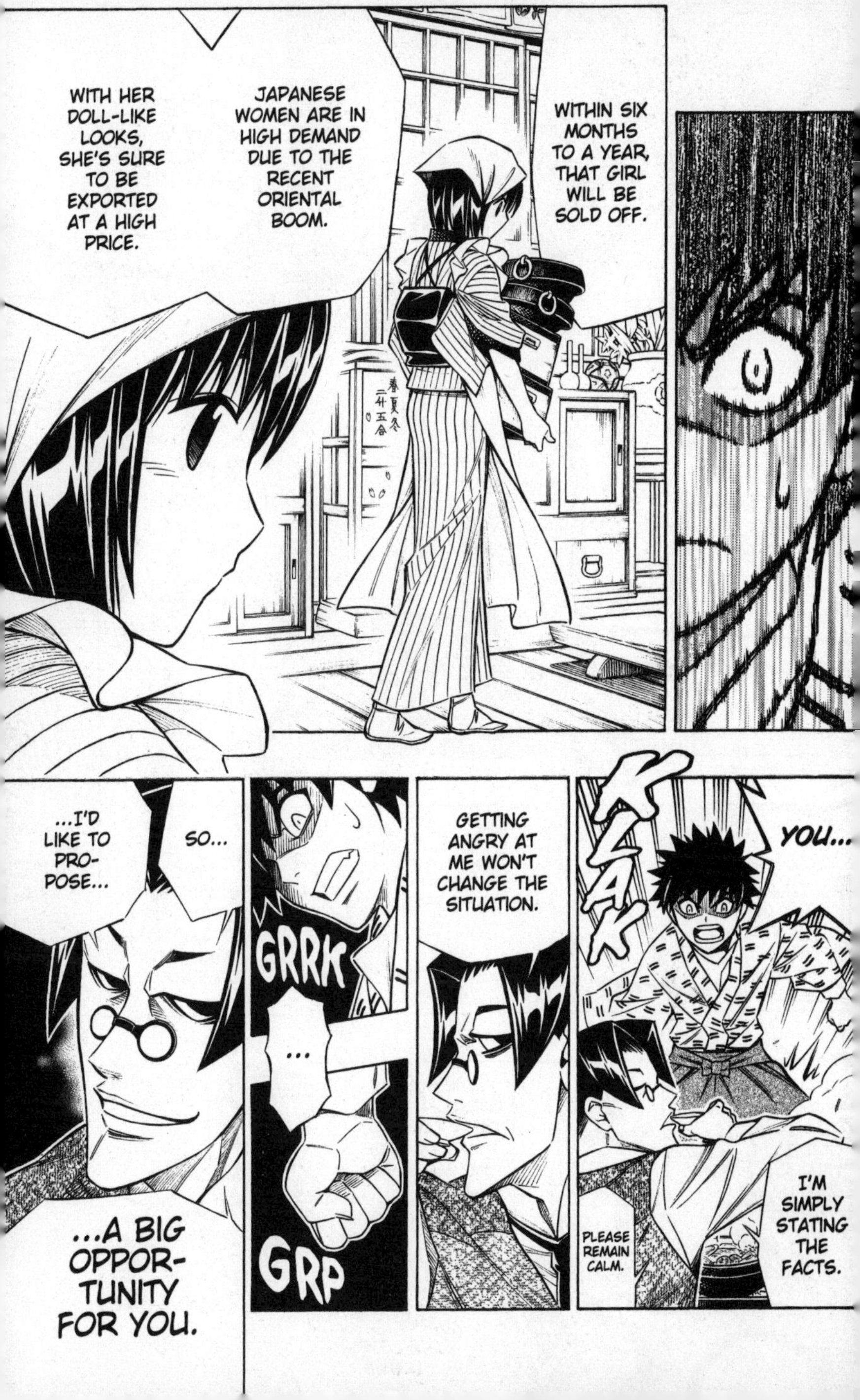
WITHIN SIX MONTHS TO A YEAR, THAT GIRL WILL BE SOLD OFF.
JAPANESE WOMEN ARE IN HIGH DEMAND DUE TO THE RECENT ORIENTAL BOOM.
WITH HER DOLL-LIKE LOOKS, SHE'S SURE TO BE EXPORTED AT A HIGH PRICE.
春夏冬
二升五合
KLAK
YOU...
I'M SIMPLY STATING THE FACTS.
PLEASE REMAIN CALM.
GETTING ANGRY AT ME WON'T CHANGE THE SITUATION.
GRRK
...
GRP
SO...
...I'D LIKE TO PRO-POSE...
...A BIG OPPOR-TUNITY FOR YOU.

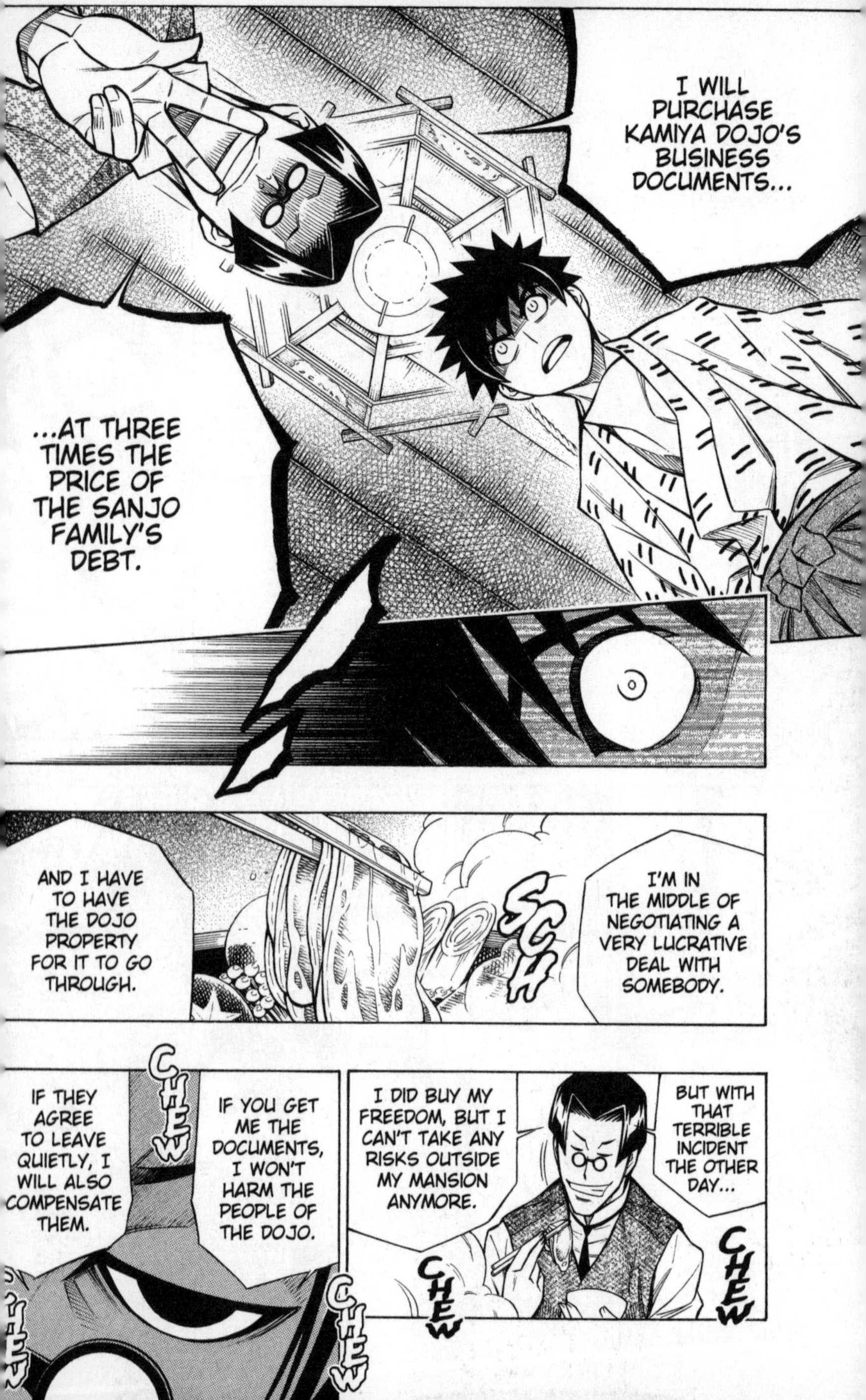
I WILL PURCHASE KAMIYA DOJO'S BUSINESS DOCUMENTS...
...AT THREE TIMES THE PRICE OF THE SANJO FAMILY'S DEBT.
I'M IN THE MIDDLE OF NEGOTIATING A VERY LUCRATIVE DEAL WITH SOMEBODY.
SCH
AND I HAVE TO HAVE THE DOJO PROPERTY FOR IT TO GO THROUGH.
BUT WITH THAT TERRIBLE INCIDENT THE OTHER DAY...
I DID BUY MY FREEDOM, BUT I CAN'T TAKE ANY RISKS OUTSIDE MY MANSION ANYMORE.
CHEW
CHEW
CHEW
IF YOU GET ME THE DOCUMENTS, I WON'T HARM THE PEOPLE OF THE DOJO.
CHEW
IF THEY AGREE TO LEAVE QUIETLY, I WILL ALSO COMPENSATE THEM.

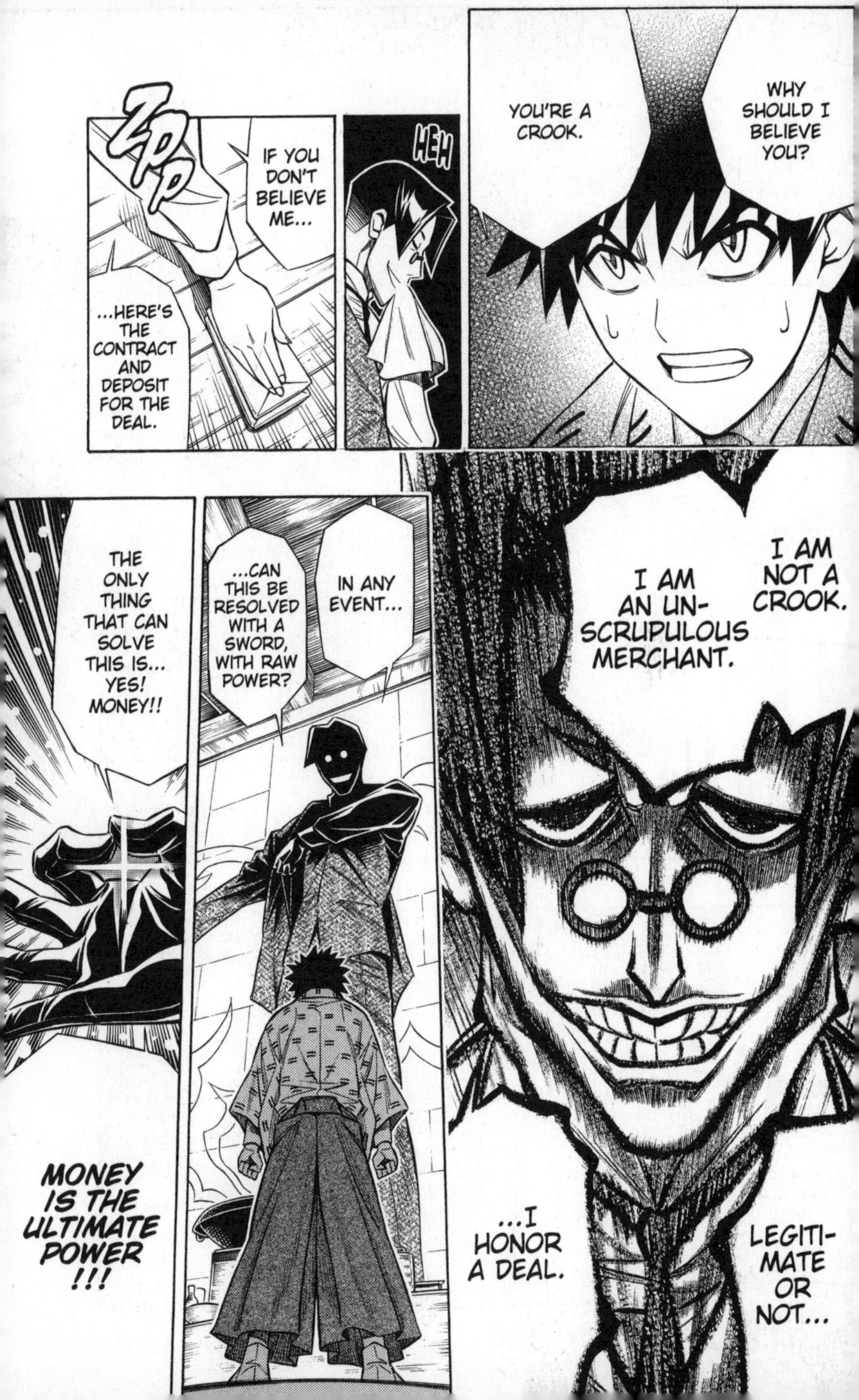
WHY SHOULD I BELIEVE YOU?
YOU'RE A CROOK.
HEH
IF YOU DON'T BELIEVE ME...
ZPP
...HERE'S THE CONTRACT AND DEPOSIT FOR THE DEAL.
I AM NOT A CROOK.
I AM AN UN-SCRUPULOUS MERCHANT.
LEGITI-MATE OR NOT...
...I HONOR A DEAL.
IN ANY EVENT...
...CAN THIS BE RESOLVED WITH A SWORD, WITH RAW POWER?
THE ONLY THING THAT CAN SOLVE THIS IS... YES! MONEY!!
MONEY IS THE ULTIMATE POWER!!!

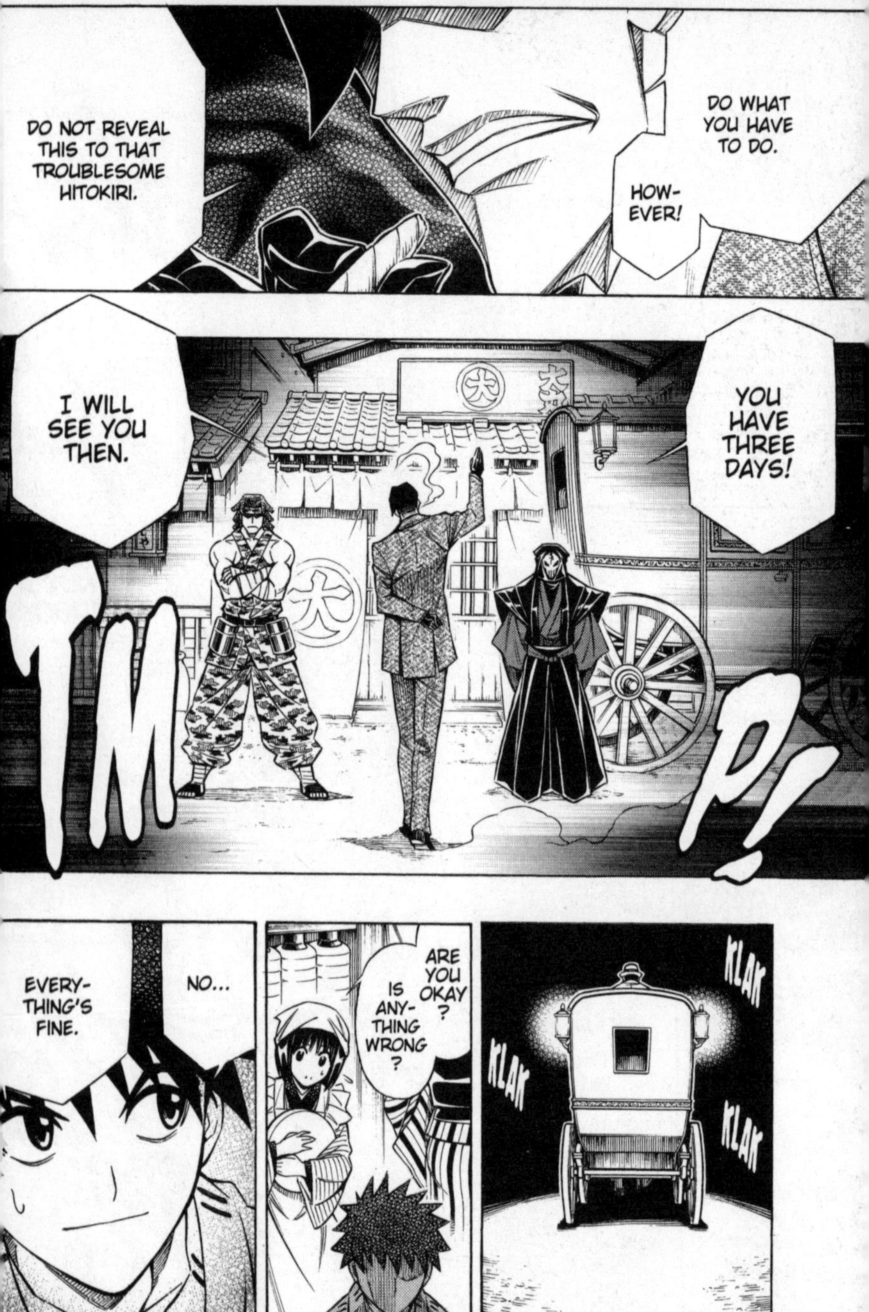
DO WHAT YOU HAVE TO DO.
HOW-EVER!
DO NOT REVEAL THIS TO THAT TROUBLESOME HITOKIRI.
YOU HAVE THREE DAYS!
I WILL SEE YOU THEN.
TMP!
KLAK
KLAK
KLAK
ARE YOU OKAY?
IS ANYTHING WRONG?
NO...
EVERYTHING'S FINE.

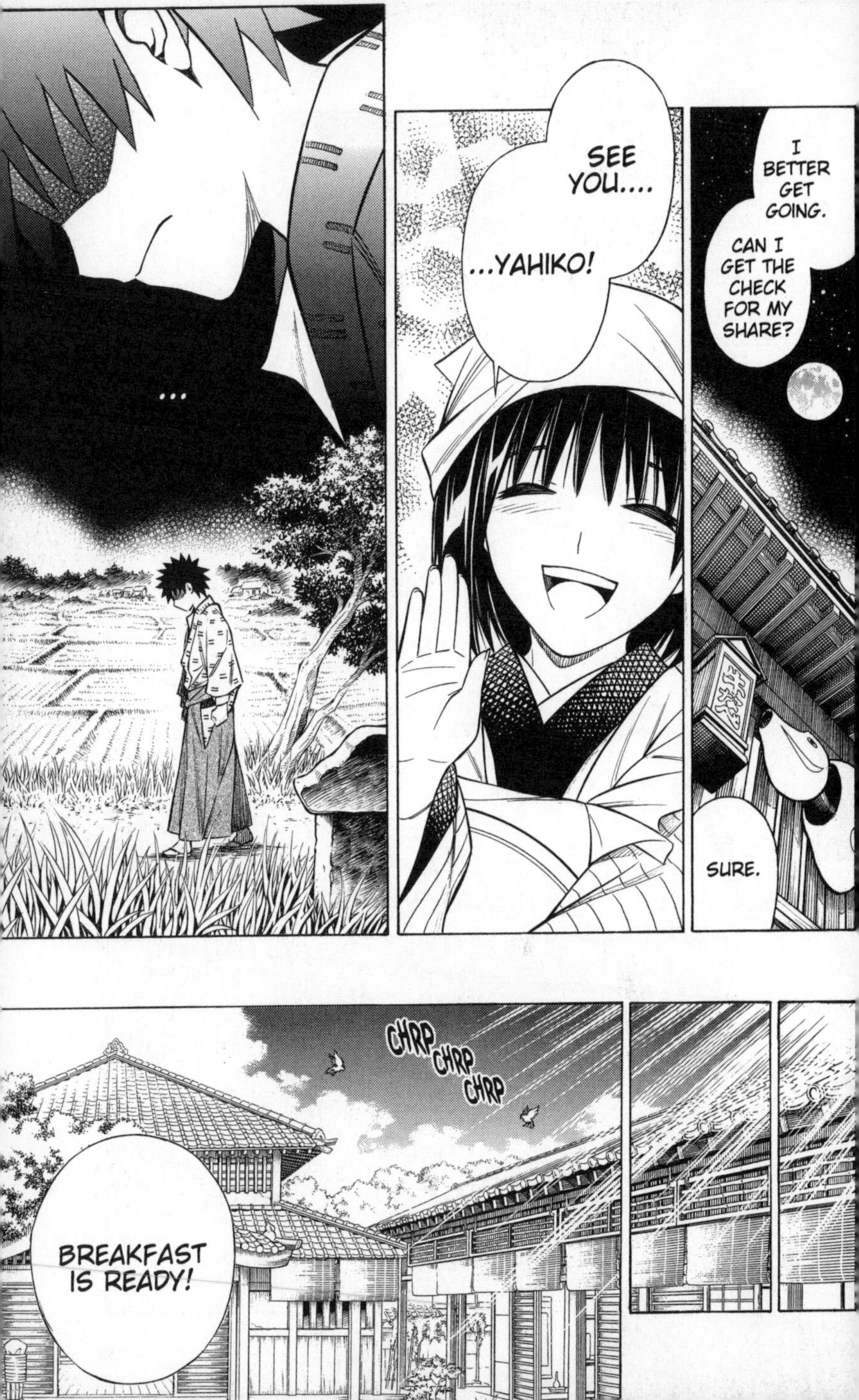
I BETTER GET GOING.
CAN I GET THE CHECK FOR MY SHARE?
SURE.
SEE YOU....
...YAHIKO!
...
CHRP CHRP CHRP
BREAKFAST IS READY!

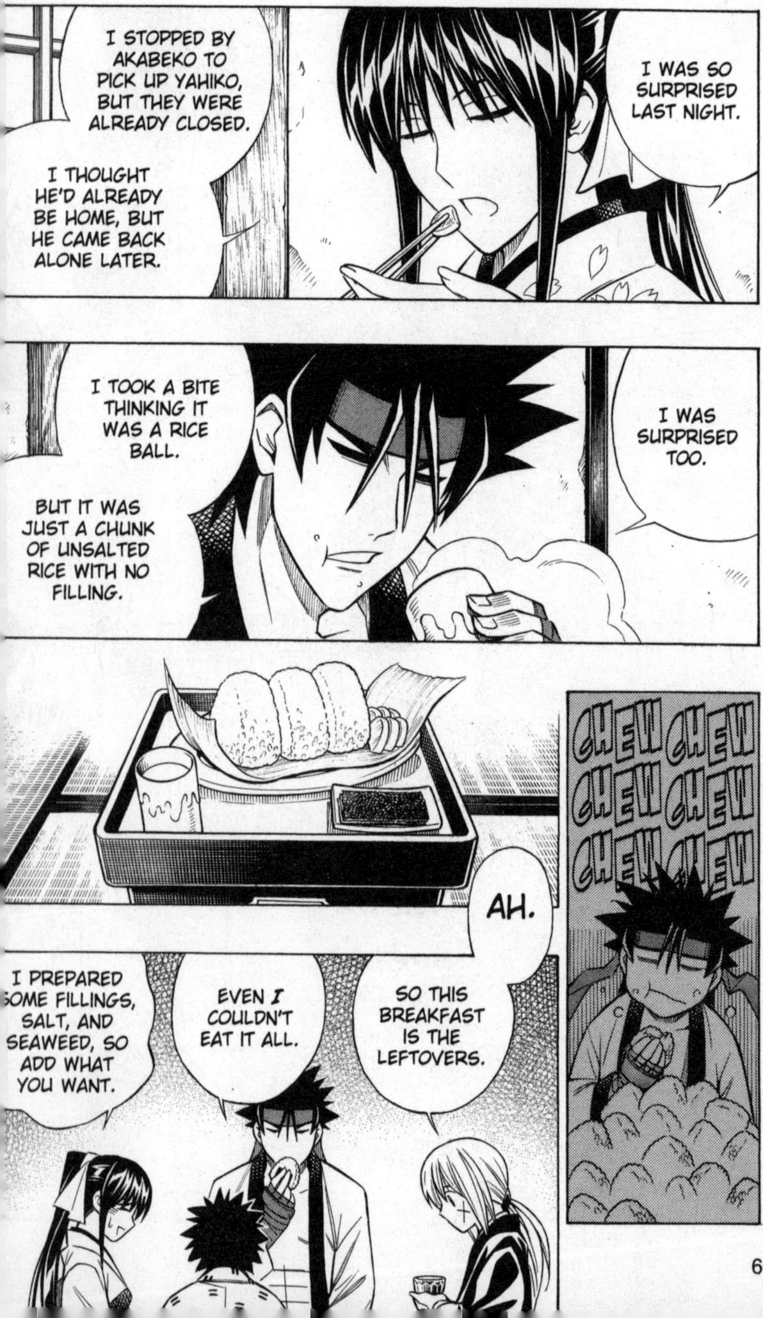
I WAS SO SURPRISED LAST NIGHT.
I STOPPED BY AKABEKO TO PICK UP YAHIKO, BUT THEY WERE ALREADY CLOSED.
I THOUGHT HE'D ALREADY BE HOME, BUT HE CAME BACK ALONE LATER.
I WAS SURPRISED TOO.
I TOOK A BITE THINKING IT WAS A RICE BALL.
BUT IT WAS JUST A CHUNK OF UNSALTED RICE WITH NO FILLING.
CHEW CHEW
CHEW CHEW
CHEW CHEW
AH.
SO THIS BREAKFAST IS THE LEFTOVERS.
EVEN *I* COULDN'T EAT IT ALL.
I PREPARED SOME FILLINGS, SALT, AND SEAWEED, SO ADD WHAT YOU WANT.

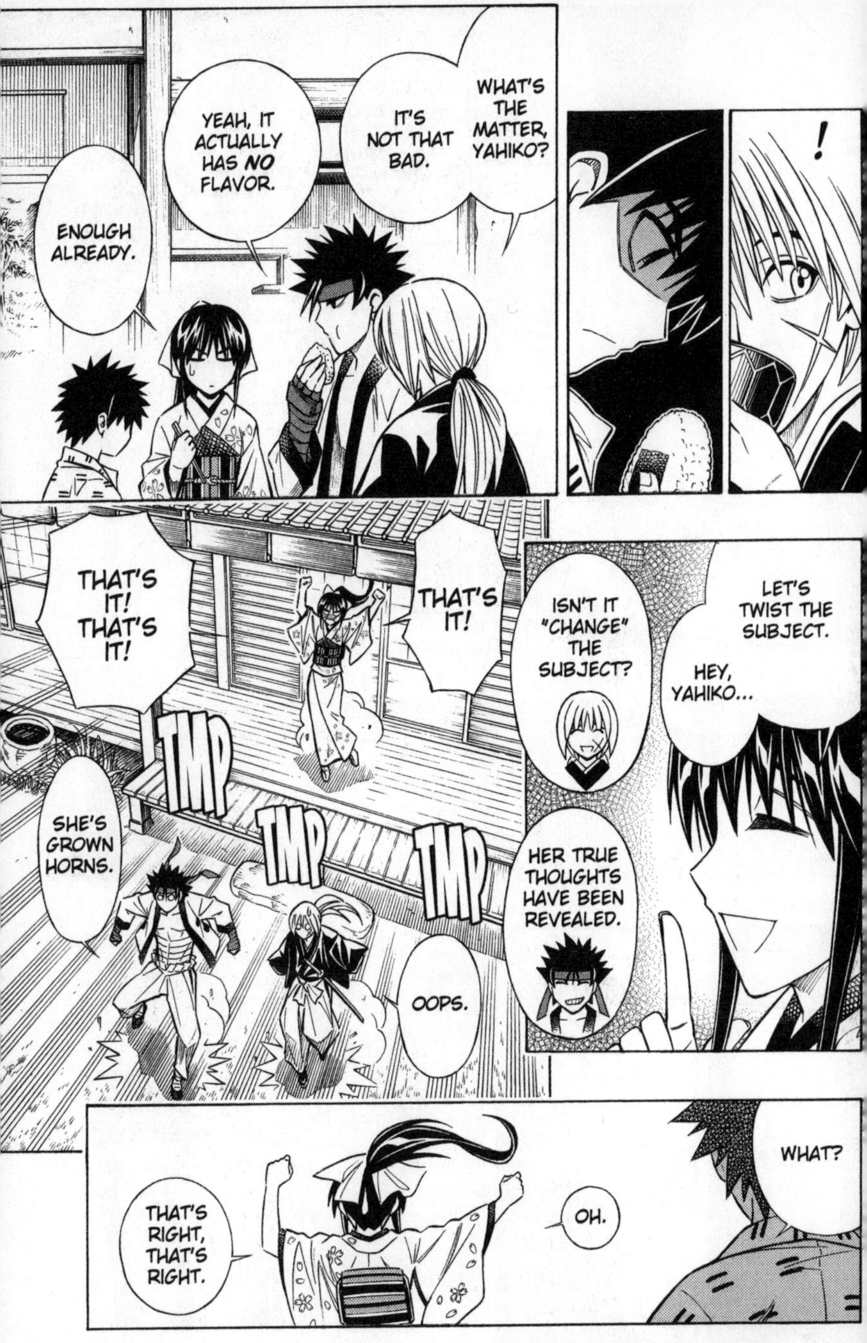
!
WHAT'S THE MATTER, YAHIKO?
IT'S NOT THAT BAD.
YEAH, IT ACTUALLY HAS *NO* FLAVOR.
ENOUGH ALREADY.
LET'S TWIST THE SUBJECT.
HEY, YAHIKO...
ISN'T IT "CHANGE" THE SUBJECT?
HER TRUE THOUGHTS HAVE BEEN REVEALED.
THAT'S IT!
THAT'S IT! THAT'S IT!
TMP
TMP
TMP
OOPS.
SHE'S GROWN HORNS.
WHAT?
OH.
THAT'S RIGHT, THAT'S RIGHT.

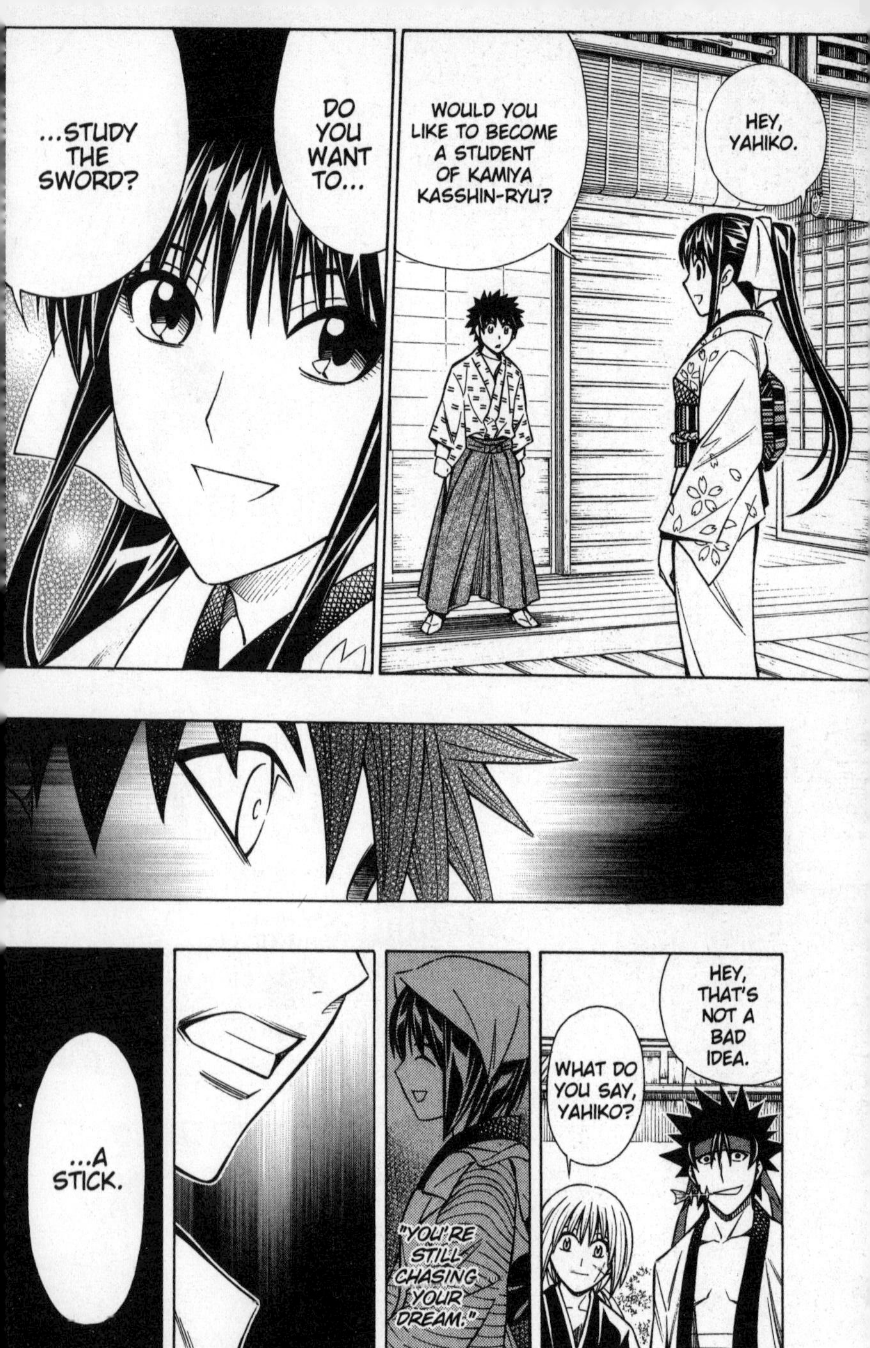
HEY, YAHIKO.
WOULD YOU LIKE TO BECOME A STUDENT OF KAMIYA KASSHIN-RYU?
DO YOU WANT TO...
...STUDY THE SWORD?
HEY, THAT'S NOT A BAD IDEA.
WHAT DO YOU SAY, YAHIKO?
"YOU'RE STILL CHASING YOUR DREAM."
...A STICK.

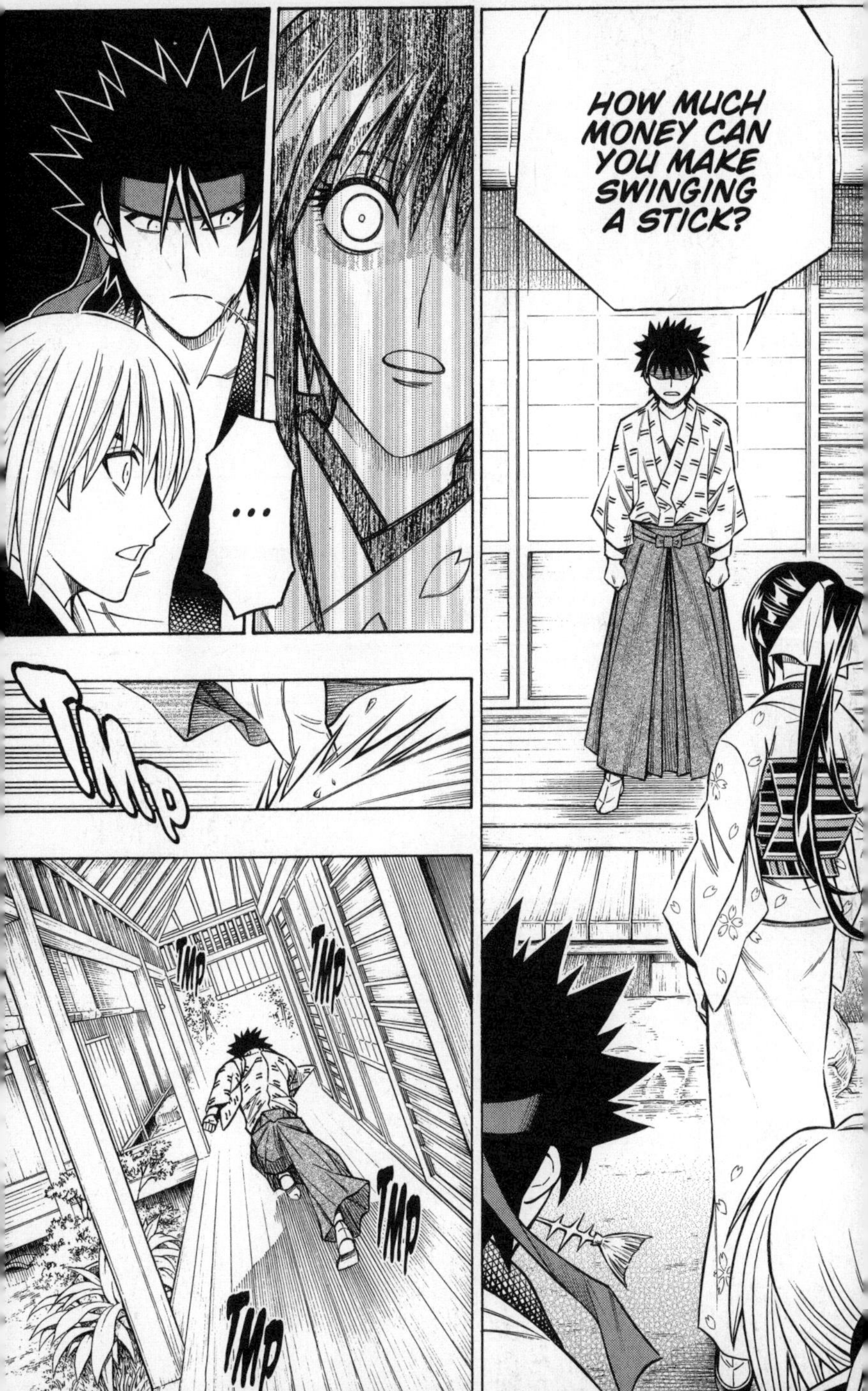
HOW MUCH MONEY CAN YOU MAKE SWINGING A STICK?
...
TMMP
TMP
TMP
TMP
TMP

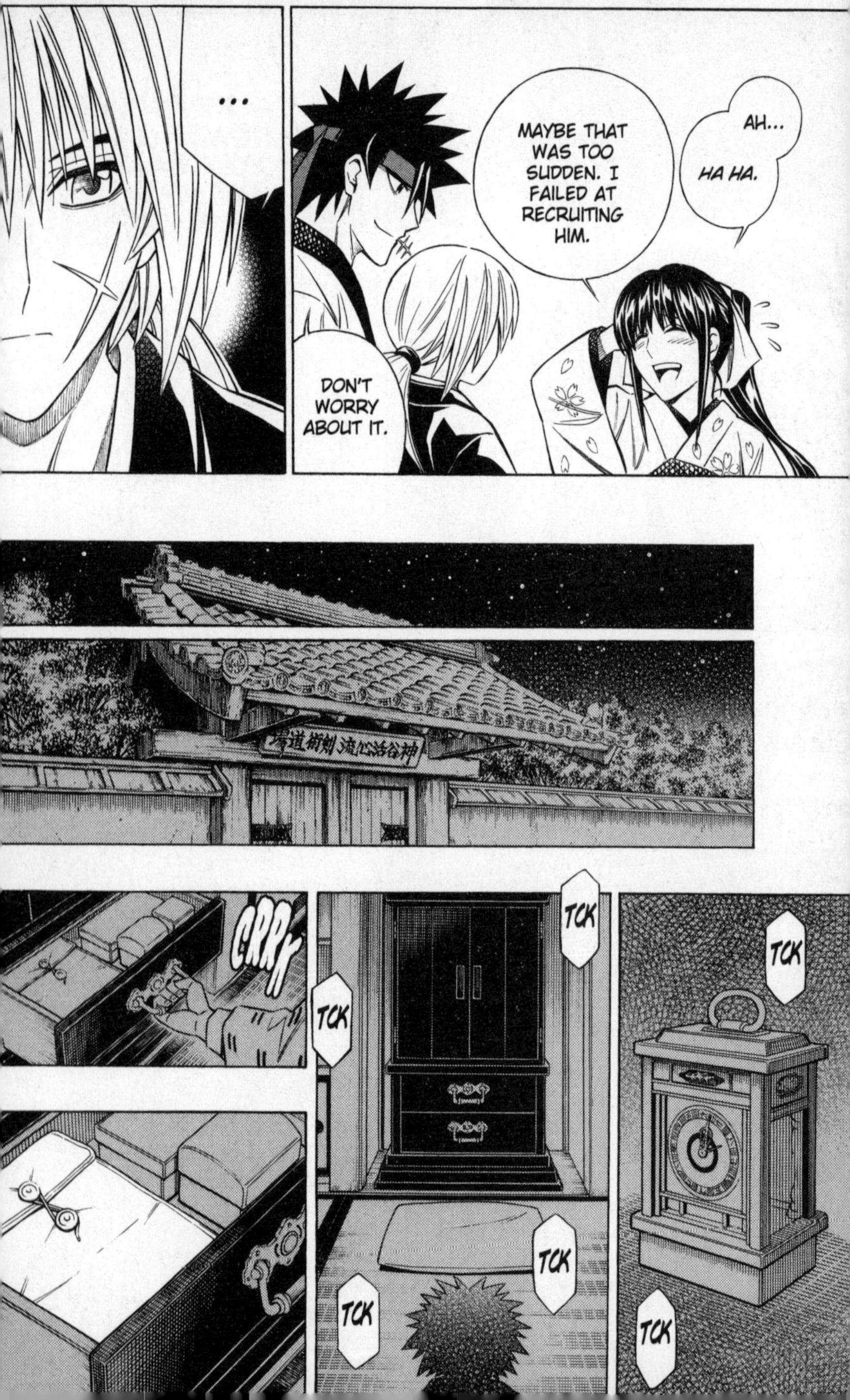
AH... HA HA.
MAYBE THAT WAS TOO SUDDEN. I FAILED AT RECRUITING HIM.
DON'T WORRY ABOUT IT.
...
神谷活心流剣術道場
TCK
TCK
TCK
TCK
TCK
TCK
CRRK

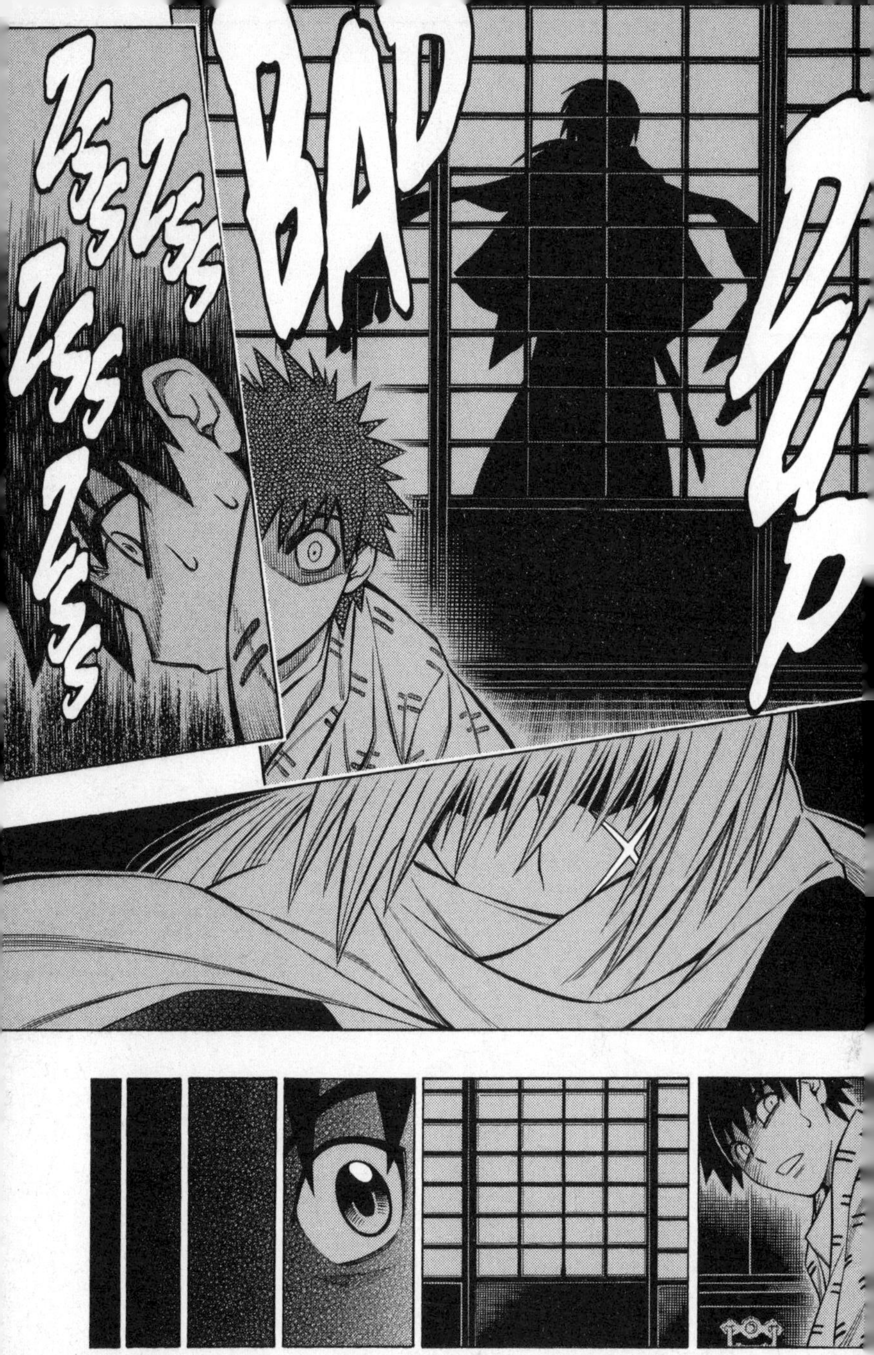
DUUP
BAD
ZSS
ZSS
ZSS
ZSSS

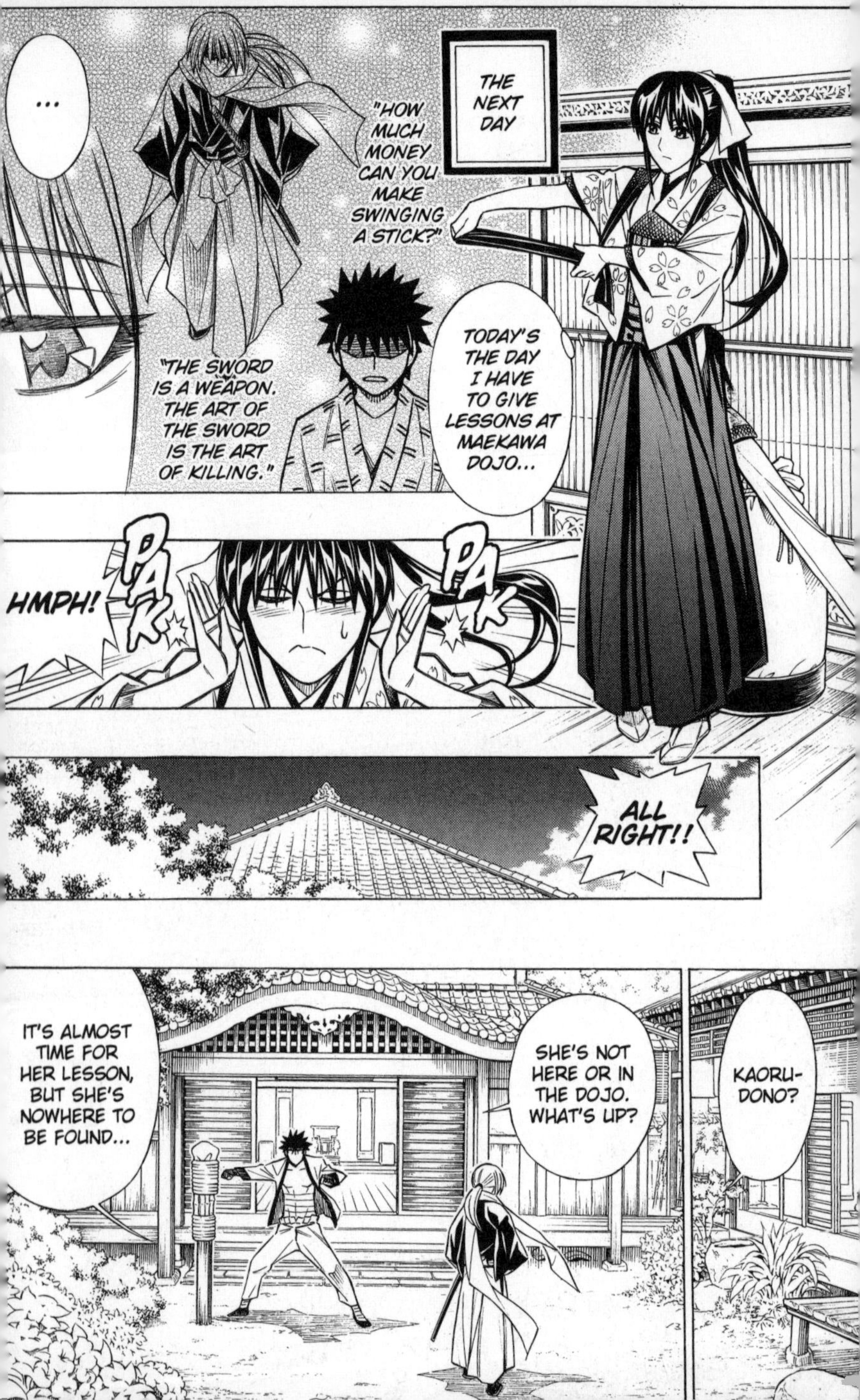
THE NEXT DAY
TODAY'S THE DAY I HAVE TO GIVE LESSONS AT MAEKAWA DOJO...
"HOW MUCH MONEY CAN YOU MAKE SWINGING A STICK?"
"THE SWORD IS A WEAPON. THE ART OF THE SWORD IS THE ART OF KILLING."
...
PAK
PAK
HMPH!
ALL RIGHT!!
KAORU-DONO?
SHE'S NOT HERE OR IN THE DOJO. WHAT'S UP?
IT'S ALMOST TIME FOR HER LESSON, BUT SHE'S NOWHERE TO BE FOUND...

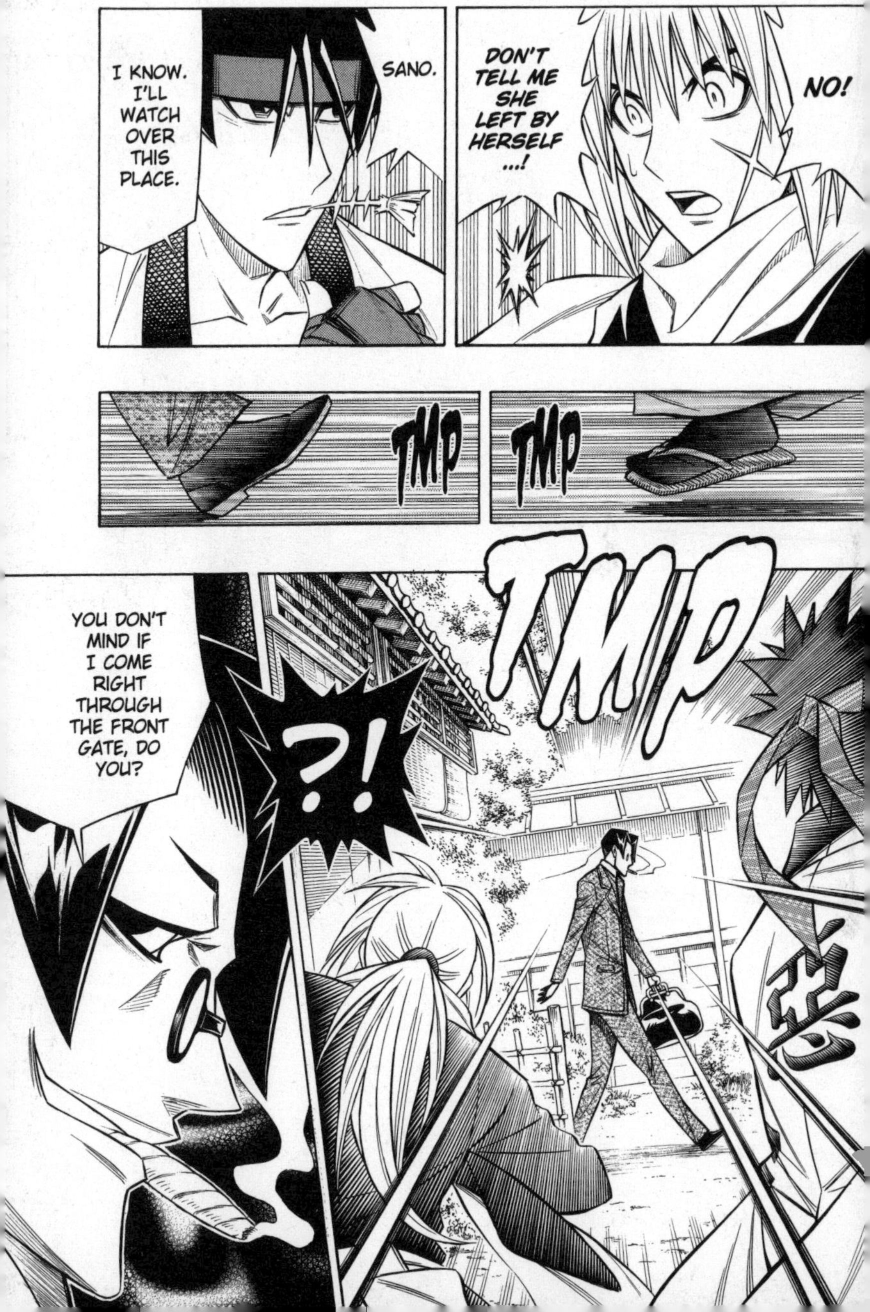

NO!
DON'T TELL ME SHE LEFT BY HERSELF ...!
SANO.
I KNOW. I'LL WATCH OVER THIS PLACE.
TMP
TMP
TMP
?!
YOU DON'T MIND IF I COME RIGHT THROUGH THE FRONT GATE, DO YOU?

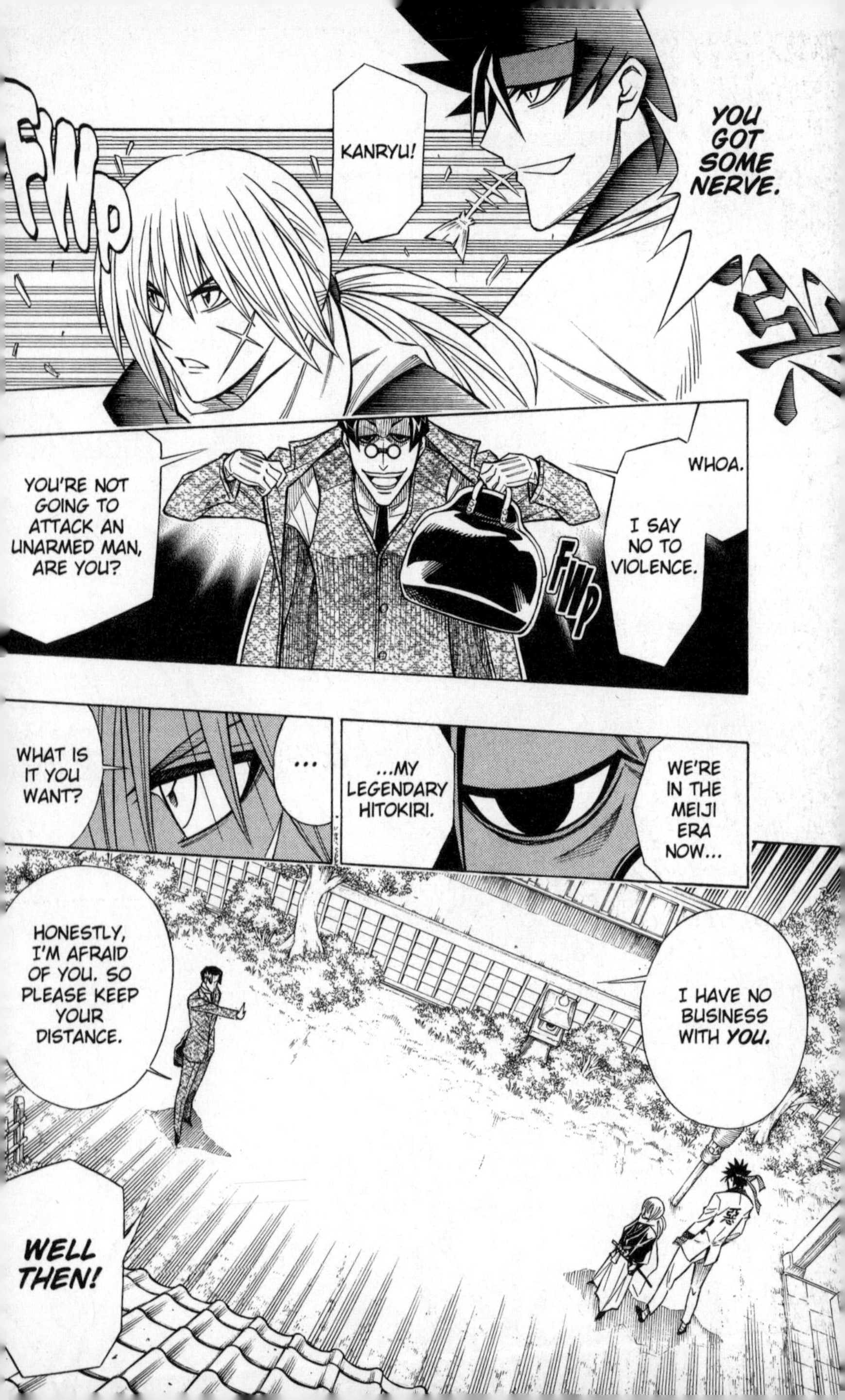
YOU GOT SOME NERVE.
KANRYU!
FWP
WHOA.
I SAY NO TO VIOLENCE.
FWP
YOU'RE NOT GOING TO ATTACK AN UNARMED MAN, ARE YOU?
WE'RE IN THE MEIJI ERA NOW...
...MY LEGENDARY HITOKIRI.
...
WHAT IS IT YOU WANT?
I HAVE NO BUSINESS WITH *YOU*.
HONESTLY, I'M AFRAID OF YOU. SO PLEASE KEEP YOUR DISTANCE.
WELL THEN!

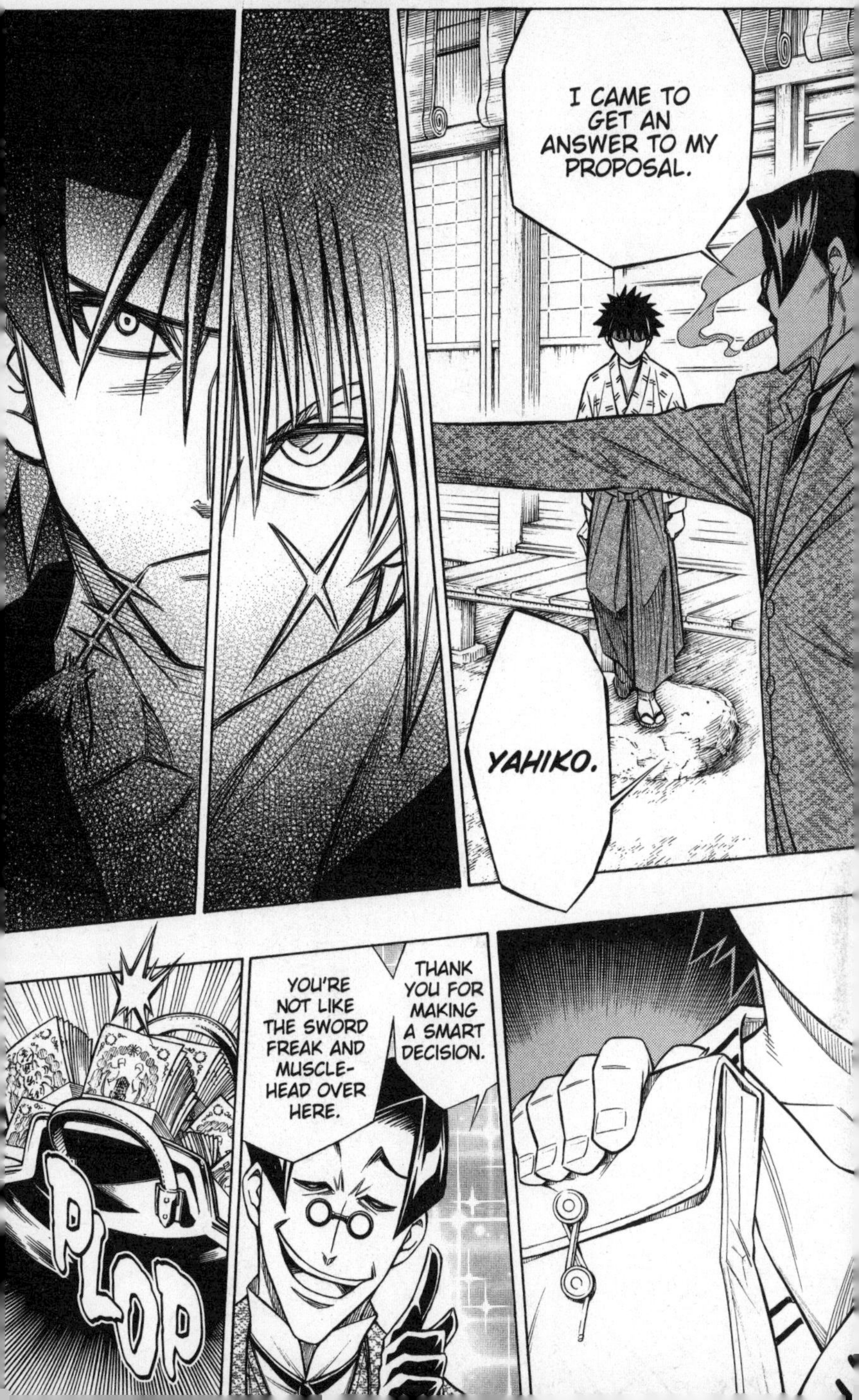
I CAME TO GET AN ANSWER TO MY PROPOSAL.
YAHIKO.
THANK YOU FOR MAKING A SMART DECISION.
YOU'RE NOT LIKE THE SWORD FREAK AND MUSCLE-HEAD OVER HERE.
PLOP

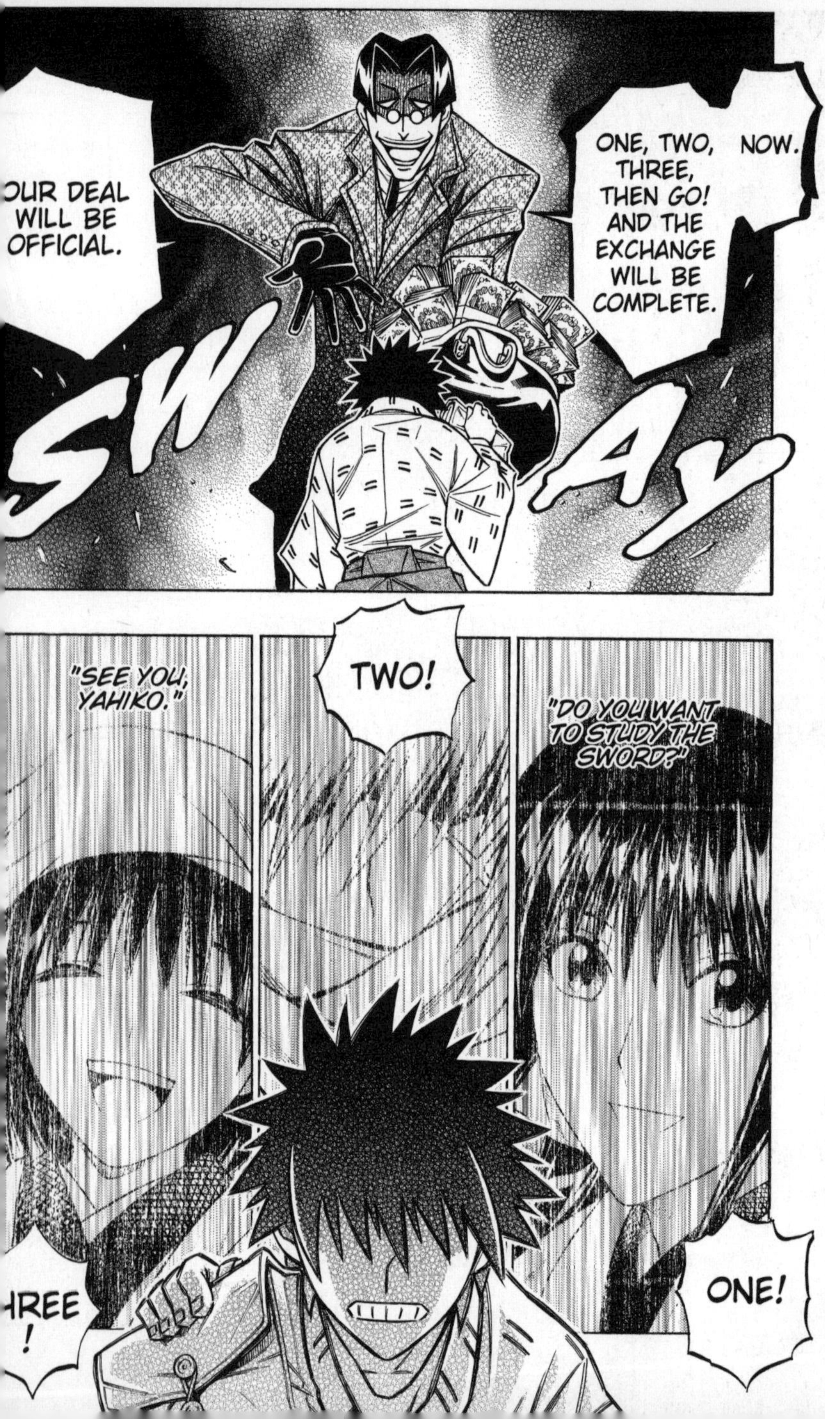
NOW.
ONE, TWO, THREE, THEN GO! AND THE EXCHANGE WILL BE COMPLETE.
SWAY
OUR DEAL WILL BE OFFICIAL.
"DO YOU WANT TO STUDY THE SWORD?"
ONE!
TWO!
"SEE YOU, YAHIKO."
HREE!

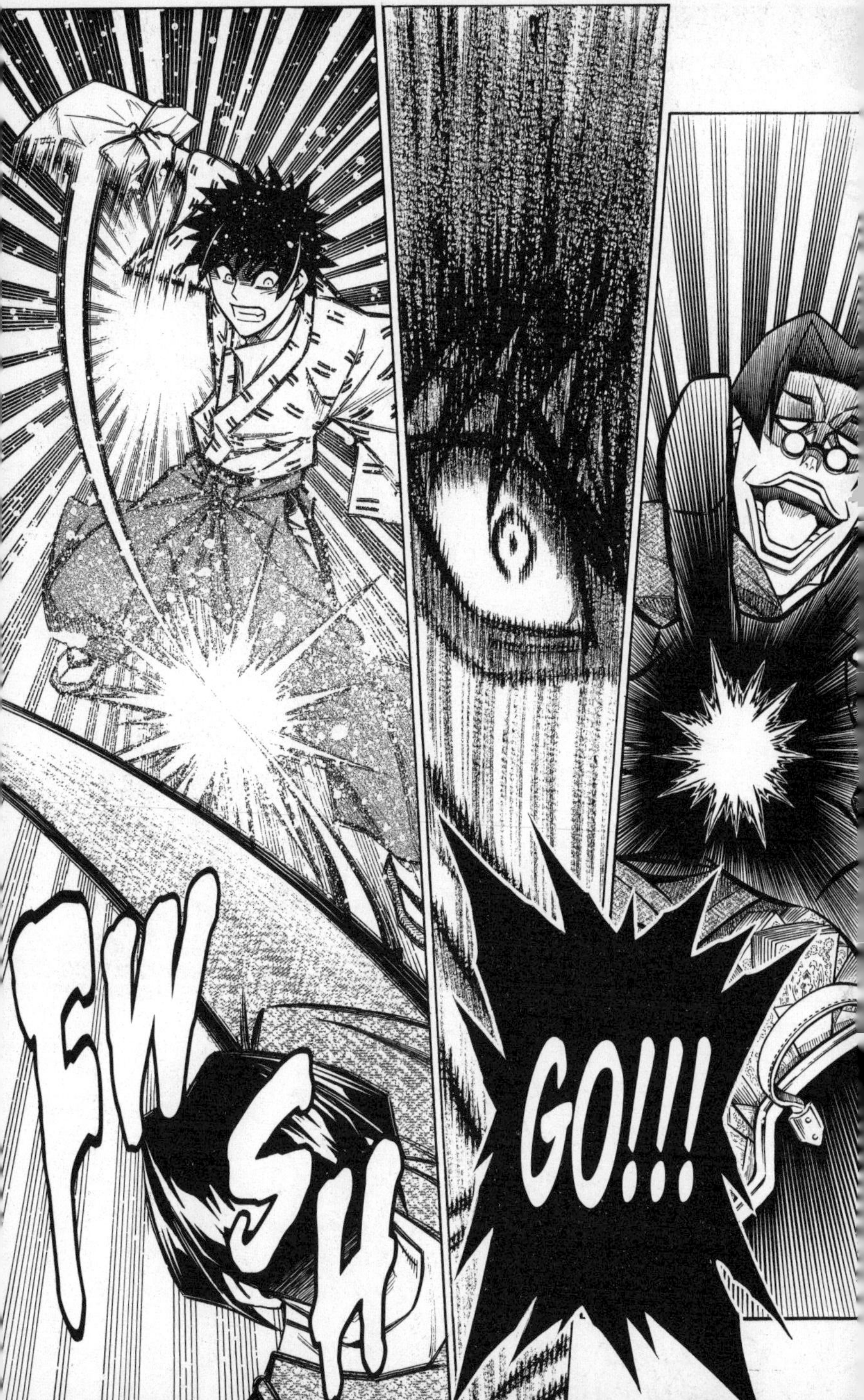
GO!!!
FWSH

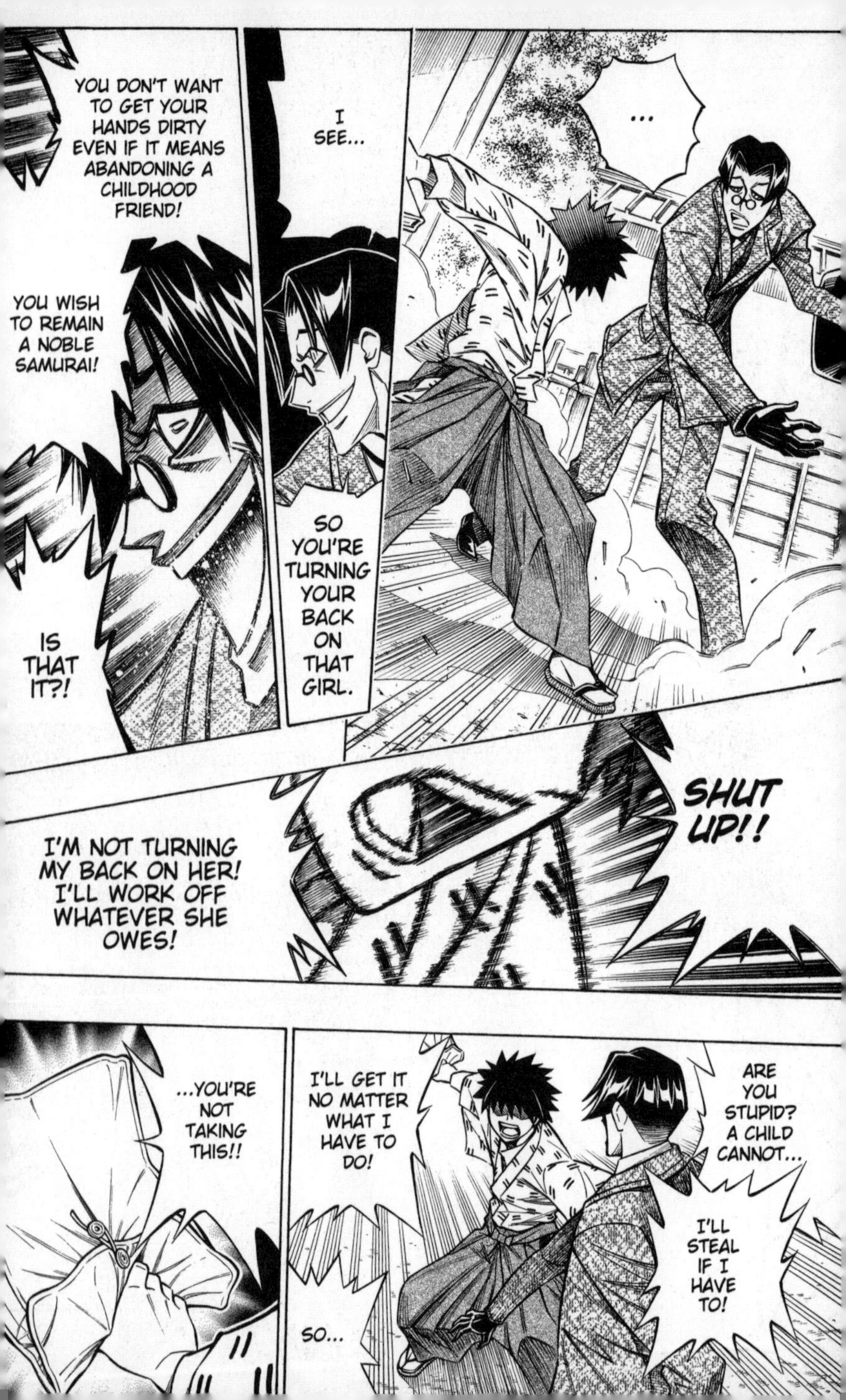
...
I SEE...
SO YOU'RE TURNING YOUR BACK ON THAT GIRL.
YOU DON'T WANT TO GET YOUR HANDS DIRTY EVEN IF IT MEANS ABANDONING A CHILDHOOD FRIEND!
YOU WISH TO REMAIN A NOBLE SAMURAI!
IS THAT IT?!
SHUT UP!!
I'M NOT TURNING MY BACK ON HER! I'LL WORK OFF WHATEVER SHE OWES!
ARE YOU STUPID? A CHILD CANNOT...
I'LL GET IT NO MATTER WHAT I HAVE TO DO!
I'LL STEAL IF I HAVE TO!
SO...
...YOU'RE NOT TAKING THIS!!

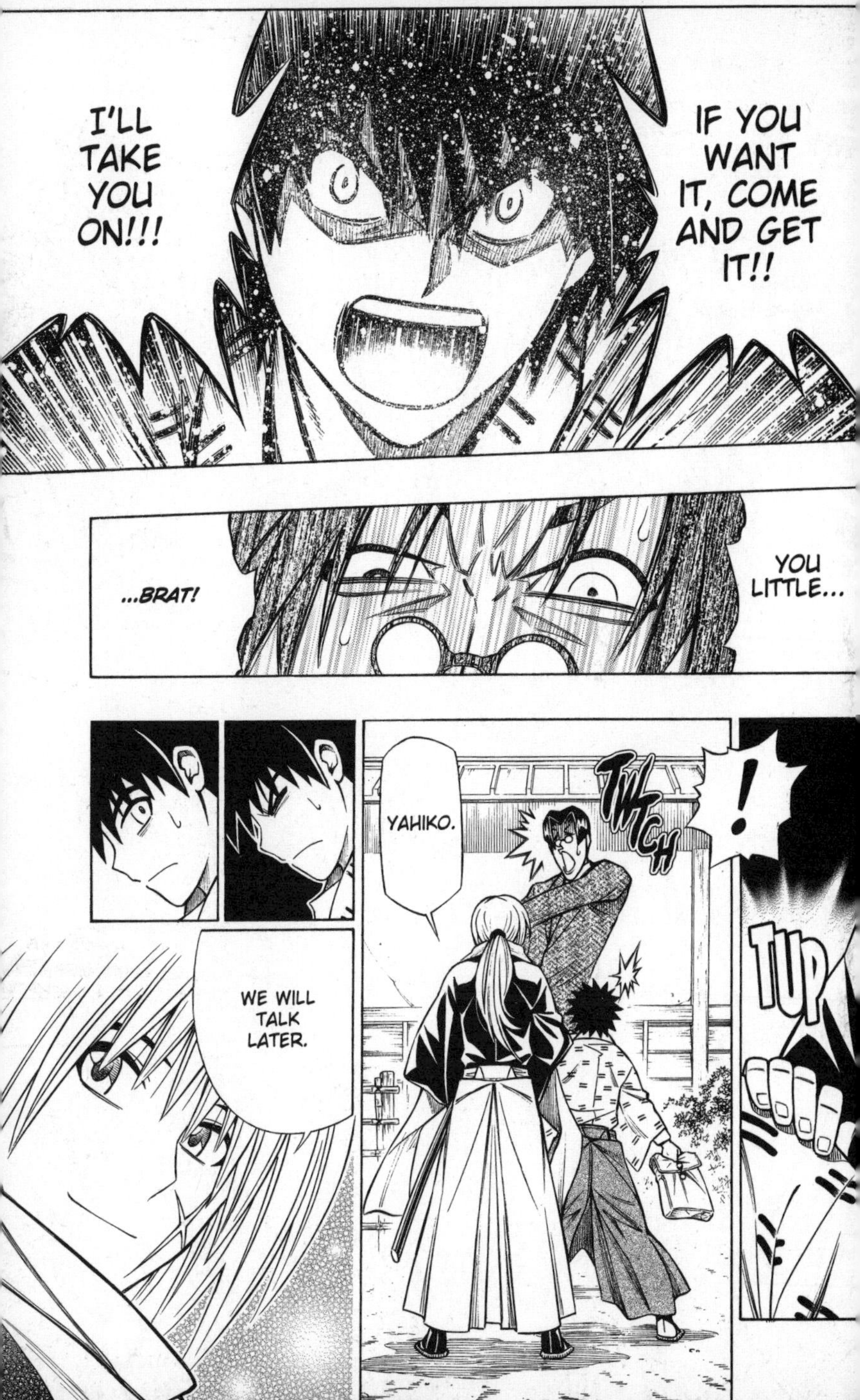
IF YOU WANT IT, COME AND GET IT!!
I'LL TAKE YOU ON!!!
YOU LITTLE...
...BRAT!
TUP
!
TWITCH
YAHIKO.
WE WILL TALK LATER.

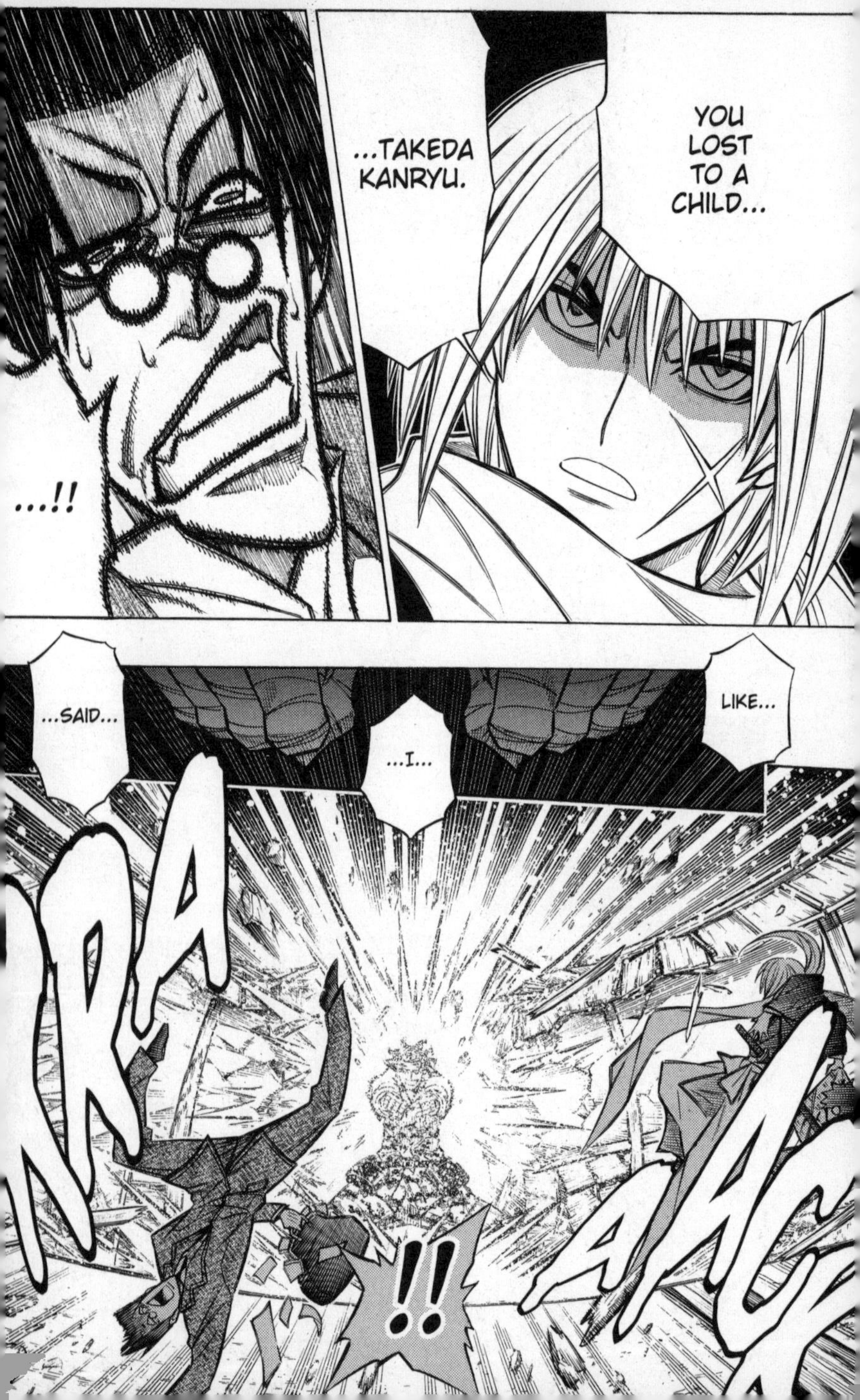
YOU LOST TO A CHILD...
...TAKEDA KANRYU.
...!!
LIKE...
...I...
...SAID...
!!

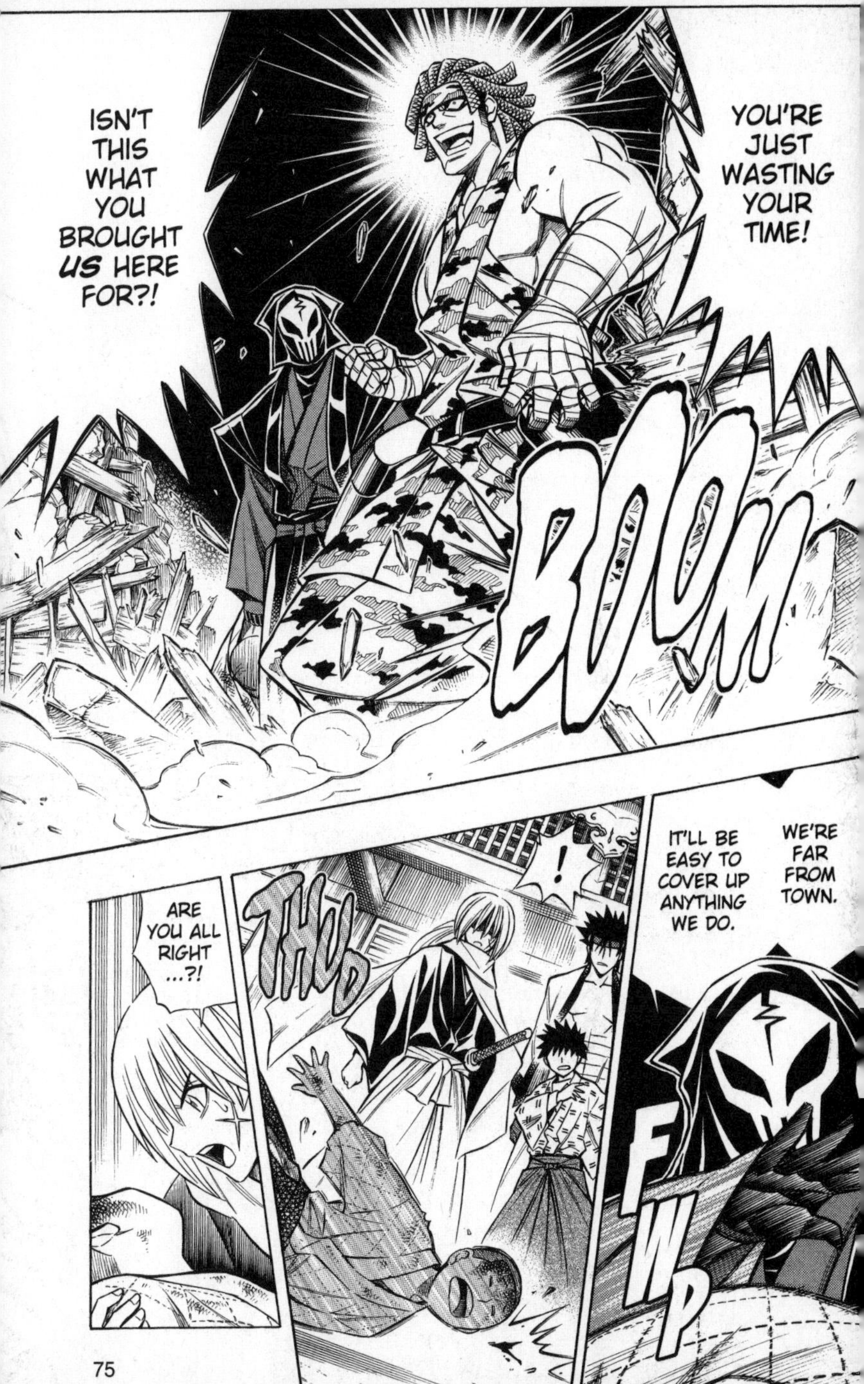
YOU'RE JUST WASTING YOUR TIME!
ISN'T THIS WHAT YOU BROUGHT *US* HERE FOR?!
BOOM
WE'RE FAR FROM TOWN.
IT'LL BE EASY TO COVER UP ANYTHING WE DO.
FWIP
!
THUD
ARE YOU ALL RIGHT ...?!

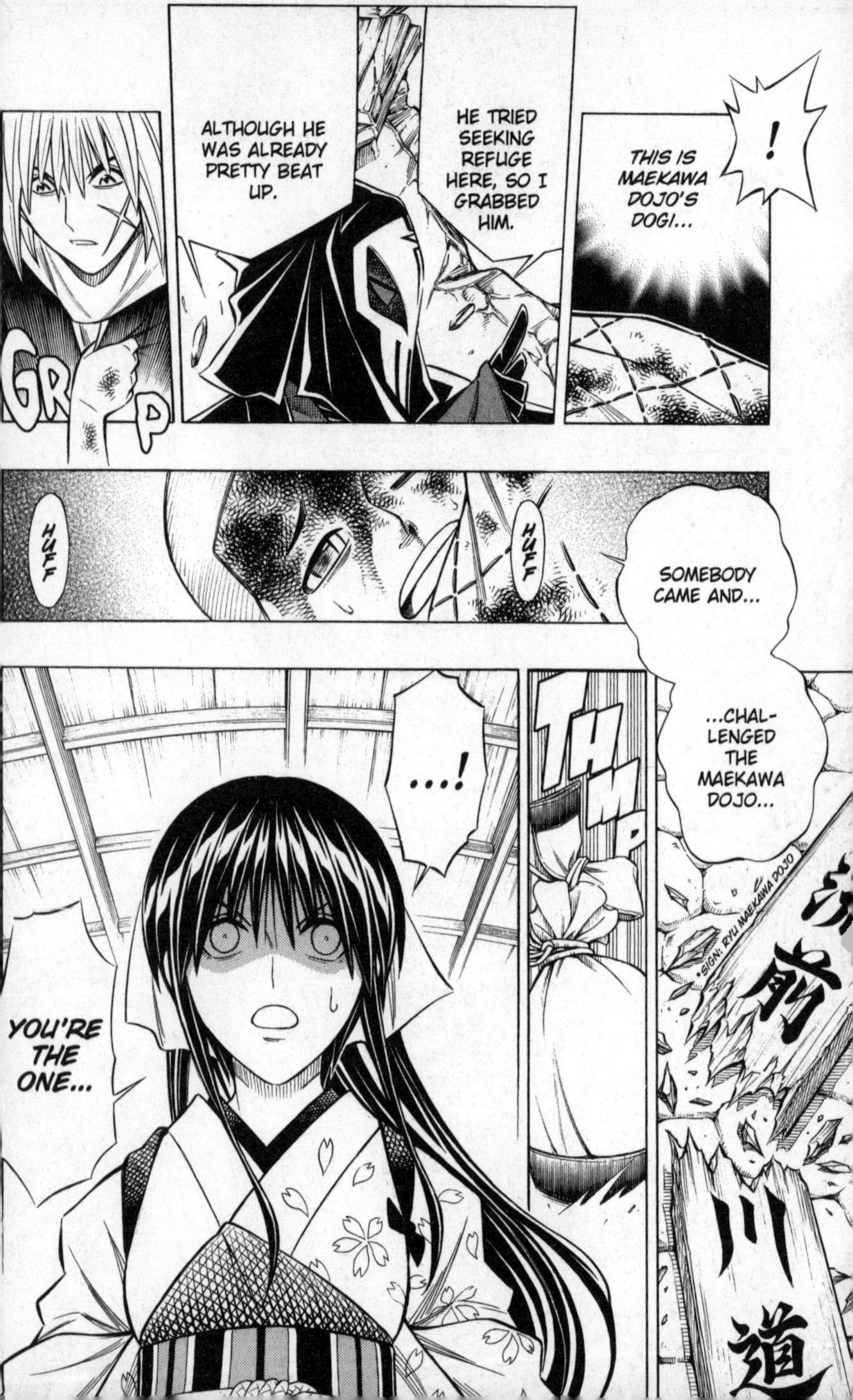
!
THIS IS MAEKAWA DOJO'S DOGI...
HE TRIED SEEKING REFUGE HERE, SO I GRABBED HIM.
ALTHOUGH HE WAS ALREADY PRETTY BEAT UP.
GRIP
SOMEBODY CAME AND...
HUFF
HUFF
...CHAL-LENGED THE MAEKAWA DOJO...
•SIGN: RYU MAEKAWA DOJO
THMP
...!
YOU'RE THE ONE...

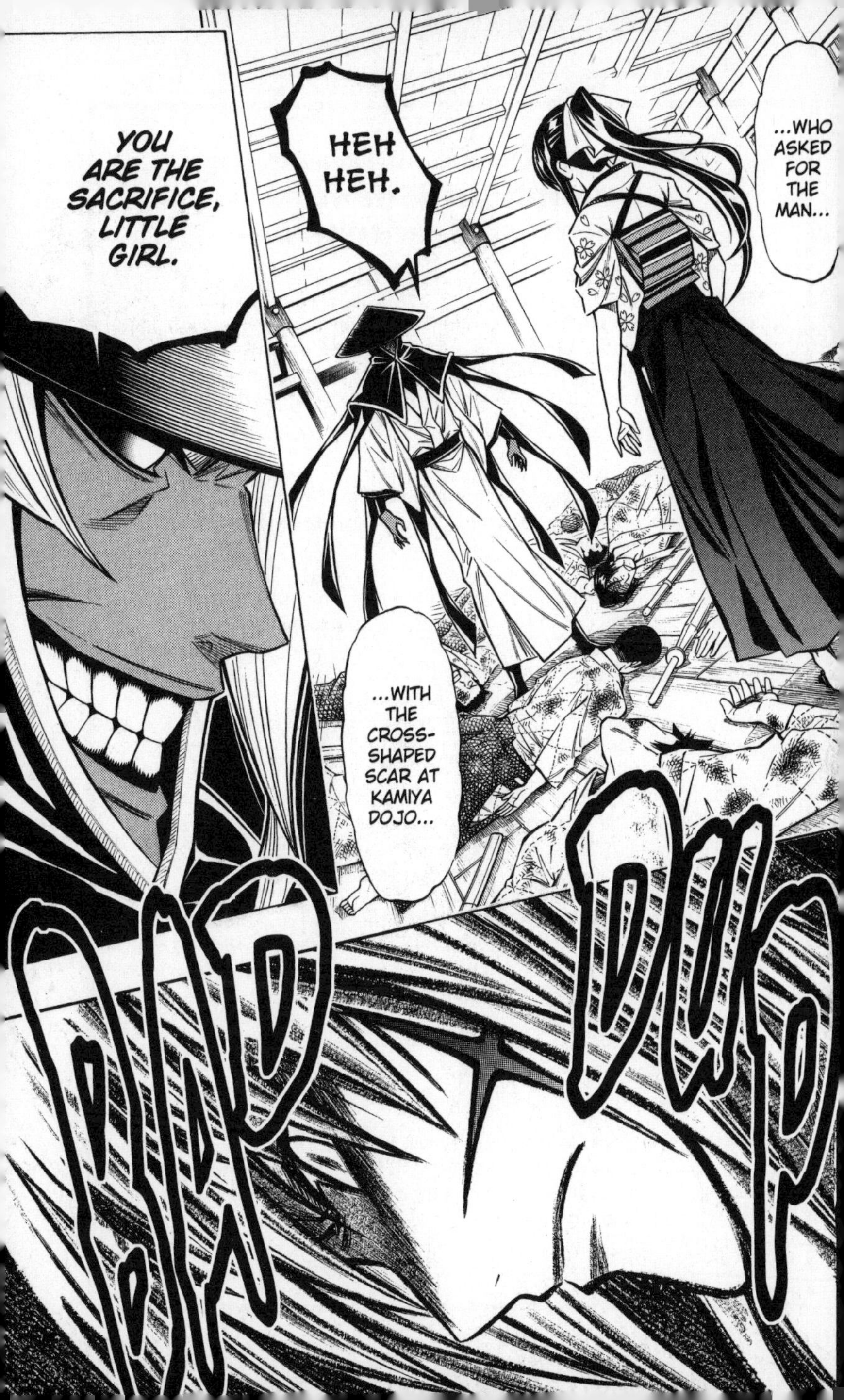
...WHO ASKED FOR THE MAN...
...WITH THE CROSS-SHAPED SCAR AT KAMIYA DOJO...
HEH HEH.
YOU ARE THE SACRIFICE, LITTLE GIRL.

(Note: Character/Production anecdotes includes spoilers for this volume. Those who have not yet read it should be warned.)

Character/Production Anecdotes Part 56

-People of *Rurouni Kenshin: Restoration*-

Himura Kenshin

I tried expressing more of his inner feelings this time. I'll explain in greater detail later. A man who brought about a peaceful new era can't find his place because of the acts he committed in the past. I tried expressing that with the theme "pool of blood." I like the image of his hands soaked in blood.

Because he's a bit more reserved and excitable compared to the original Kenshin, he seems slightly immature. To a forty-something-year-old like myself, he seems like he's in his late twenties. Perhaps he isn't too hero-like.

The way Hiten Mitsuryugi-ryu is written and why its techniques are different is purely out of fun. The editorial office received a phone call pointing out that Tensho Ryusen was read using the Chinese pronunciation. I'm sorry for the confusion.

The most obvious change in his appearance was his white scarf. "Scarf = hero" is imprinted in my mind.

Besides the expressions of his eyes and speech, I changed Kenshin's cross-shaped scar→ white (crimson), Battosai's cross-shaped scar →black (deep crimson). Many of the readers didn't notice until the end...

I struggled most with his hairstyle. With the way I draw now, I couldn't quite recreate his original bushy hair. I finally regained that touch toward the end.

Kamiya Kaoru

With Kenshin a bit more immature, Kaoru ended up being slightly more mature. I didn't realize it at the time, but I mixed in some "older sister" qualities in her.

One thing I paid close attention to was removing violent expressions when she calls people out. The aversion for a violent heroine has been strong the past few years. I kept it to her raising her arms and chasing people around this time.

Continued on page 110.

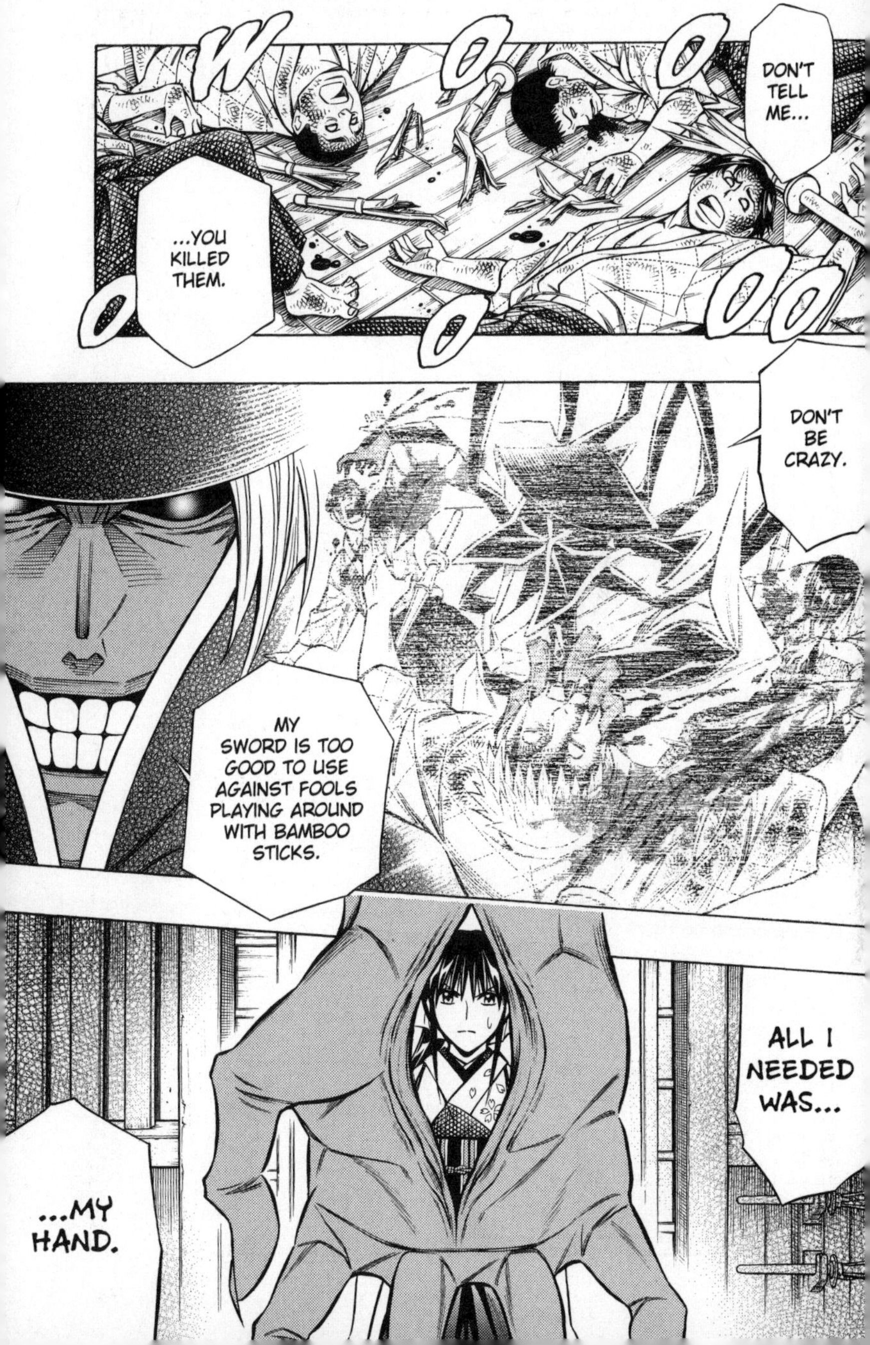
DON'T TELL ME...
...YOU KILLED THEM.
WOOOOOO
DON'T BE CRAZY.
MY SWORD IS TOO GOOD TO USE AGAINST FOOLS PLAYING AROUND WITH BAMBOO STICKS.
ALL I NEEDED WAS...
...MY HAND.

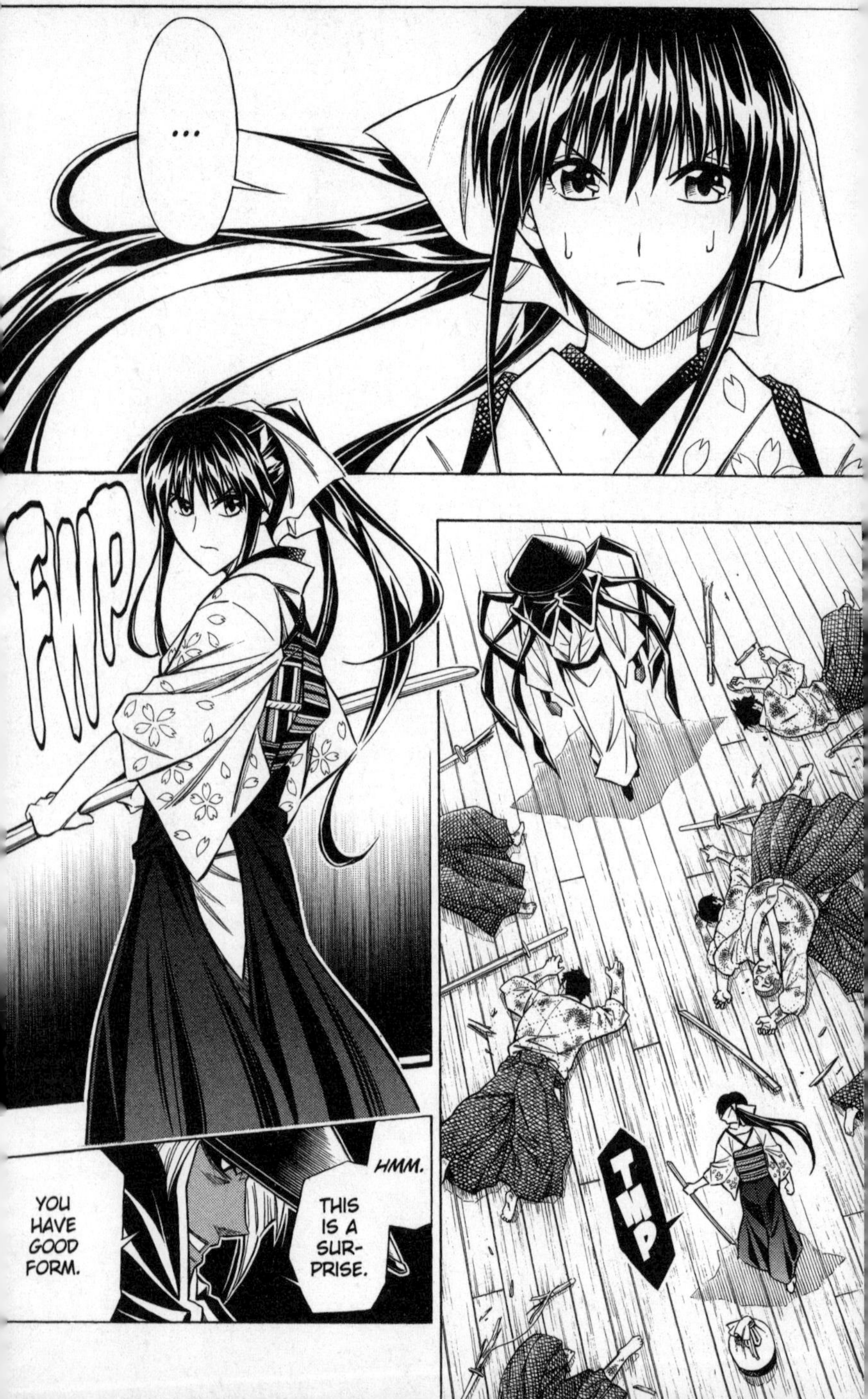
...
TMP
FWP
HMM.
THIS IS A SUR-PRISE.
YOU HAVE GOOD FORM.

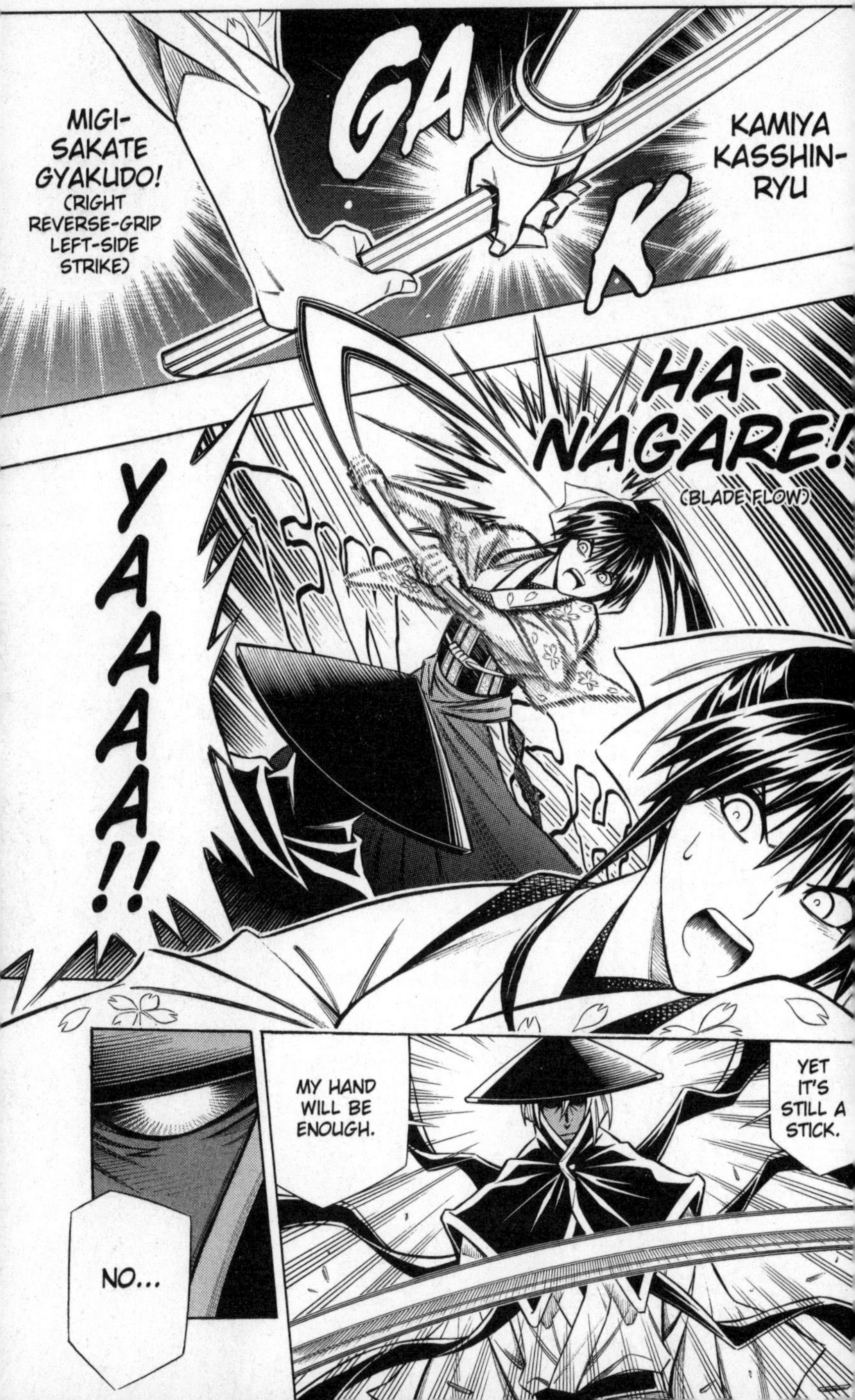
KAMIYA KASSHIN-RYU
GAK
MIGI-SAKATE GYAKUDO!
(RIGHT REVERSE-GRIP LEFT-SIDE STRIKE)
HA-NAGARE!
(BLADE FLOW)
YAAAAA!!
YET IT'S STILL A STICK.
MY HAND WILL BE ENOUGH.
NO...

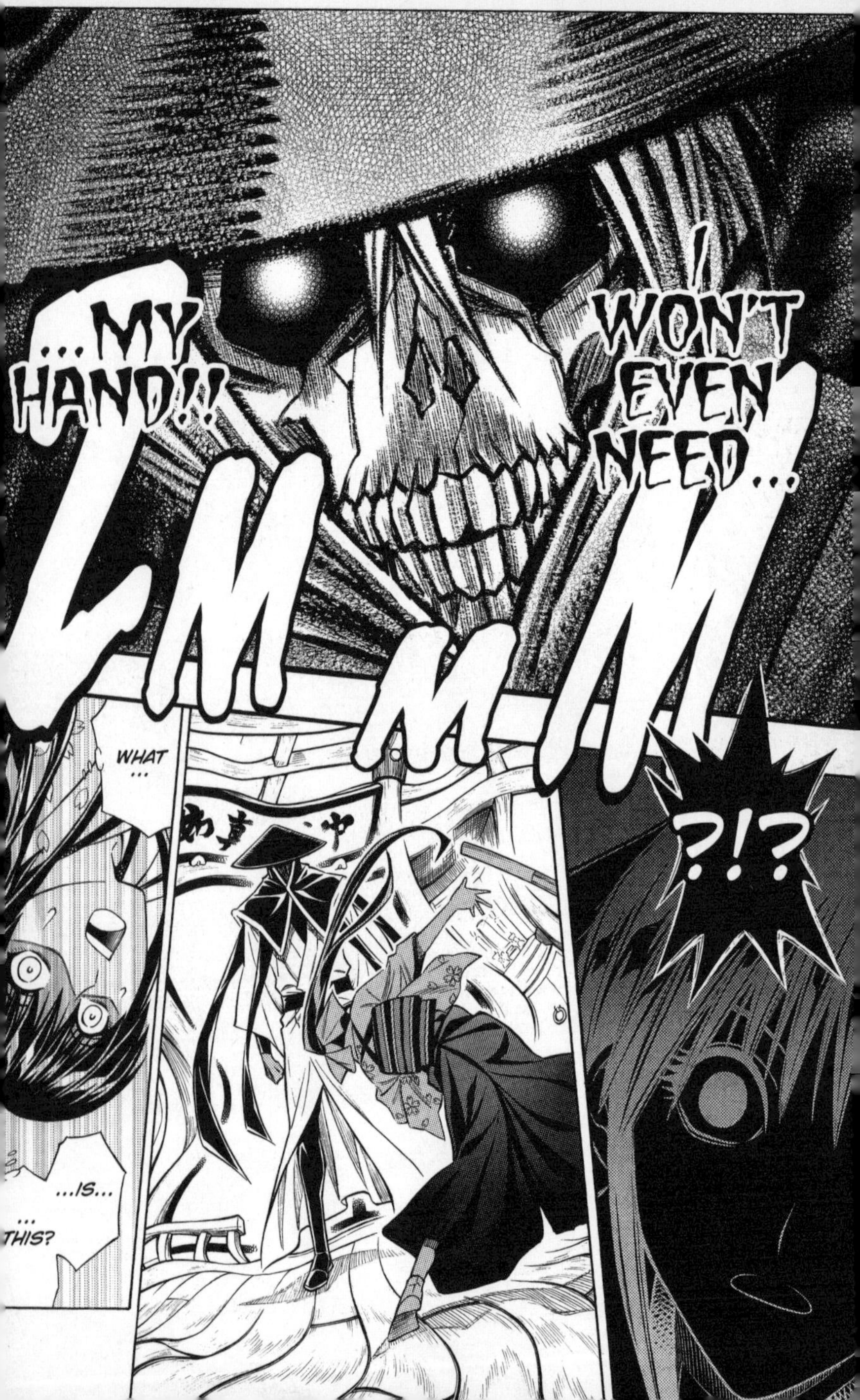
I WON'T EVEN NEED...
...MY HAND!!
?!?
WHAT ...
...IS...
... THIS?

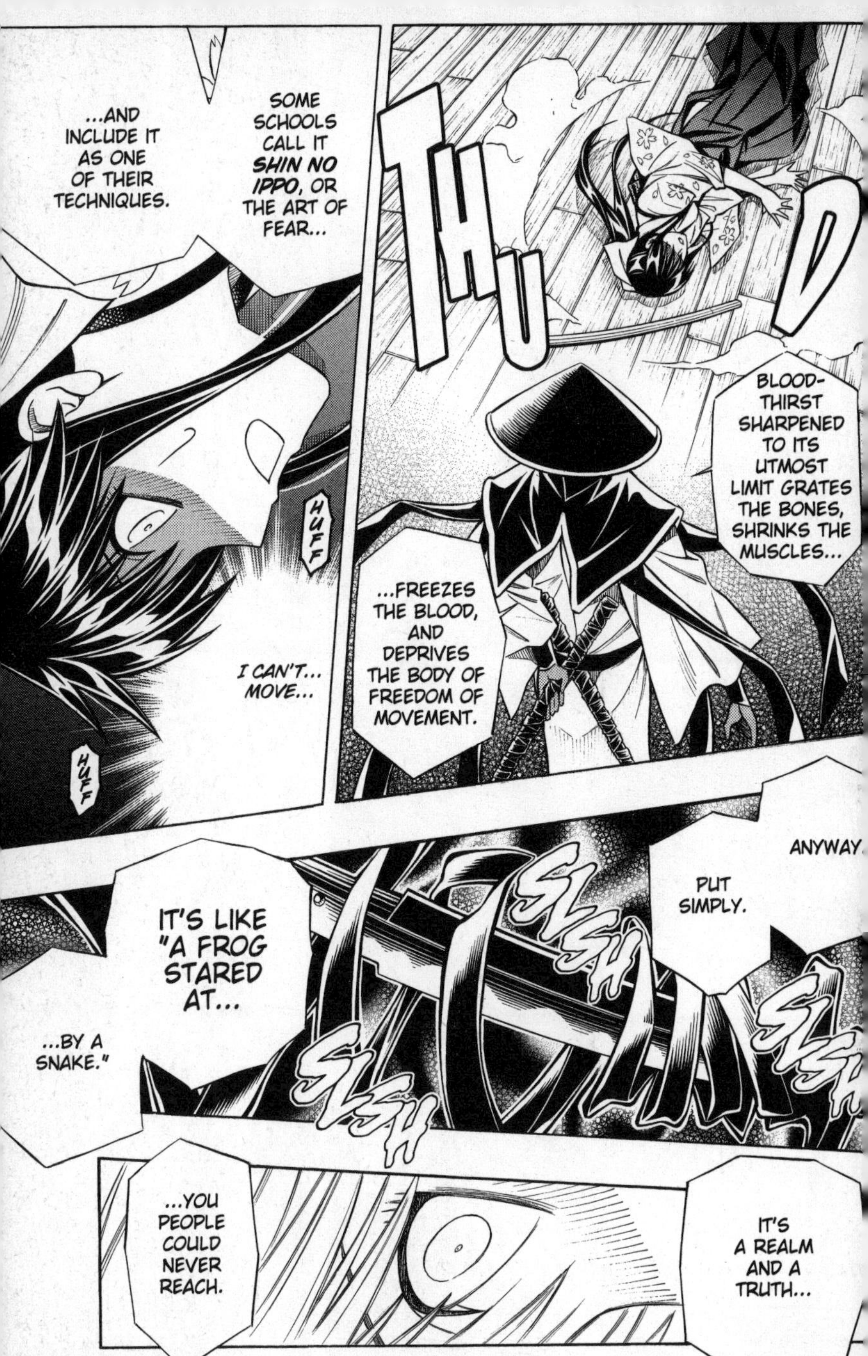
THUD
BLOOD-THIRST SHARPENED TO ITS UTMOST LIMIT GRATES THE BONES, SHRINKS THE MUSCLES...
...FREEZES THE BLOOD, AND DEPRIVES THE BODY OF FREEDOM OF MOVEMENT.
SOME SCHOOLS CALL IT *SHIN NO IPPO*, OR THE ART OF FEAR...
...AND INCLUDE IT AS ONE OF THEIR TECHNIQUES.
HUFF
I CAN'T... MOVE...
HUFF
ANYWAY.
PUT SIMPLY.
IT'S LIKE "A FROG STARED AT...
...BY A SNAKE."
SLSH
SLSH
SLSH
IT'S A REALM AND A TRUTH...
...YOU PEOPLE COULD NEVER REACH.

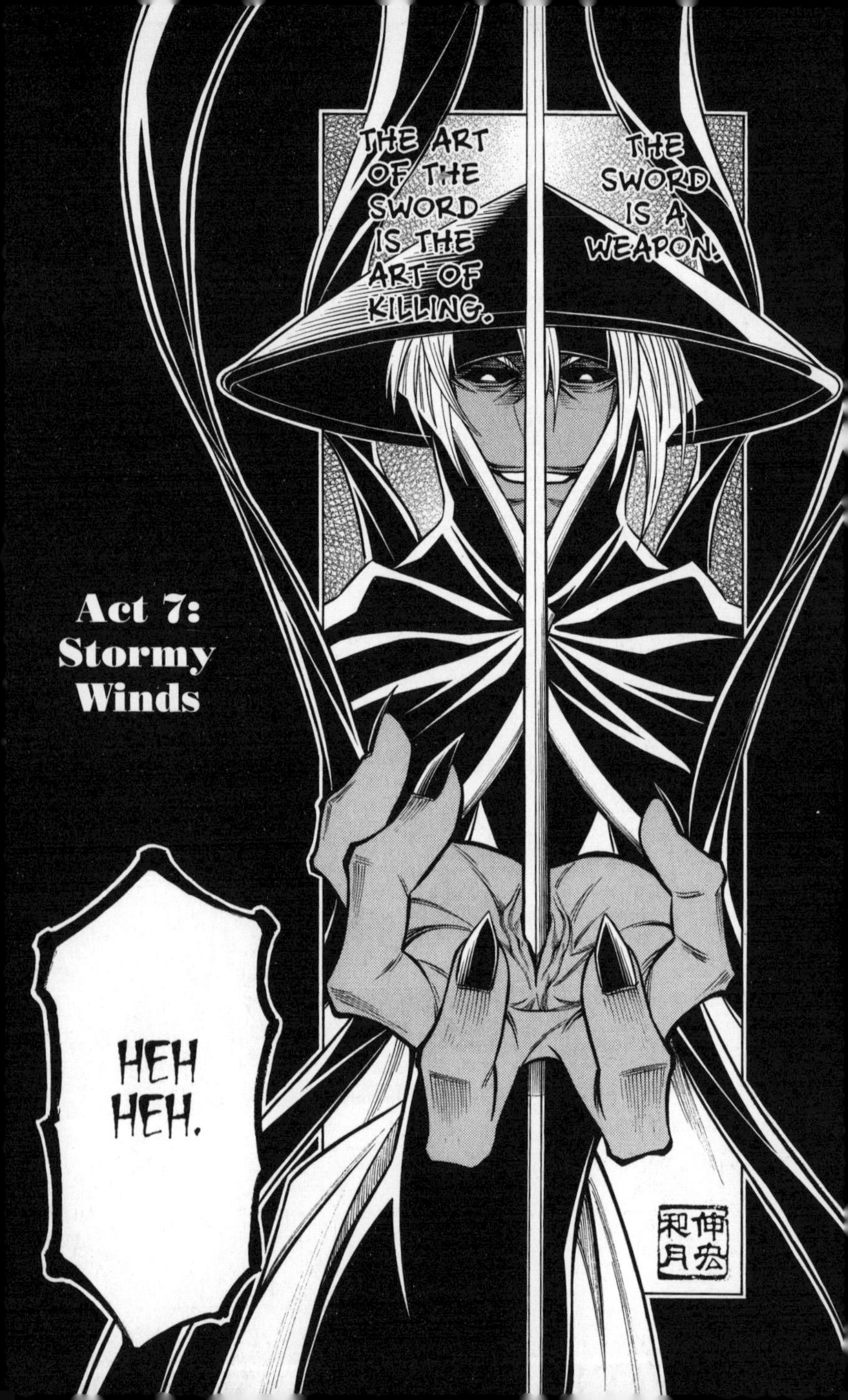
THE SWORD IS A WEAPON.
THE ART OF THE SWORD IS THE ART OF KILLING.
Act 7: Stormy Winds
HEH HEH.
伸宏和月

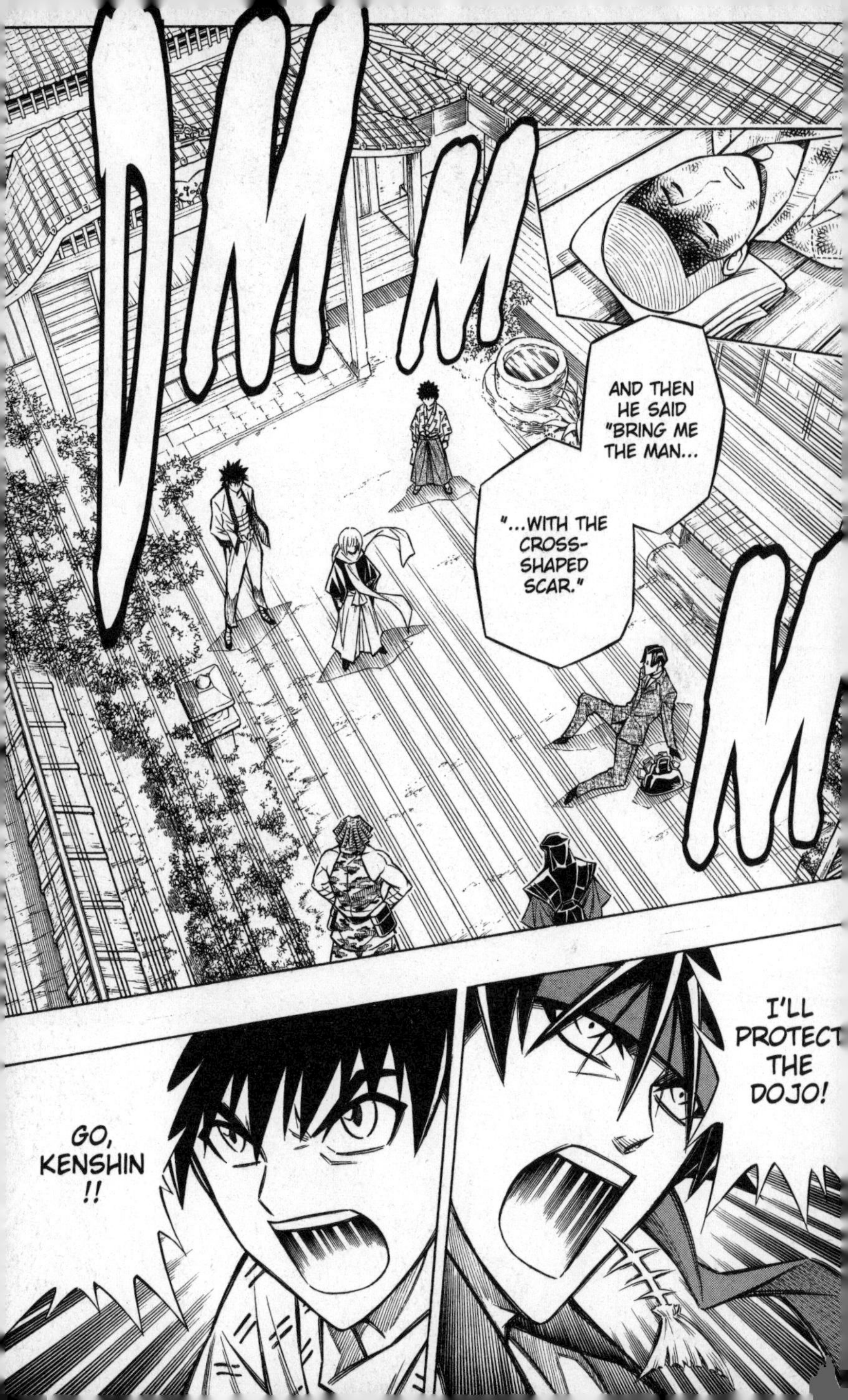
AND THEN HE SAID "BRING ME THE MAN...
"...WITH THE CROSS-SHAPED SCAR."
DMMM
I'LL PROTECT THE DOJO!
GO, KENSHIN!!

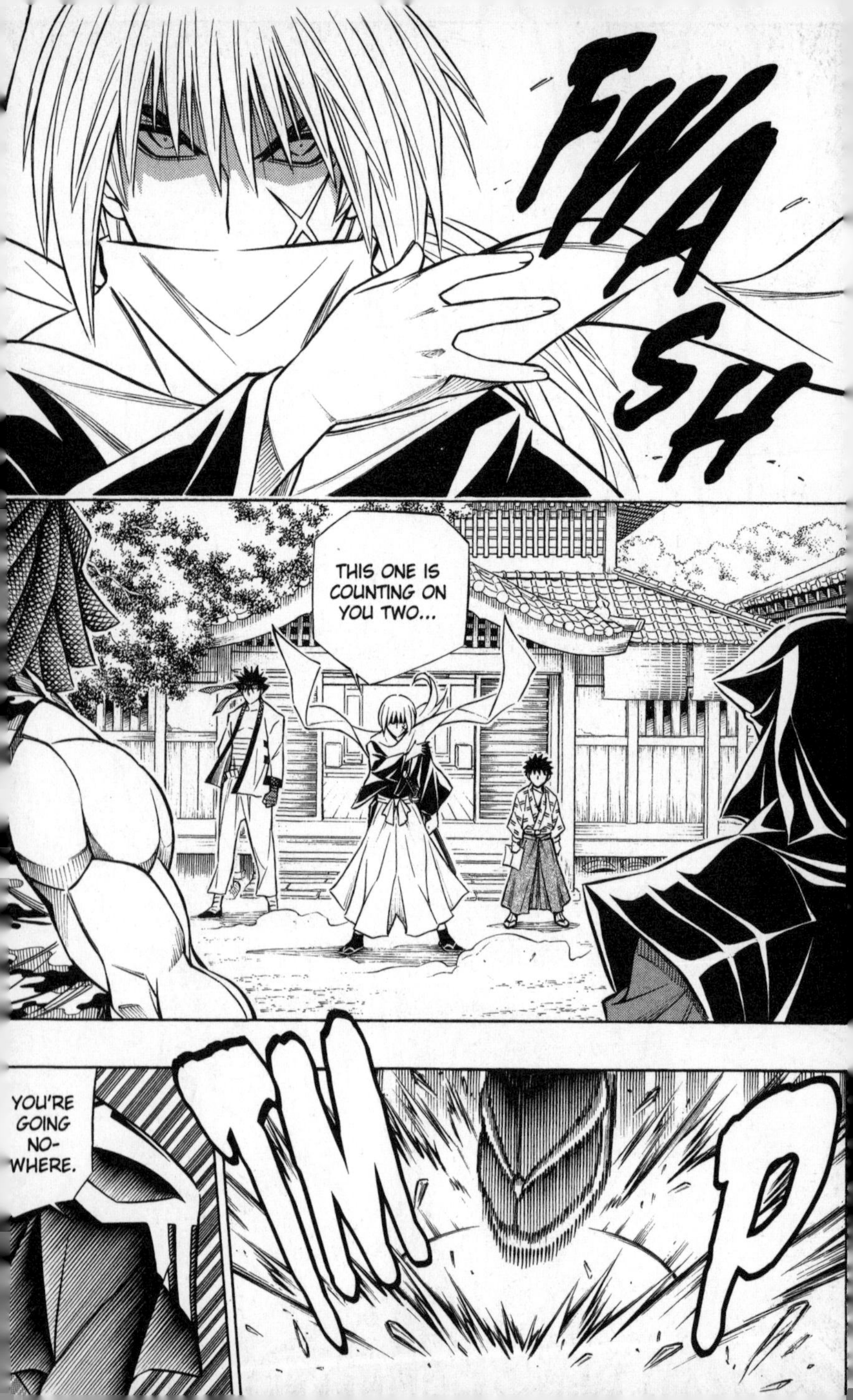
FWASH
THIS ONE IS COUNTING ON YOU TWO...
TMP
YOU'RE GOING NO-WHERE.

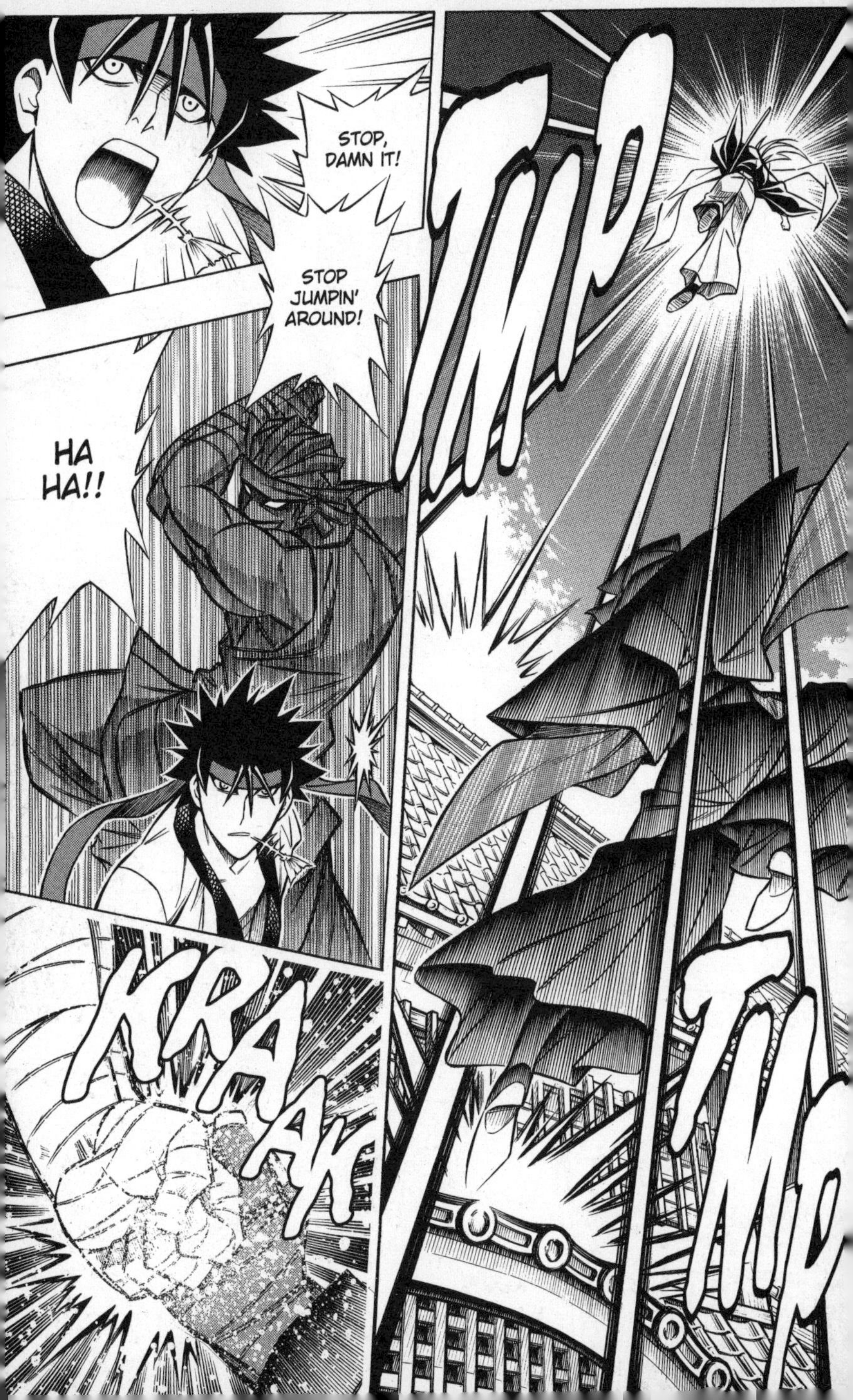
TMP
TMP
STOP, DAMN IT!
STOP JUMPIN' AROUND!
HA HA!!
KRAAK

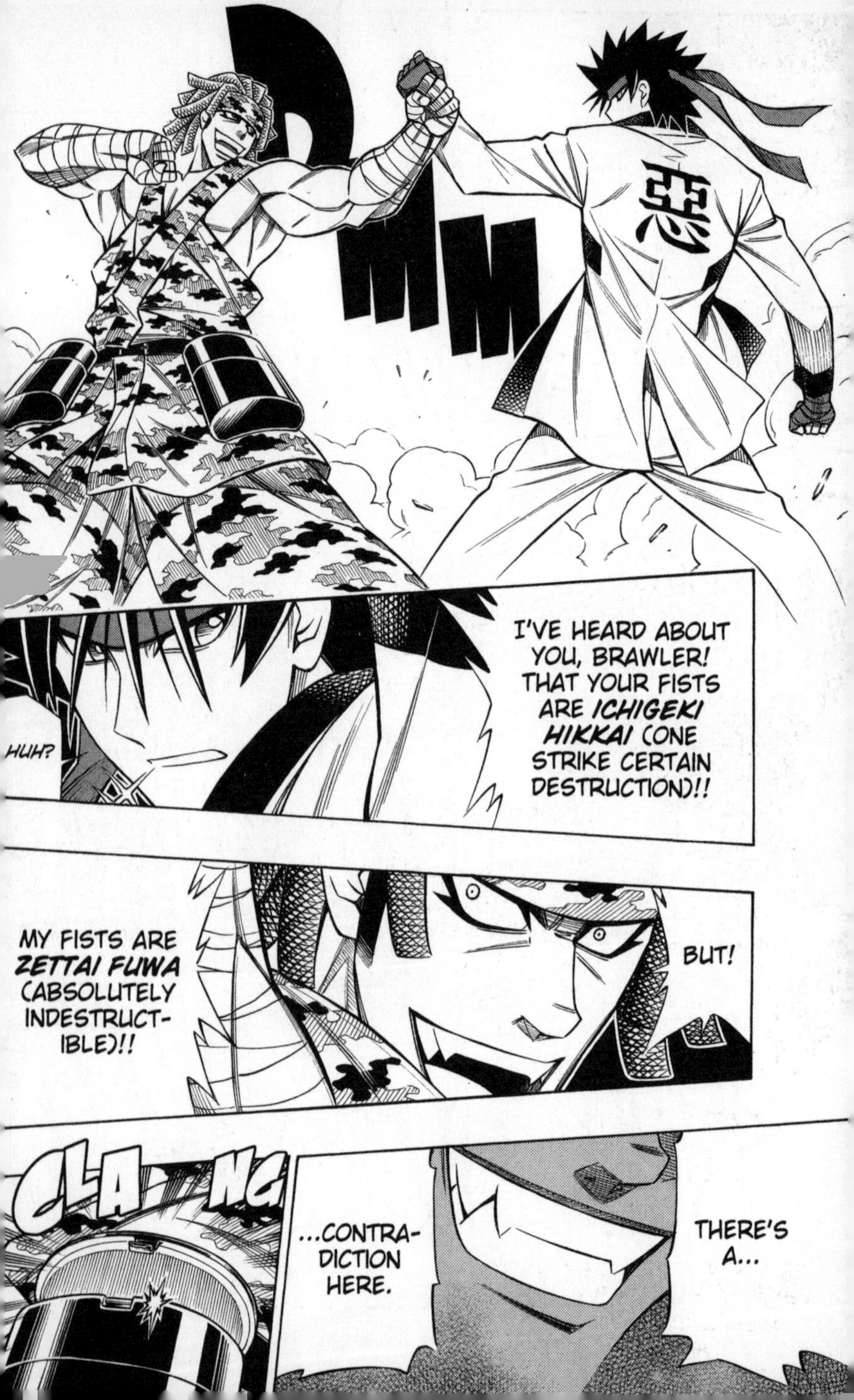

I'VE HEARD ABOUT YOU, BRAWLER! THAT YOUR FISTS ARE *ICHIGEKI HIKKAI* (ONE STRIKE CERTAIN DESTRUCTION)!!
HUH?
BUT!
MY FISTS ARE *ZETTAI FUWA* (ABSOLUTELY INDESTRUCT-IBLE)!!
THERE'S A...
...CONTRA-DICTION HERE.

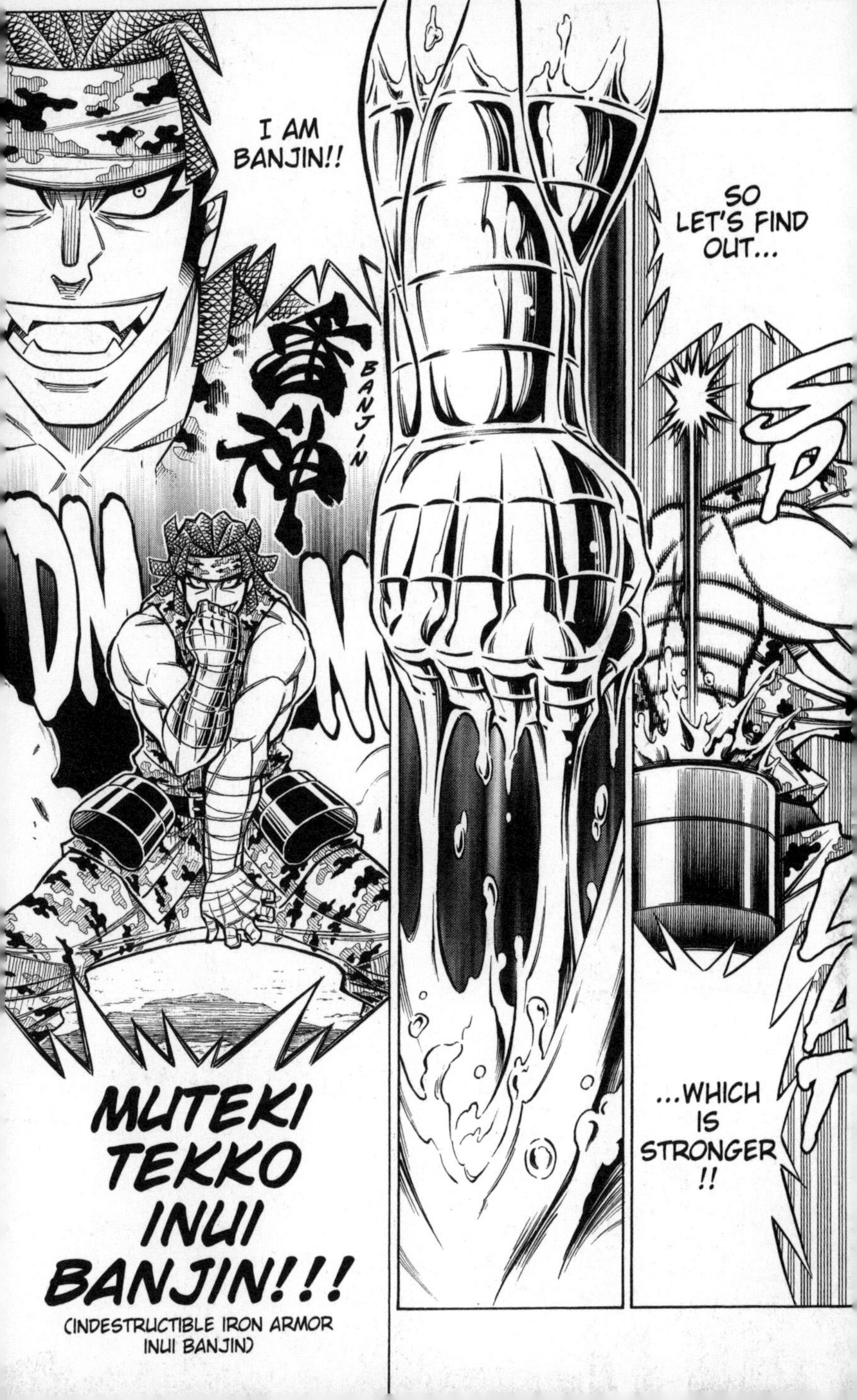
SO LET'S FIND OUT...
...WHICH IS STRONGER!!
I AM BANJIN!!
番神
BANJIN
MUTEKI TEKKO INUI BANJIN!!!
(INDESTRUCTIBLE IRON ARMOR INUI BANJIN)

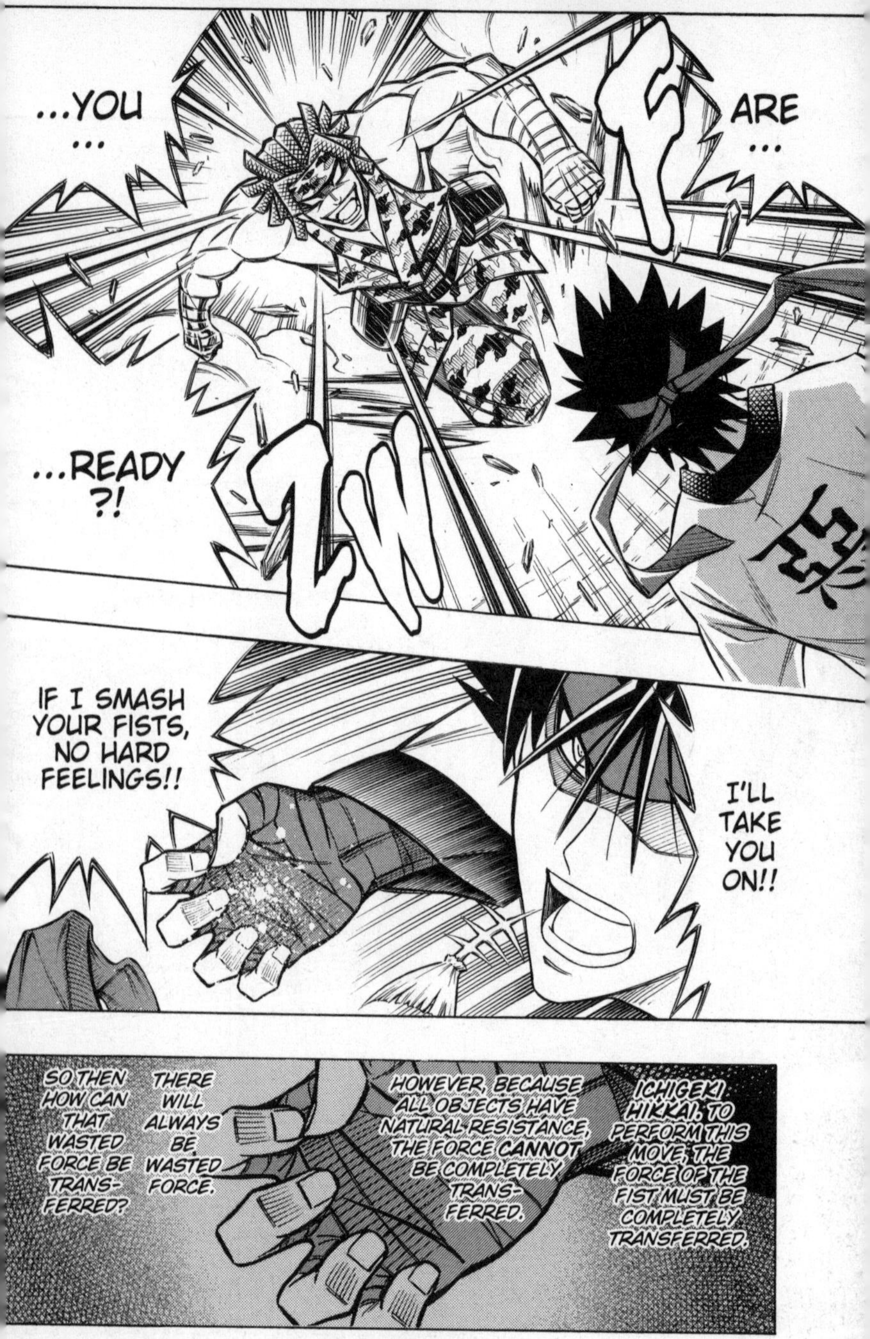
...YOU ...
ARE ...
...READY ?!
I'LL TAKE YOU ON!!
IF I SMASH YOUR FISTS, NO HARD FEELINGS!!
ICHIGEKI HIKKAI. TO PERFORM THIS MOVE, THE FORCE OF THE FIST MUST BE COMPLETELY TRANSFERRED.
HOWEVER, BECAUSE ALL OBJECTS HAVE NATURAL RESISTANCE, THE FORCE CANNOT BE COMPLETELY TRANS-FERRED.
THERE WILL ALWAYS BE WASTED FORCE.
SO THEN HOW CAN THAT WASTED FORCE BE TRANS-FERRED?

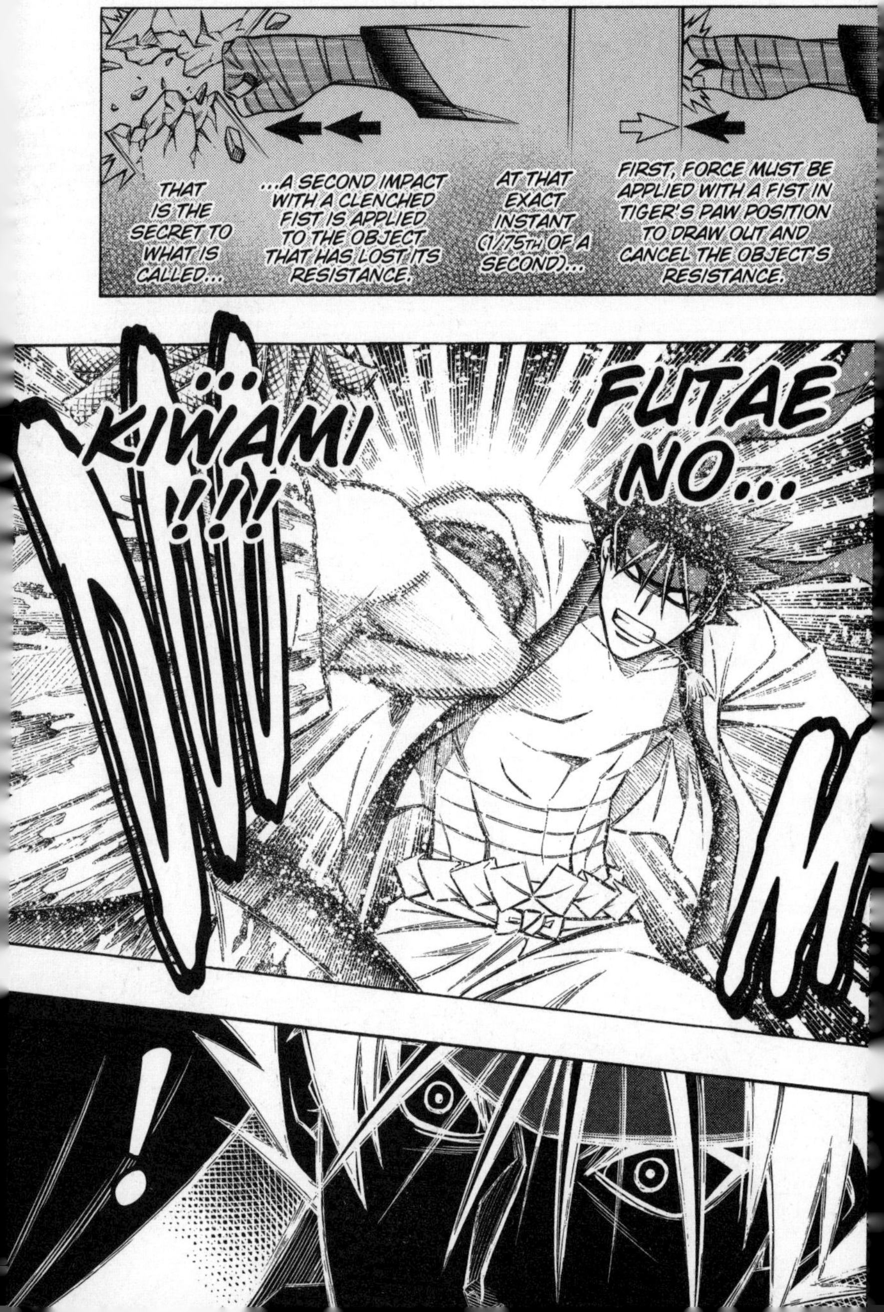
FIRST, FORCE MUST BE APPLIED WITH A FIST IN TIGER'S PAW POSITION TO DRAW OUT AND CANCEL THE OBJECT'S RESISTANCE.
AT THAT EXACT INSTANT (1/75TH OF A SECOND)...
...A SECOND IMPACT WITH A CLENCHED FIST IS APPLIED TO THE OBJECT THAT HAS LOST ITS RESISTANCE.
THAT IS THE SECRET TO WHAT IS CALLED...
FUTAE NO...
...KIWAMI!!!
!

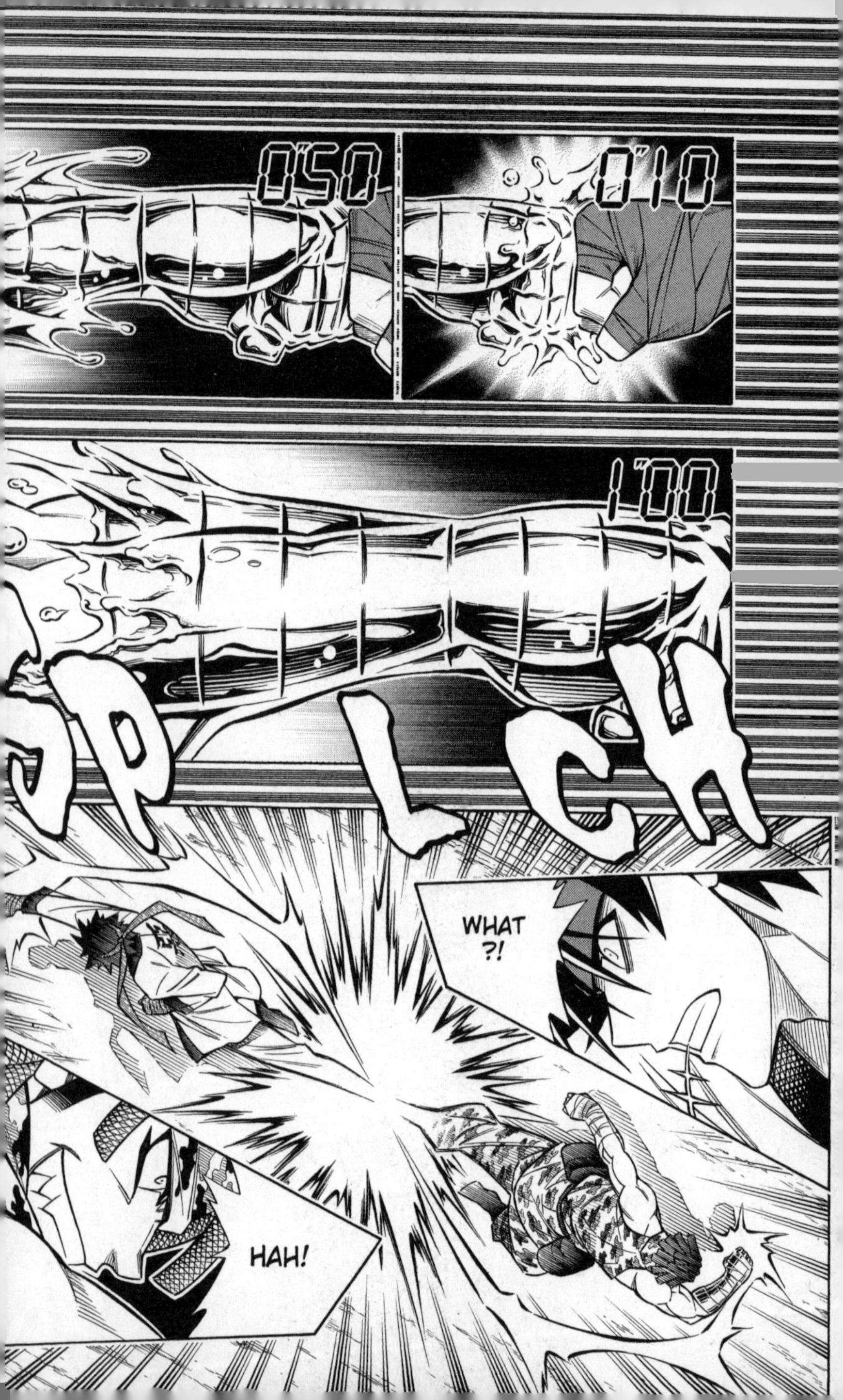
0"10
0"50
1"00
SPLCH
WHAT ?!
HAH!

HIS SYRUP-LIKE METAL IS THROWING OFF THE TIMING OF MY FORCE TRANSFER.

I CAN'T PULL OFF FUTAE...!!

HA HA!!

FISTS, BLADES, BULLETS! NOTHING...

...CAN DESTROY THIS **SOFT METAL!!**

WELL?! WHADDAYA THINK OF THIS **MUTEKI TEKKO INDESTRUCTIBLE** ARMOR? IT'S MADE FROM MERCURY!!

BUT IT'S **PERFECT** FOR **SMASHIN'** THINGS!!

SPLCH

ALTHOUGH IT SUCKS THAT I CAN'T USE MY HANDS WHEN IT HARDENS!!

94

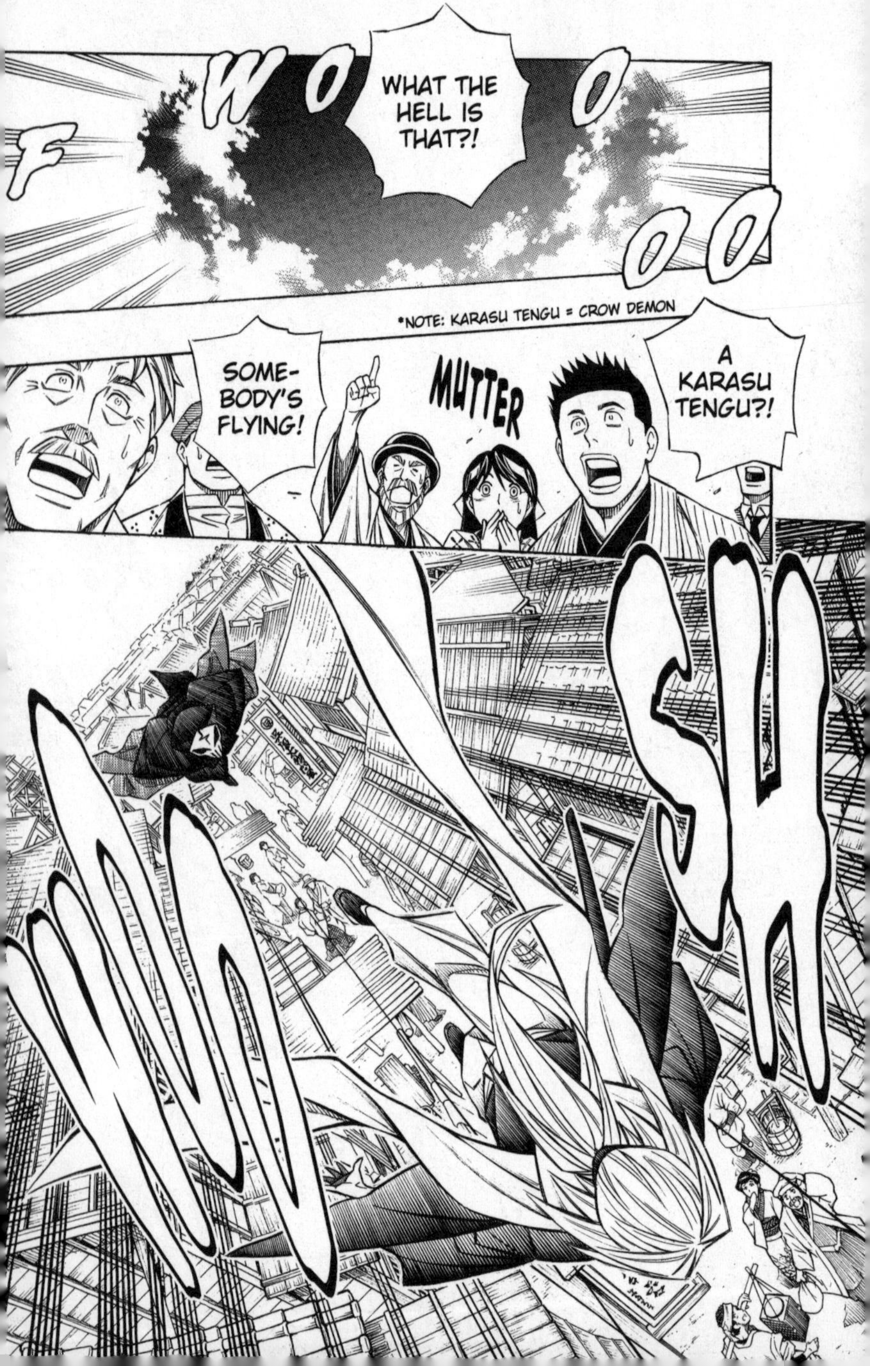
FWOOOO
WHAT THE HELL IS THAT?!
*NOTE: KARASU TENGU = CROW DEMON
A KARASU TENGU?!
MUTTER
SOME-BODY'S FLYING!
WOOSH

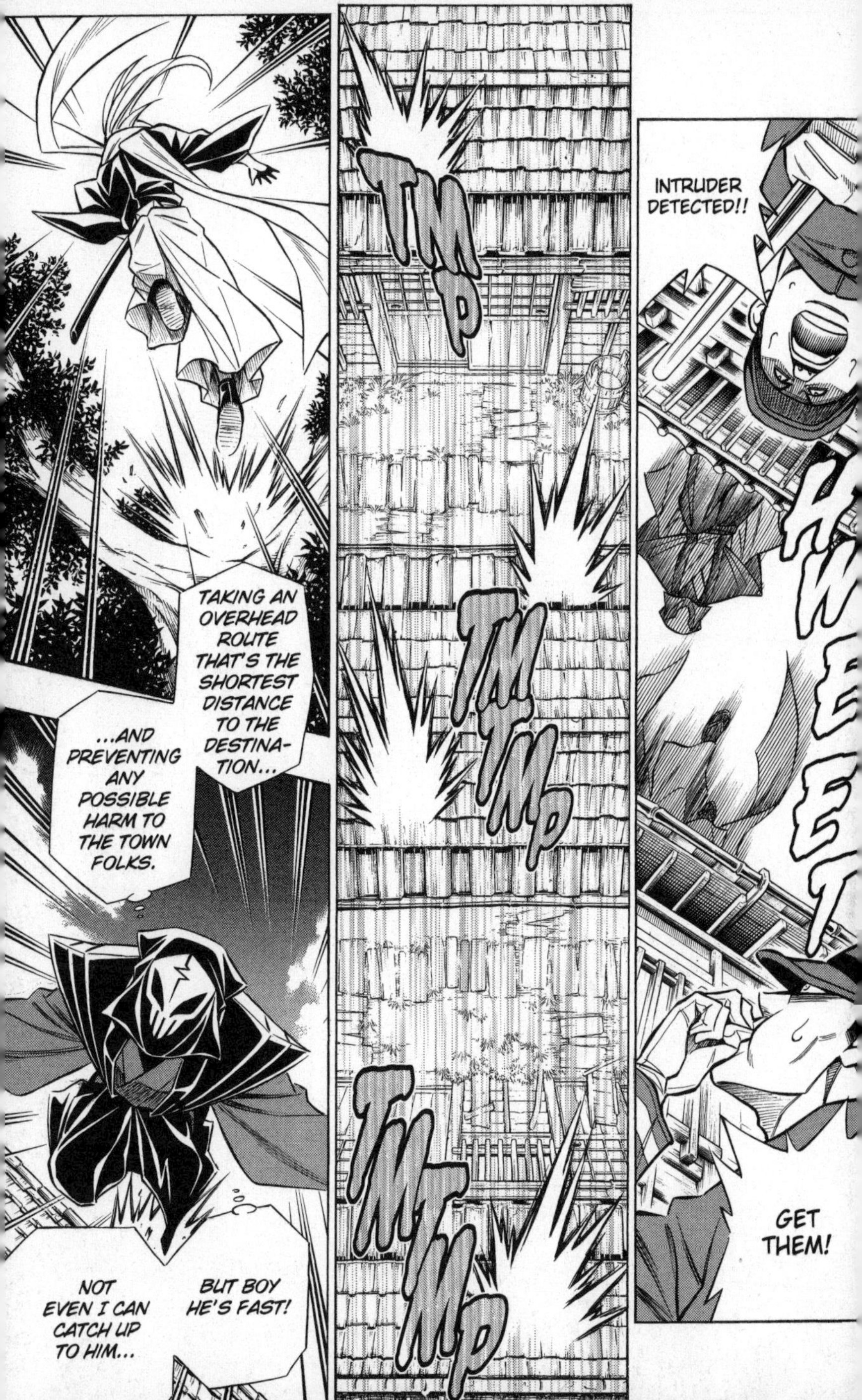
INTRUDER DETECTED!!
HWEET
GET THEM!
TMP
TMTMP
TMTMP
TAKING AN OVERHEAD ROUTE THAT'S THE SHORTEST DISTANCE TO THE DESTINA-TION...
...AND PREVENTING ANY POSSIBLE HARM TO THE TOWN FOLKS.
BUT BOY HE'S FAST!
NOT EVEN I CAN CATCH UP TO HIM...

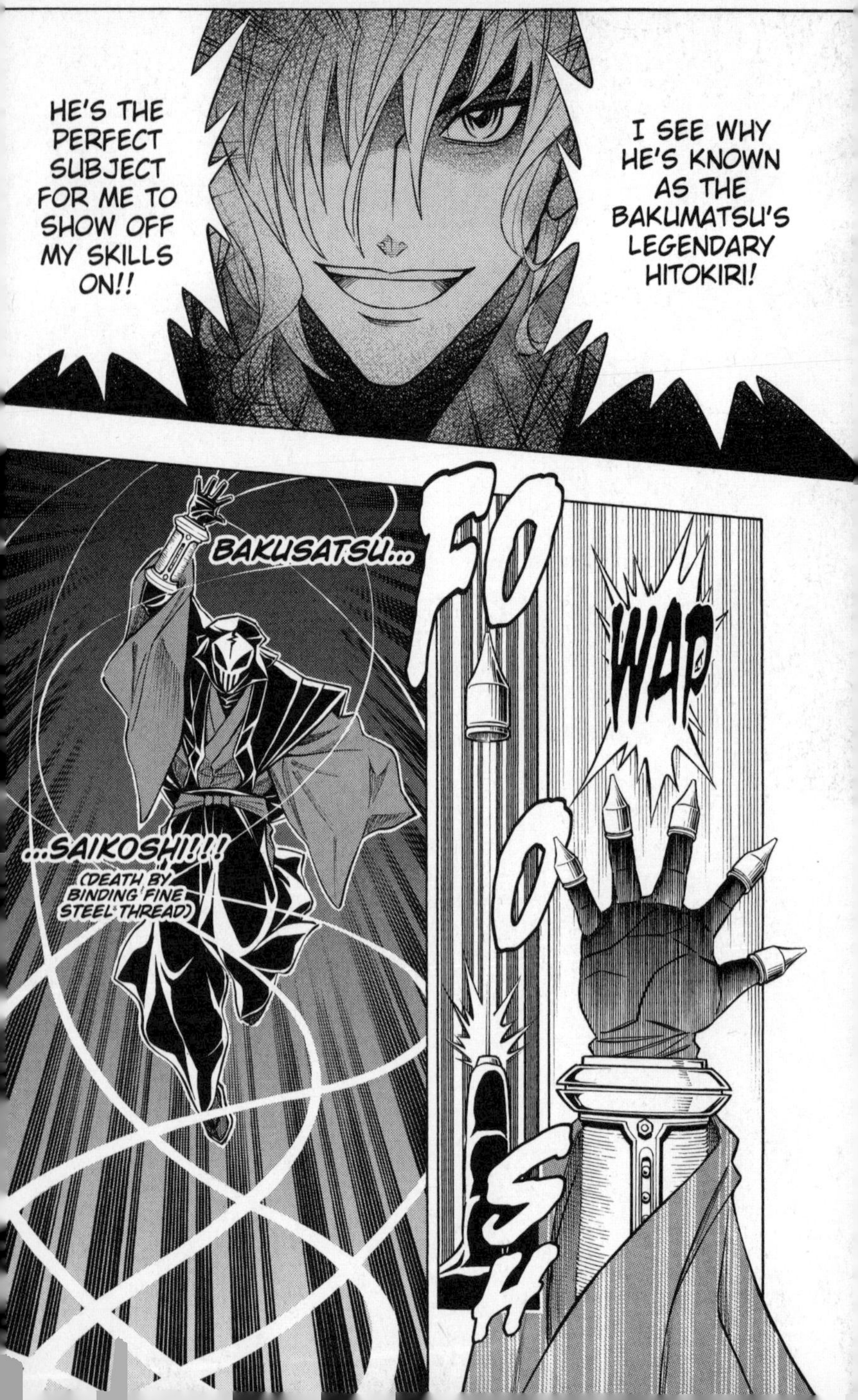
I SEE WHY HE'S KNOWN AS THE BAKUMATSU'S LEGENDARY HITOKIRI!
HE'S THE PERFECT SUBJECT FOR ME TO SHOW OFF MY SKILLS ON!!
FOOSH
WAP
BAKUSATSU...
...SAIKOSHI!!!
(DEATH BY BINDING FINE STEEL THREAD)

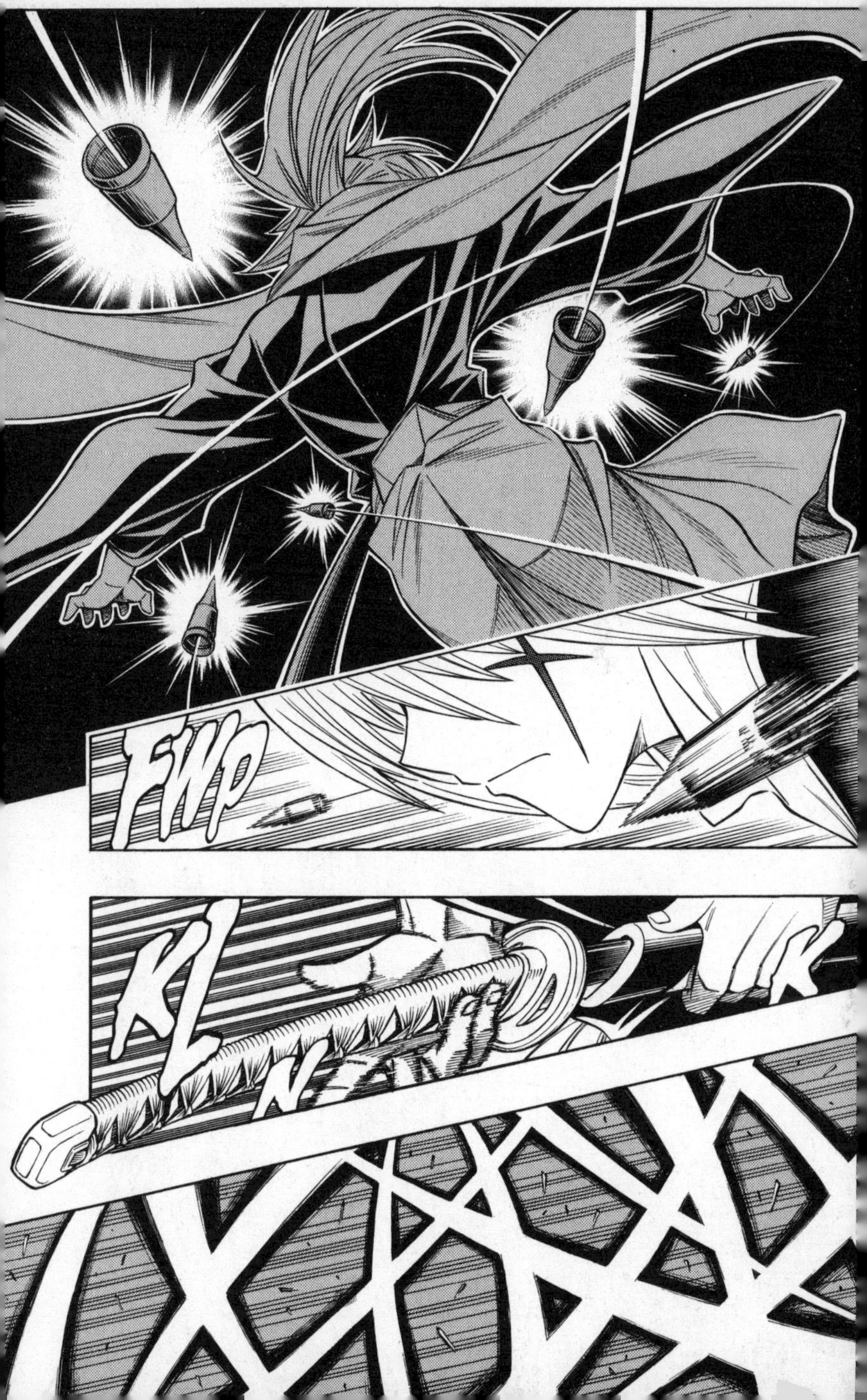
FWP
KLINK

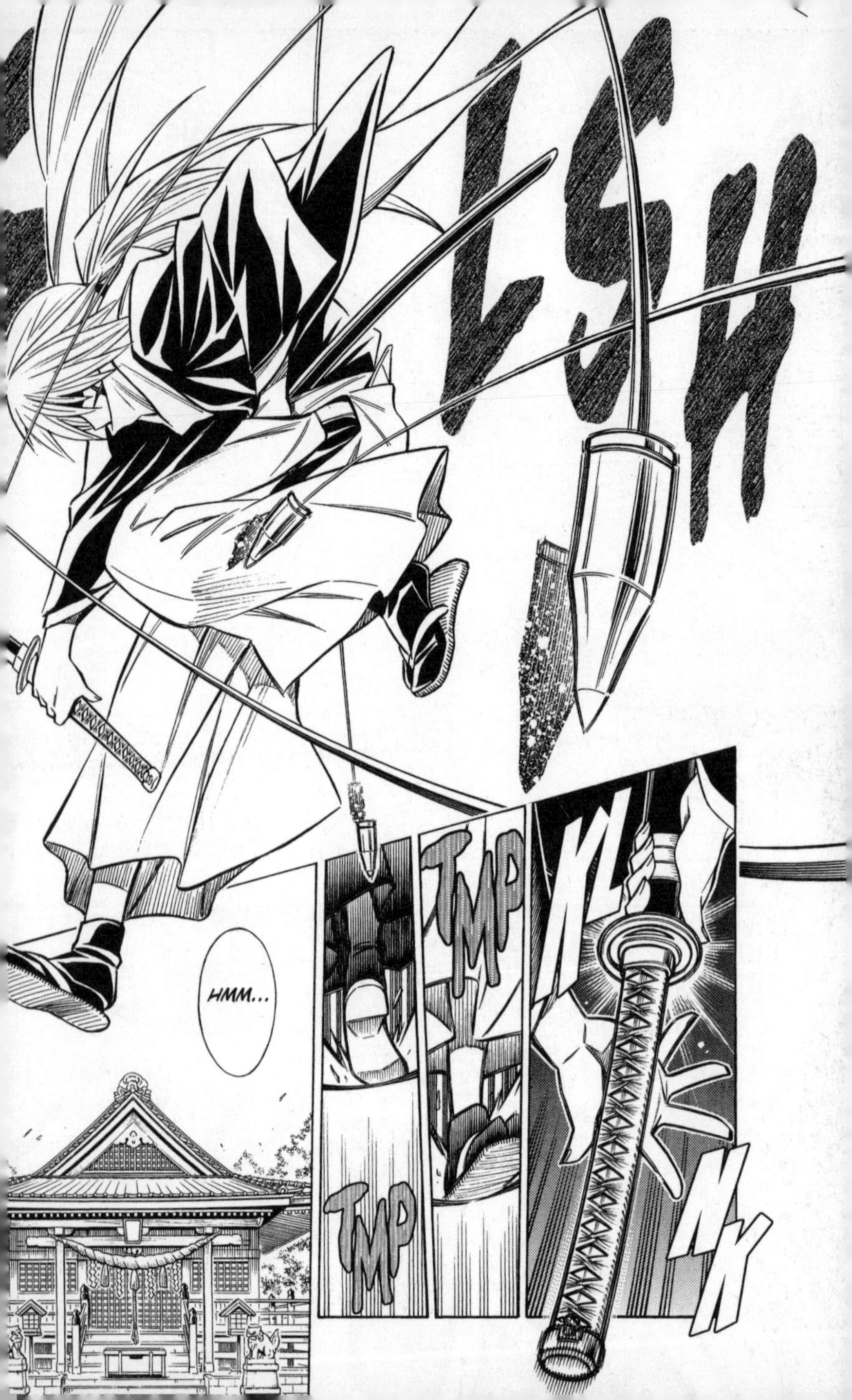
LSH
KL
NK
TMP
TMP
HMM...

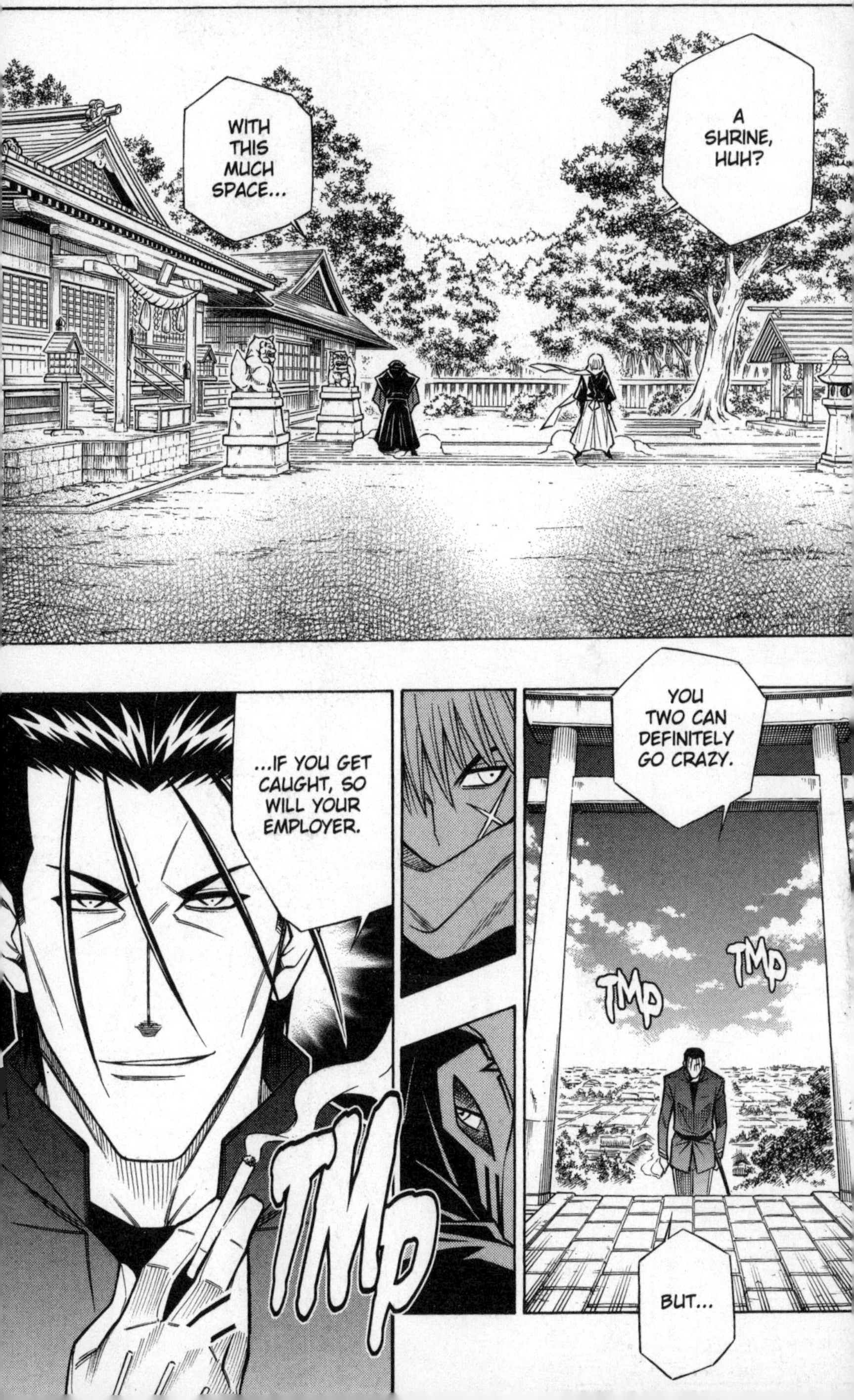
A SHRINE, HUH?
WITH THIS MUCH SPACE...
YOU TWO CAN DEFINITELY GO CRAZY.
TMP
TMP
BUT...
...IF YOU GET CAUGHT, SO WILL YOUR EMPLOYER.
TMP

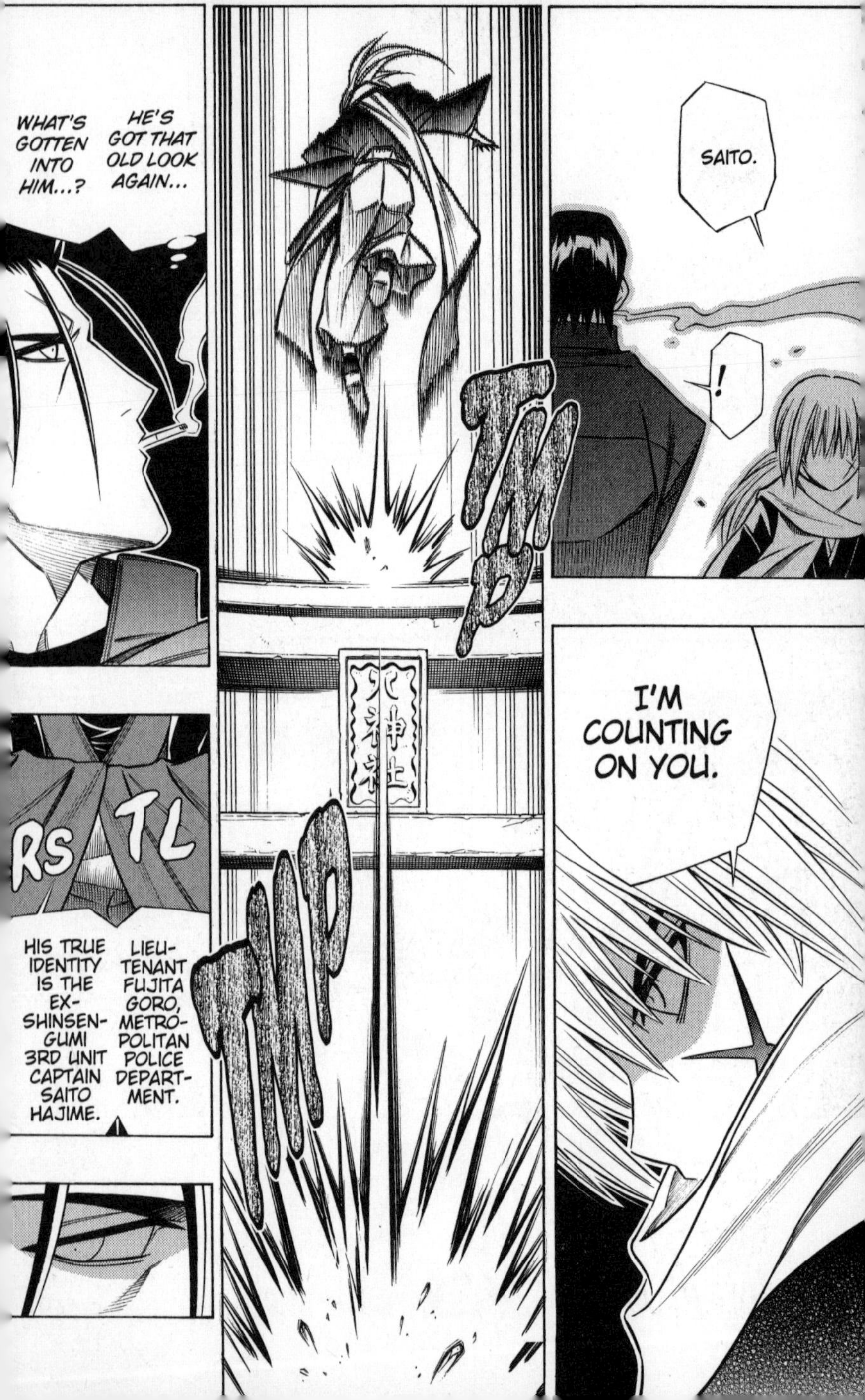
SAITO.
!
I'M COUNTING ON YOU.
HE'S GOT THAT OLD LOOK AGAIN...
WHAT'S GOTTEN INTO HIM...?
RSTL
LIEUTENANT FUJITA GORO, METROPOLITAN POLICE DEPARTMENT.
HIS TRUE IDENTITY IS THE EX-SHINSENGUMI 3RD UNIT CAPTAIN SAITO HAJIME.

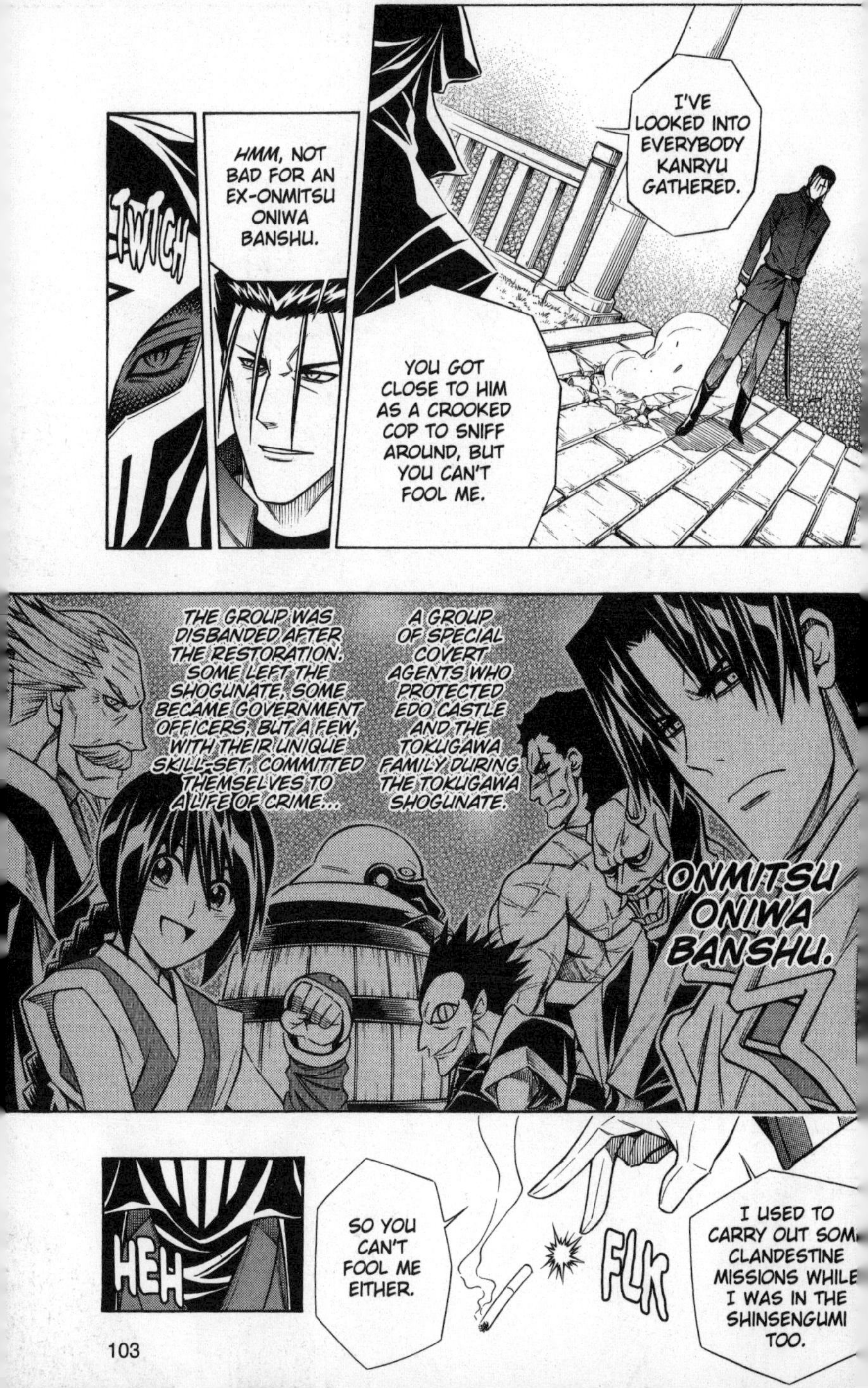
I'VE LOOKED INTO EVERYBODY KANRYU GATHERED.
YOU GOT CLOSE TO HIM AS A CROOKED COP TO SNIFF AROUND, BUT YOU CAN'T FOOL ME.
HMM, NOT BAD FOR AN EX-ONMITSU ONIWA BANSHU.
TWITCH
ONMITSU ONIWA BANSHU.
A GROUP OF SPECIAL COVERT AGENTS WHO PROTECTED EDO CASTLE AND THE TOKUGAWA FAMILY DURING THE TOKUGAWA SHOGUNATE.
THE GROUP WAS DISBANDED AFTER THE RESTORATION. SOME LEFT THE SHOGUNATE, SOME BECAME GOVERNMENT OFFICERS, BUT A FEW, WITH THEIR UNIQUE SKILL-SET, COMMITTED THEMSELVES TO A LIFE OF CRIME...
I USED TO CARRY OUT SOM CLANDESTINE MISSIONS WHILE I WAS IN THE SHINSENGUMI TOO.
FLK
SO YOU CAN'T FOOL ME EITHER.
HEH

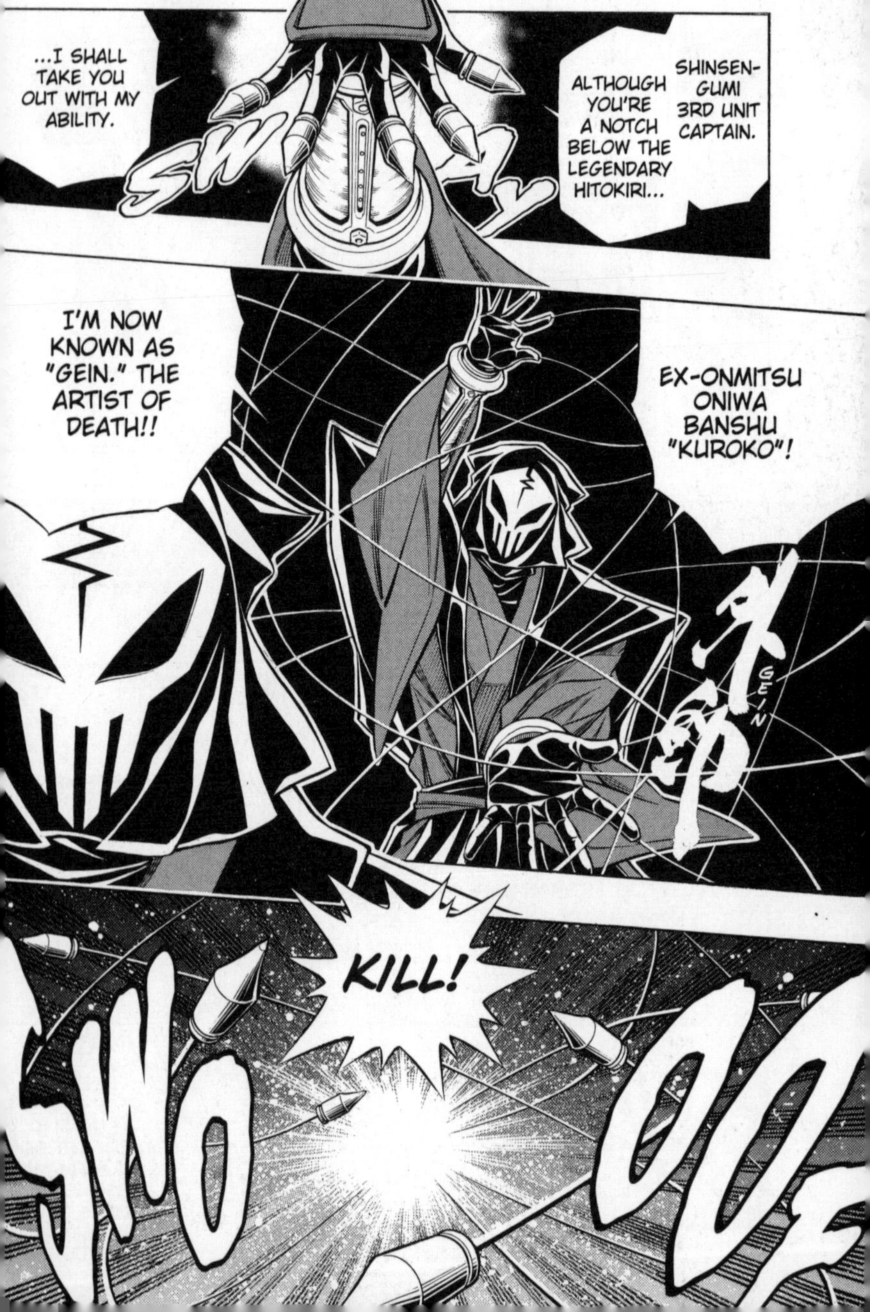
SHINSEN-GUMI 3RD UNIT CAPTAIN.
ALTHOUGH YOU'RE A NOTCH BELOW THE LEGENDARY HITOKIRI...
...I SHALL TAKE YOU OUT WITH MY ABILITY.
SWAY
EX-ONMITSU ONIWA BANSHU "KUROKO"!
I'M NOW KNOWN AS "GEIN." THE ARTIST OF DEATH!!
GEIN
KILL!

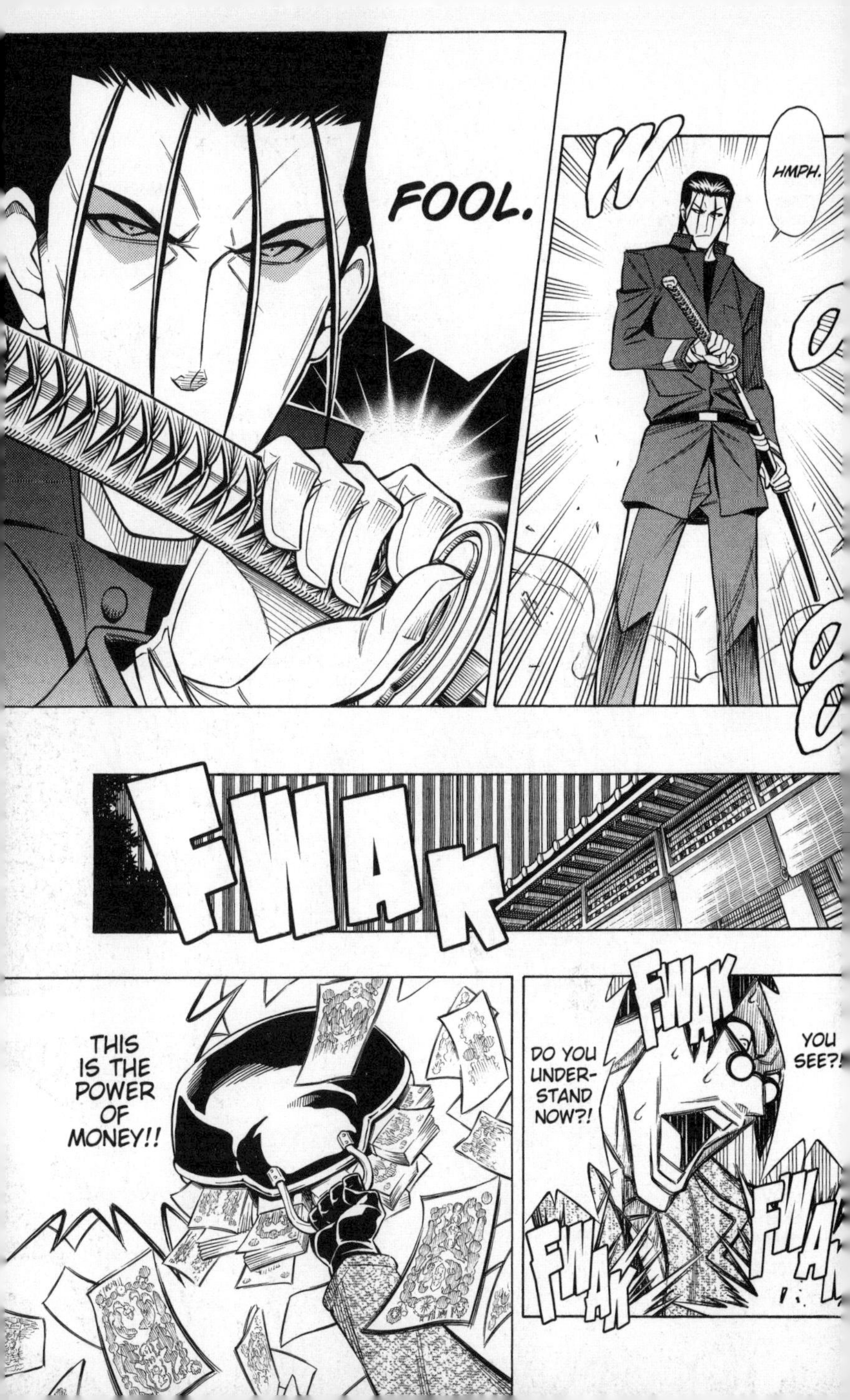
HMPH.
FOOL.
FWAK
YOU SEE?!
DO YOU UNDERSTAND NOW?!
FWAK
FWAK
FWAK
THIS IS THE POWER OF MONEY!!

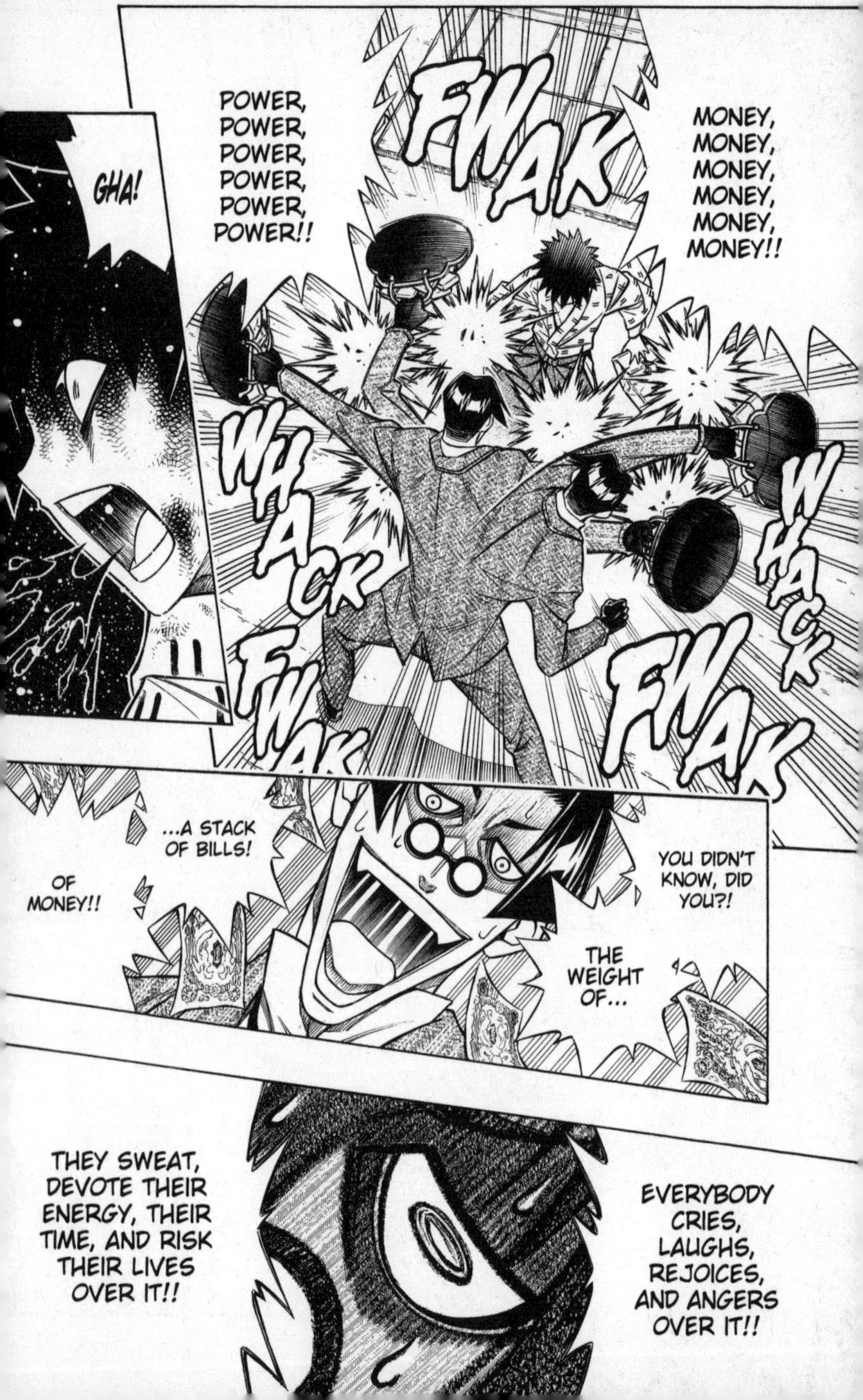
MONEY, MONEY, MONEY, MONEY, MONEY, MONEY!!
FWAK
POWER, POWER, POWER, POWER, POWER, POWER!!
WHACK
WHACK
FWAK
FWAK
GHA!
YOU DIDN'T KNOW, DID YOU?!
THE WEIGHT OF...
...A STACK OF BILLS!
OF MONEY!!
EVERYBODY CRIES, LAUGHS, REJOICES, AND ANGERS OVER IT!!
THEY SWEAT, DEVOTE THEIR ENERGY, THEIR TIME, AND RISK THEIR LIVES OVER IT!!

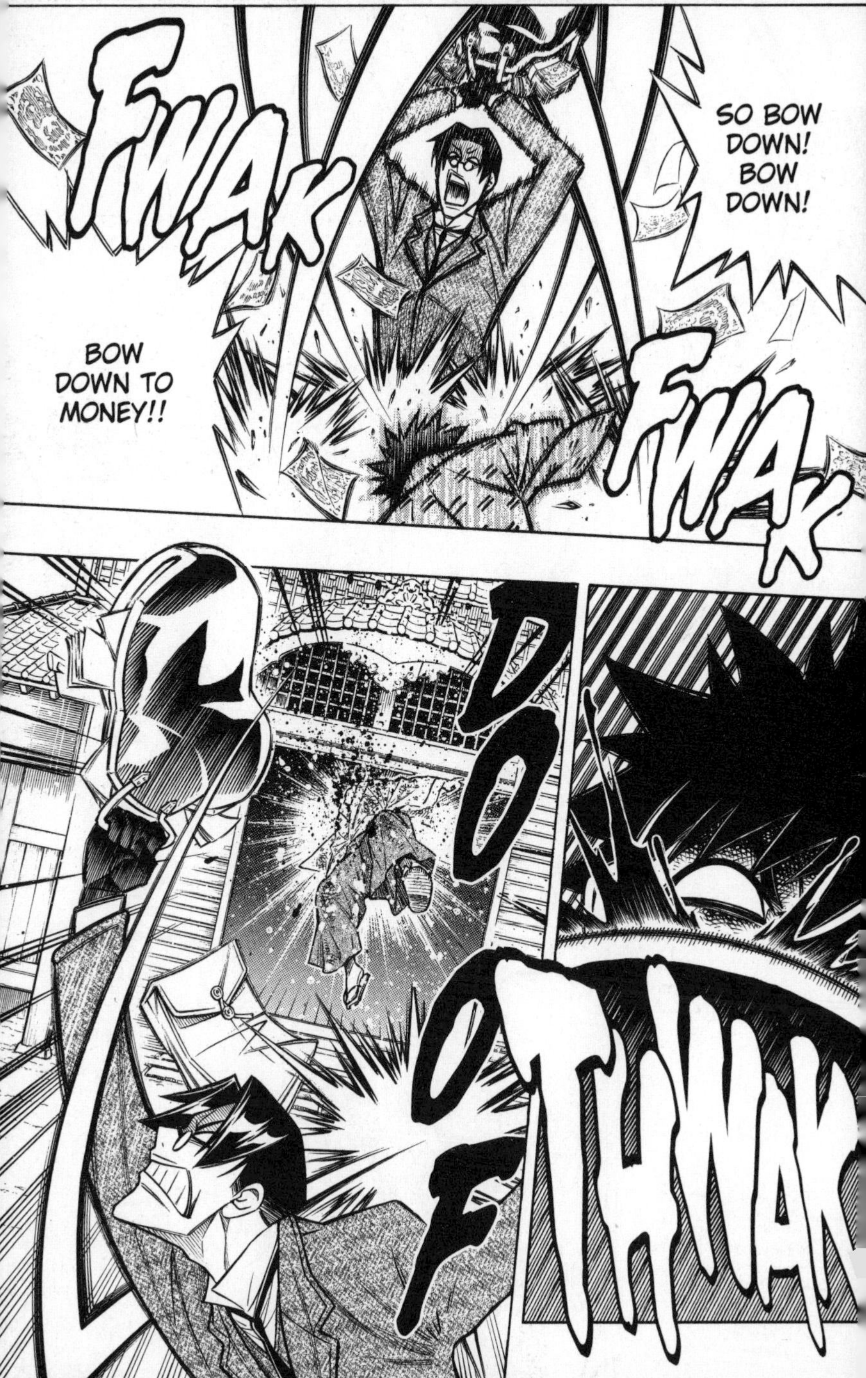
SO BOW DOWN! BOW DOWN!
FWAK
BOW DOWN TO MONEY!!
FWAK
THWAK
DOOF

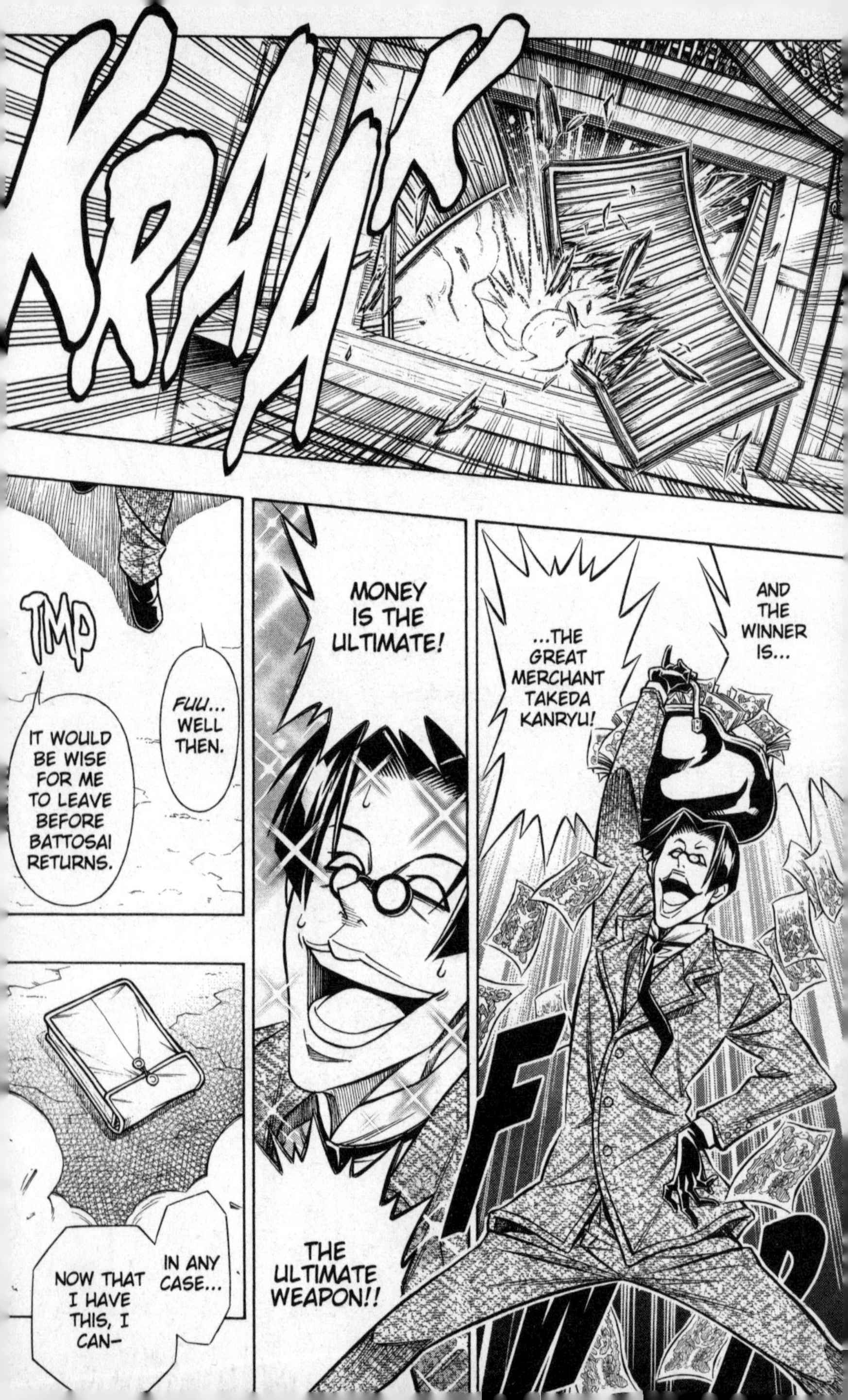
AND THE WINNER IS...
...THE GREAT MERCHANT TAKEDA KANRYU!
MONEY IS THE ULTIMATE!
THE ULTIMATE WEAPON!!
TMP
FUU... WELL THEN.
IT WOULD BE WISE FOR ME TO LEAVE BEFORE BATTOSAI RETURNS.
IN ANY CASE...
NOW THAT I HAVE THIS, I CAN-

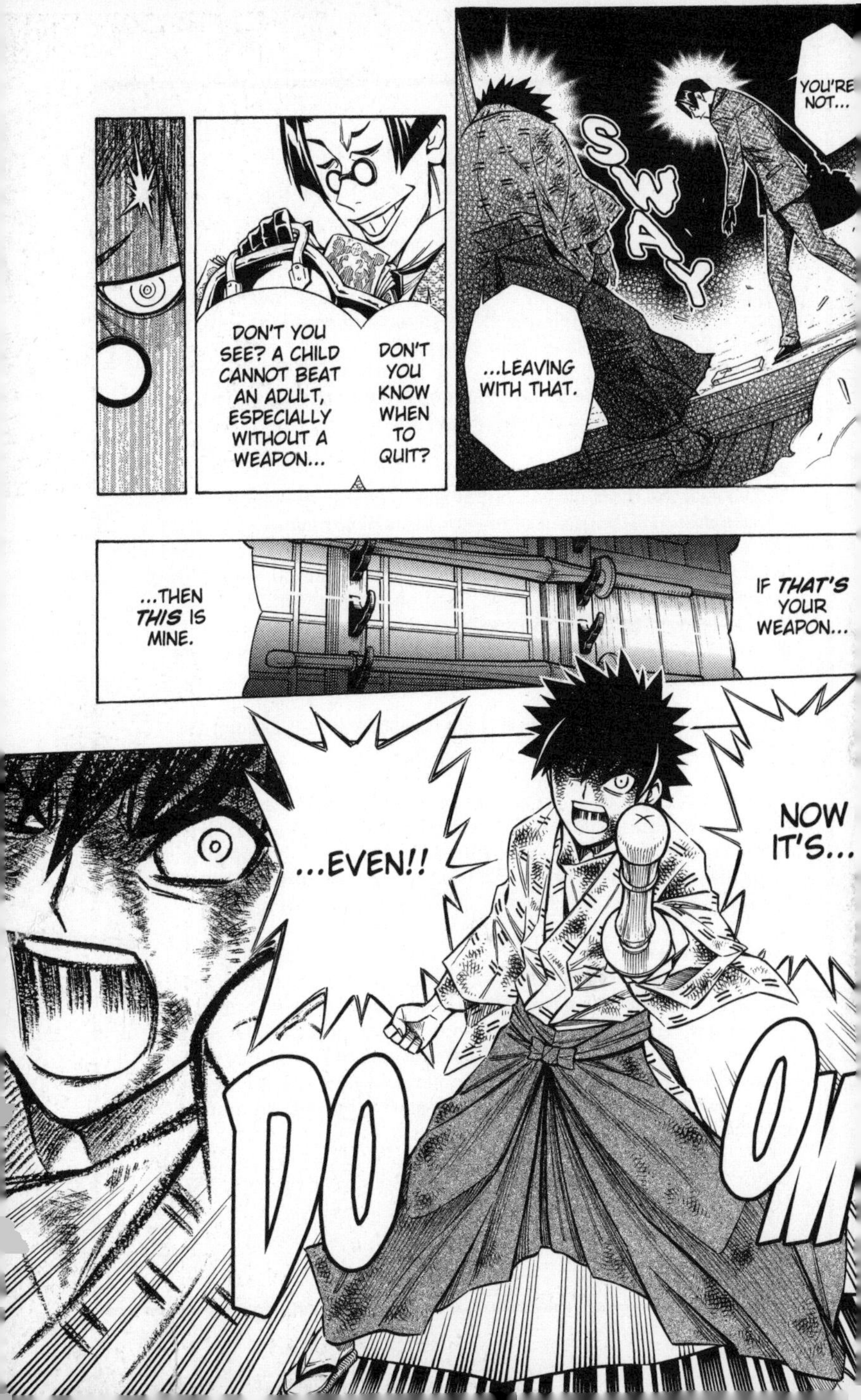
YOU'RE NOT...
SWAY
...LEAVING WITH THAT.
DON'T YOU KNOW WHEN TO QUIT?
DON'T YOU SEE? A CHILD CANNOT BEAT AN ADULT, ESPECIALLY WITHOUT A WEAPON...
IF *THAT'S* YOUR WEAPON...
...THEN *THIS* IS MINE.
NOW IT'S...
...EVEN!!
DOOM

I really like the scene of Kaoru talking to Kenshin on the bridge, both staging and design-wise. The most notable change in her appearance is the presence or absence of a part in her bangs. When I was still beginning as a manga artist, I worried too much about drawing distinctive hairstyles, hardly paying attention to the flow of the hair. Because of that, I struggled with the sheen and shading. So this time around, I narrowed it down to a ponytail.

As far as her wardrobe, I had to emphasize that she was a female samurai, so she wore a kimono + hakama.

Myojin Yahiko

Yahiko saw the most growth out of all the characters in *Restoration*. He was originally born out of my concerns over having a thirty-something-year-old main character in a shonen manga. I included him to add a child's perspective. But in reality, the main demographic of *Jump* readers were middle school and high school kids, slightly older than Yahiko. In addition, the age of *my* readers was slightly higher than that. So my intentions may have been misguided. This time around, I had him as a character who evolves through the story.

Yahiko rejecting Kanryu's deal is his climactic scene. The fight afterwards is just a bonus.

The biggest changes in his appearance are to his hair and eyes. His hairstyle was quite similar to Sanosuke's in the original, so I made it a little shorter. I wanted his growth to be apparent with his eyes, so I drew his pupils a bit smaller and gave him a more menacing look in the first half.

Sagara Sanosuke

There was a bold idea of removing Sanosuke from the story when the film adaptation was being discussed, since he wasn't involved in the main plot. However, he ranks in the top 3 most popular *Rurouni Kenshin* characters. It would've been a waste not to take advantage of the way he livens up the story and imagery. He played the exact same role in *Restoration*. The rowdiness at Kamiya Dojo dramatically increases with him around.

Continued on page 142.

Act 8: Eve of Convergence

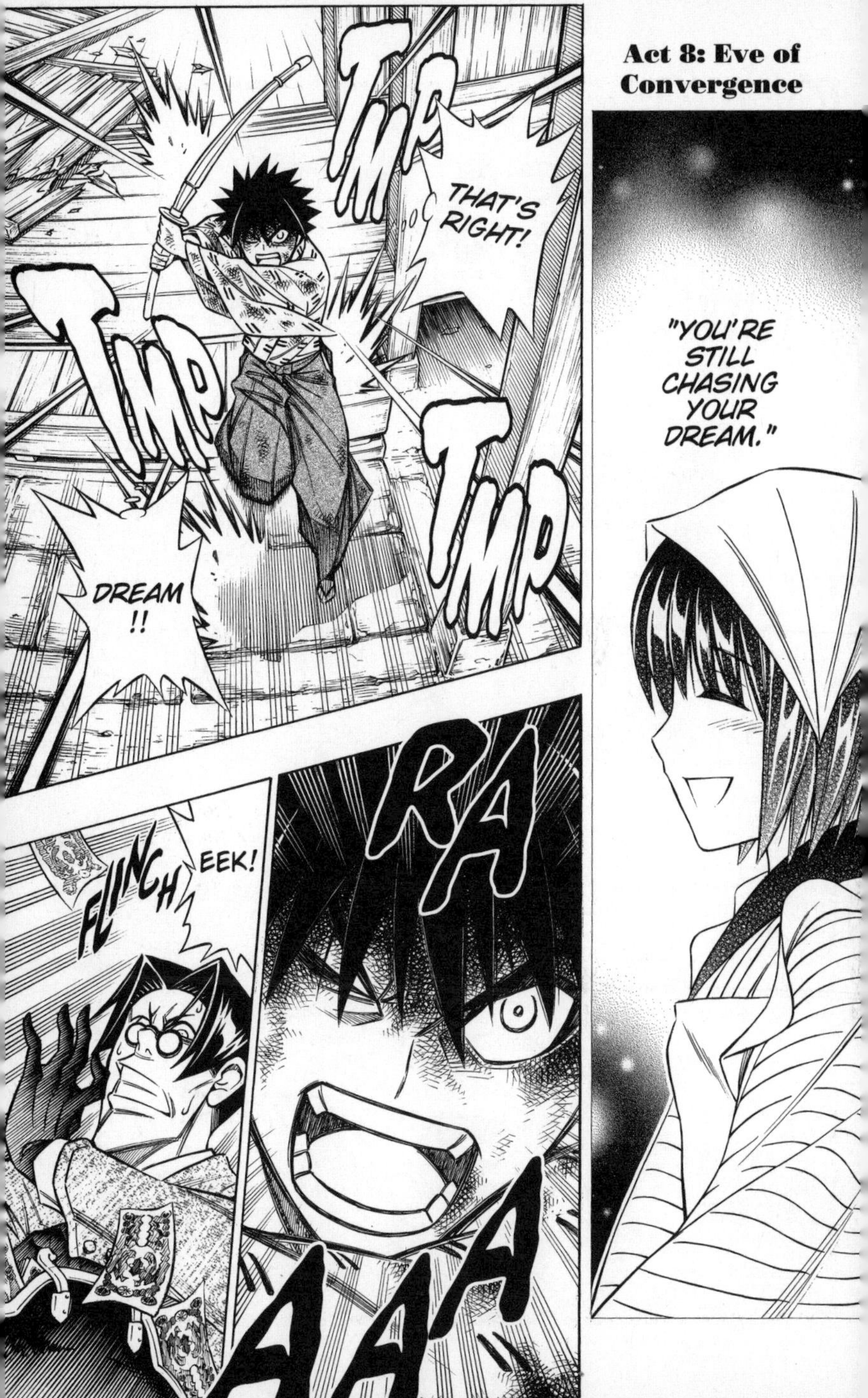
"YOU'RE STILL CHASING YOUR DREAM."
TMP
THAT'S RIGHT!
TMP
TMP
DREAM !!
RA
AAA
EEK!
FLINCH

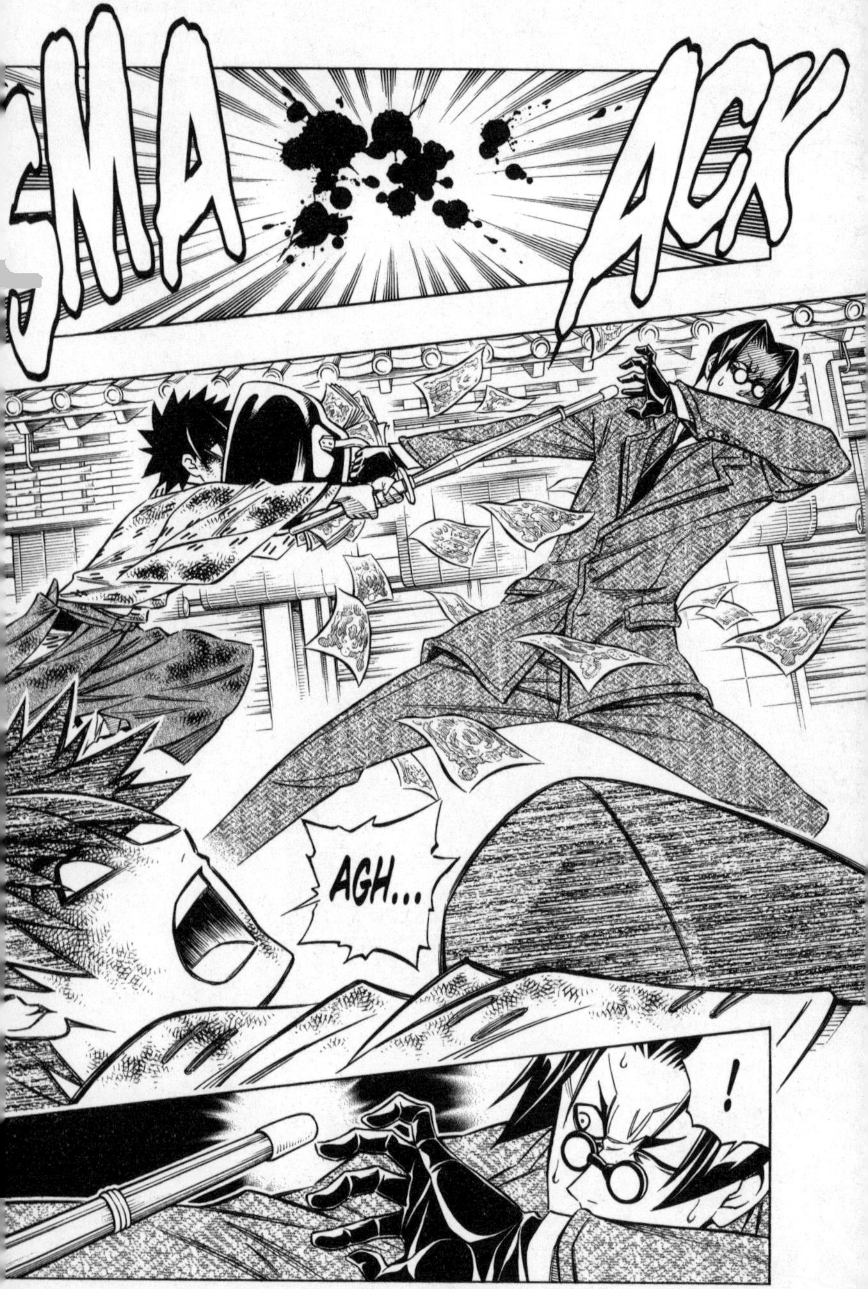
SMA
ACK
AGH...
!

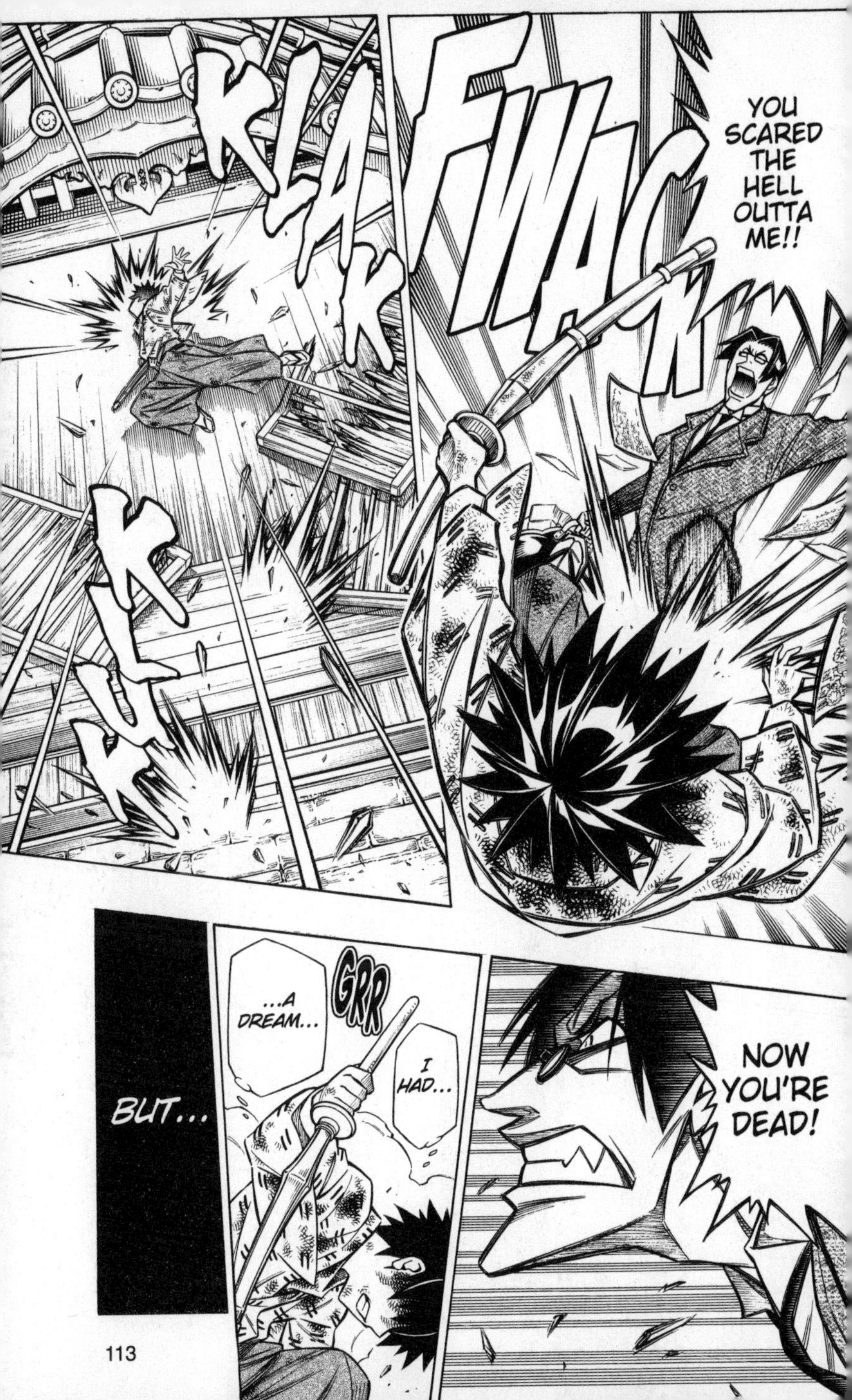
FWACK
YOU SCARED THE HELL OUTTA ME!!
KLAK
KLUK
NOW YOU'RE DEAD!
GRR
...A DREAM...
I HAD...
BUT...

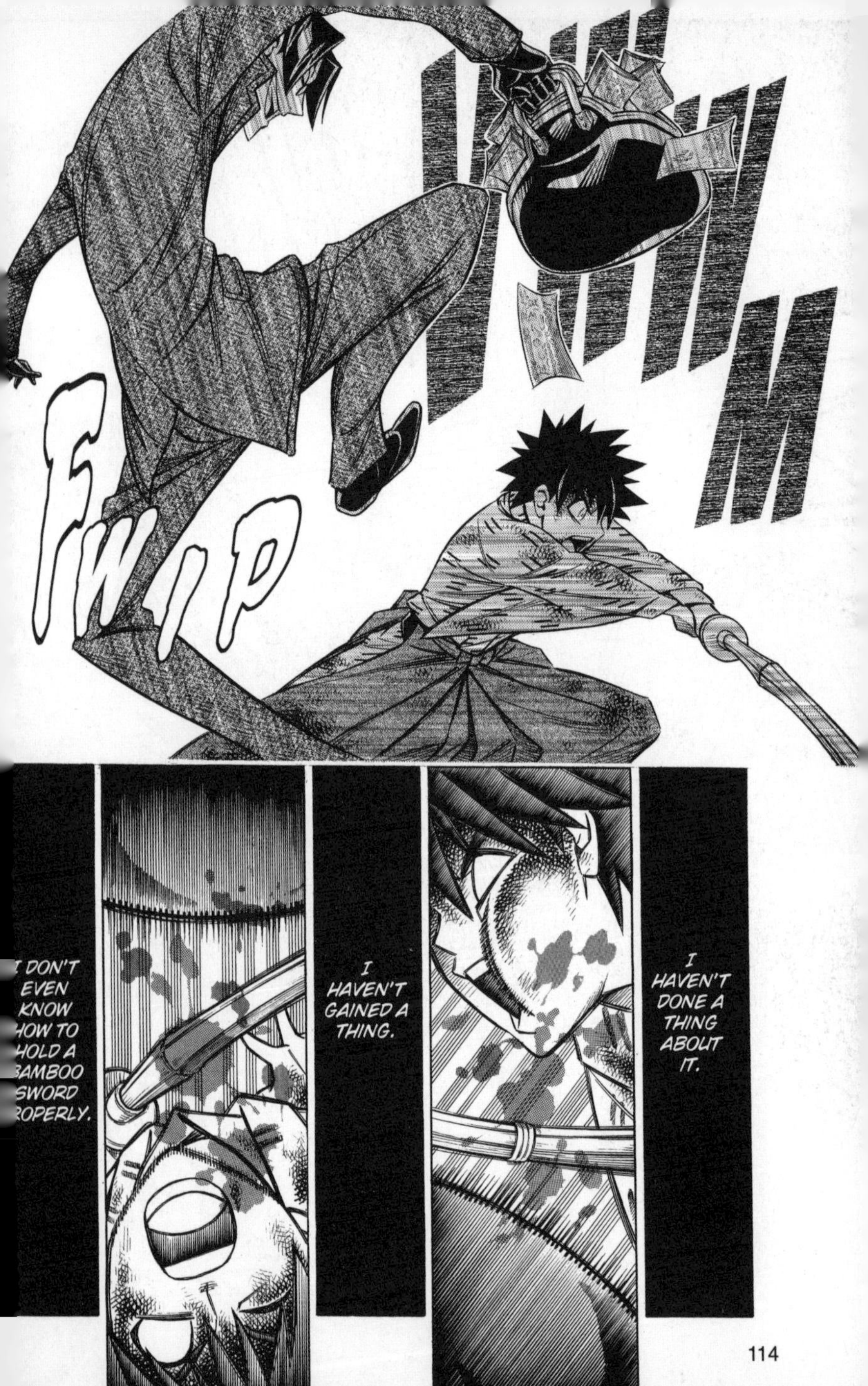
FWIP
I HAVEN'T DONE A THING ABOUT IT.
I HAVEN'T GAINED A THING.
I DON'T EVEN KNOW HOW TO HOLD A BAMBOO SWORD PROPERLY.

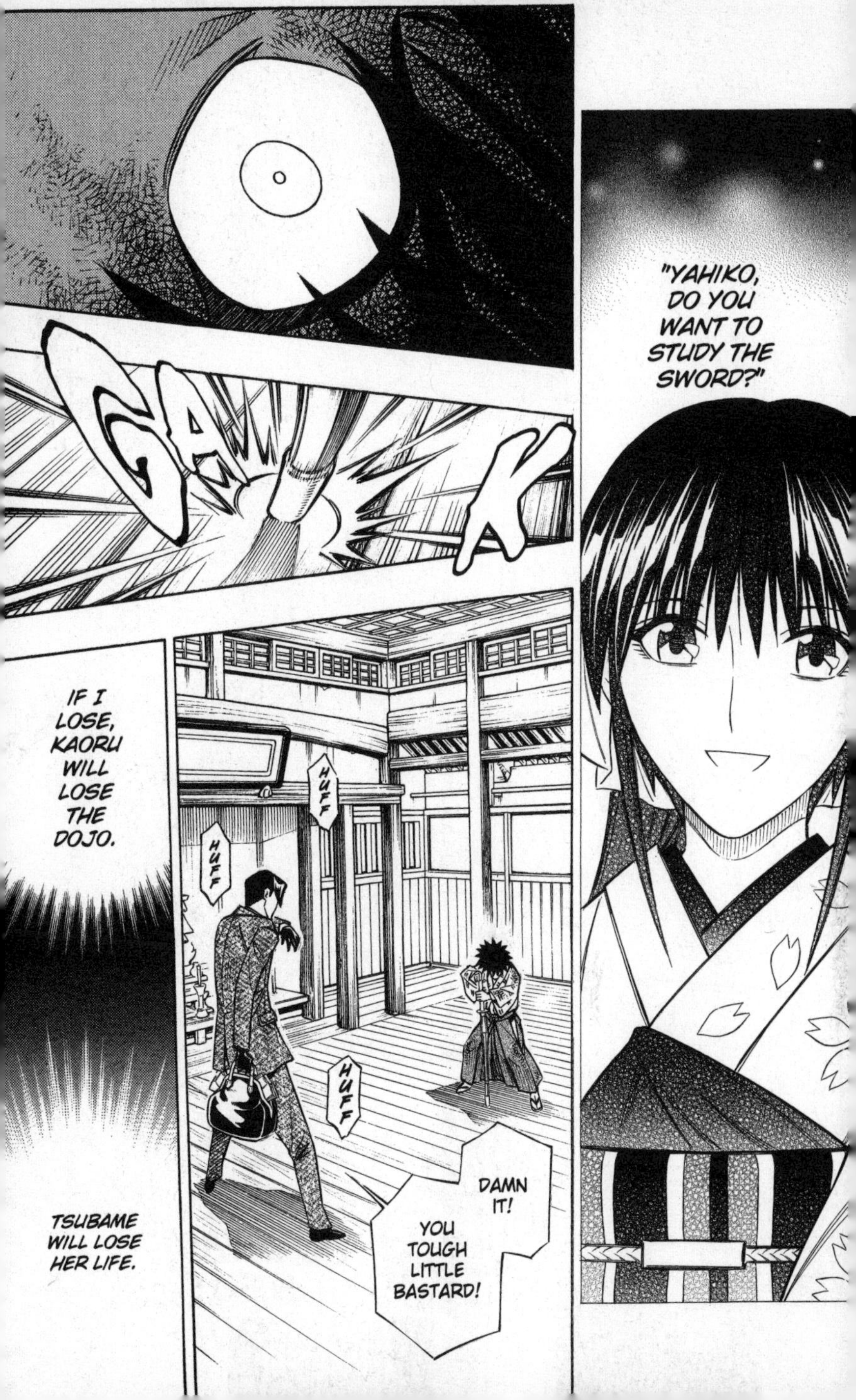
GAWK
"YAHIKO, DO YOU WANT TO STUDY THE SWORD?"
IF I LOSE, KAORU WILL LOSE THE DOJO.
HUFF HUFF
HUFF HUFF
HUFF HUFF
DAMN IT! YOU TOUGH LITTLE BASTARD!
TSUBAME WILL LOSE HER LIFE.

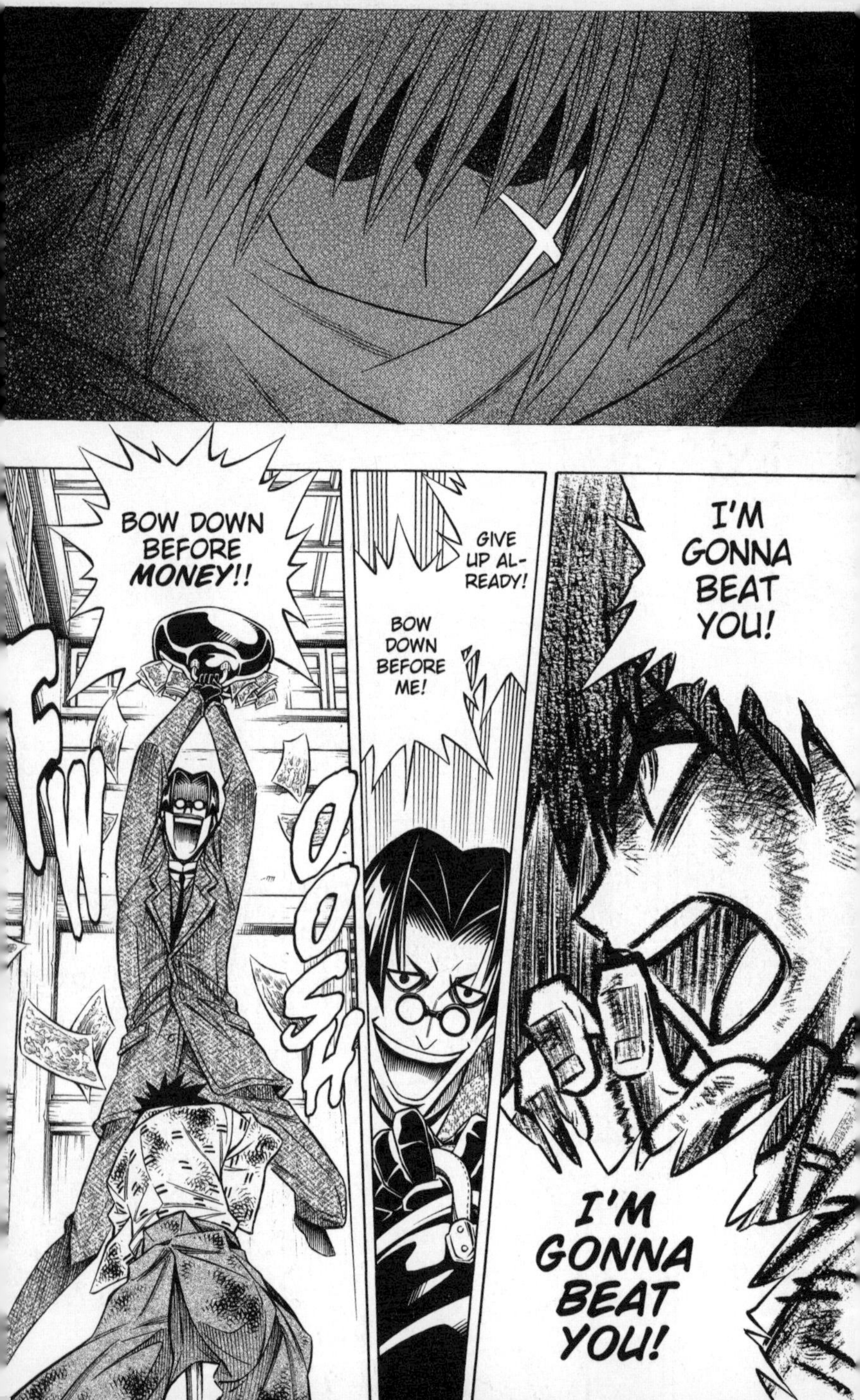
I'M GONNA BEAT YOU!
I'M GONNA BEAT YOU!
GIVE UP AL-READY!
BOW DOWN BEFORE ME!
BOW DOWN BEFORE **MONEY**!!

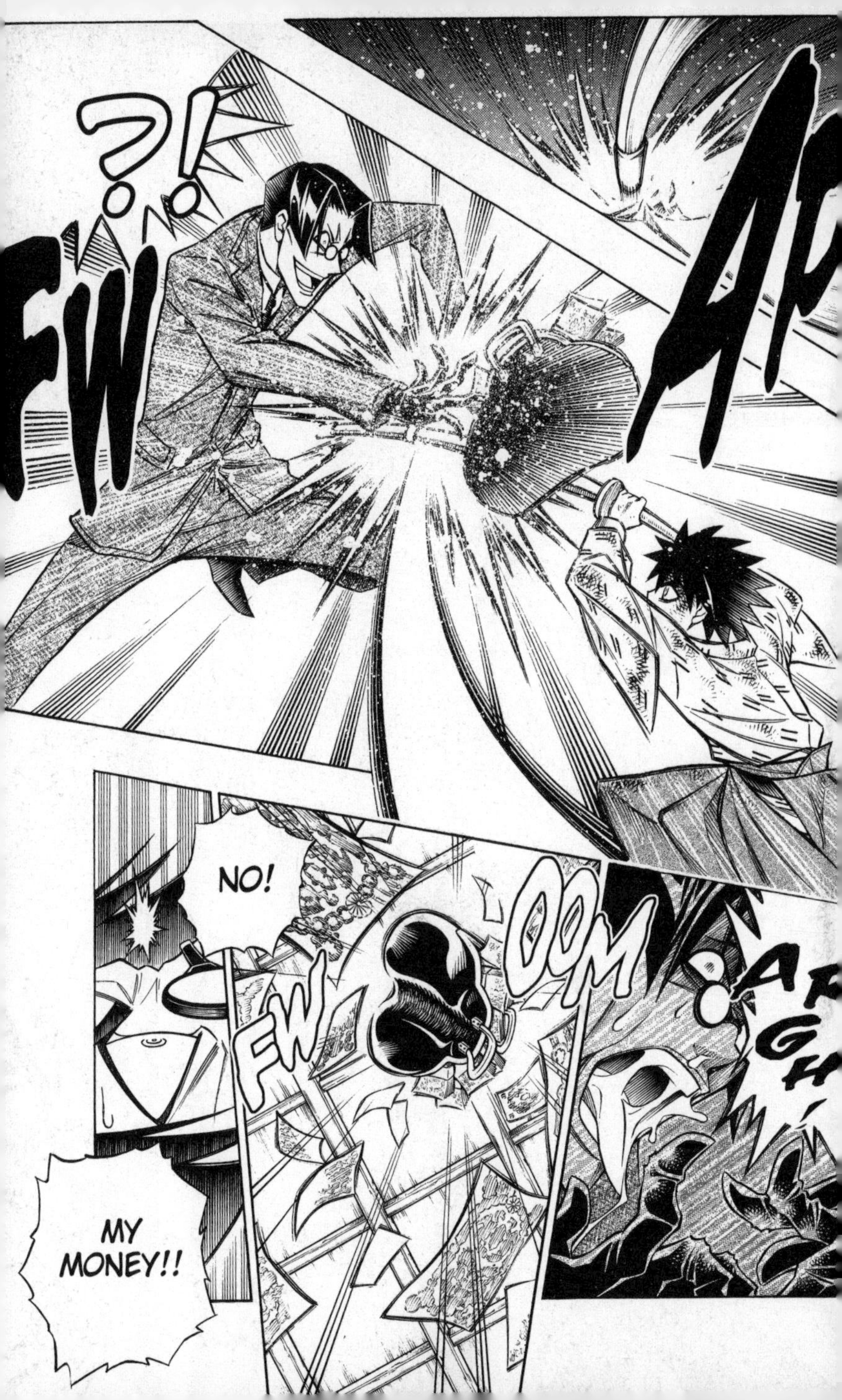
AP
?!
FW
ARGH
FWOOM
NO!
MY MONEY!!

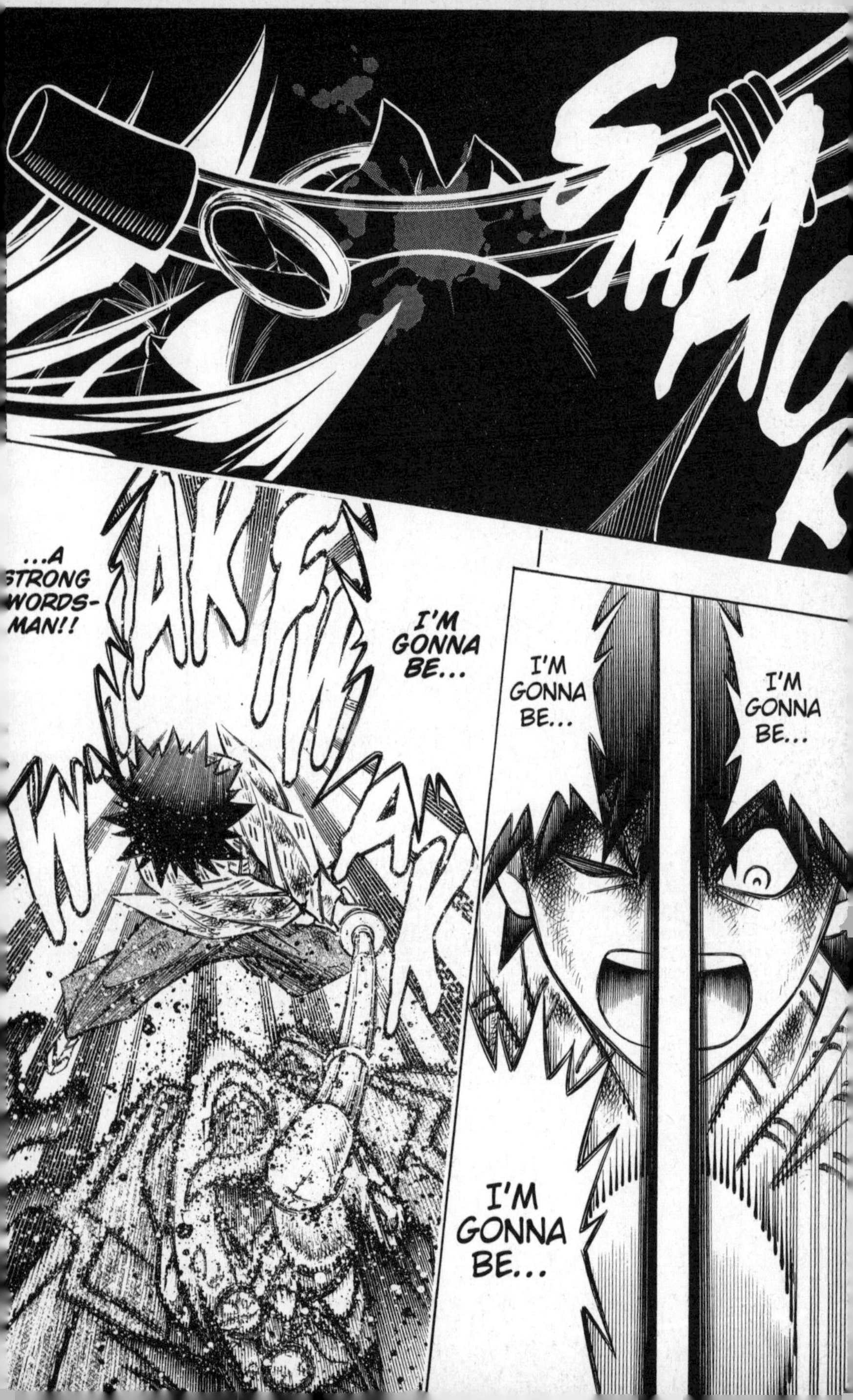
I'M GONNA BE...
I'M GONNA BE...
I'M GONNA BE...
I'M GONNA BE...
...A STRONG WORDS-MAN!!

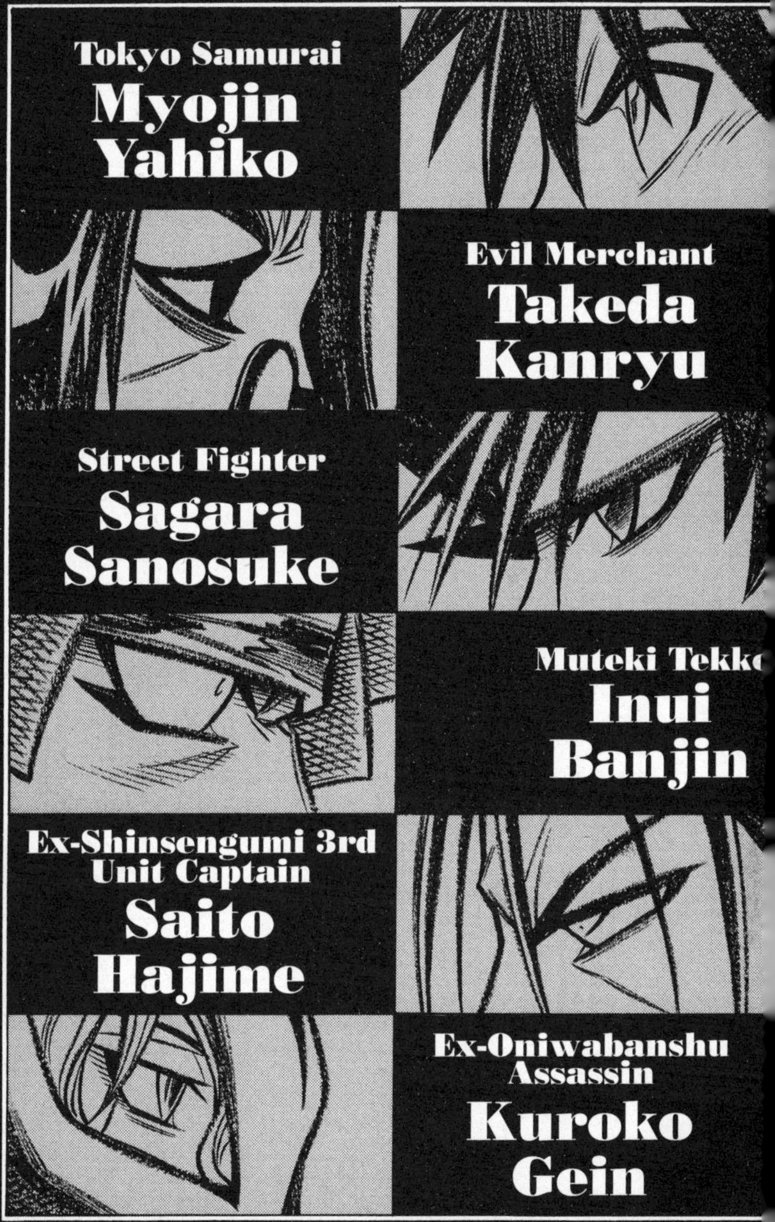
Tokyo Samurai
Myojin Yahiko
Evil Merchant
Takeda Kanryu
Street Fighter
Sagara Sanosuke
Muteki Tekko
Inui Banjin
Ex-Shinsengumi 3rd Unit Captain
Saito Hajime
Ex-Oniwabanshu Assassin
Kuroko Gein

Act 8: Eve of Convergence

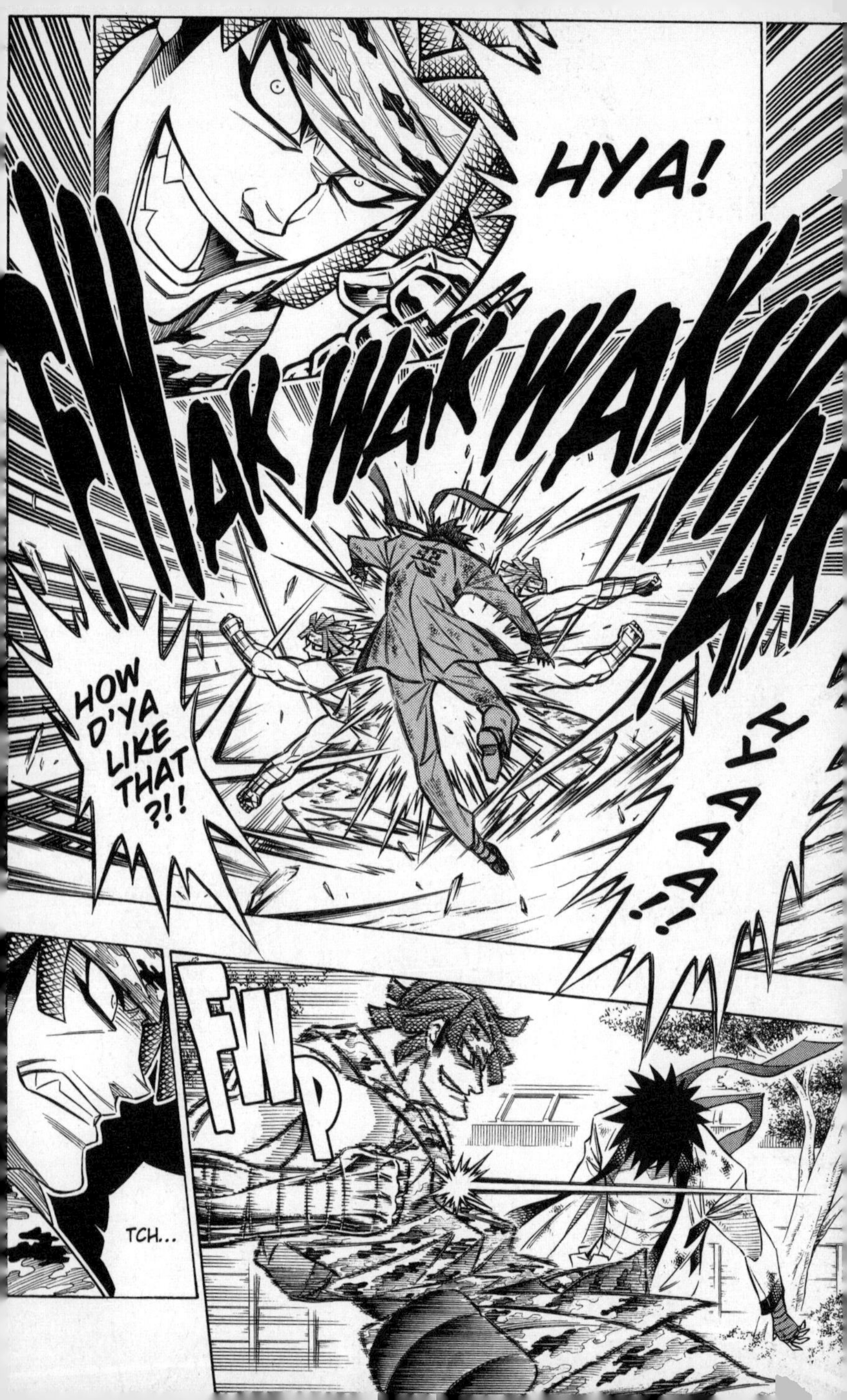
HYA!
HYAAAA!!
THWAKWAKWAKWAK
HOW D'YA LIKE THAT?!!
FWP
TCH...

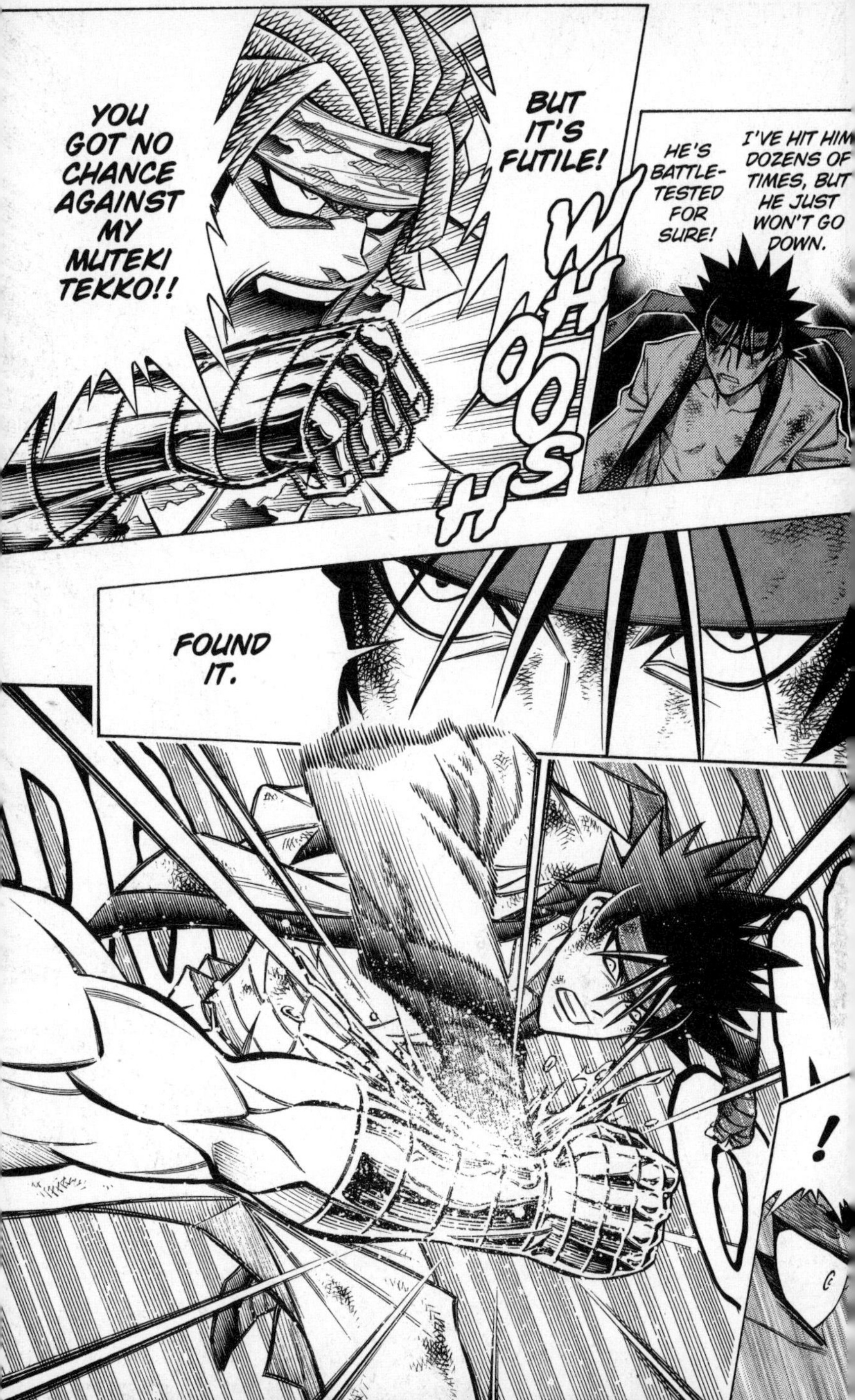
I'VE HIT HIM DOZENS OF TIMES, BUT HE JUST WON'T GO DOWN.
HE'S BATTLE-TESTED FOR SURE!
BUT IT'S FUTILE!
YOU GOT NO CHANCE AGAINST MY MUTEKI TEKKO!!
WHOOSH
FOUND IT.
!

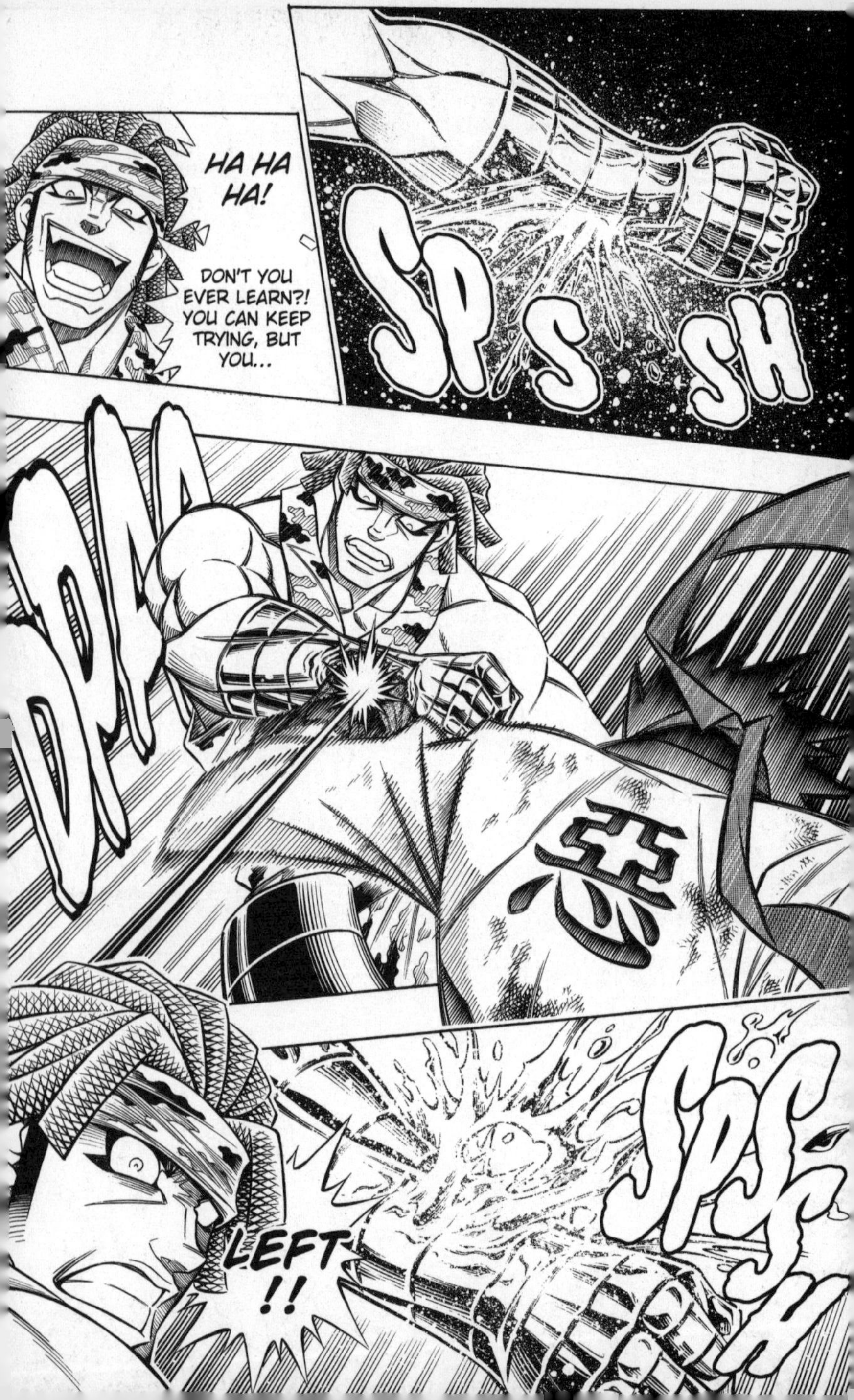
SPSSH
HA HA HA!
DON'T YOU EVER LEARN?! YOU CAN KEEP TRYING, BUT YOU...
LEFT !!

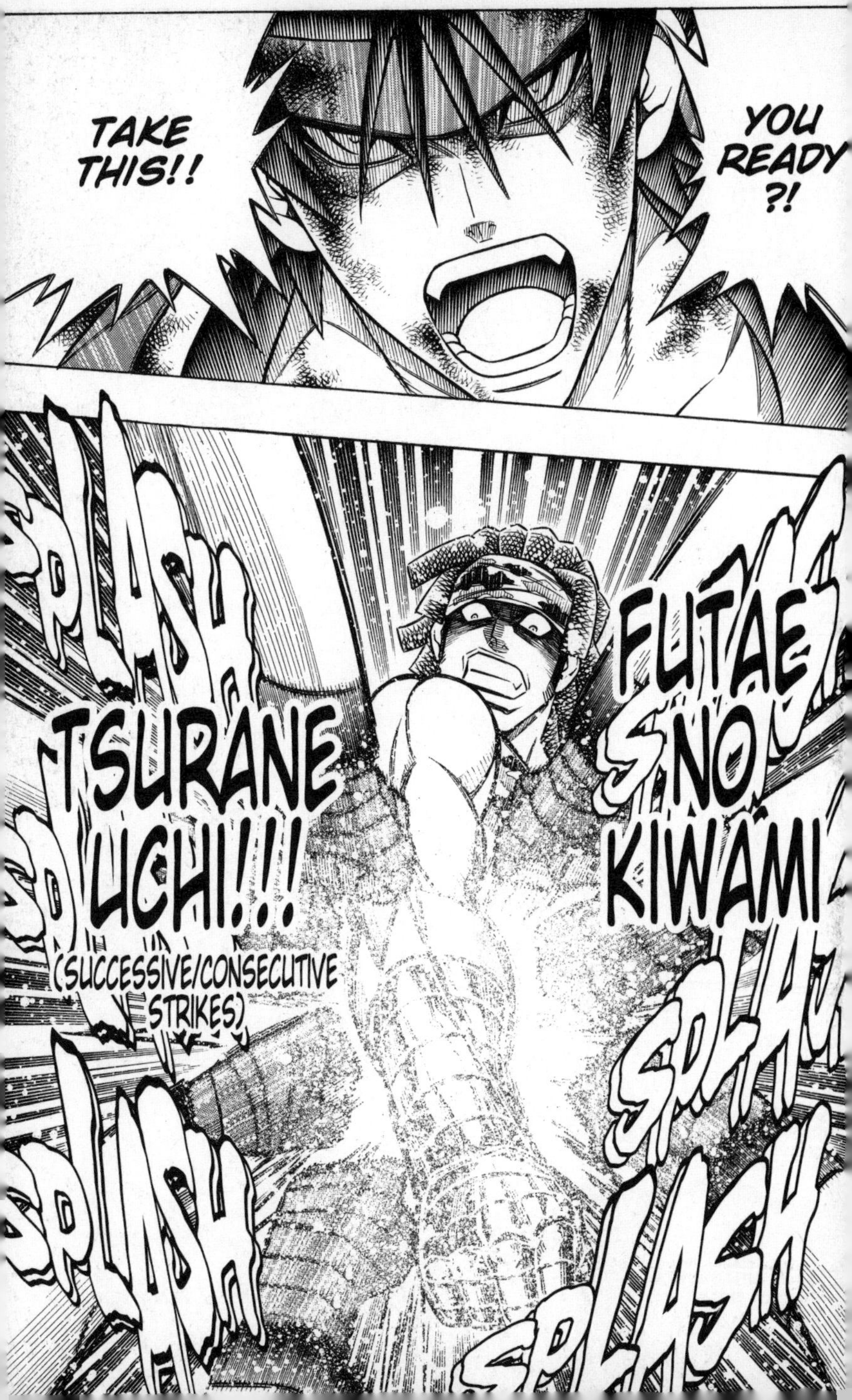
YOU READY?!
TAKE THIS!!
FUTAE NO KIWAMI
TSURANE UCHI!!!
(SUCCESSIVE/CONSECUTIVE STRIKES)
SPLASH
SPLASH
SPLASH

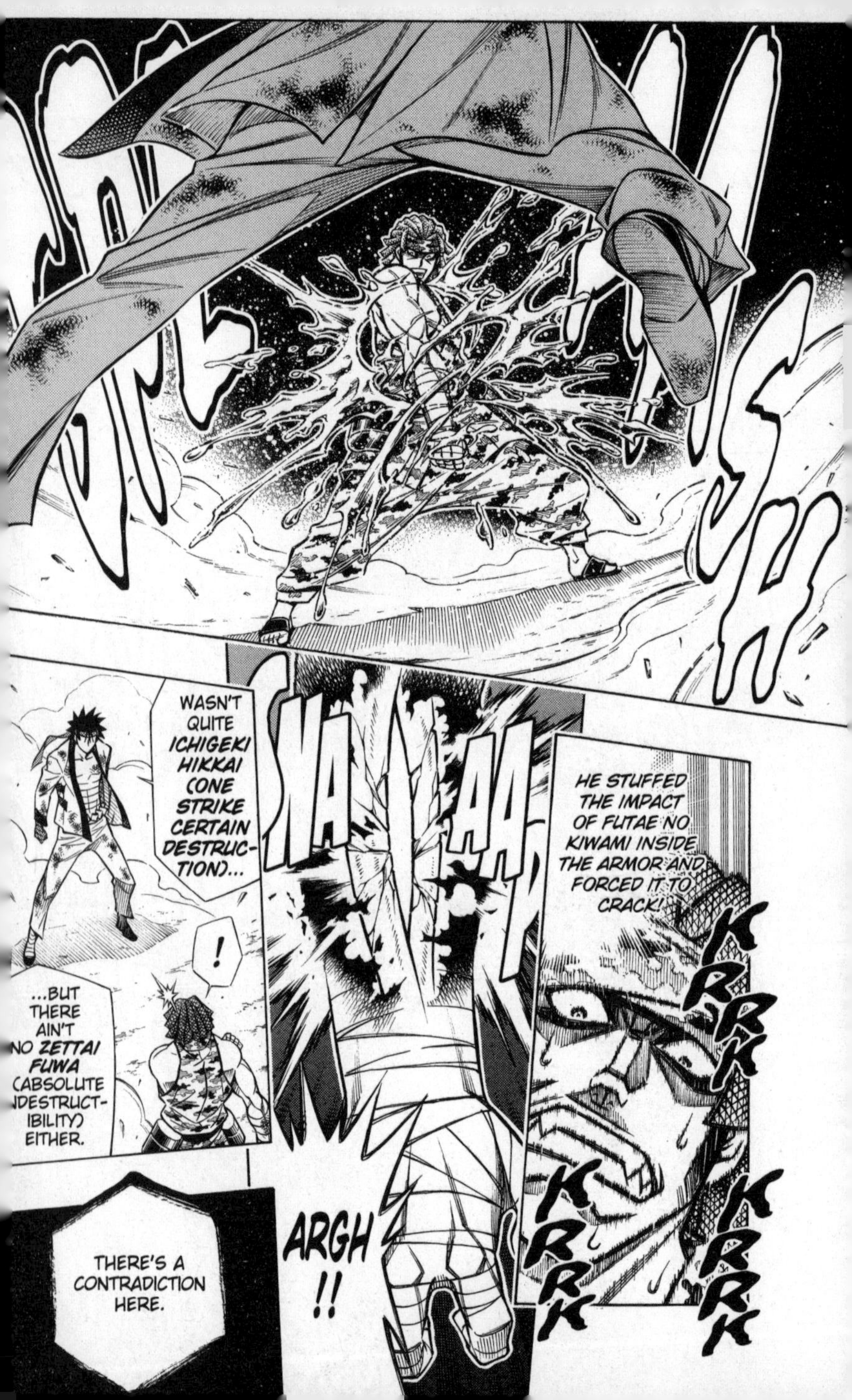

HE STUFFED THE IMPACT OF FUTAE NO KIWAMI INSIDE THE ARMOR AND FORCED IT TO CRACK!
KRRK KRRK
KRRK KRRK
ARGH !!
WASN'T QUITE *ICHIGEKI HIKKAI* (ONE STRIKE CERTAIN DESTRUCTION)...
!
...BUT THERE AIN'T NO *ZETTAI FUWA* (ABSOLUTE INDESTRUCTIBILITY) EITHER.
THERE'S A CONTRADICTION HERE.

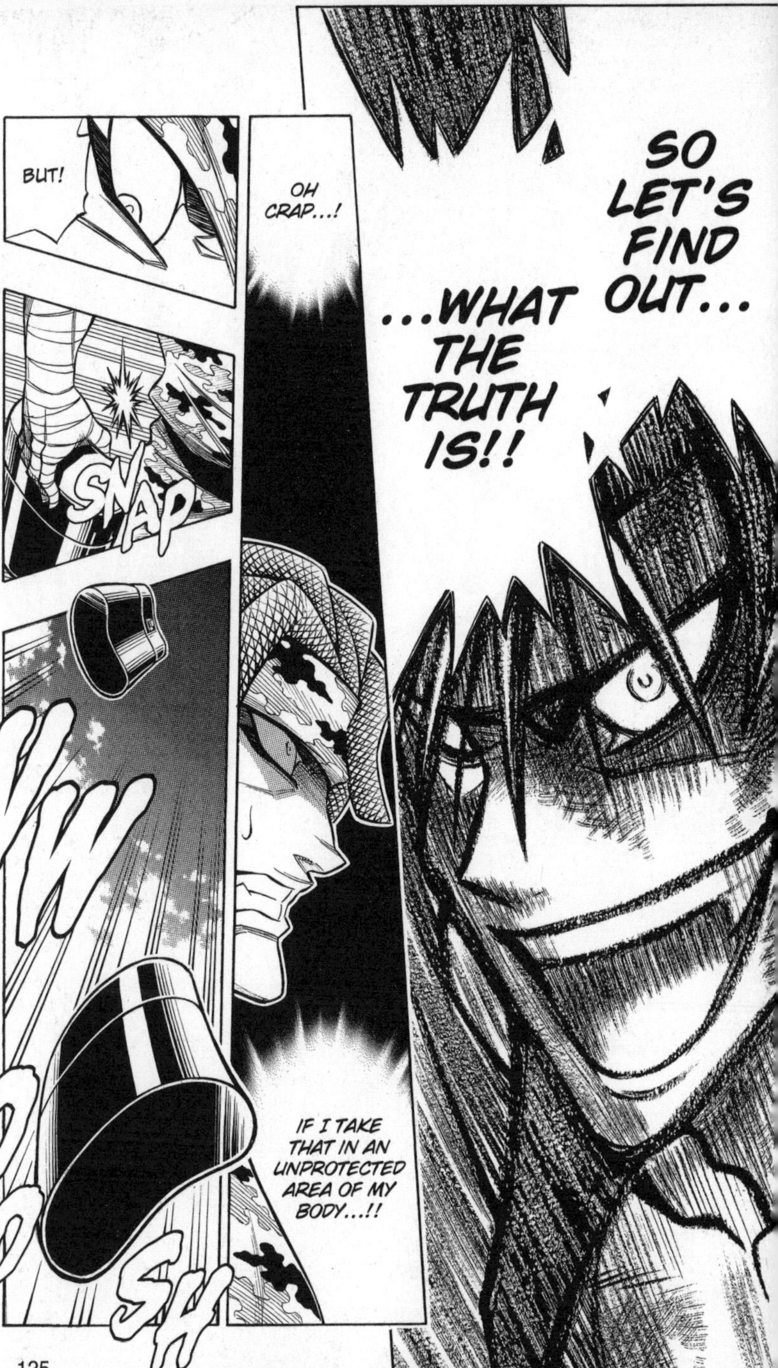
SO LET'S FIND OUT...
...WHAT THE TRUTH IS!!
OH CRAP...!
IF I TAKE THAT IN AN UNPROTECTED AREA OF MY BODY...!!
BUT!
SNAP
VWOOSH

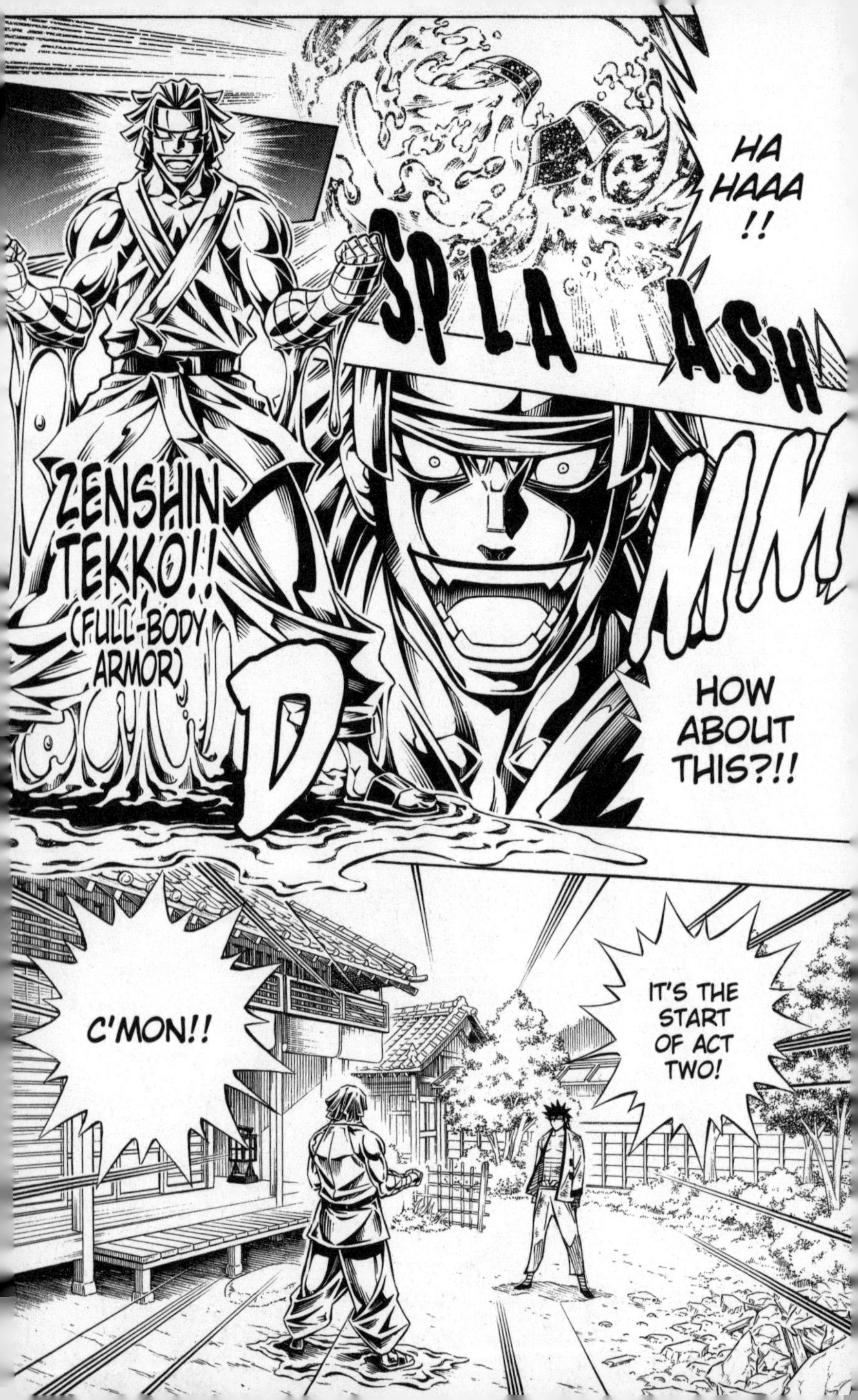
HA HAAA!!
SPLAASH
HOW ABOUT THIS?!!
ZENSHIN TEKKO!! (FULL-BODY ARMOR)
IT'S THE START OF ACT TWO!
C'MON!!

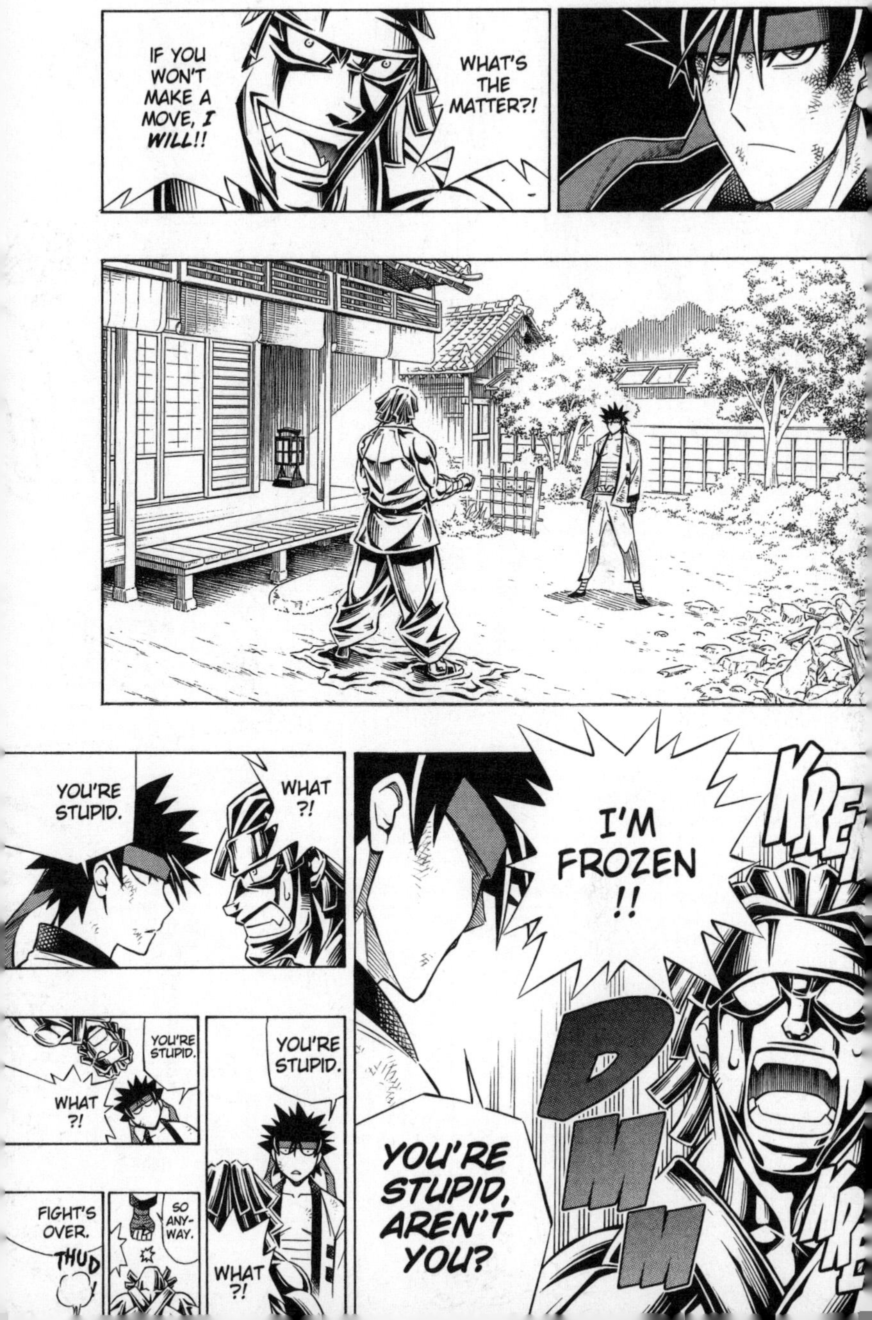
WHAT'S THE MATTER?!
IF YOU WON'T MAKE A MOVE, I WILL!!
KRE
I'M FROZEN!!
DMM
YOU'RE STUPID, AREN'T YOU?
WHAT ?!
YOU'RE STUPID.
YOU'RE STUPID.
WHAT ?!
YOU'RE STUPID.
WHAT ?!
SO ANYWAY.
FIGHT'S OVER.
THUD

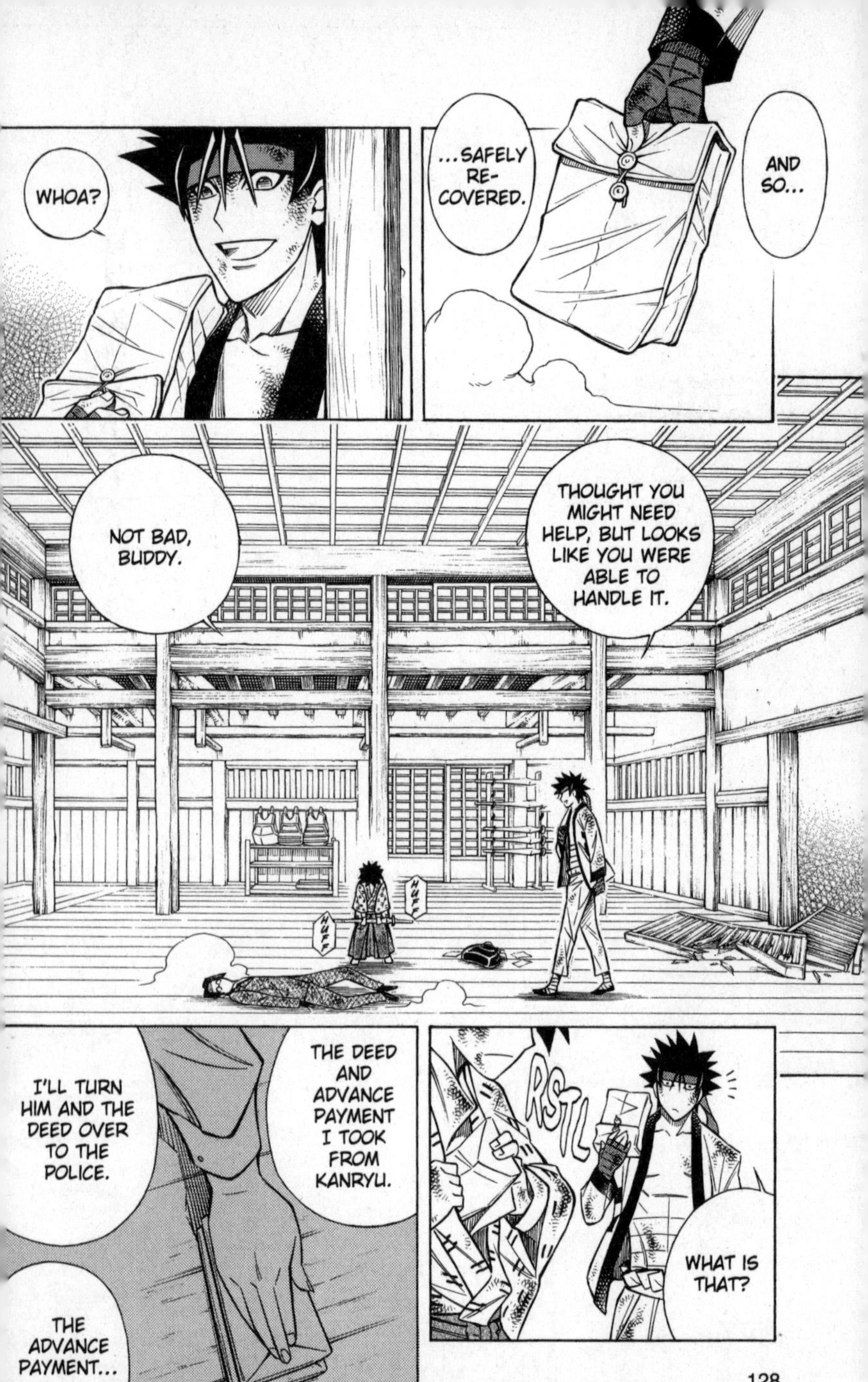
AND SO...
...SAFELY RE-COVERED.
WHOA?
THOUGHT YOU MIGHT NEED HELP, BUT LOOKS LIKE YOU WERE ABLE TO HANDLE IT.
NOT BAD, BUDDY.
HUFF
HUFF
RSTL
WHAT IS THAT?
THE DEED AND ADVANCE PAYMENT I TOOK FROM KANRYU.
I'LL TURN HIM AND THE DEED OVER TO THE POLICE.
THE ADVANCE PAYMENT...

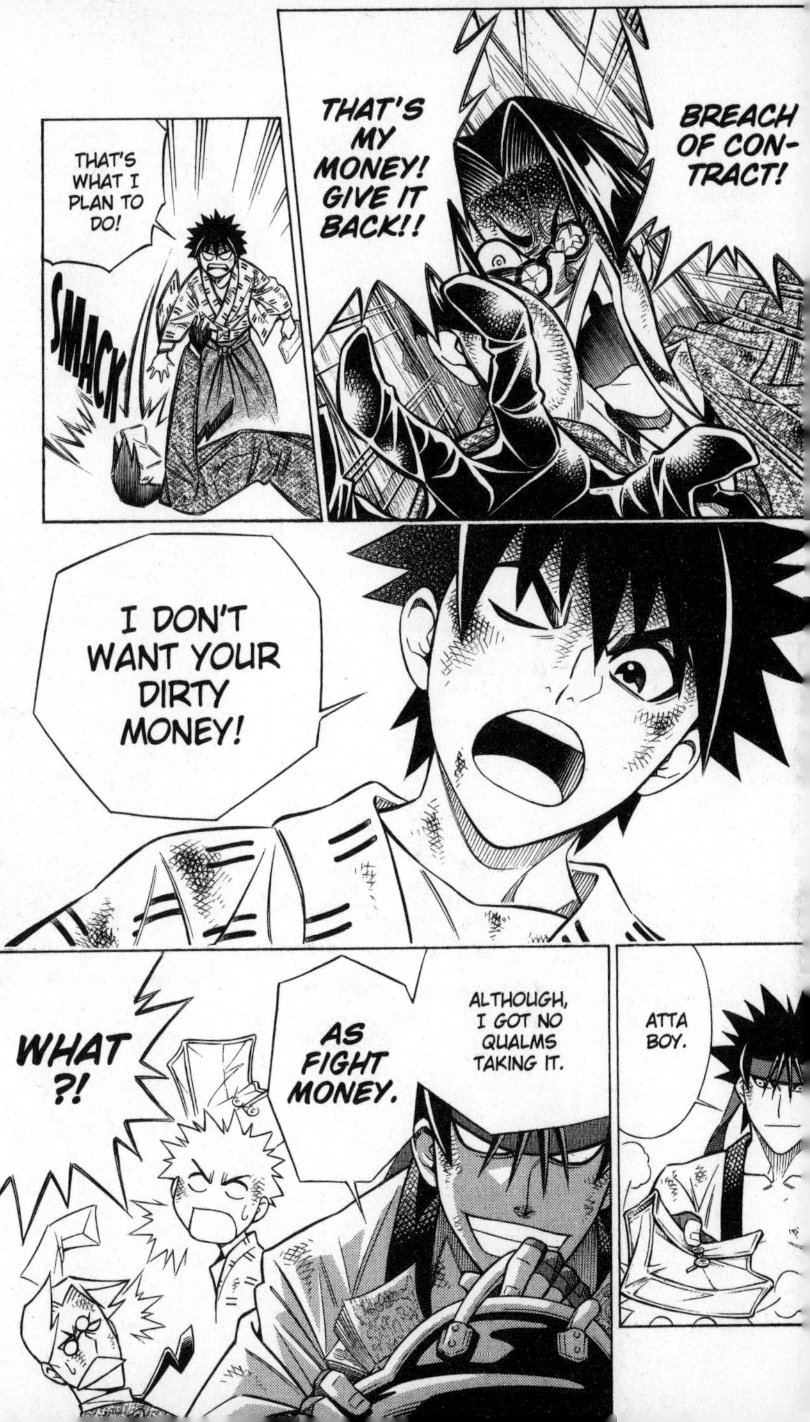
BREACH OF CON-TRACT!
THAT'S MY MONEY! GIVE IT BACK!!
THAT'S WHAT I PLAN TO DO!
SMACK
I DON'T WANT YOUR DIRTY MONEY!
ATTA BOY.
ALTHOUGH, I GOT NO QUALMS TAKING IT.
AS FIGHT MONEY.
WHAT ?!

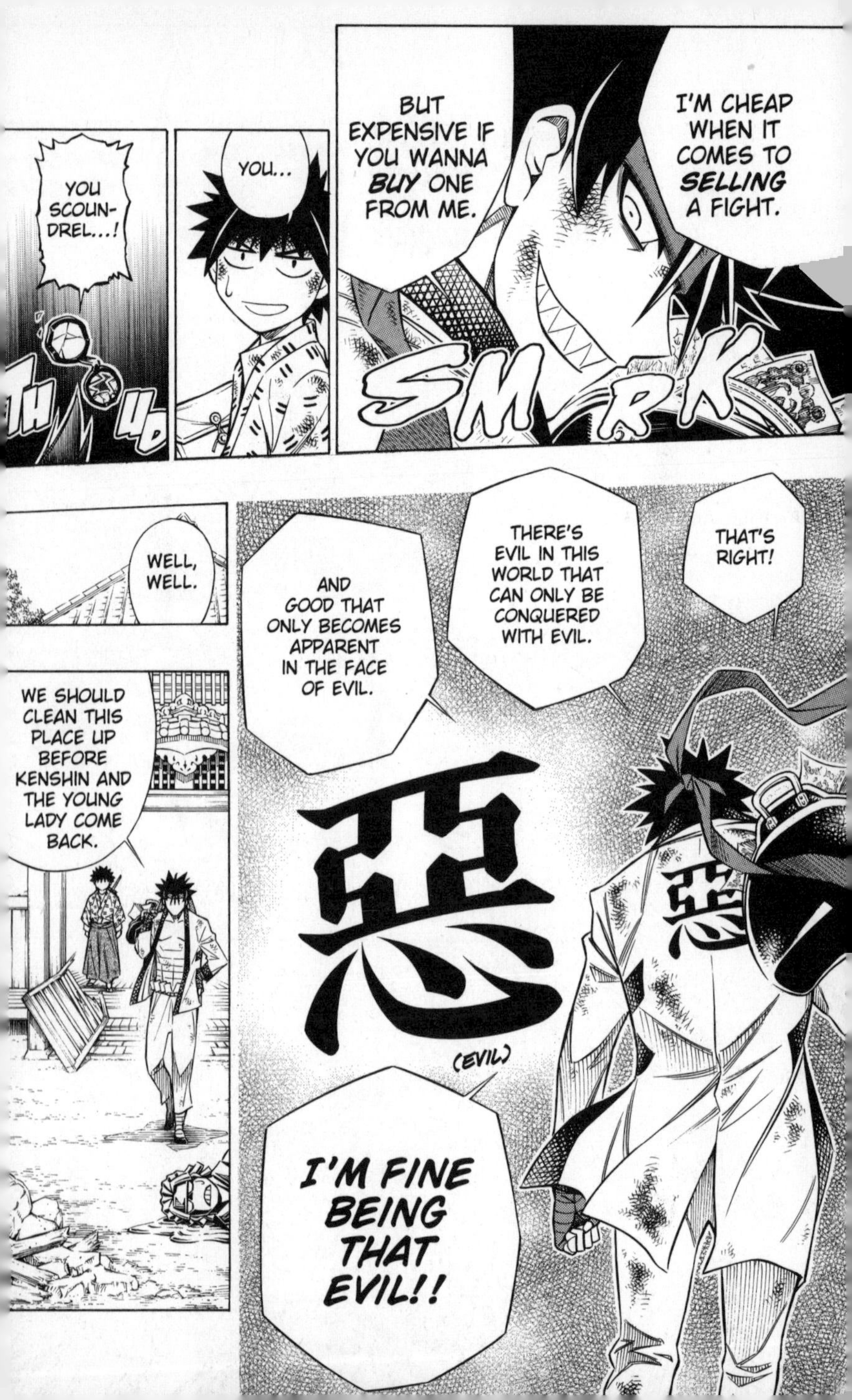
I'M CHEAP WHEN IT COMES TO *SELLING* A FIGHT.
BUT EXPENSIVE IF YOU WANNA *BUY* ONE FROM ME.
SMRK
YOU...
YOU SCOUN-DREL...!
TH UD
THAT'S RIGHT!
THERE'S EVIL IN THIS WORLD THAT CAN ONLY BE CONQUERED WITH EVIL.
AND GOOD THAT ONLY BECOMES APPARENT IN THE FACE OF EVIL.
悪
(EVIL)
I'M FINE BEING THAT EVIL!!
WELL, WELL.
WE SHOULD CLEAN THIS PLACE UP BEFORE KENSHIN AND THE YOUNG LADY COME BACK.

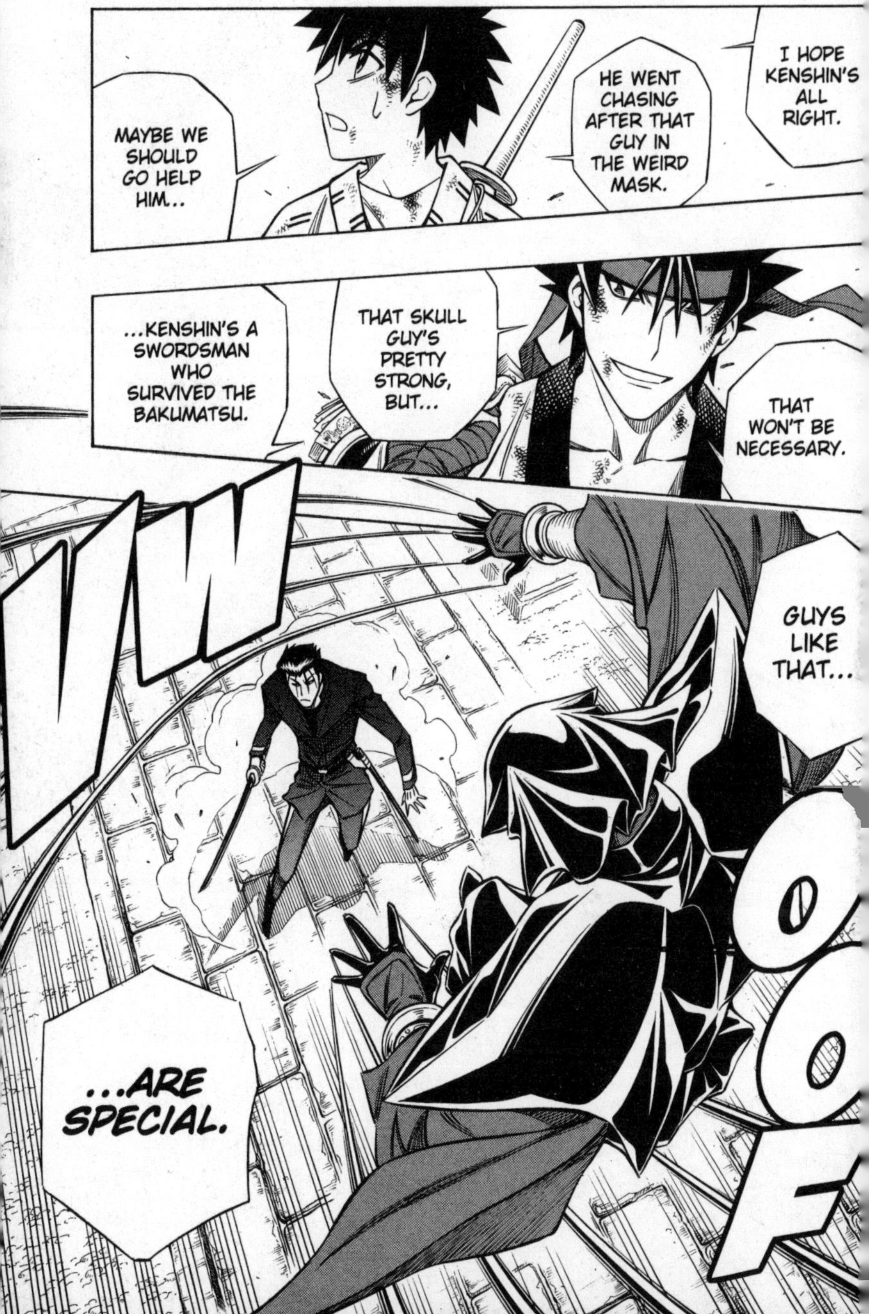
I HOPE KENSHIN'S ALL RIGHT.
HE WENT CHASING AFTER THAT GUY IN THE WEIRD MASK.
MAYBE WE SHOULD GO HELP HIM...
THAT WON'T BE NECESSARY.
THAT SKULL GUY'S PRETTY STRONG, BUT...
...KENSHIN'S A SWORDSMAN WHO SURVIVED THE BAKUMATSU.
GUYS LIKE THAT...
...ARE SPECIAL.

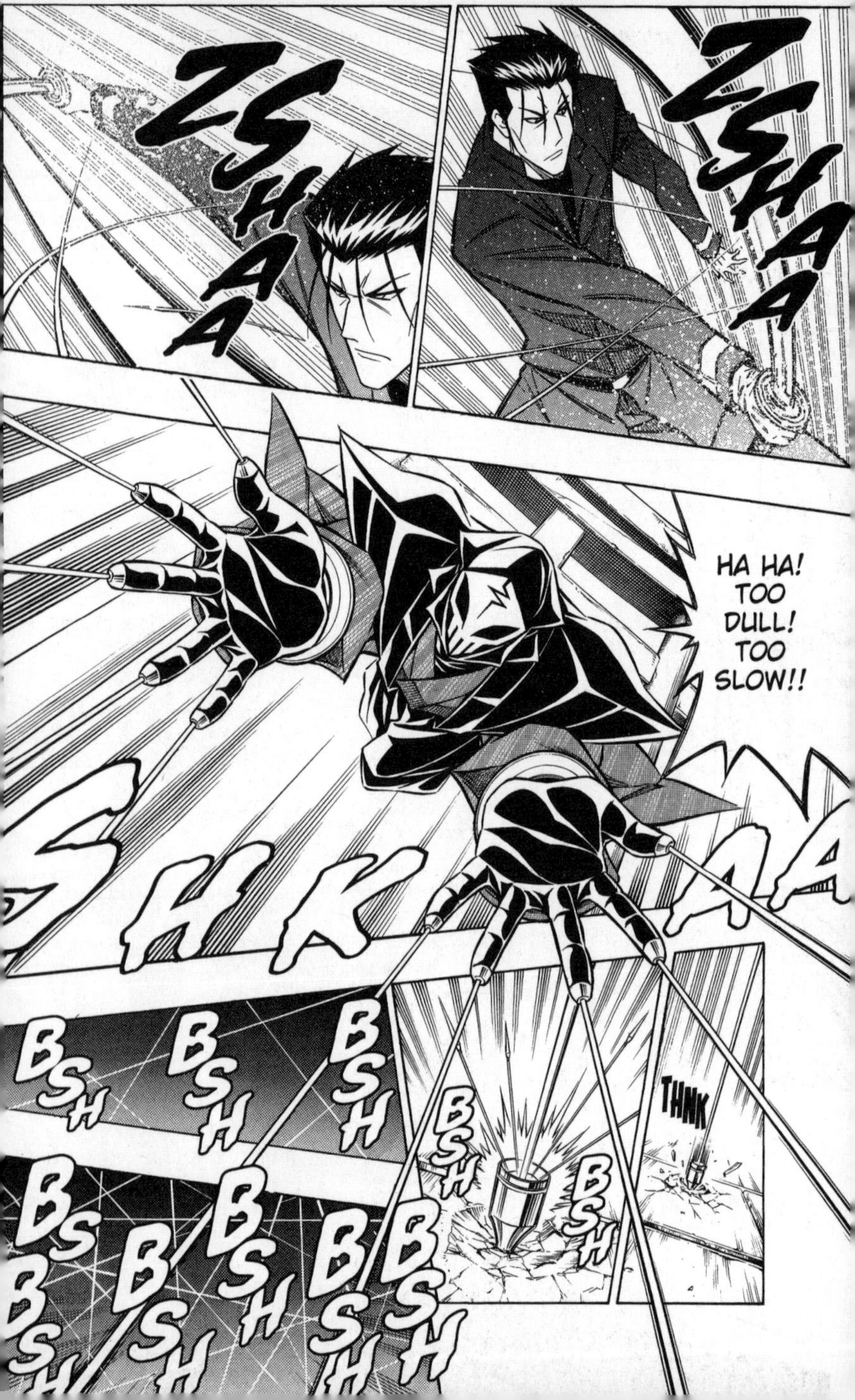
ZSHAAA
ZSHAAA
HA HA! TOO DULL! TOO SLOW!!
SHKAA
THNK
BSH
BSH
BSH
BSH
BSH
BSH
BSH
BSH
BSH
BSH
BSH

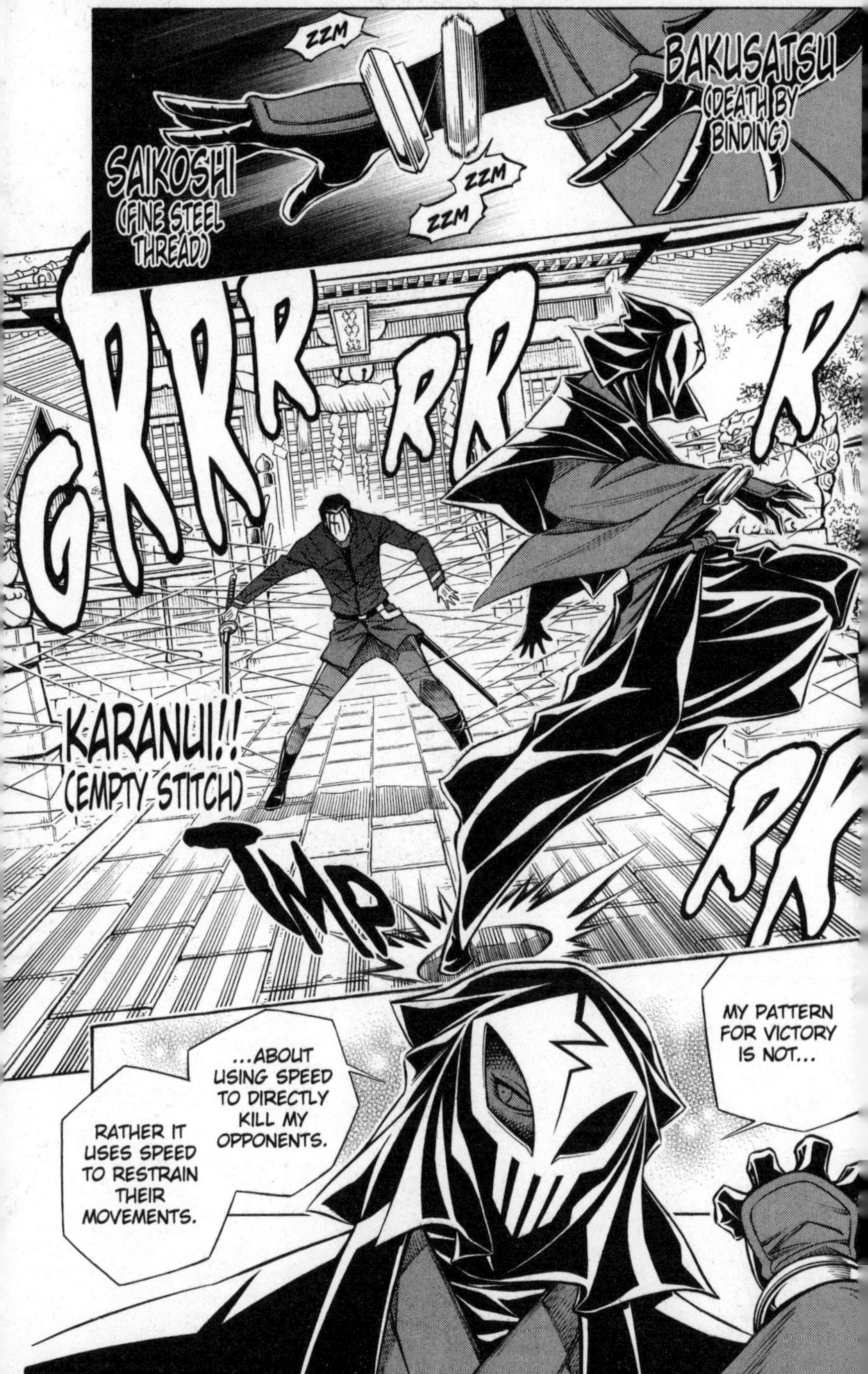
BAKUSATSU
(DEATH BY BINDING)
ZZM
ZZM
ZZM
SAIKOSHI
(FINE STEEL THREAD)
GRRRRRRRRR
KARANUI!!
(EMPTY STITCH)
TMP
MY PATTERN FOR VICTORY IS NOT...
...ABOUT USING SPEED TO DIRECTLY KILL MY OPPONENTS.
RATHER IT USES SPEED TO RESTRAIN THEIR MOVEMENTS.

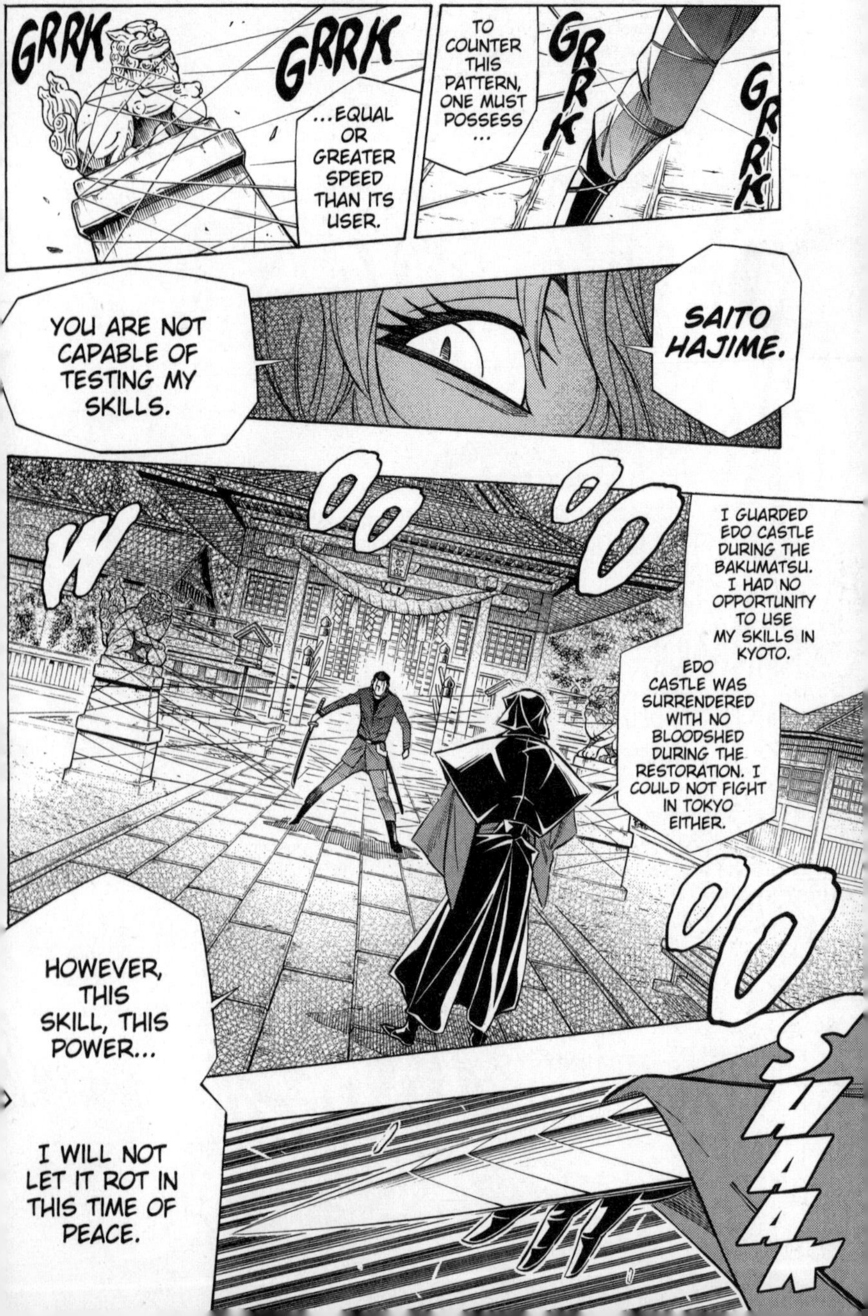
GRRK
GRRK
TO COUNTER THIS PATTERN, ONE MUST POSSESS...
GRRK
GRRK
...EQUAL OR GREATER SPEED THAN ITS USER.
SAITO HAJIME.
YOU ARE NOT CAPABLE OF TESTING MY SKILLS.
WOOOO
I GUARDED EDO CASTLE DURING THE BAKUMATSU. I HAD NO OPPORTUNITY TO USE MY SKILLS IN KYOTO.
EDO CASTLE WAS SURRENDERED WITH NO BLOODSHED DURING THE RESTORATION. I COULD NOT FIGHT IN TOKYO EITHER.
HOWEVER, THIS SKILL, THIS POWER...
SHAAK
I WILL NOT LET IT ROT IN THIS TIME OF PEACE.

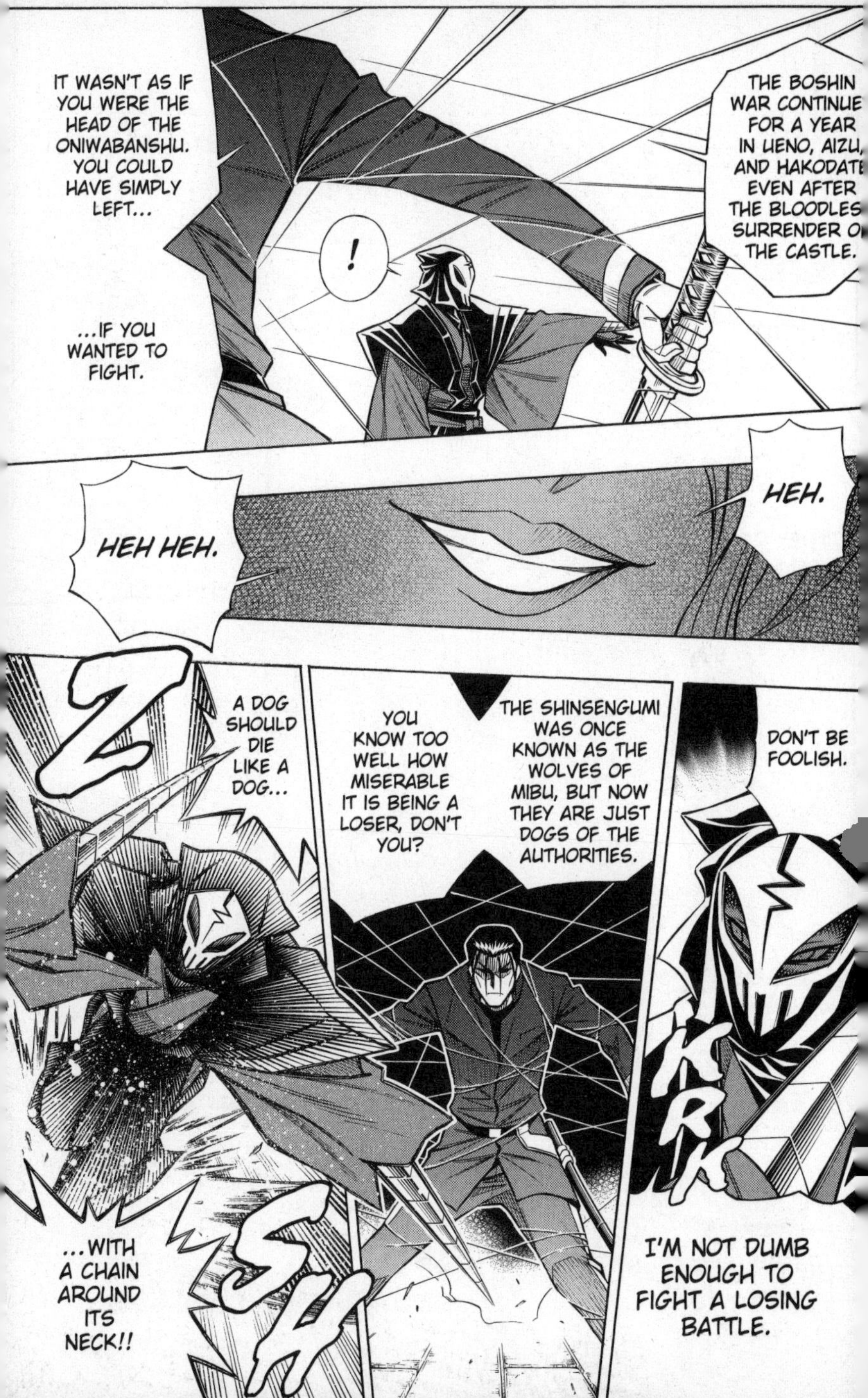
THE BOSHIN WAR CONTINUE FOR A YEAR IN UENO, AIZU, AND HAKODAT EVEN AFTER THE BLOODLES SURRENDER O THE CASTLE.
IT WASN'T AS IF YOU WERE THE HEAD OF THE ONIWABANSHU. YOU COULD HAVE SIMPLY LEFT...
!
...IF YOU WANTED TO FIGHT.
HEH.
HEH HEH.
DON'T BE FOOLISH.
KRK
I'M NOT DUMB ENOUGH TO FIGHT A LOSING BATTLE.
THE SHINSENGUMI WAS ONCE KNOWN AS THE WOLVES OF MIBU, BUT NOW THEY ARE JUST DOGS OF THE AUTHORITIES.
YOU KNOW TOO WELL HOW MISERABLE IT IS BEING A LOSER, DON'T YOU?
A DOG SHOULD DIE LIKE A DOG...
Z
...WITH A CHAIN AROUND ITS NECK!!
SH

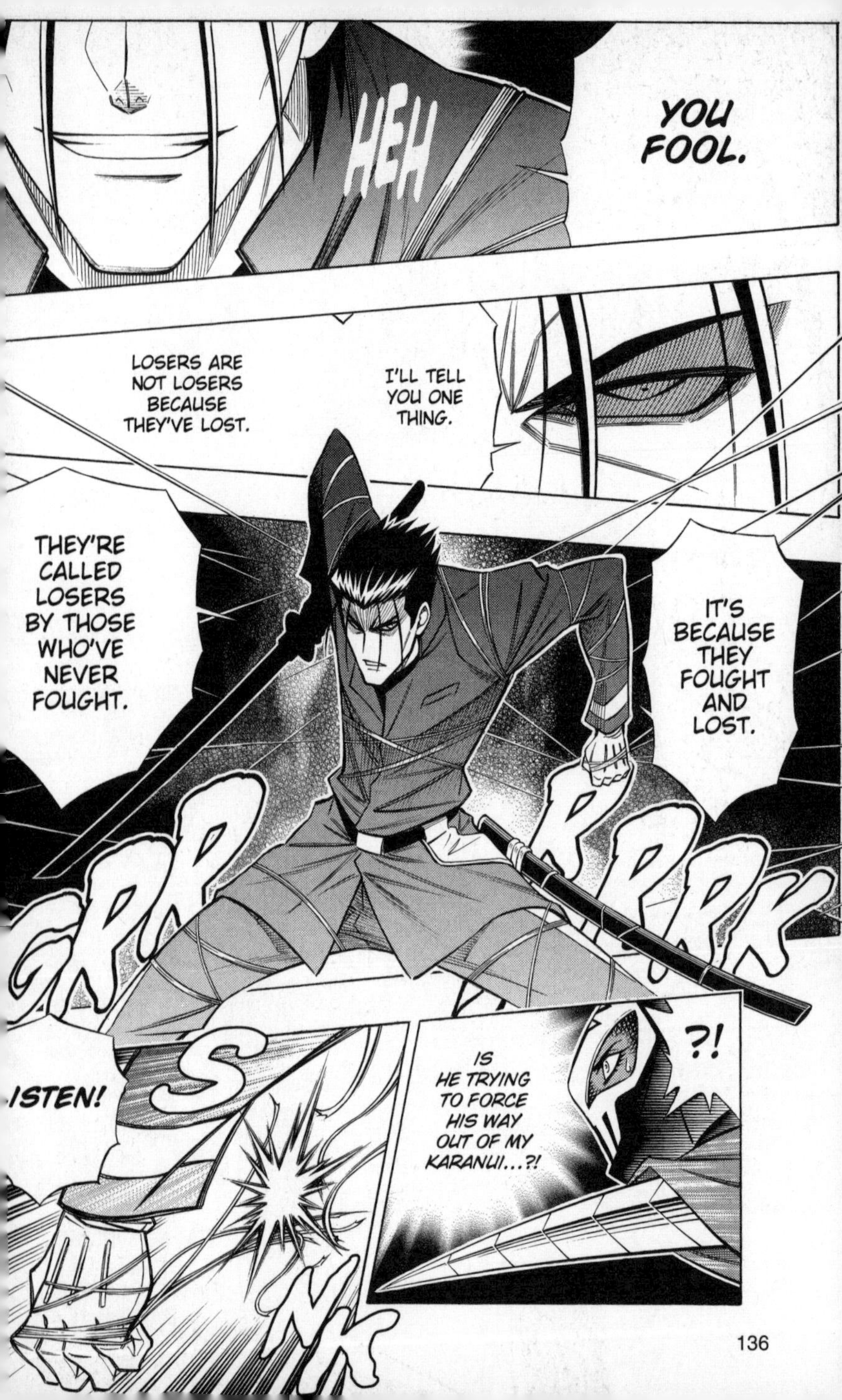
HEH
YOU FOOL.
I'LL TELL YOU ONE THING.
LOSERS ARE NOT LOSERS BECAUSE THEY'VE LOST.
IT'S BECAUSE THEY FOUGHT AND LOST.
THEY'RE CALLED LOSERS BY THOSE WHO'VE NEVER FOUGHT.
GRR
RRRK
?!
IS HE TRYING TO FORCE HIS WAY OUT OF MY KARANUI...?!
ISTEN!
S
NK

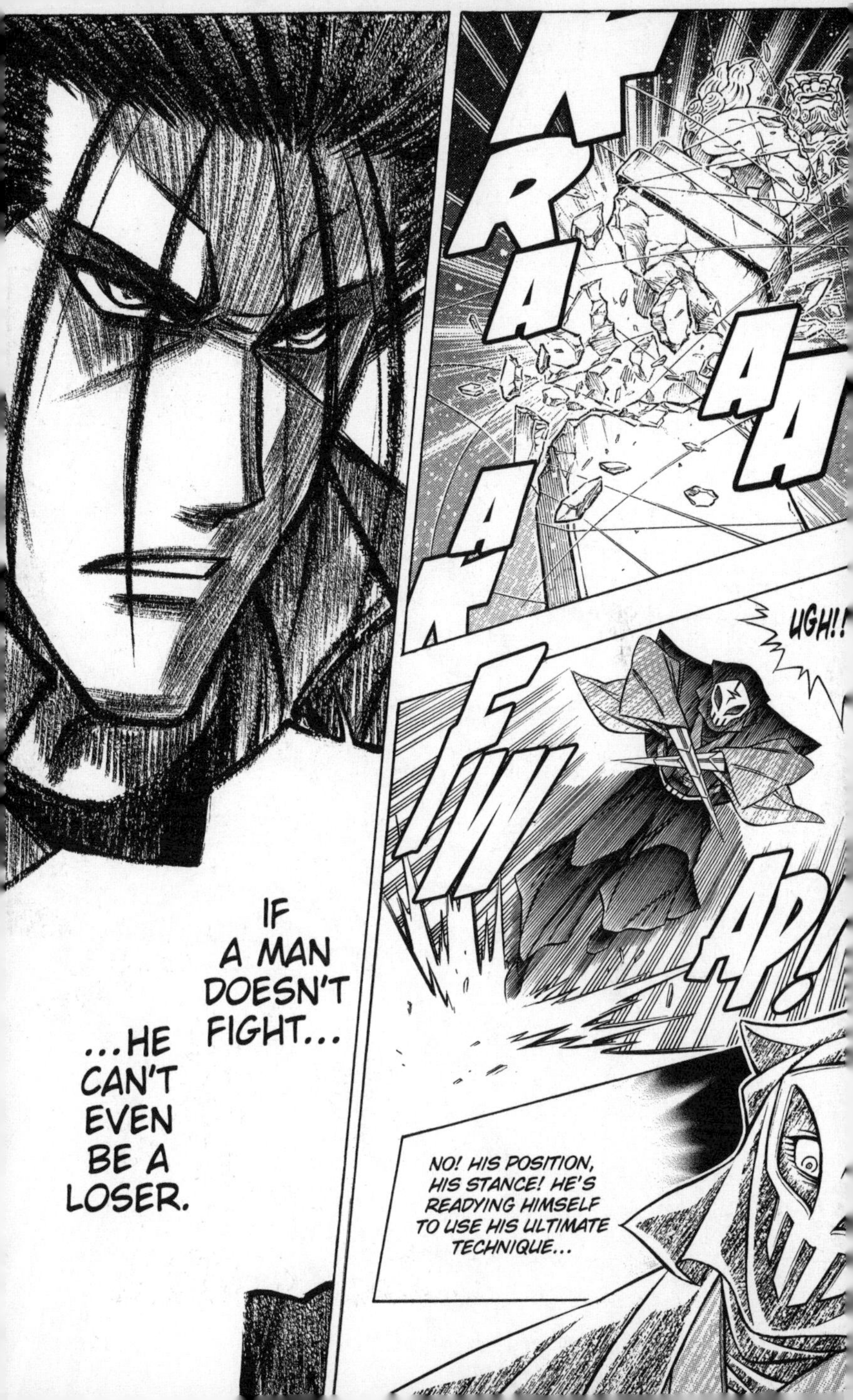
UGH!!
FWAP!
NO! HIS POSITION, HIS STANCE! HE'S READYING HIMSELF TO USE HIS ULTIMATE TECHNIQUE...
IF A MAN DOESN'T FIGHT...
...HE CAN'T EVEN BE A LOSER.

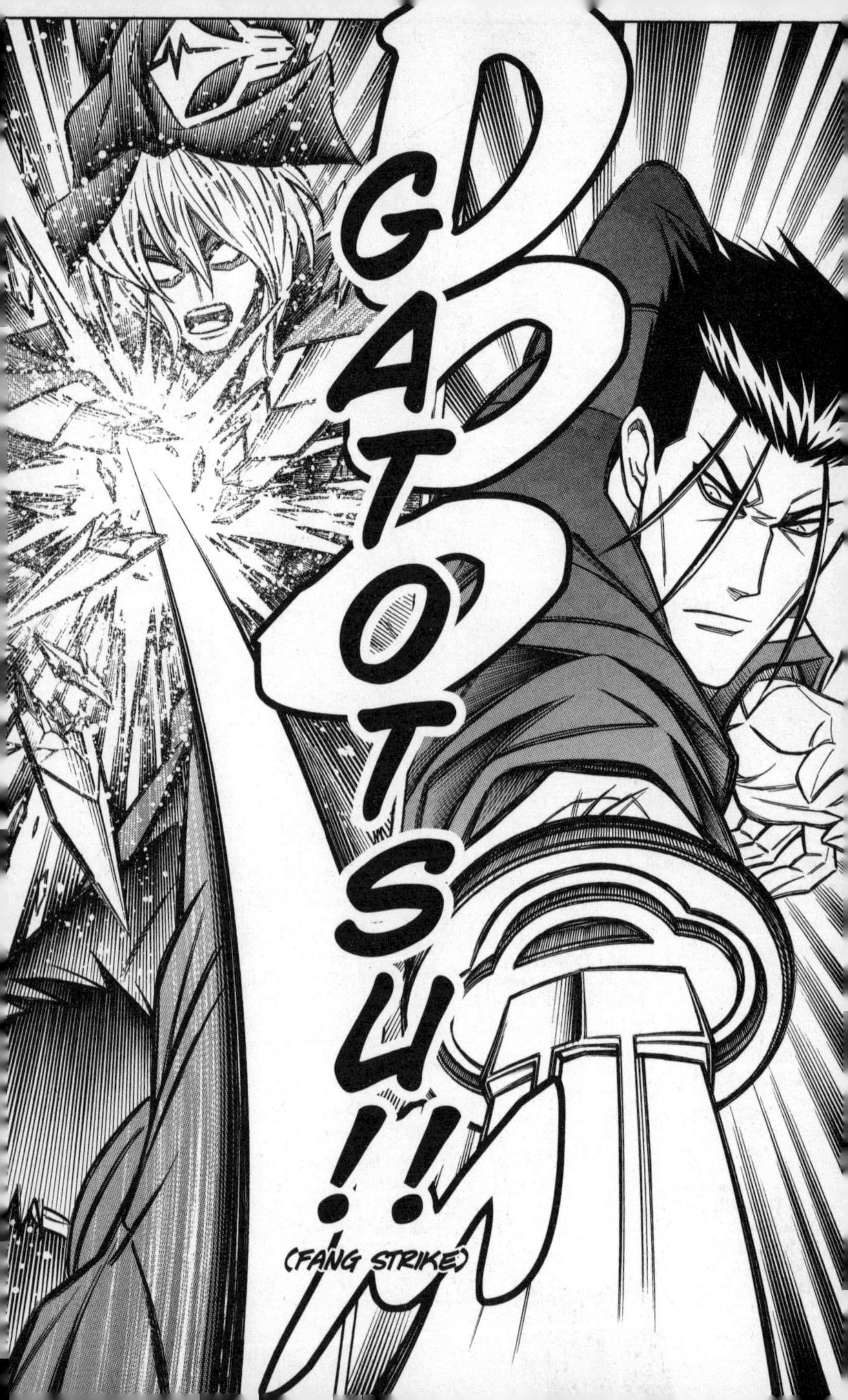
GATOTSU!!
(FANG STRIKE)

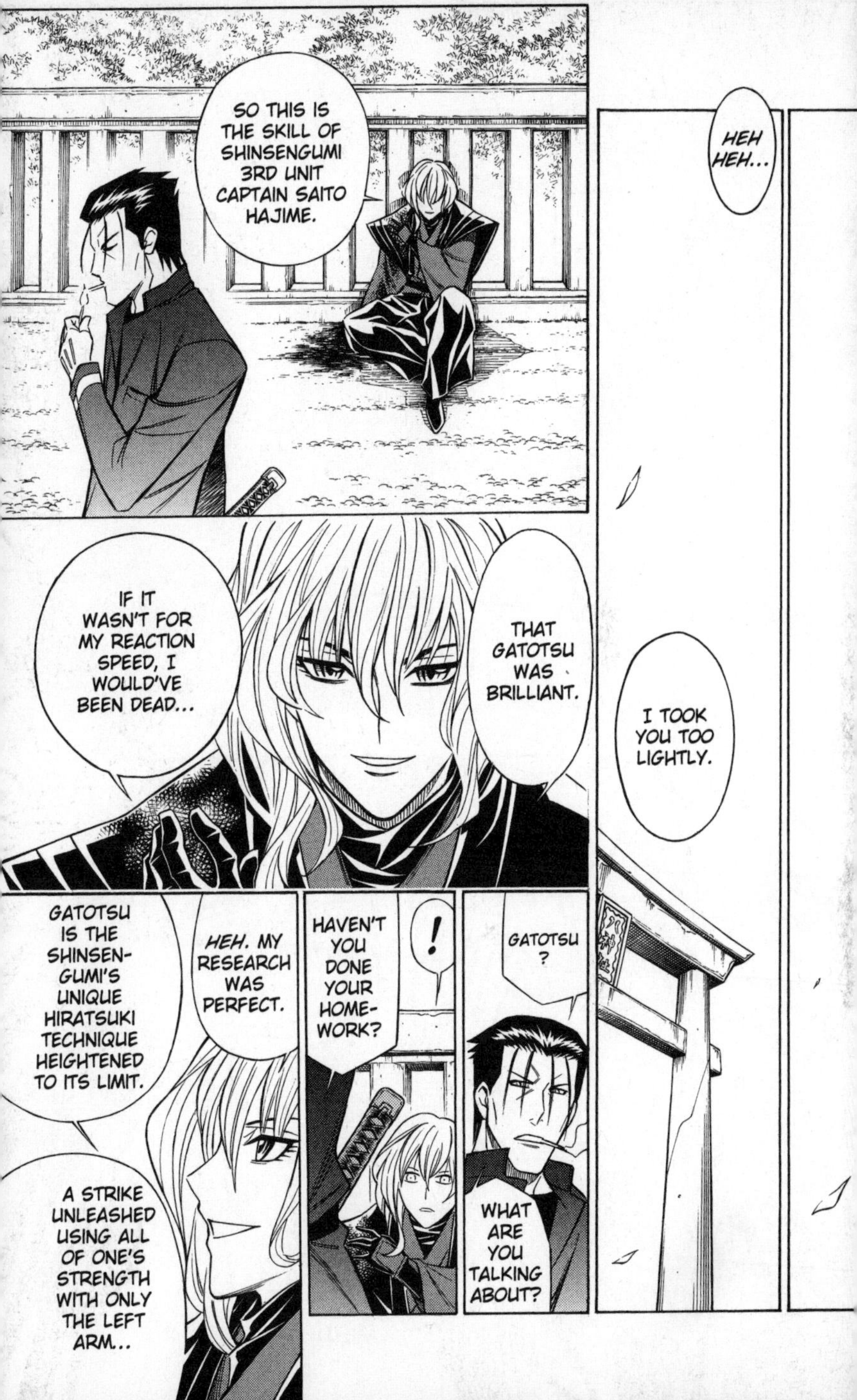
HEH HEH...
I TOOK YOU TOO LIGHTLY.
SO THIS IS THE SKILL OF SHINSENGUMI 3RD UNIT CAPTAIN SAITO HAJIME.
THAT GATOTSU WAS BRILLIANT.
IF IT WASN'T FOR MY REACTION SPEED, I WOULD'VE BEEN DEAD...
GATOTSU?
WHAT ARE YOU TALKING ABOUT?
!
HAVEN'T YOU DONE YOUR HOME-WORK?
HEH. MY RESEARCH WAS PERFECT.
GATOTSU IS THE SHINSEN-GUMI'S UNIQUE HIRATSUKI TECHNIQUE HEIGHTENED TO ITS LIMIT.
A STRIKE UNLEASHED USING ALL OF ONE'S STRENGTH WITH ONLY THE LEFT ARM...

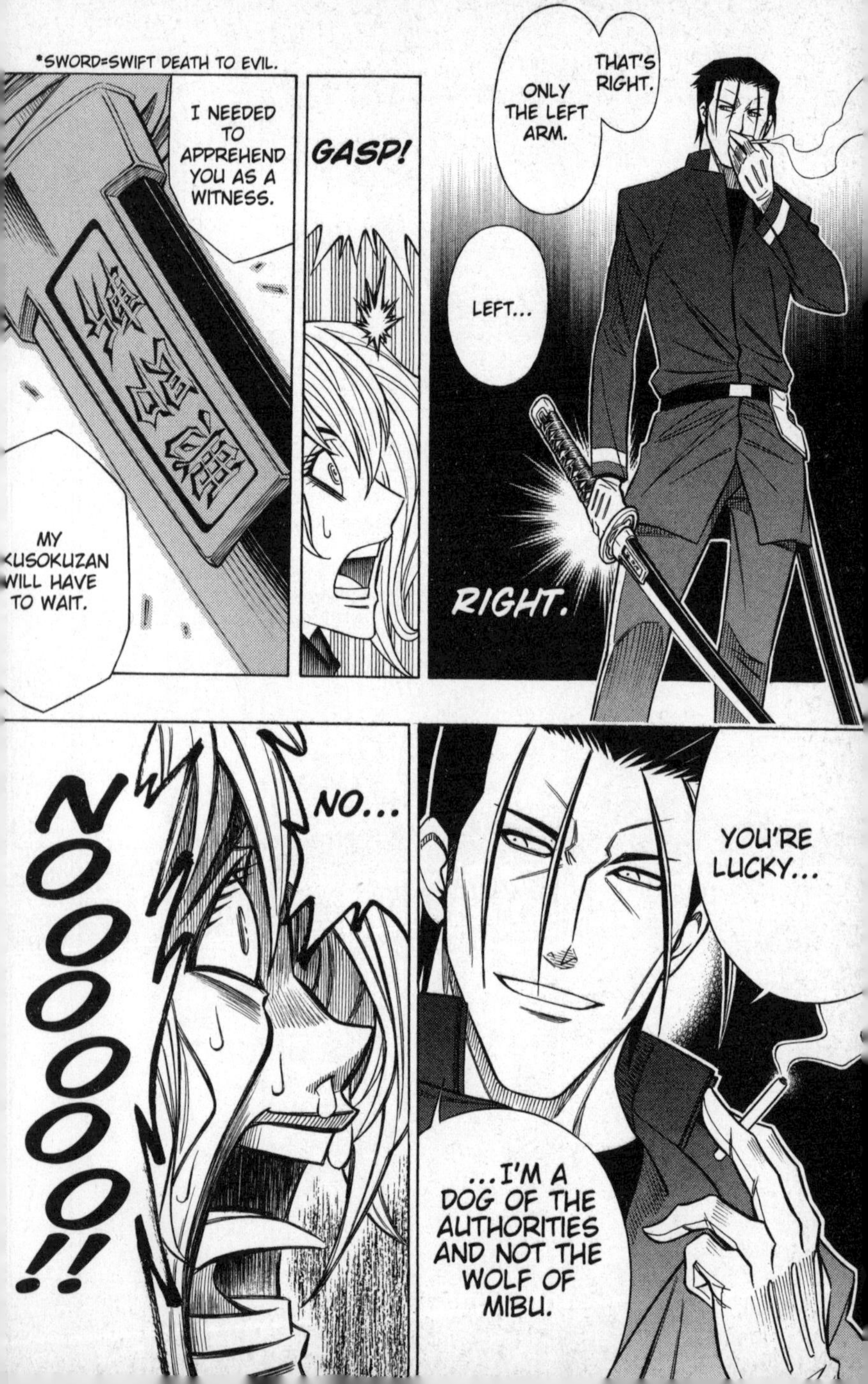
THAT'S RIGHT.
ONLY THE LEFT ARM.
LEFT...
RIGHT.
GASP!
I NEEDED TO APPREHEND YOU AS A WITNESS.
MY KUSOKUZAN WILL HAVE TO WAIT.
YOU'RE LUCKY...
...I'M A DOG OF THE AUTHORITIES AND NOT THE WOLF OF MIBU.
NO...
NOOOOOOO!!

*SWORD=SWIFT DEATH TO EVIL.

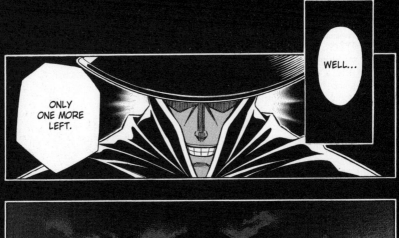

WELL...

ONLY ONE MORE LEFT.

...CAN LIVE.

AND ONLY ONE...

I struggled most with how in depth to write about the Sekiho Army. It was unrelated to the story, but it was an important part of Sanosuke's character. In the end, I only touched on it due to length restrictions. I'm a little disappointed about that.

The most notable change in his appearance was his red knuckle gloves. I wanted to emphasize him as a barehanded fighter, and I thought it would be cooler if he removed them before firing Futae no Kiwami. I also added a touch of *Kamen Rider 2*.

Saito Hajime
He seems like Kenshin's nemesis, but in fact he's his #1 supporter. I kept his role as Kenshin's comrade connected by a strange friendship. I think condensing the story strengthened their bond even more.

I came up with the line "If a man doesn't fight, he can't even be a loser" while I was walking my dog. I figured it was fitting for Saito. I'm really happy I got to include it in this version.

The biggest change in his appearance was his uniform. I had very little reference material while working on the original version. I compared his original uniform to the reference material I had this time around to make it more historically accurate. The internet is really helpful. It's so helpful I can't put out anything that's halfhearted.

Udo Jin-e
He's the biggest enemy early in the original series and the last boss in *Restoration* and the film. I initially depicted him as being crazy and attacking Kenshin out of sheer madness, but then gave him a motive. As a result, his level of madness diminished compared to the original. That was a slight miscalculation on my part. I left out Shin no Ippo because I felt it was too supernatural, but that too diminished some of the excitement unique to a shonen manga. That was also a miscalculation.

The biggest change in his appearance is his skin tone. I changed it hoping to increase his oddity, but that led to difficulties in keeping the tone of the entire script consistent. It's best not to do anything you're not used to. A lot of things didn't work out in *Restoration* for Jin-e. It drove home that the original version of Jin-e is the perfect and the ultimate.

Continued on page 174.

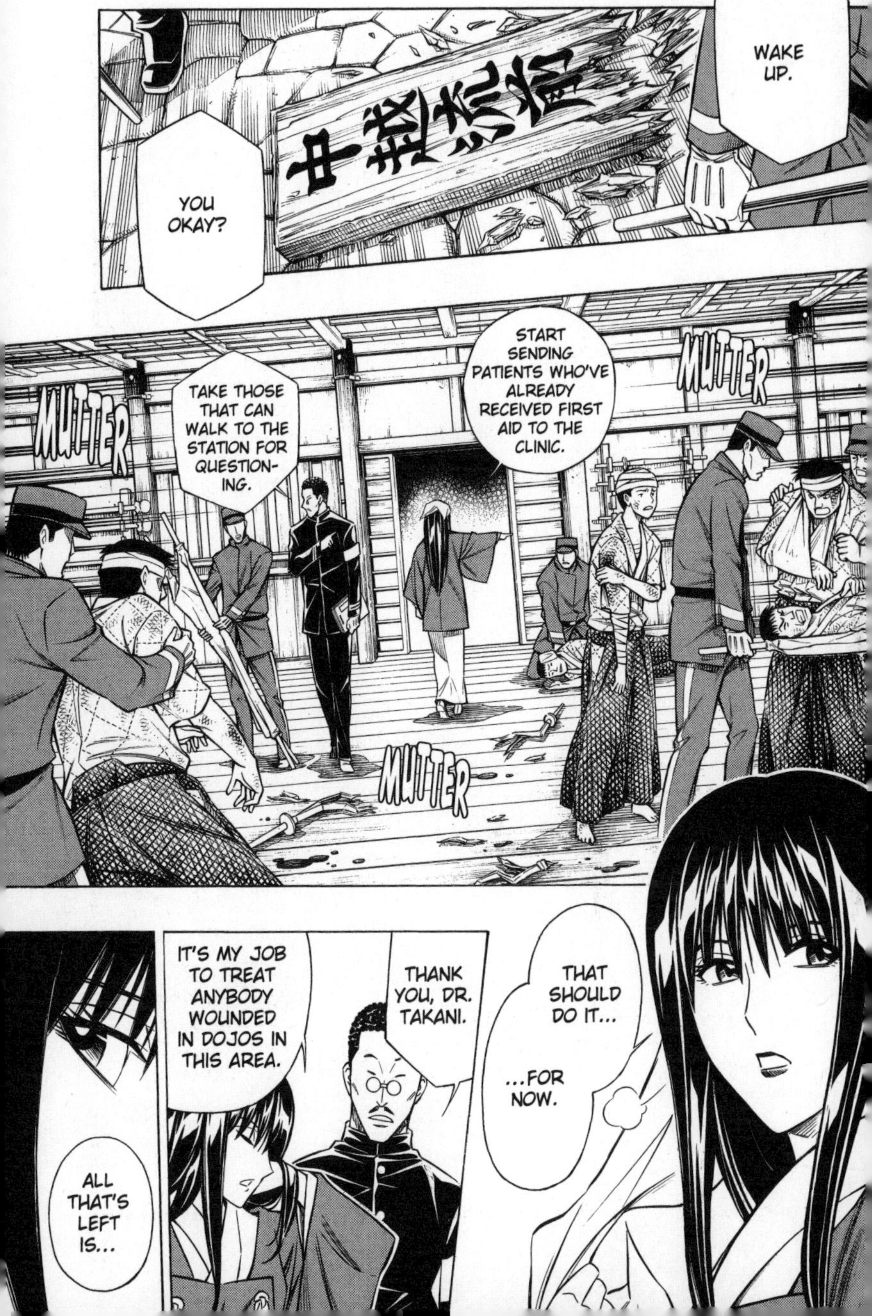
WAKE UP.
YOU OKAY?
MUTTER
START SENDING PATIENTS WHO'VE ALREADY RECEIVED FIRST AID TO THE CLINIC.
TAKE THOSE THAT CAN WALK TO THE STATION FOR QUESTION-ING.
MUTTER
MUTTER
THAT SHOULD DO IT...
...FOR NOW.
THANK YOU, DR. TAKANI.
IT'S MY JOB TO TREAT ANYBODY WOUNDED IN DOJOS IN THIS AREA.
ALL THAT'S LEFT IS...

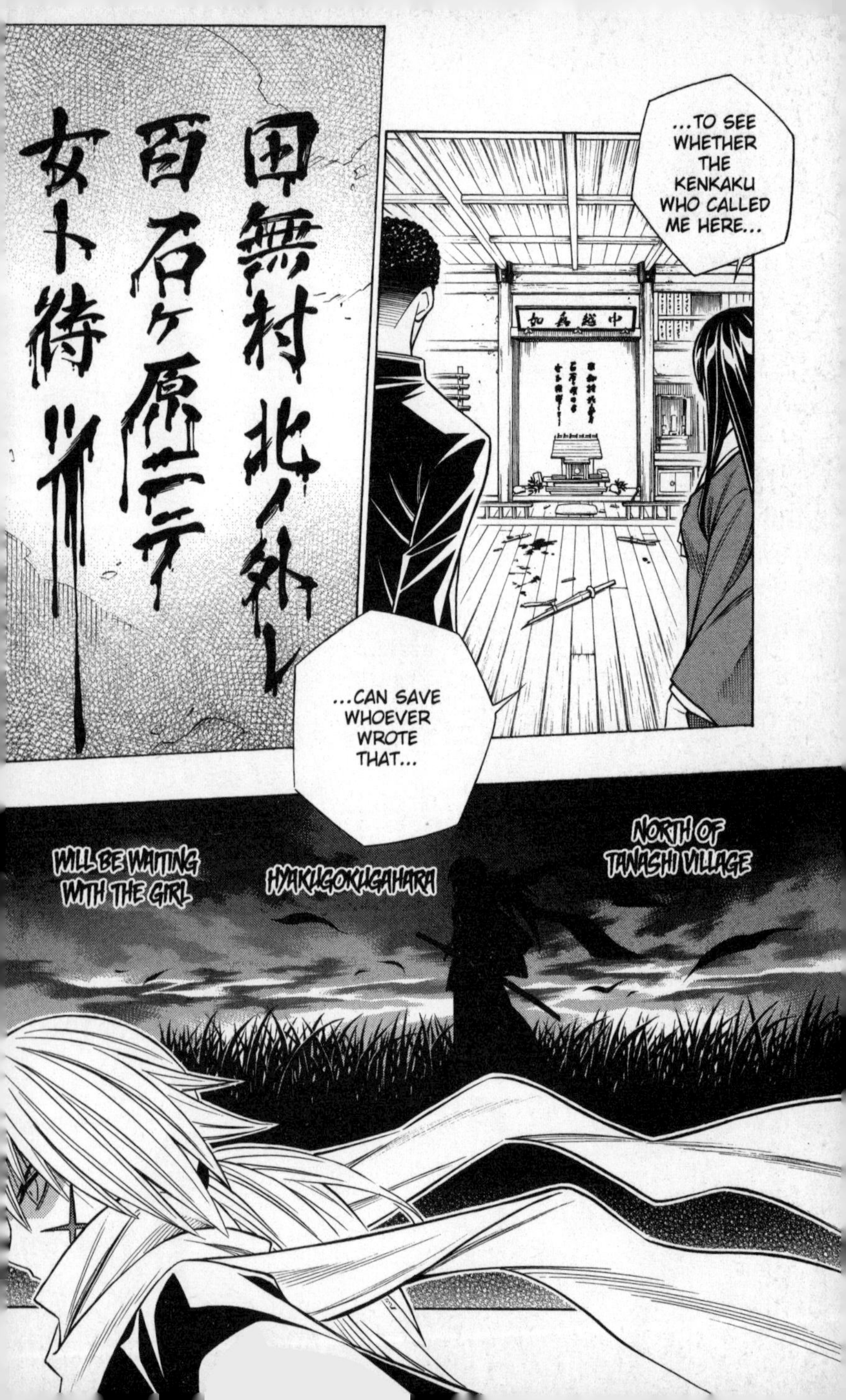
...TO SEE WHETHER THE KENKAKU WHO CALLED ME HERE...
...CAN SAVE WHOEVER WROTE THAT...
田無村北ノ外レ
百石ヶ原ニテ
女ト待ツ
NORTH OF TANASHI VILLAGE
HYAKUGOKUGAHARA
WILL BE WAITING WITH THE GIRL

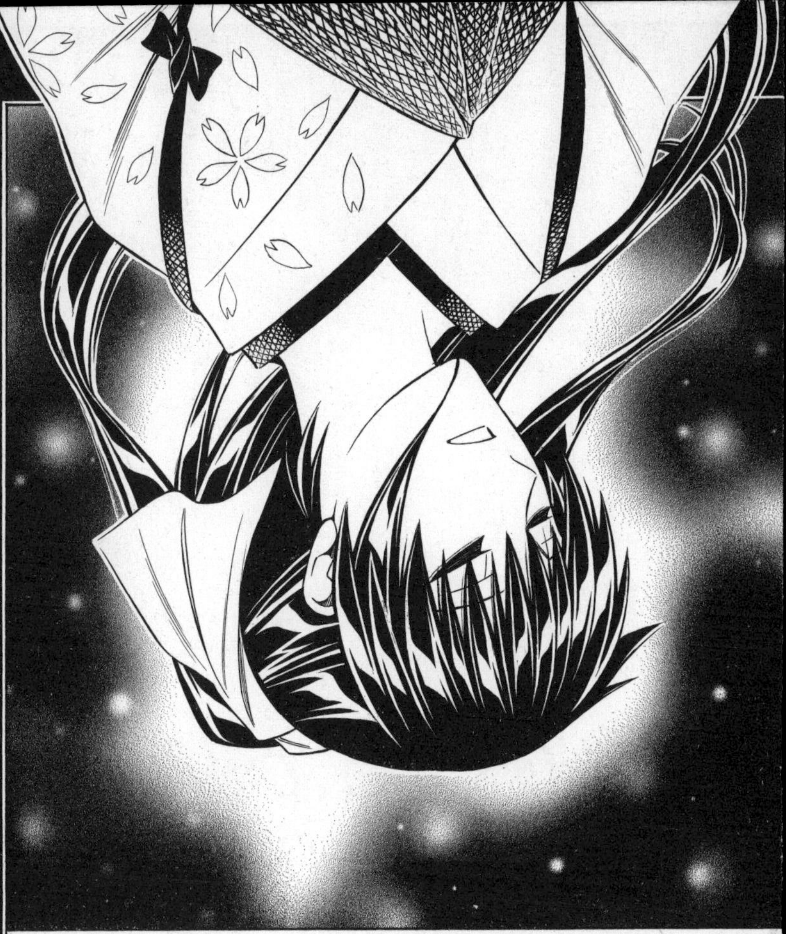

Act 9: Sacrifice

伸宏
和月

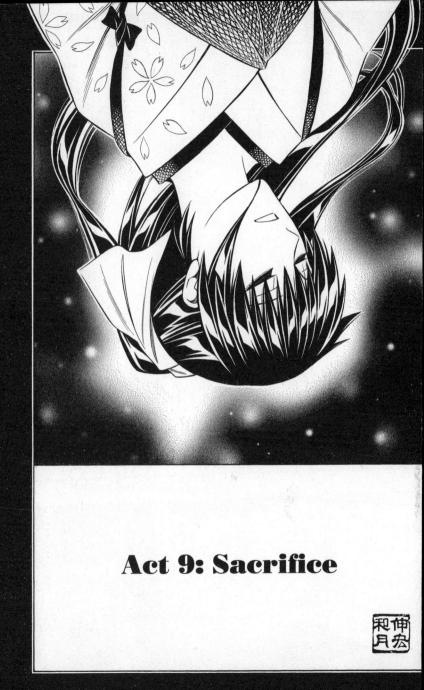

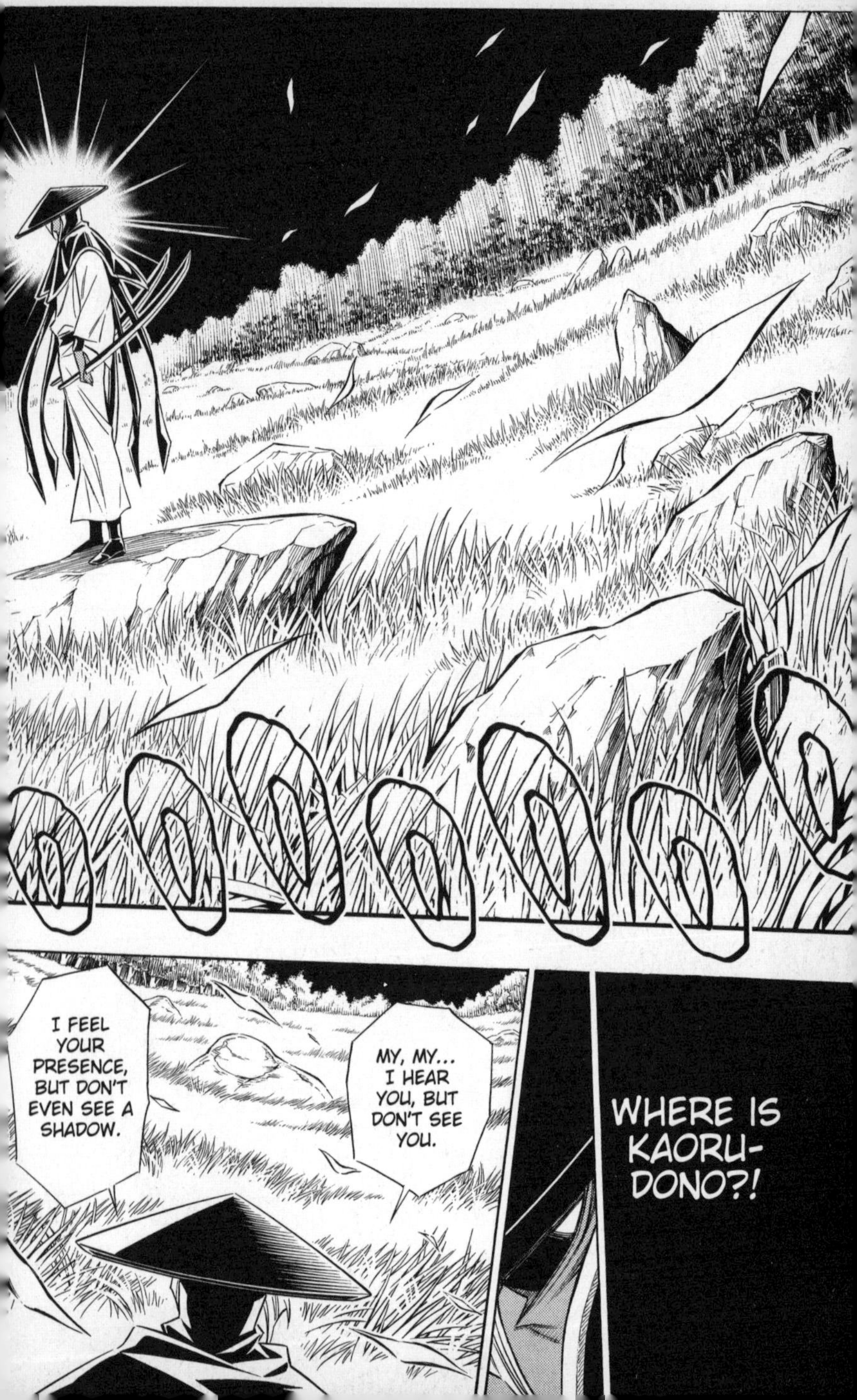
WHERE IS KAORU-DONO?!
MY, MY... I HEAR YOU, BUT DON'T SEE YOU.
I FEEL YOUR PRESENCE, BUT DON'T EVEN SEE A SHADOW.

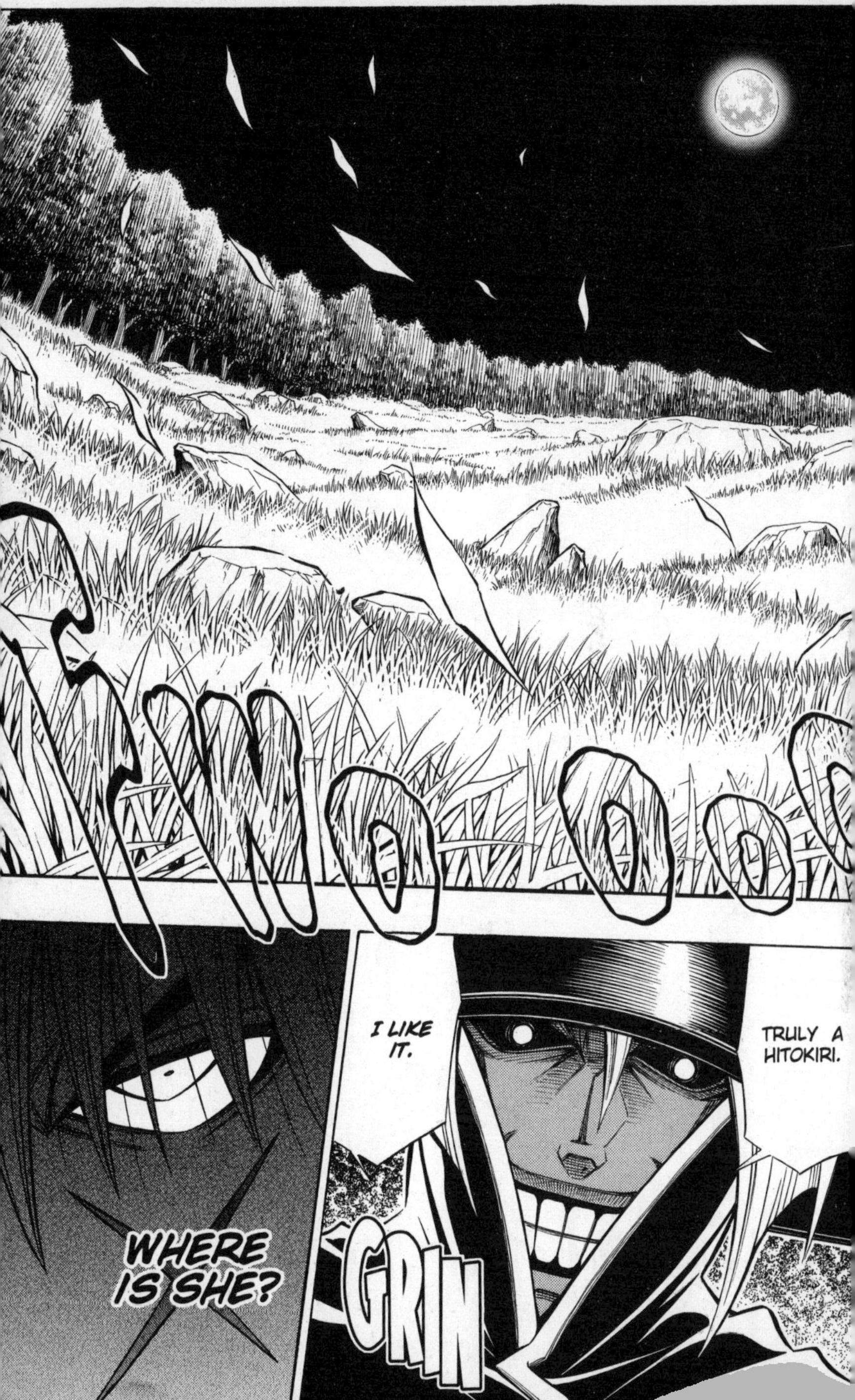
TRULY A HITOKIRI.
I LIKE IT.
GRIN
WHERE IS SHE?

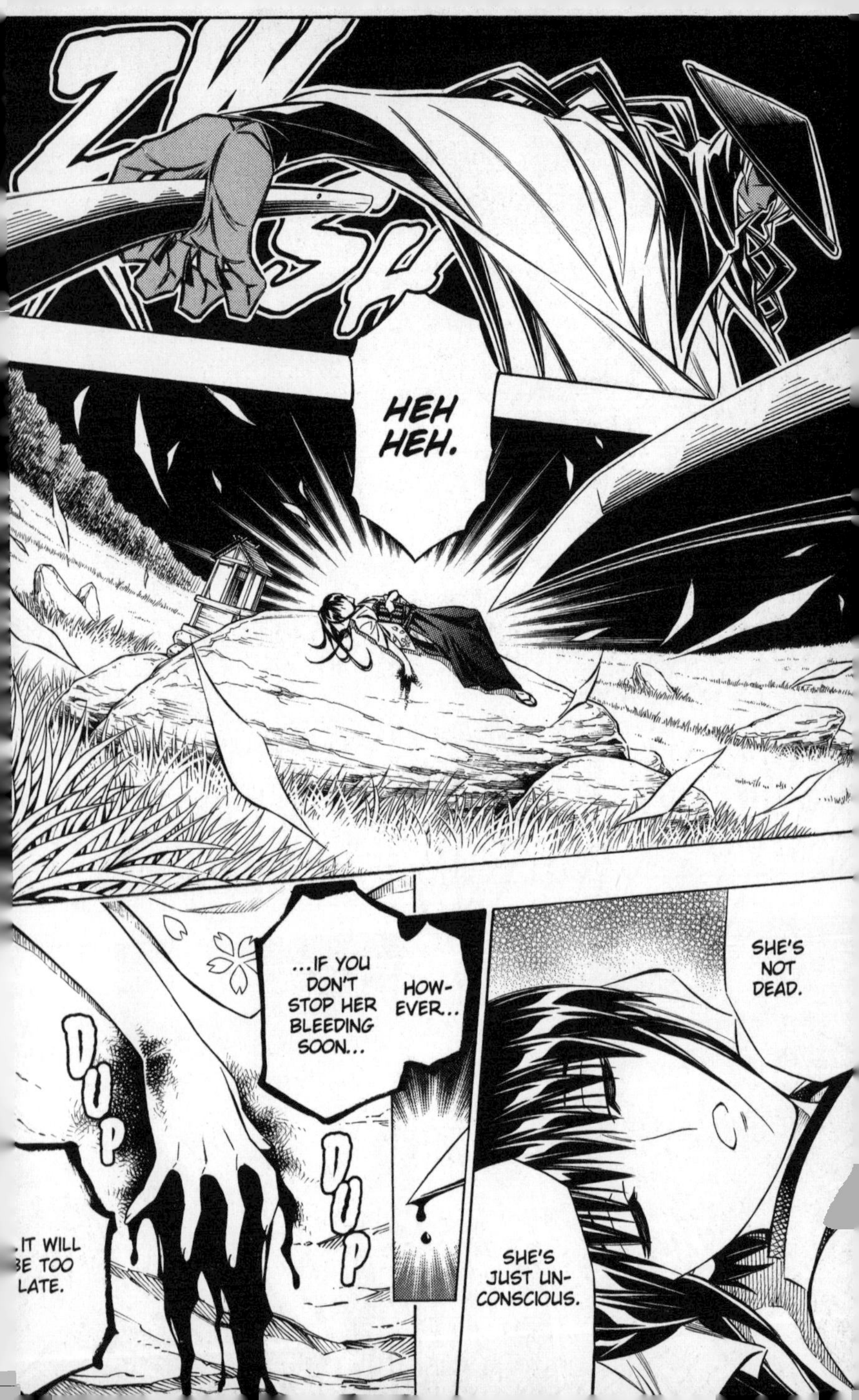
ZW
HEH HEH.
SHE'S NOT DEAD.
SHE'S JUST UN-CONSCIOUS.
HOW-EVER...
...IF YOU DON'T STOP HER BLEEDING SOON...
DUP
DUP
IT WILL BE TOO LATE.

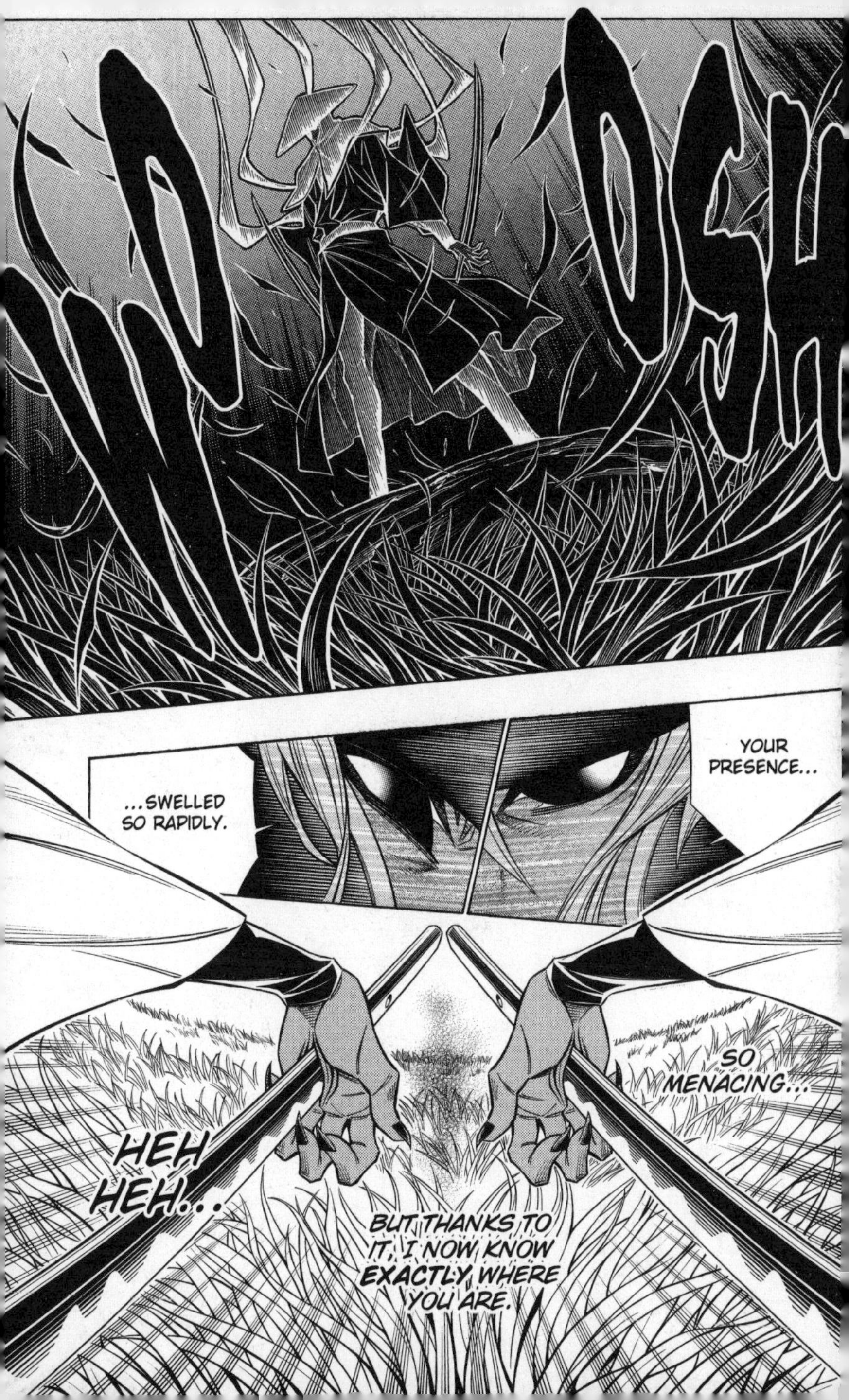
WHOOSH
YOUR PRESENCE...
...SWELLED SO RAPIDLY.
SO MENACING...
HEH HEH...
BUT THANKS TO IT, I NOW KNOW EXACTLY WHERE YOU ARE.

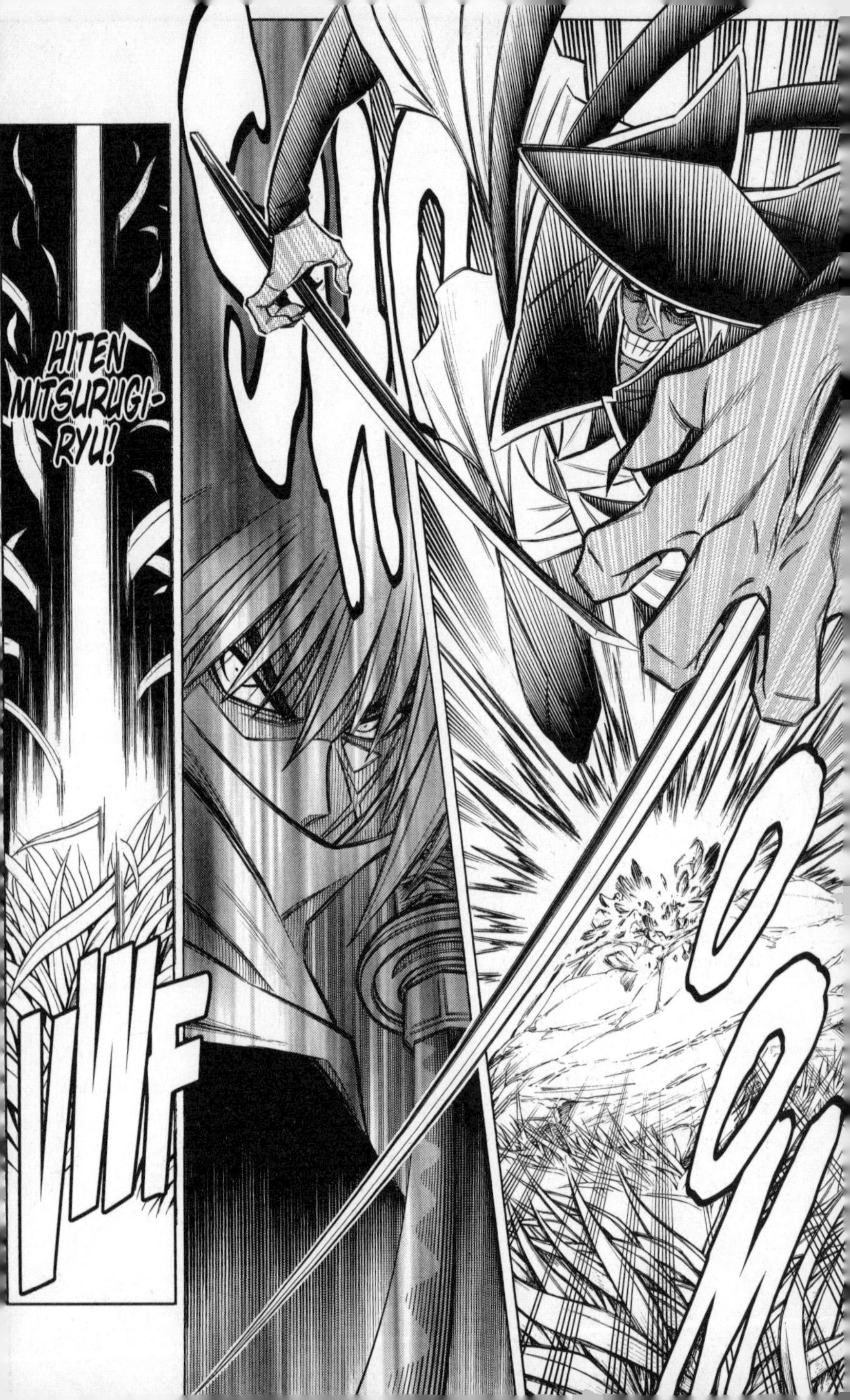
HITEN MITSURUGI-RYU!

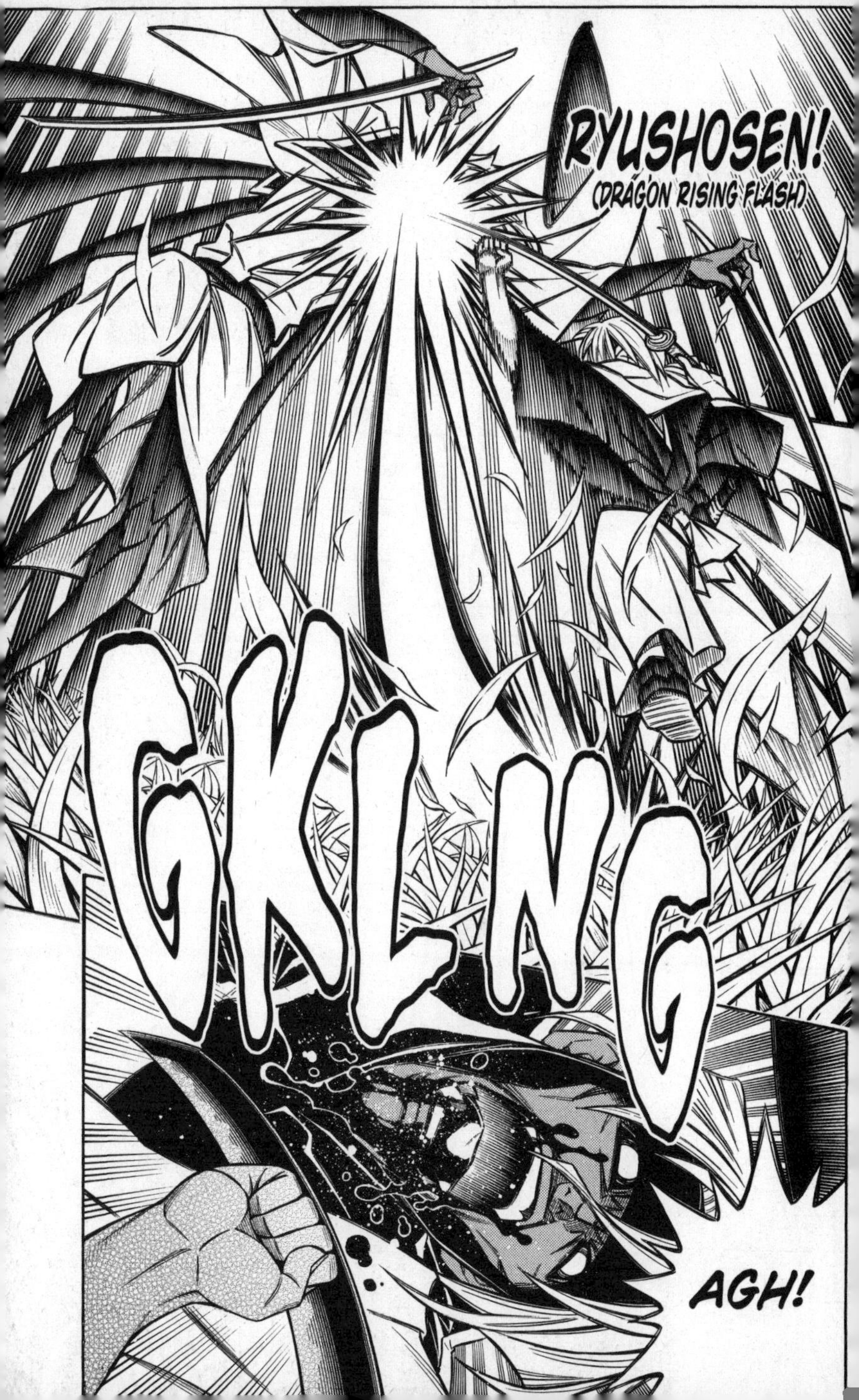
RYUSHOSEN!
(DRAGON RISING FLASH)
GKLNG
AGH!

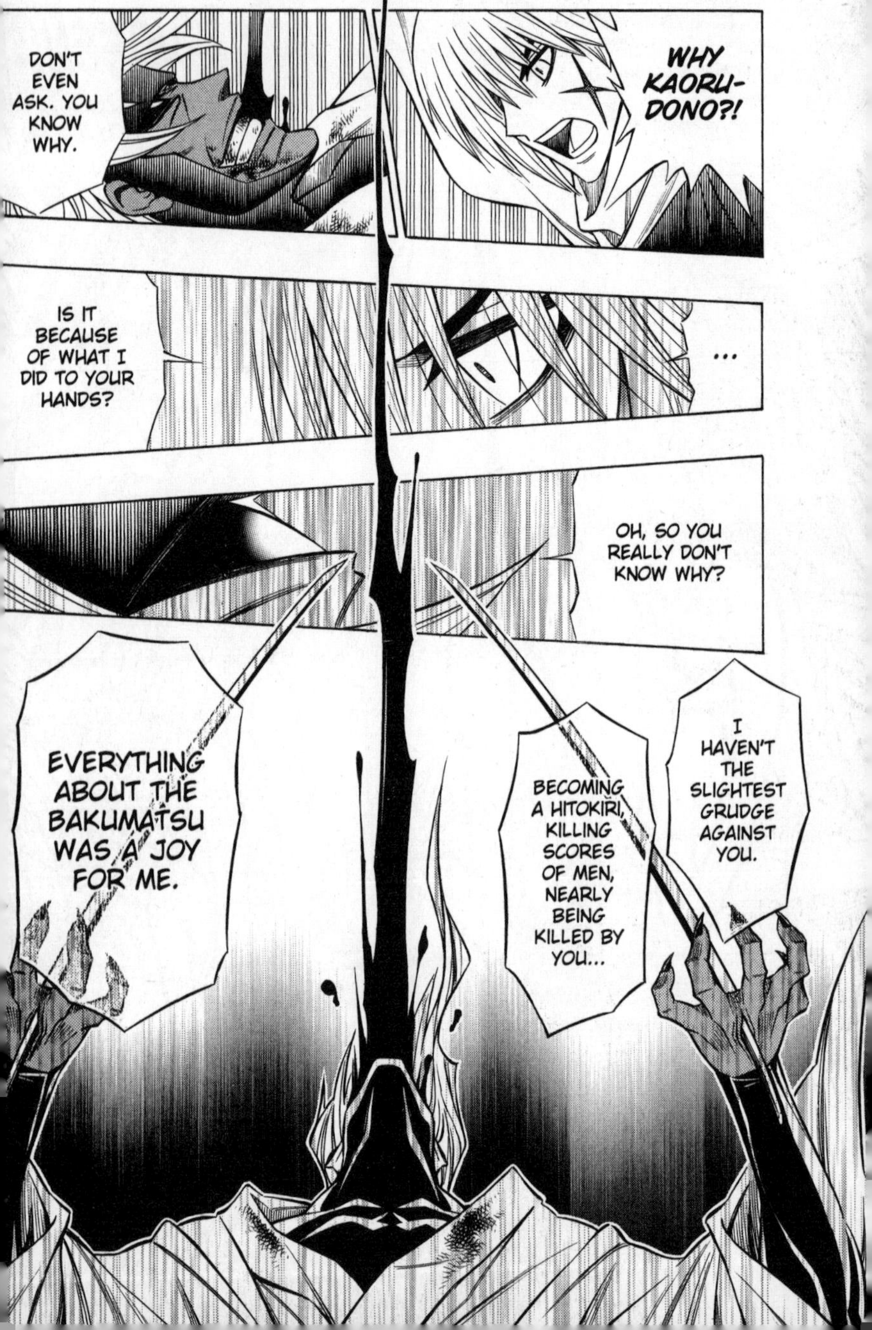
WHY KAORU-DONO?!
DON'T EVEN ASK. YOU KNOW WHY.
...
IS IT BECAUSE OF WHAT I DID TO YOUR HANDS?
OH, SO YOU REALLY DON'T KNOW WHY?
I HAVEN'T THE SLIGHTEST GRUDGE AGAINST YOU.
BECOMING A HITOKIRI, KILLING SCORES OF MEN, NEARLY BEING KILLED BY YOU...
EVERYTHING ABOUT THE BAKUMATSU WAS A JOY FOR ME.

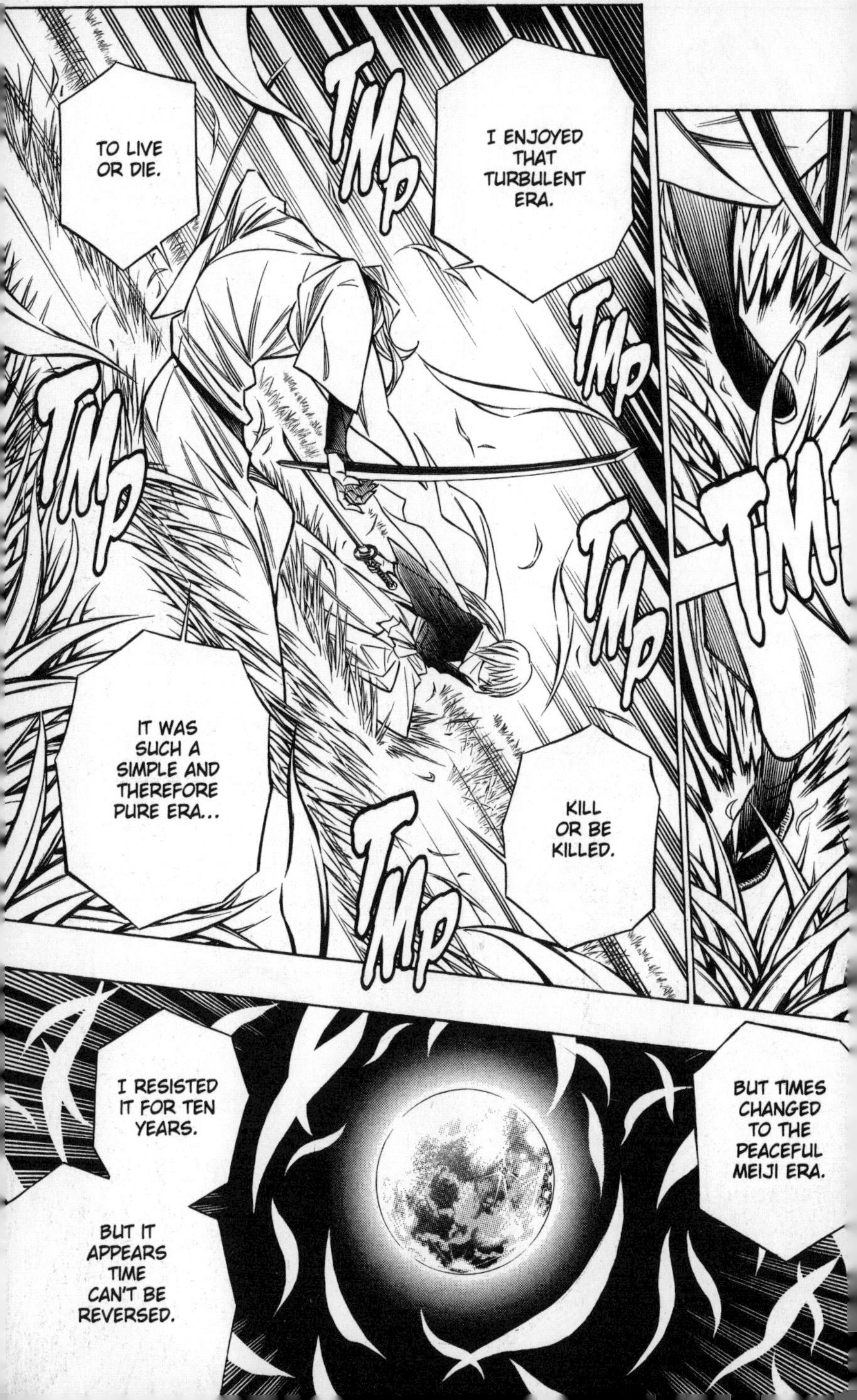
TIM
I ENJOYED THAT TURBULENT ERA.
TIMP
TO LIVE OR DIE.
TIMP
TIMP
TIMP
KILL OR BE KILLED.
IT WAS SUCH A SIMPLE AND THEREFORE PURE ERA...
TIMP
BUT TIMES CHANGED TO THE PEACEFUL MEIJI ERA.
I RESISTED IT FOR TEN YEARS.
BUT IT APPEARS TIME CAN'T BE REVERSED.

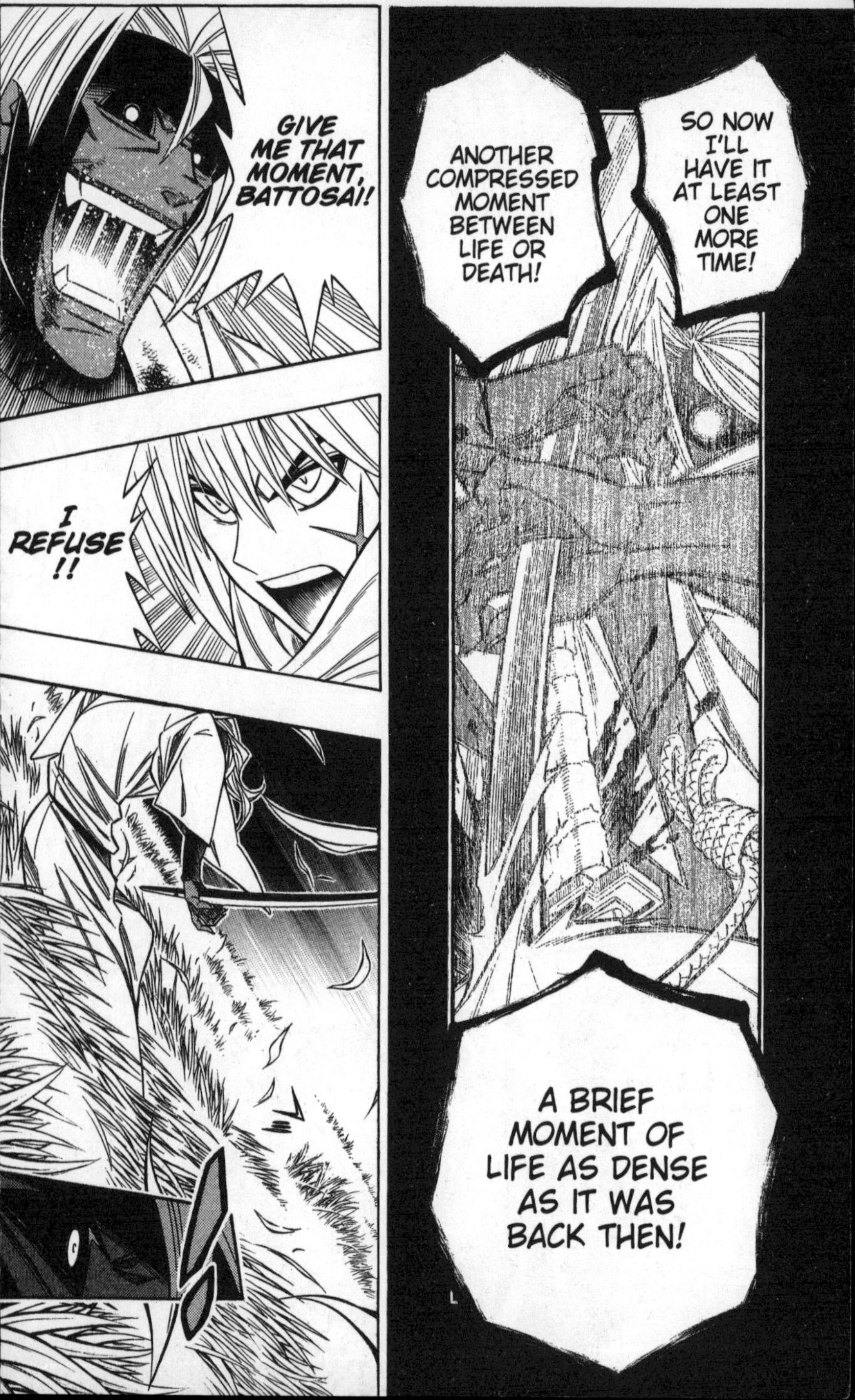
SO NOW I'LL HAVE IT AT LEAST ONE MORE TIME!
ANOTHER COMPRESSED MOMENT BETWEEN LIFE OR DEATH!
A BRIEF MOMENT OF LIFE AS DENSE AS IT WAS BACK THEN!
GIVE ME THAT MOMENT, BATTOSAI!
I REFUSE !!

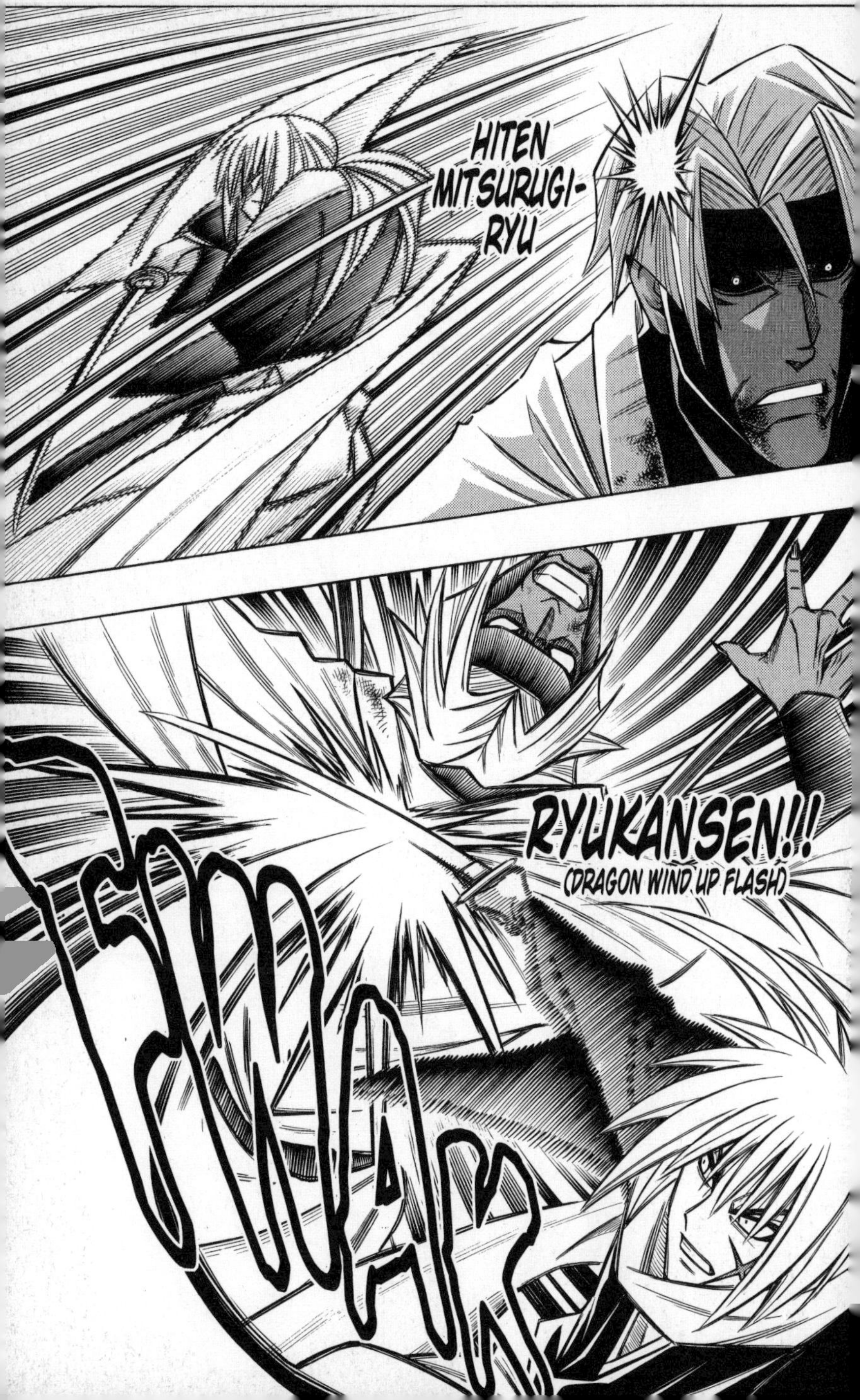
HITEN MITSURUGI-RYU
RYUKANSEN!!
(DRAGON WIND UP FLASH)

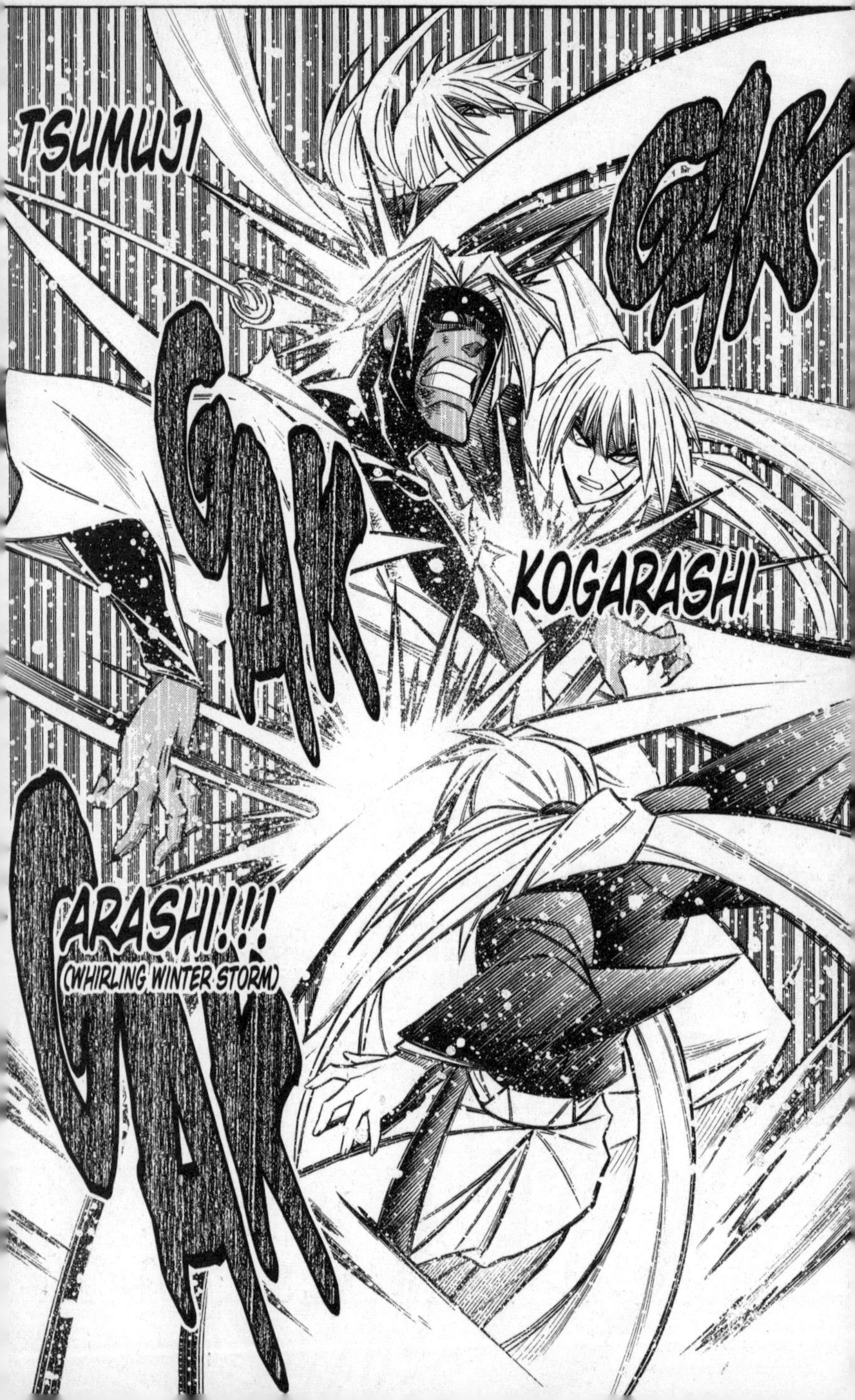
TSUMUJI
KOGARASHI
ARASHI!!!!
(WHIRLING WINTER STORM)

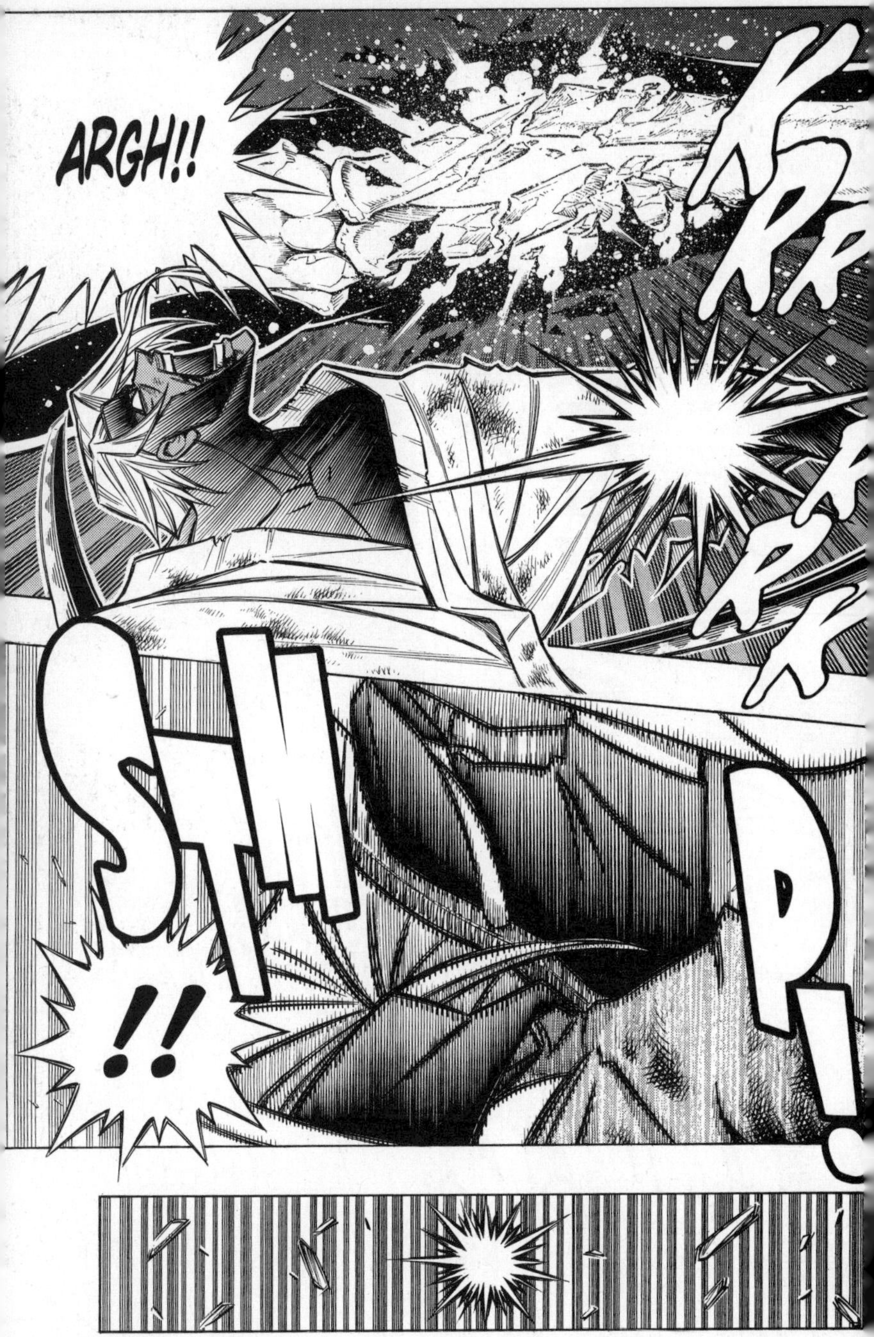
ARGH!!

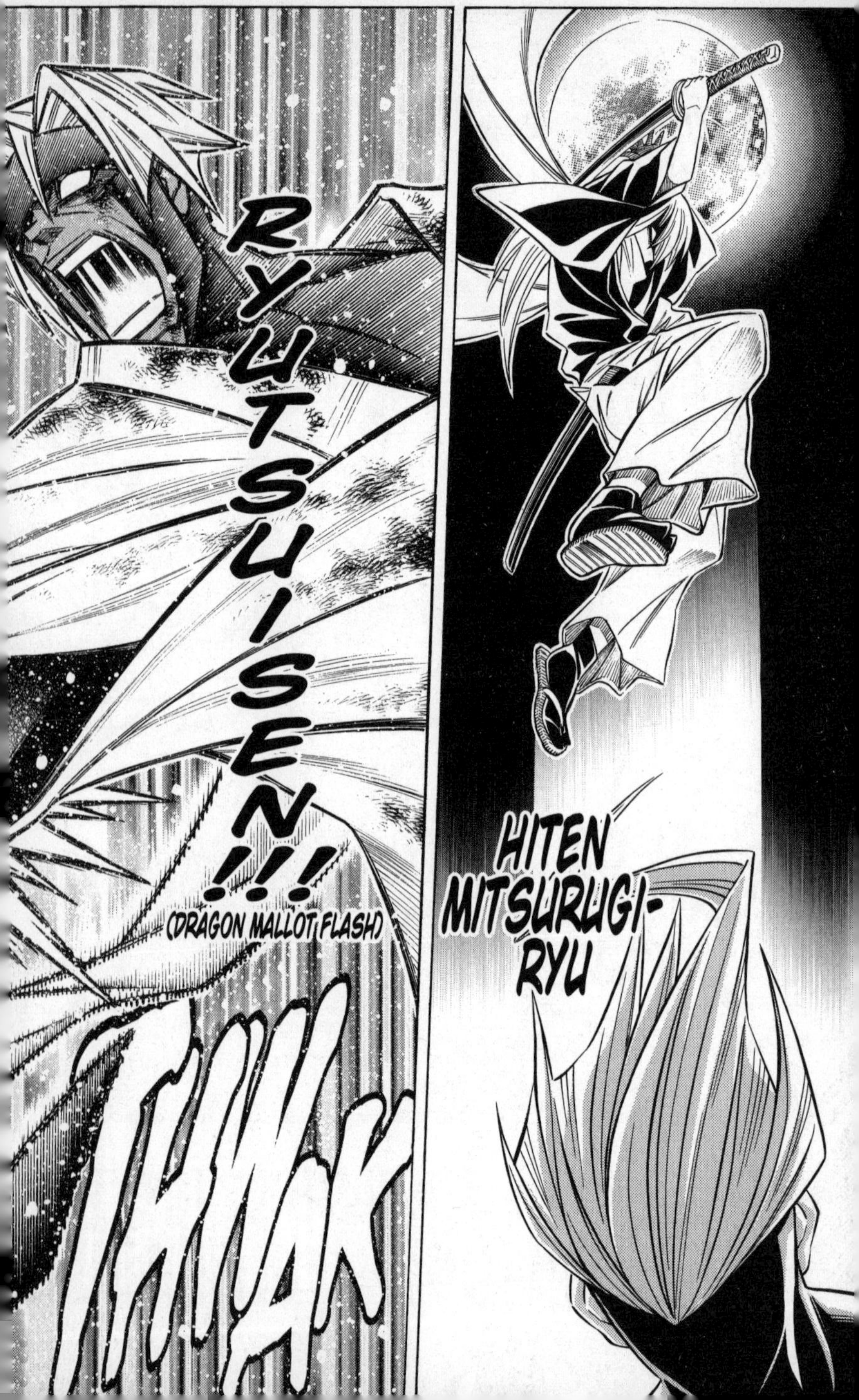
HITEN MITSURUGI-RYU
RYUTSUISEN!!!
(DRAGON MALLOT FLASH)
THWAK

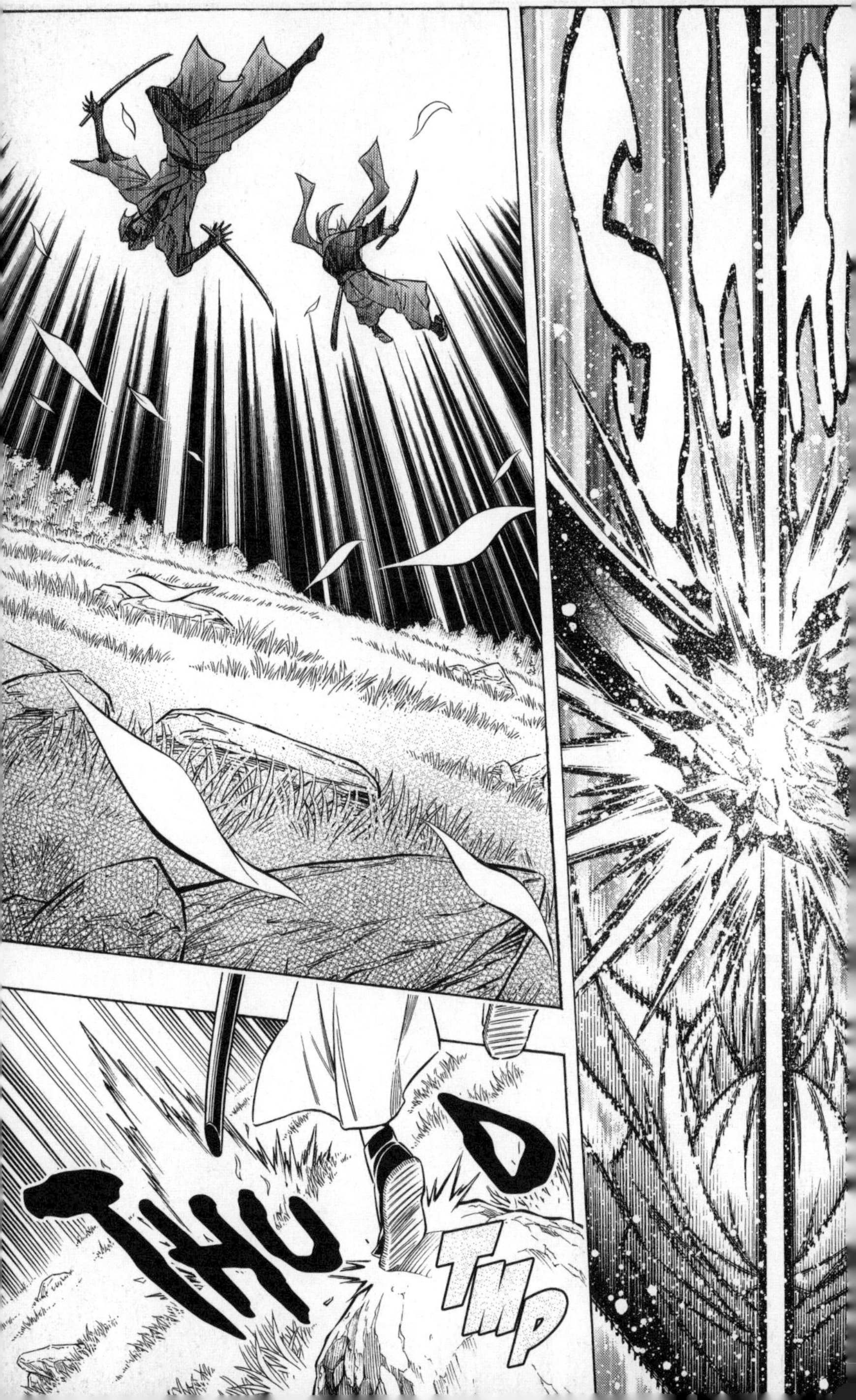
SHA
THUD
TMP

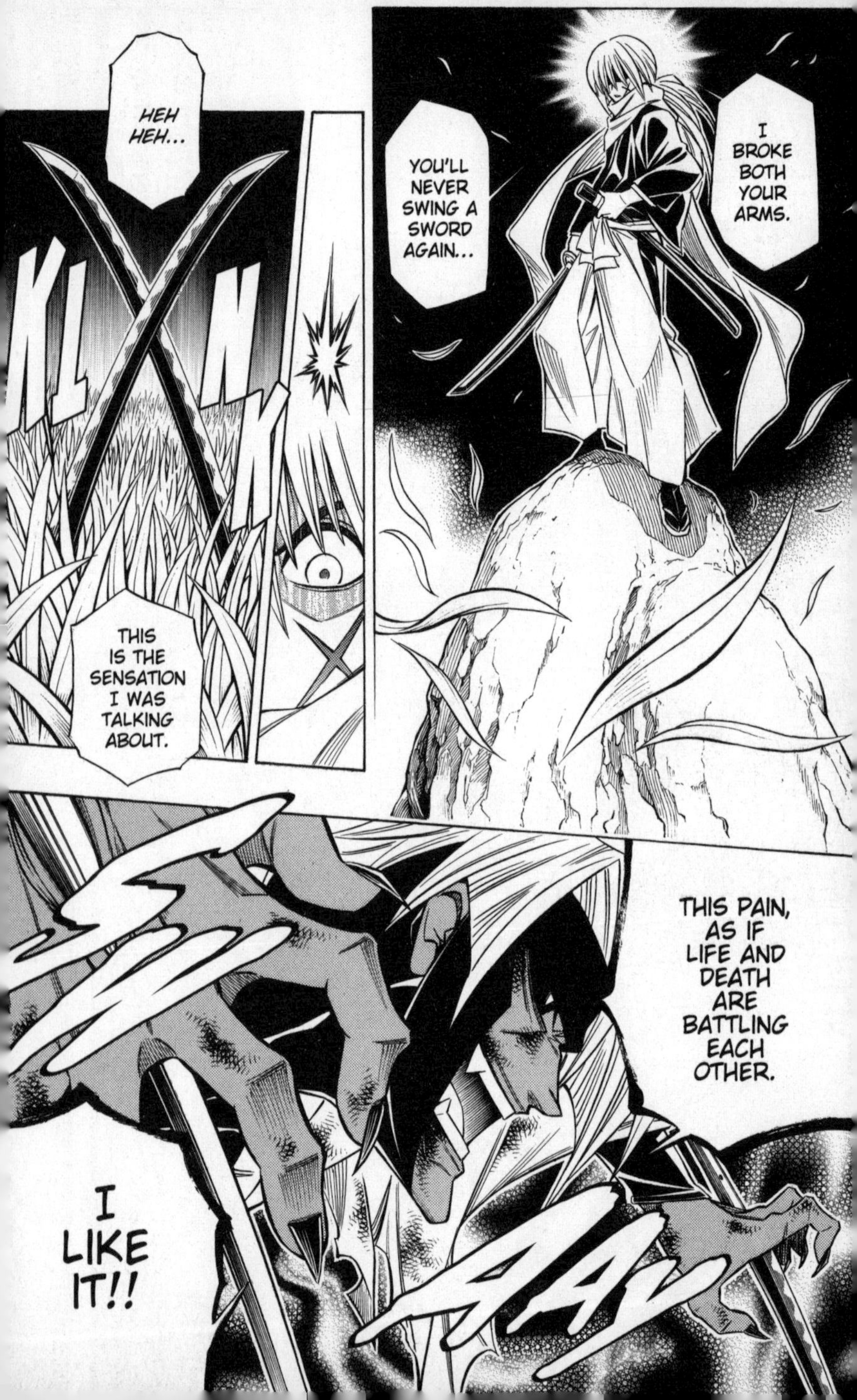
I BROKE BOTH YOUR ARMS.
YOU'LL NEVER SWING A SWORD AGAIN...
HEH HEH...
THIS IS THE SENSATION I WAS TALKING ABOUT.
THIS PAIN, AS IF LIFE AND DEATH ARE BATTLING EACH OTHER.
I LIKE IT!!

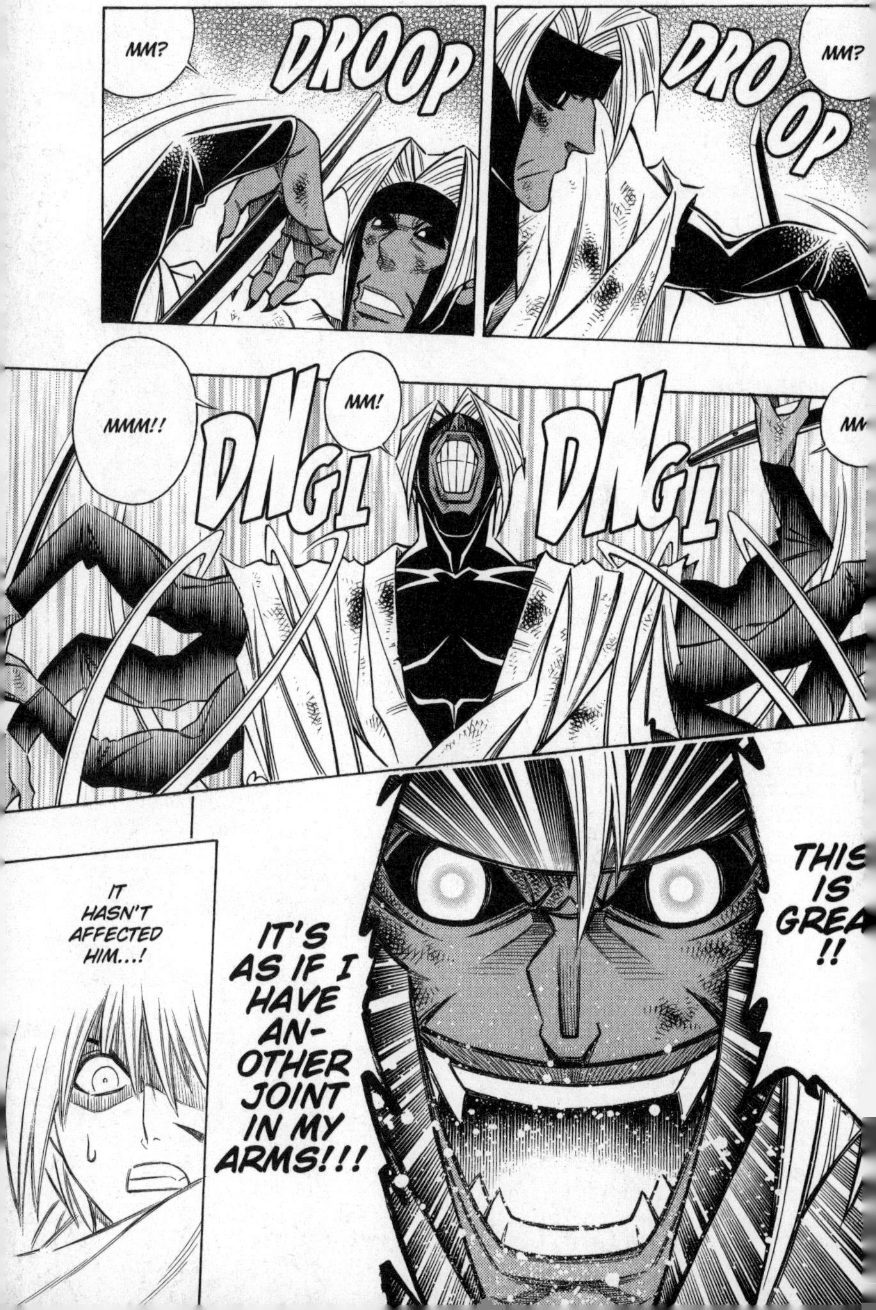

MM?
DRO OP
MM?
DROOP
MM
DNGI
DNGI
MM!
MMM!!
THIS IS GREA !!
IT'S AS IF I HAVE AN-OTHER JOINT IN MY ARMS!!!
IT HASN'T AFFECTED HIM...!

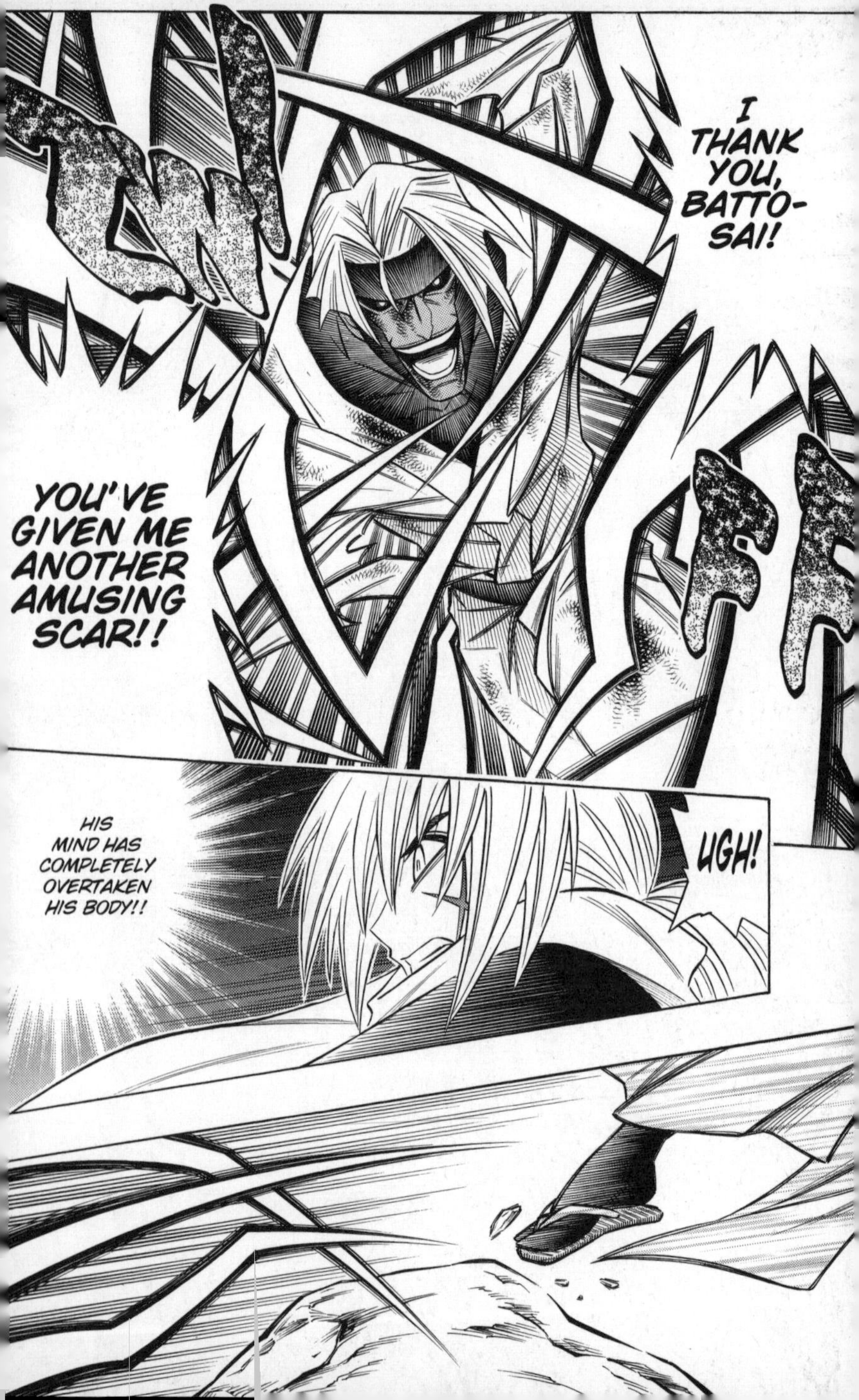
I THANK YOU, BATTO-SAI!
YOU'VE GIVEN ME ANOTHER AMUSING SCAR!!
UGH!
HIS MIND HAS COMPLETELY OVERTAKEN HIS BODY!!

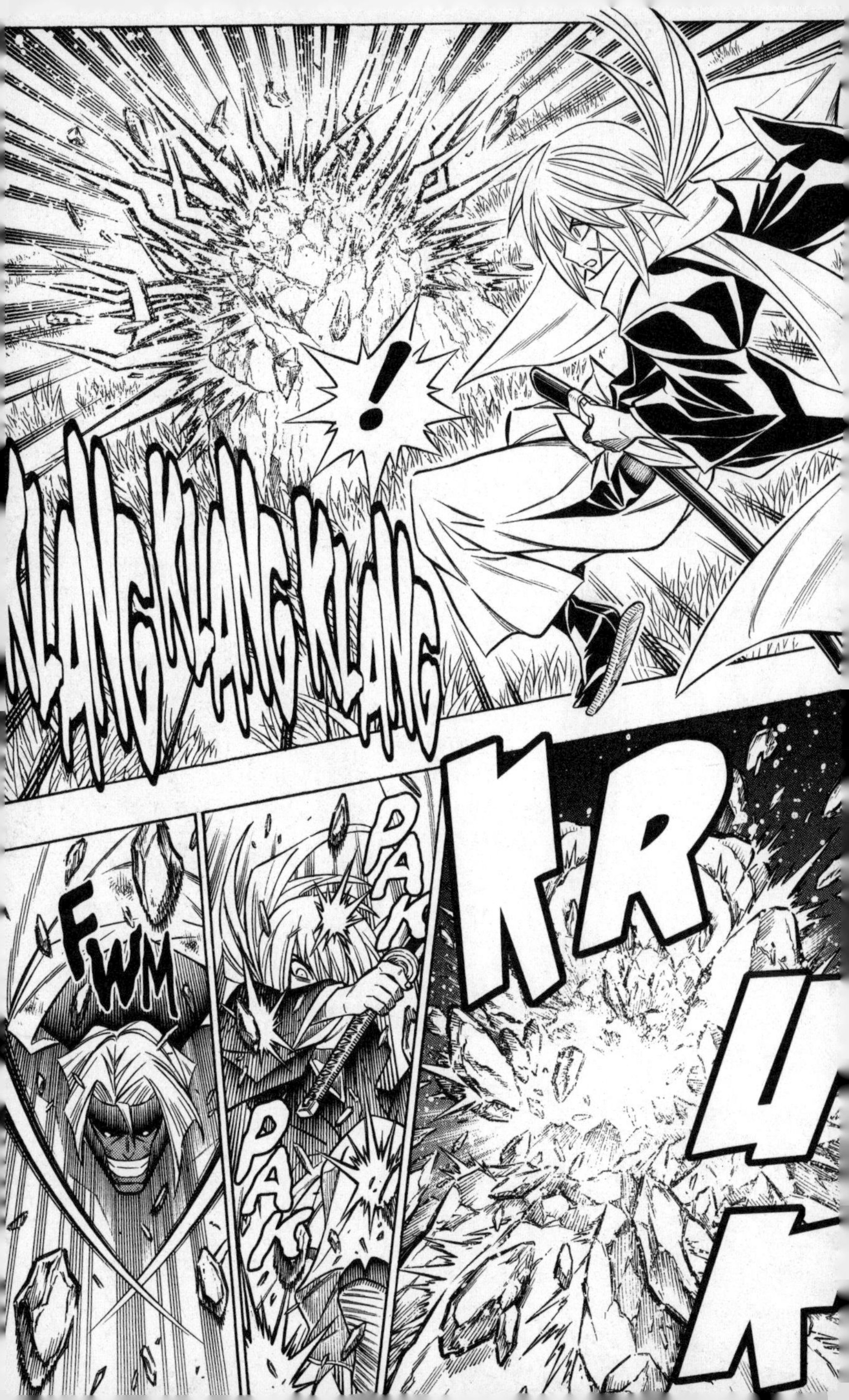
!
KLANG KLANG KLANG
KRUK
PAK
PAK
FWM

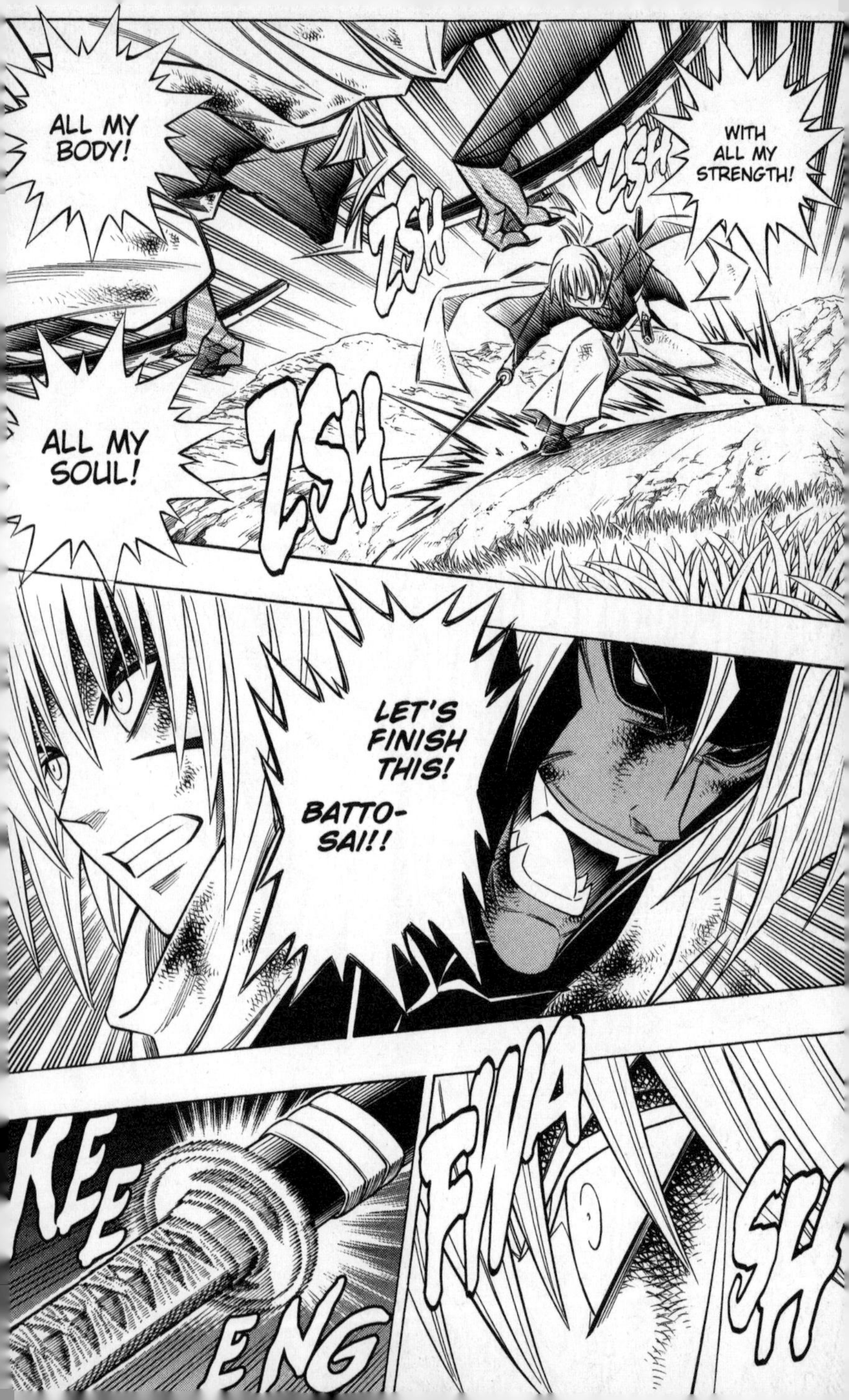
WITH ALL MY STRENGTH!
ZSH
ZSH
ALL MY BODY!
ZSH
ZSH
ALL MY SOUL!
LET'S FINISH THIS!
BATTO-SAI!!
SHA
FWA
KEE
ENG

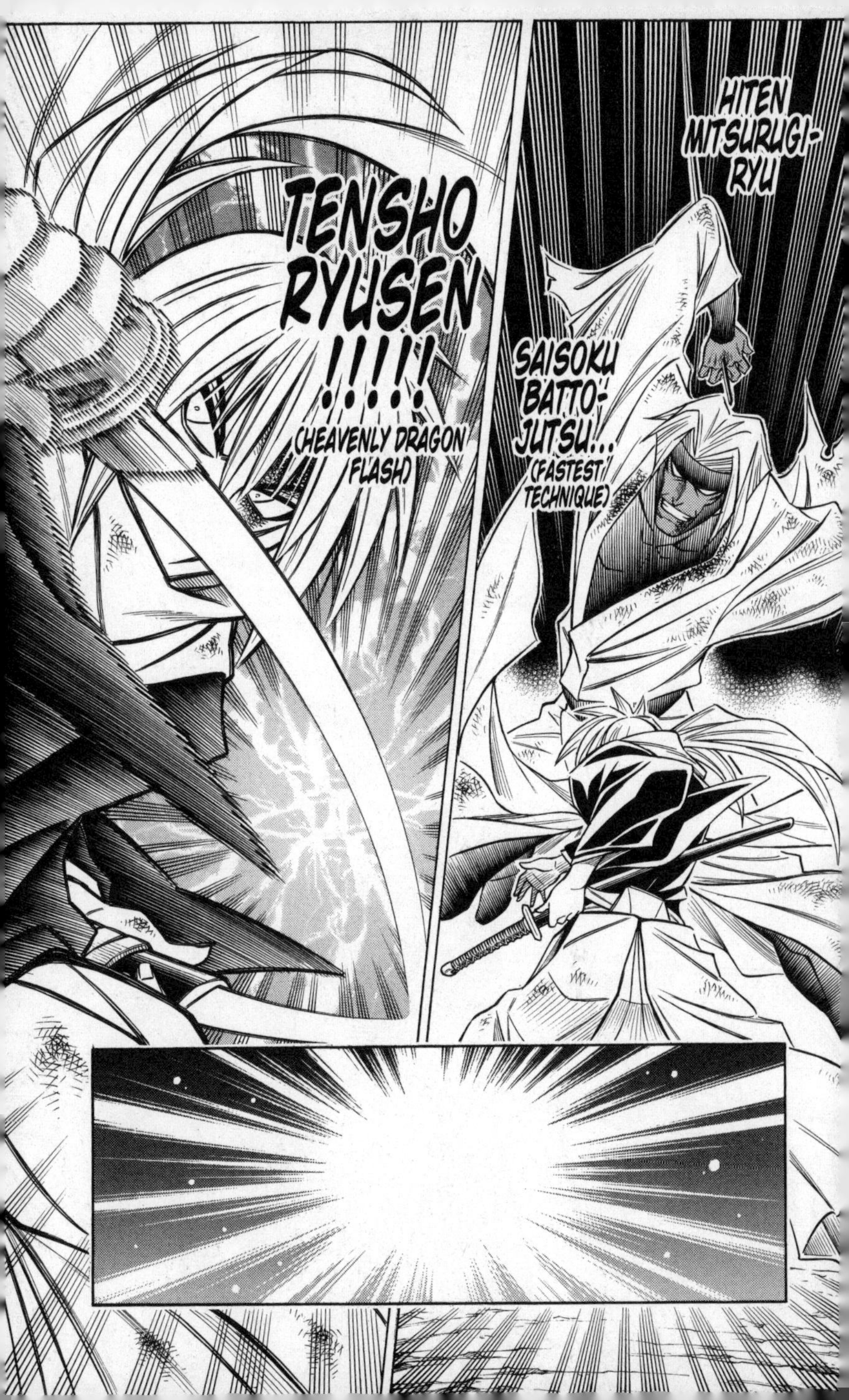
HITEN MITSURUGI-RYU
SAISOKU BATTO-JUTSU...
(FASTEST TECHNIQUE)
TENSHO RYUSEN !!!!!
(HEAVENLY DRAGON FLASH)

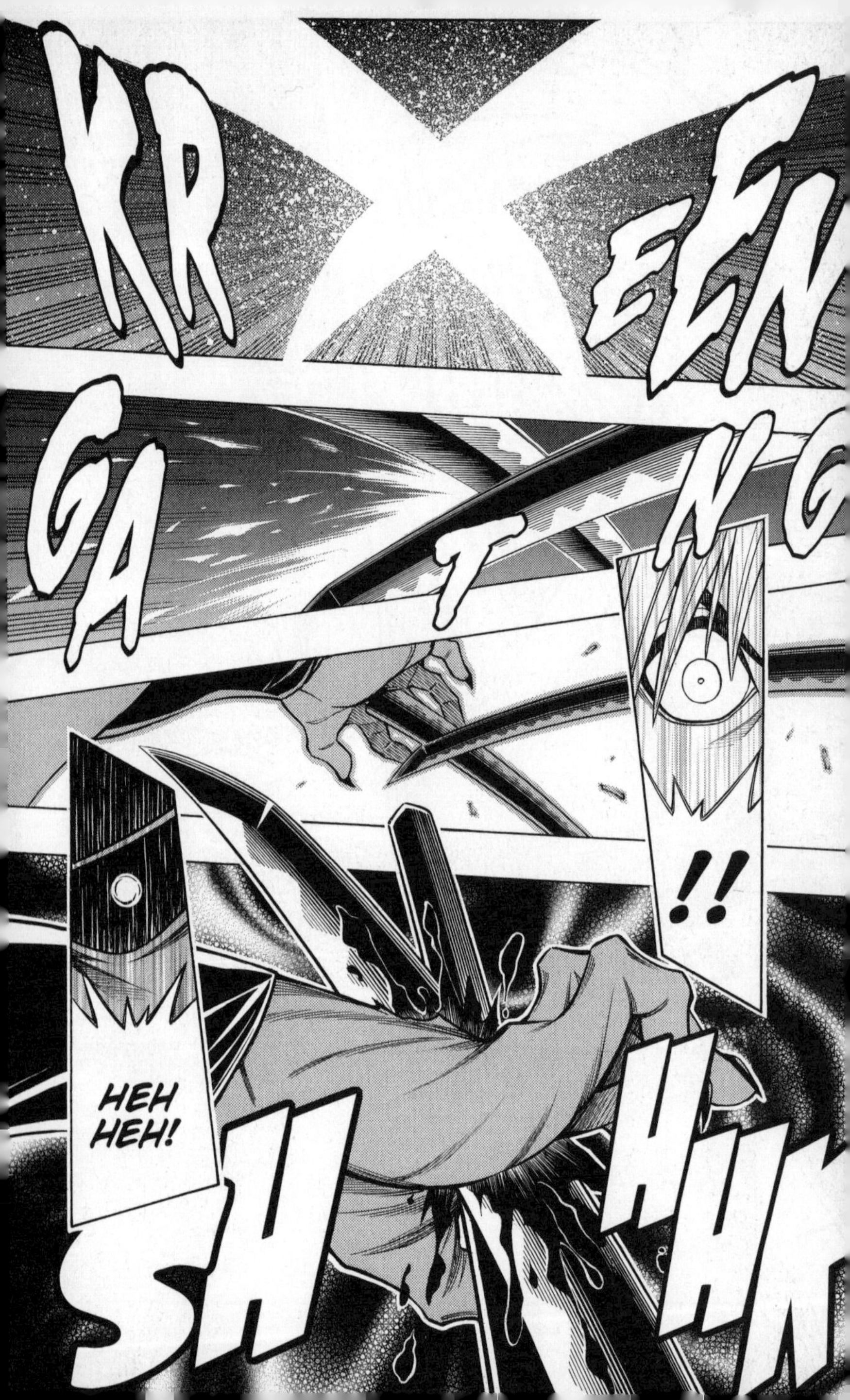
KREEN
GANG
!!
HEH HEH!
SHHHK

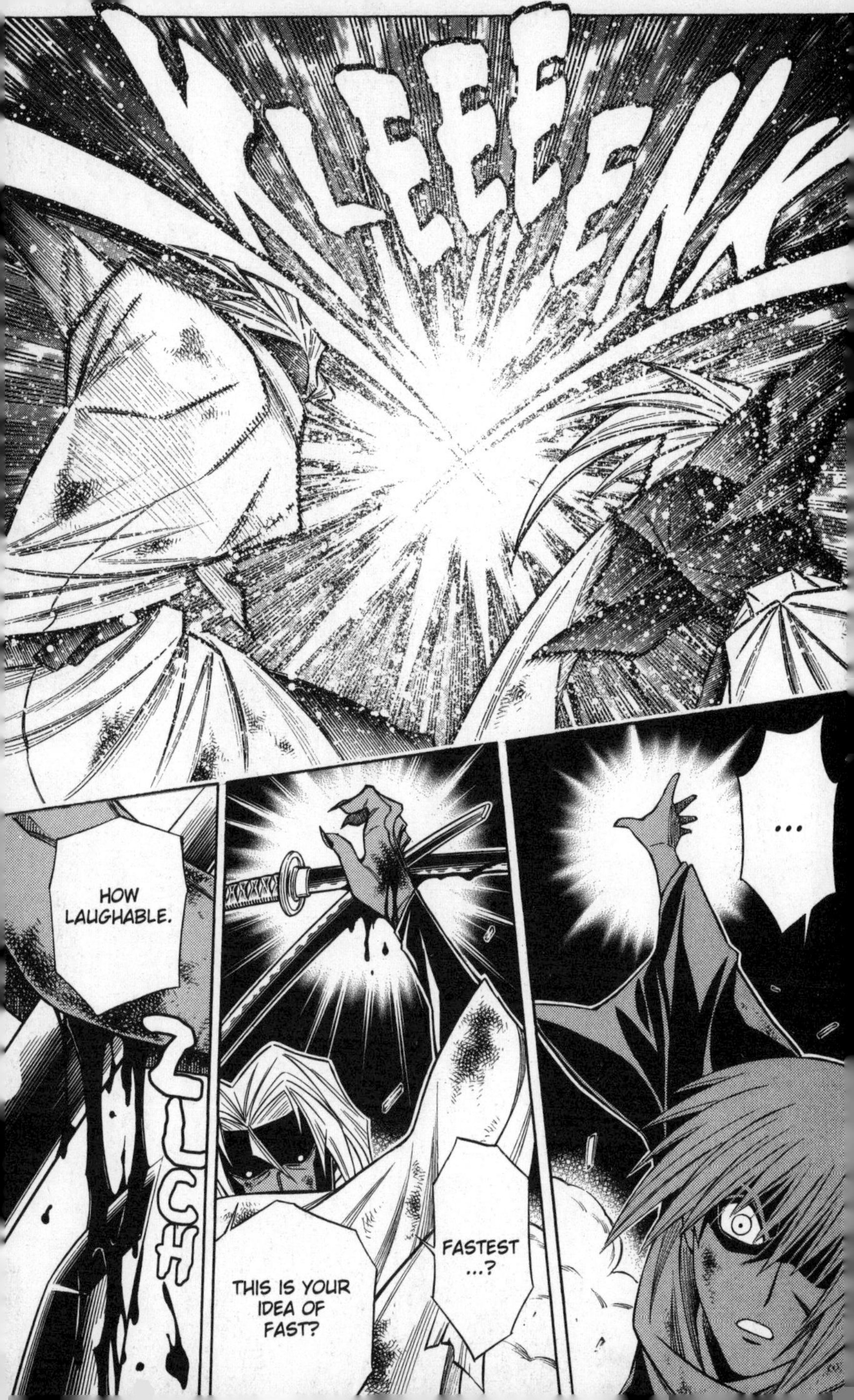
KLEEENK
...
FASTEST ...?
THIS IS YOUR IDEA OF FAST?
HOW LAUGHABLE.

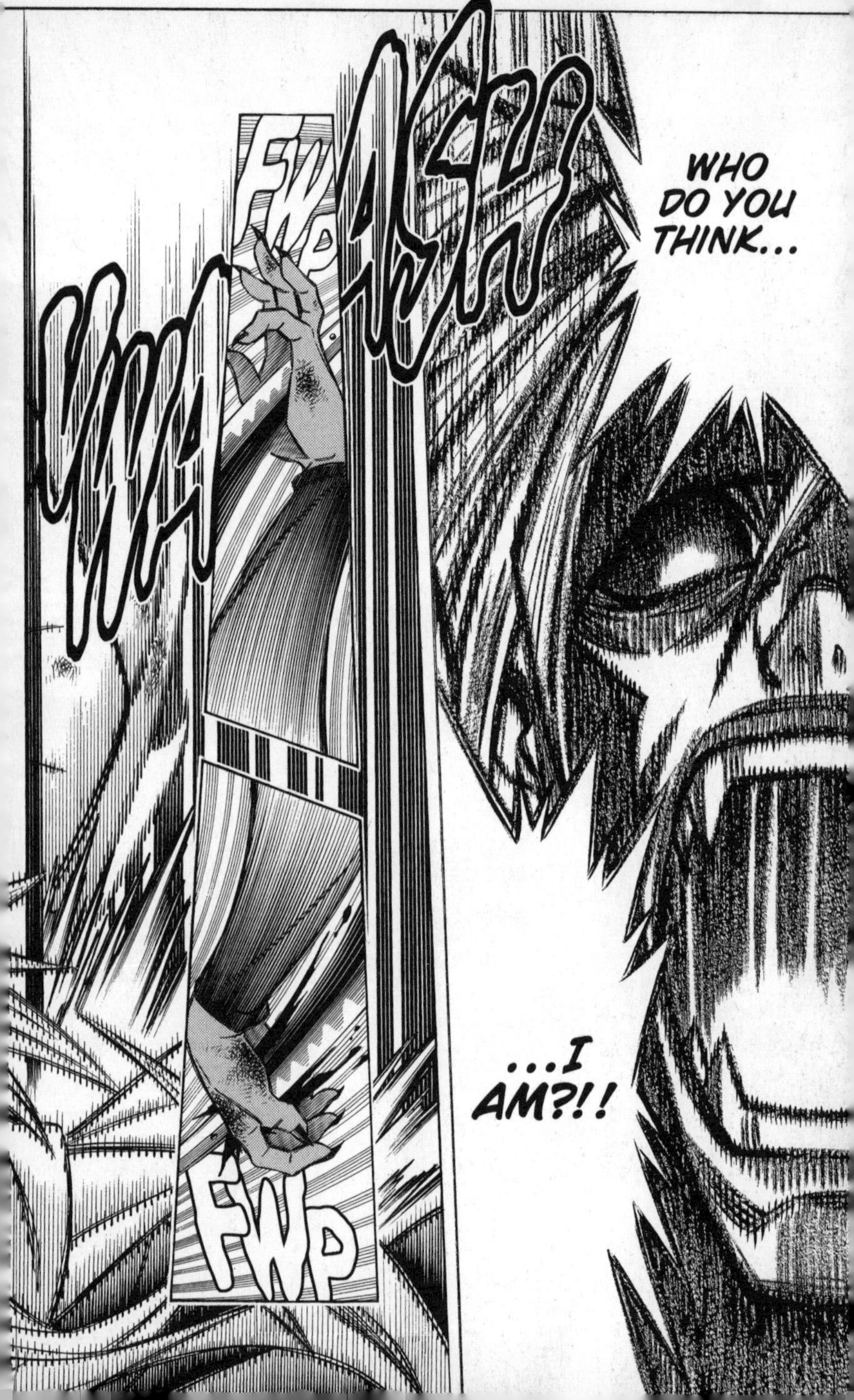
WHO DO YOU THINK...
FWP
...I AM?!!
FWP

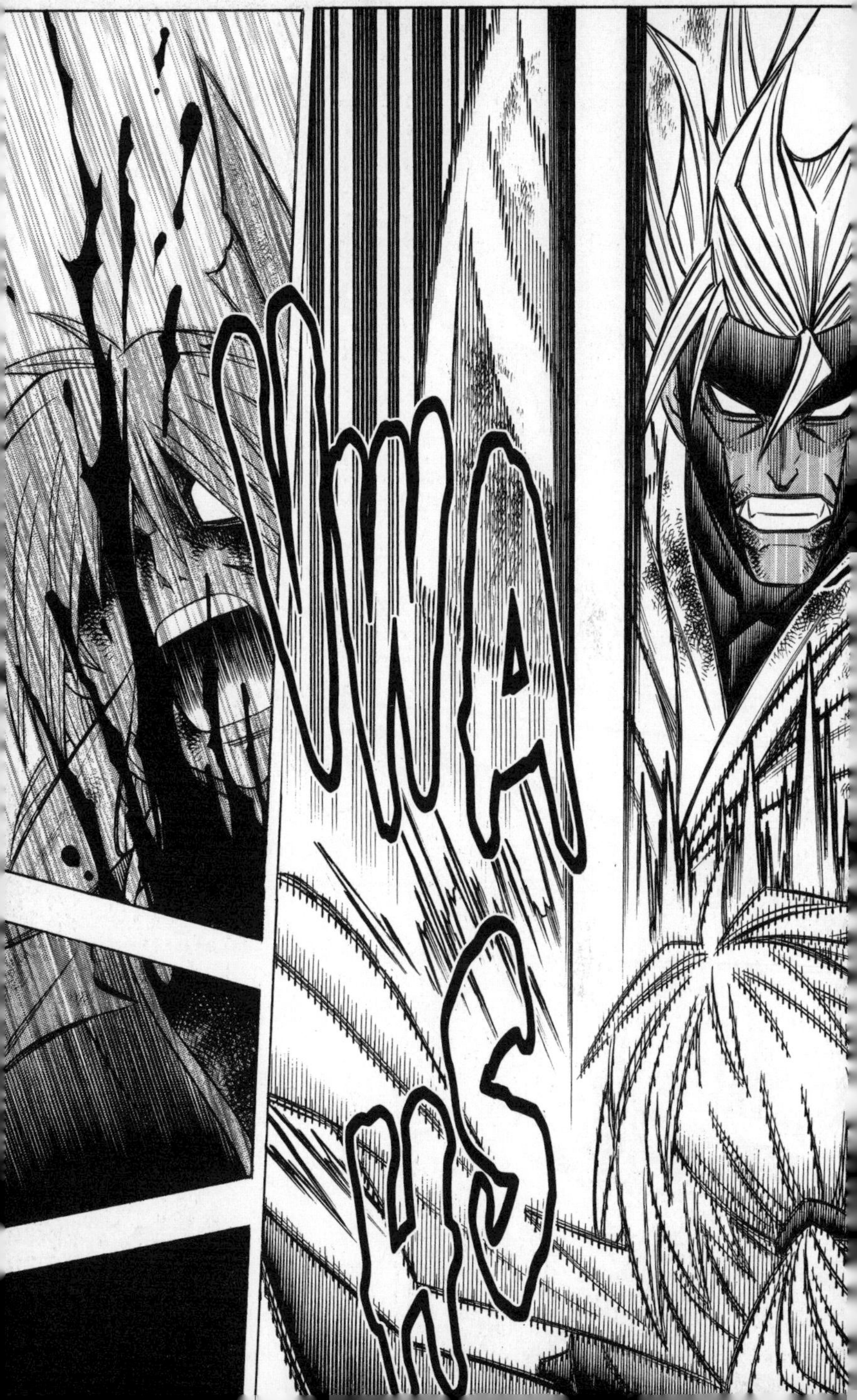

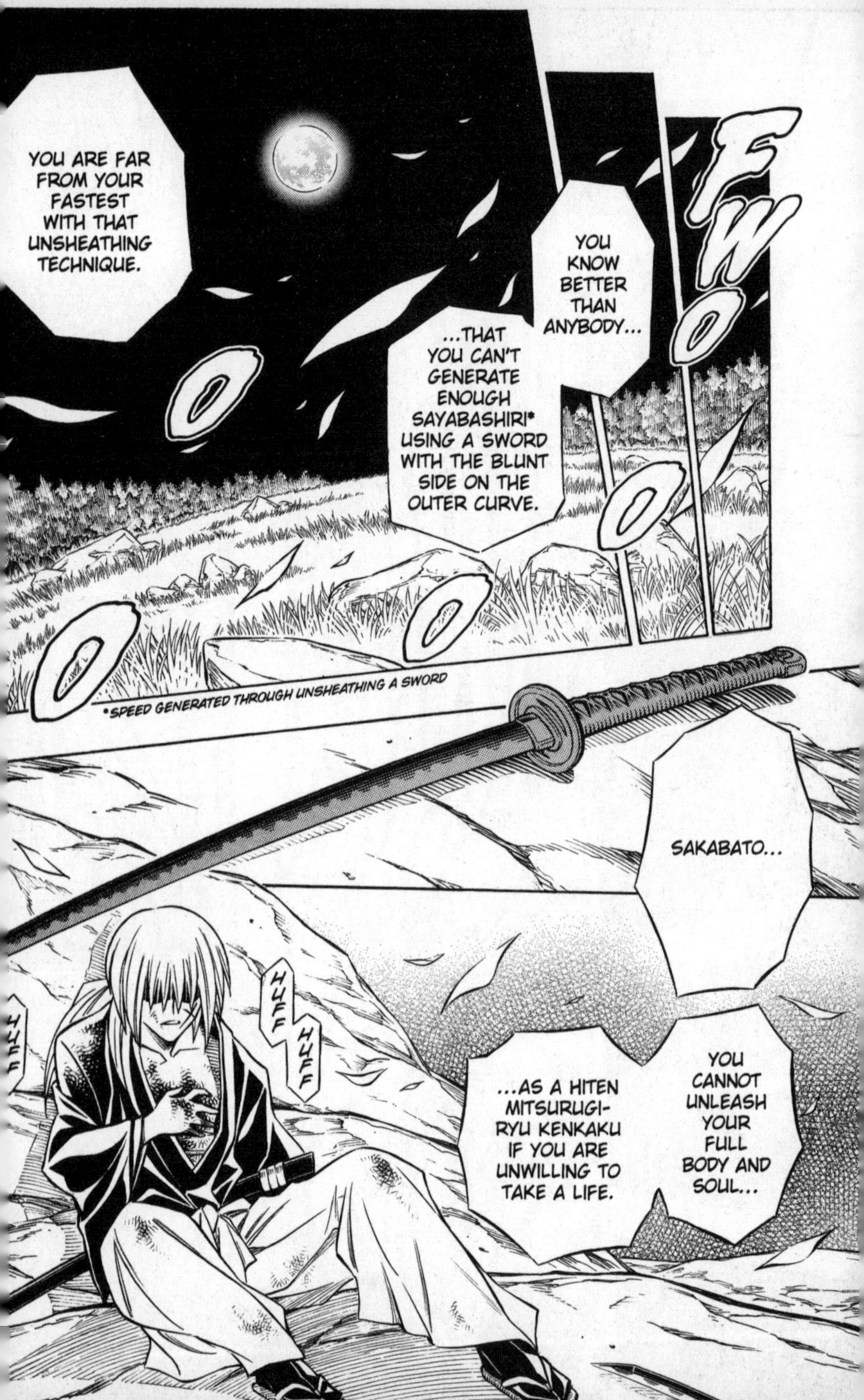
FWOOO
YOU KNOW BETTER THAN ANYBODY...
...THAT YOU CAN'T GENERATE ENOUGH SAYABASHIRI* USING A SWORD WITH THE BLUNT SIDE ON THE OUTER CURVE.
YOU ARE FAR FROM YOUR FASTEST WITH THAT UNSHEATHING TECHNIQUE.
*SPEED GENERATED THROUGH UNSHEATHING A SWORD
SAKABATO...
YOU CANNOT UNLEASH YOUR FULL BODY AND SOUL...
...AS A HITEN MITSURUGI-RYU KENKAKU IF YOU ARE UNWILLING TO TAKE A LIFE.
HUFF HUFF
HUFF

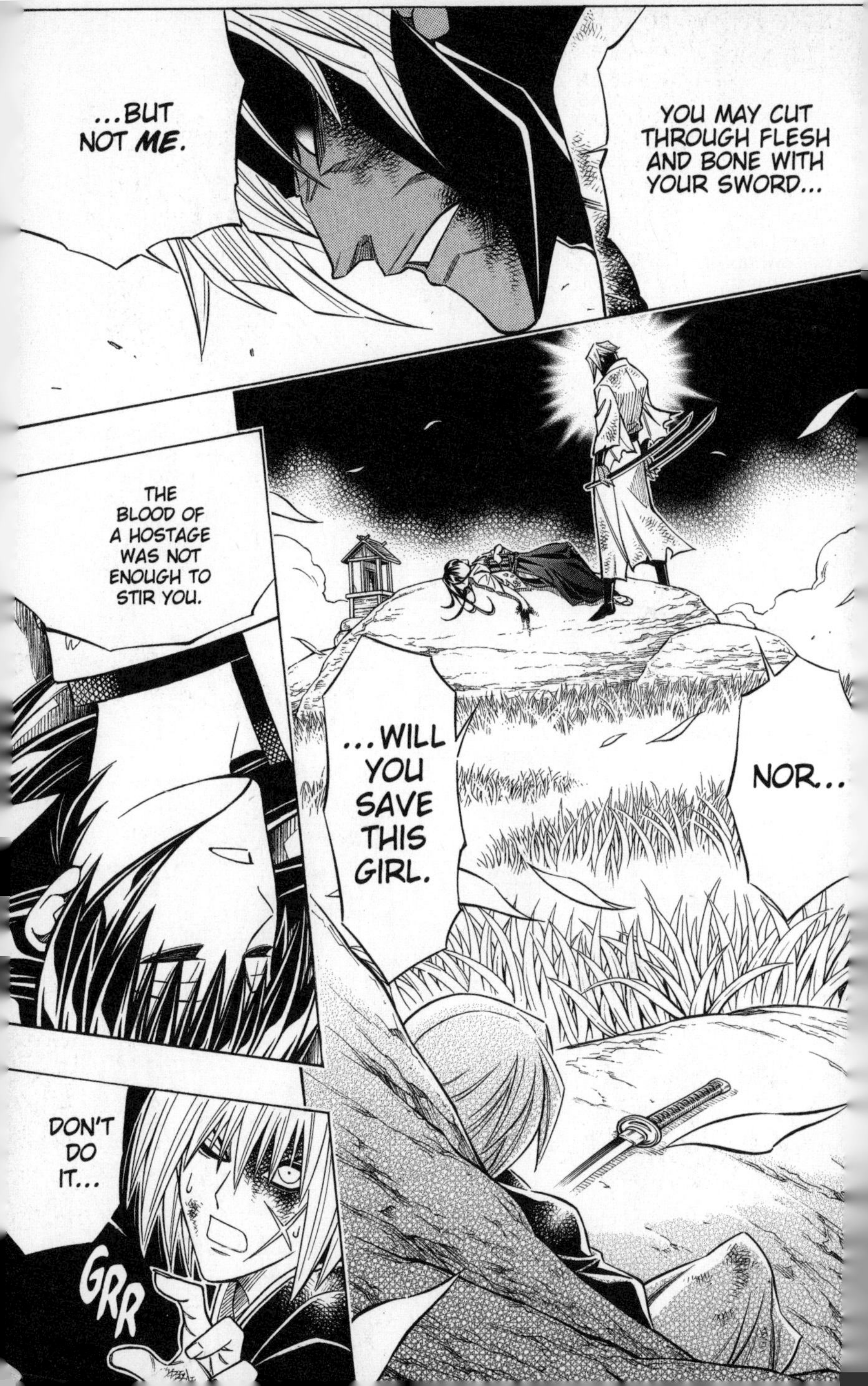
YOU MAY CUT THROUGH FLESH AND BONE WITH YOUR SWORD...
...BUT NOT ME.
NOR...
...WILL YOU SAVE THIS GIRL.
THE BLOOD OF A HOSTAGE WAS NOT ENOUGH TO STIR YOU.
DON'T DO IT...
GRR

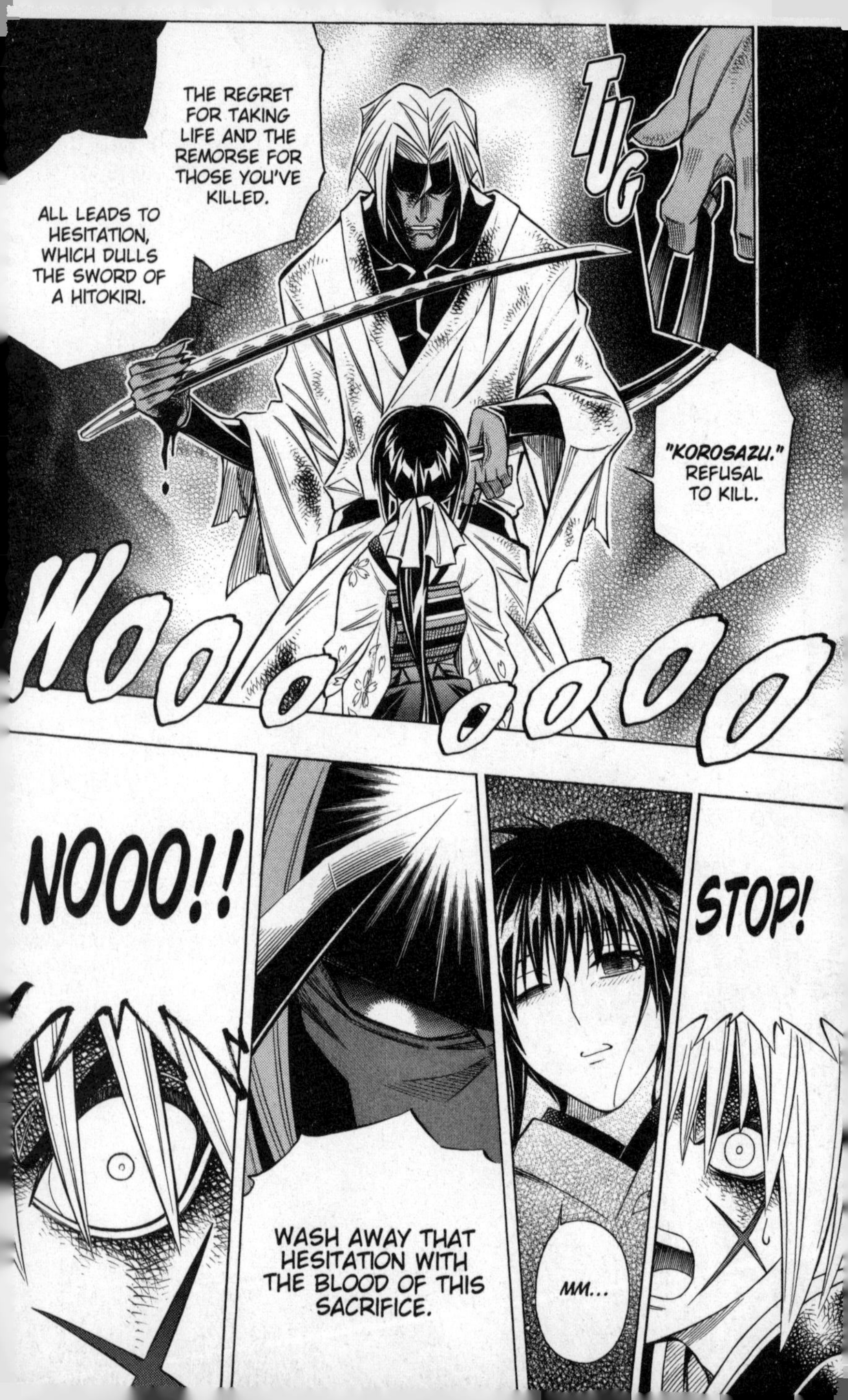
TUG
THE REGRET FOR TAKING LIFE AND THE REMORSE FOR THOSE YOU'VE KILLED.
ALL LEADS TO HESITATION, WHICH DULLS THE SWORD OF A HITOKIRI.
"KOROSAZU." REFUSAL TO KILL.
NOOOOOOO
STOP!
MM...
WASH AWAY THAT HESITATION WITH THE BLOOD OF THIS SACRIFICE.
NOOO!!

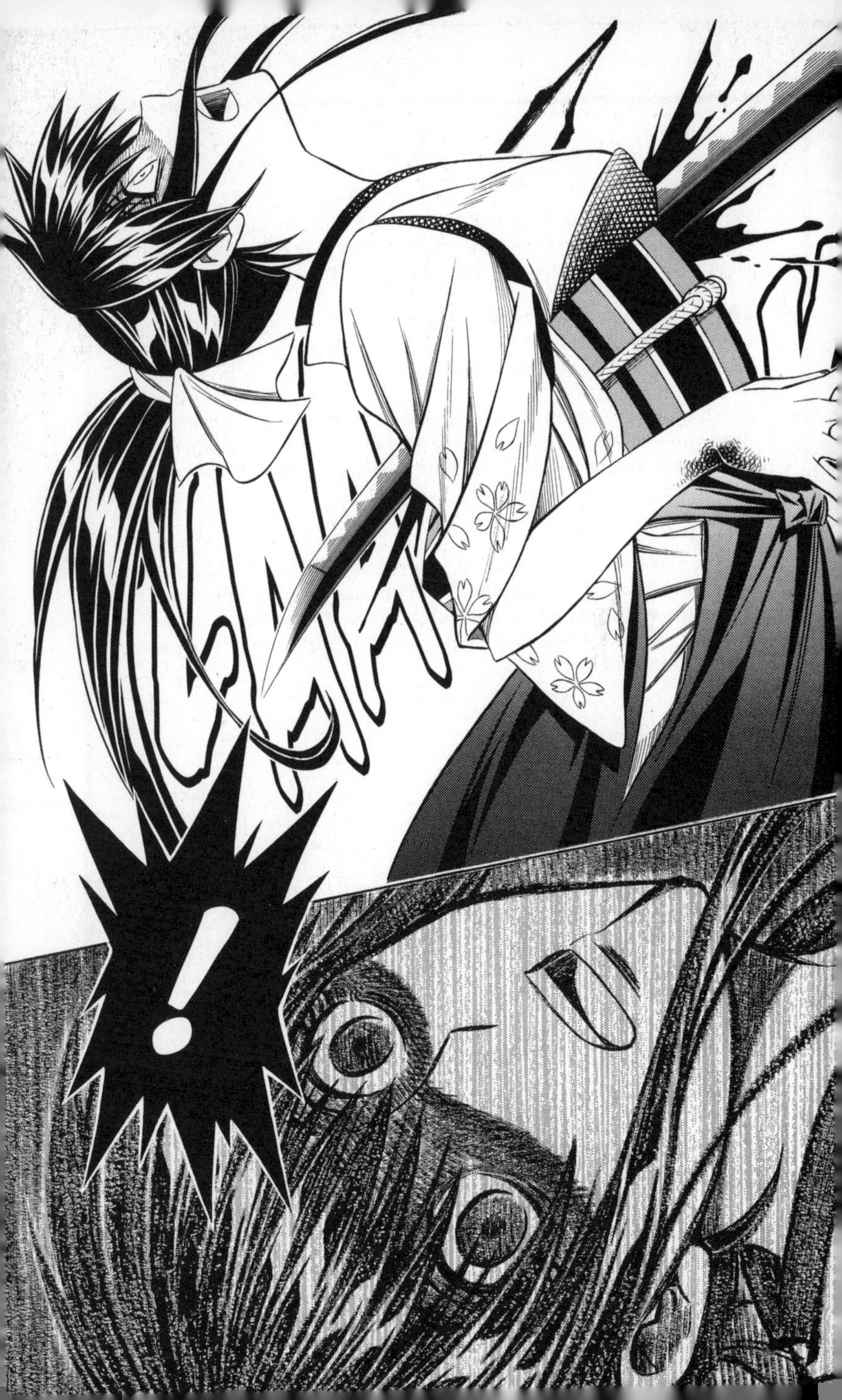
!

Takeda Kanryu
He is the last boss in both *Restoration* and the film, so I wasn't planning on making any drastic changes. But I was inspired to after seeing Teruyuki Kagawa's fanatical performance in the film.

I figured he should be proud of being a crooked merchant, so I came up with the line "I'm not a crook. I'm an unscrupulous merchant." That line is one of my favorites.

The biggest change in his appearance is the shape of his glasses. I changed them to round glasses to give him a more Meiji era feel, but I think square glasses suited his apathetic ways more. That was a mistake.

Others
Banjin and Gein's roles were so dramatically changed that I used versions of them from *Kenshin Saihitsu*. Tae, Megumi, Chief Uramura, and other minor characters stayed the same from the original version. A friend of mine insisted I keep Tsubame the same so I couldn't change her...

Final Chapter: In the New Era

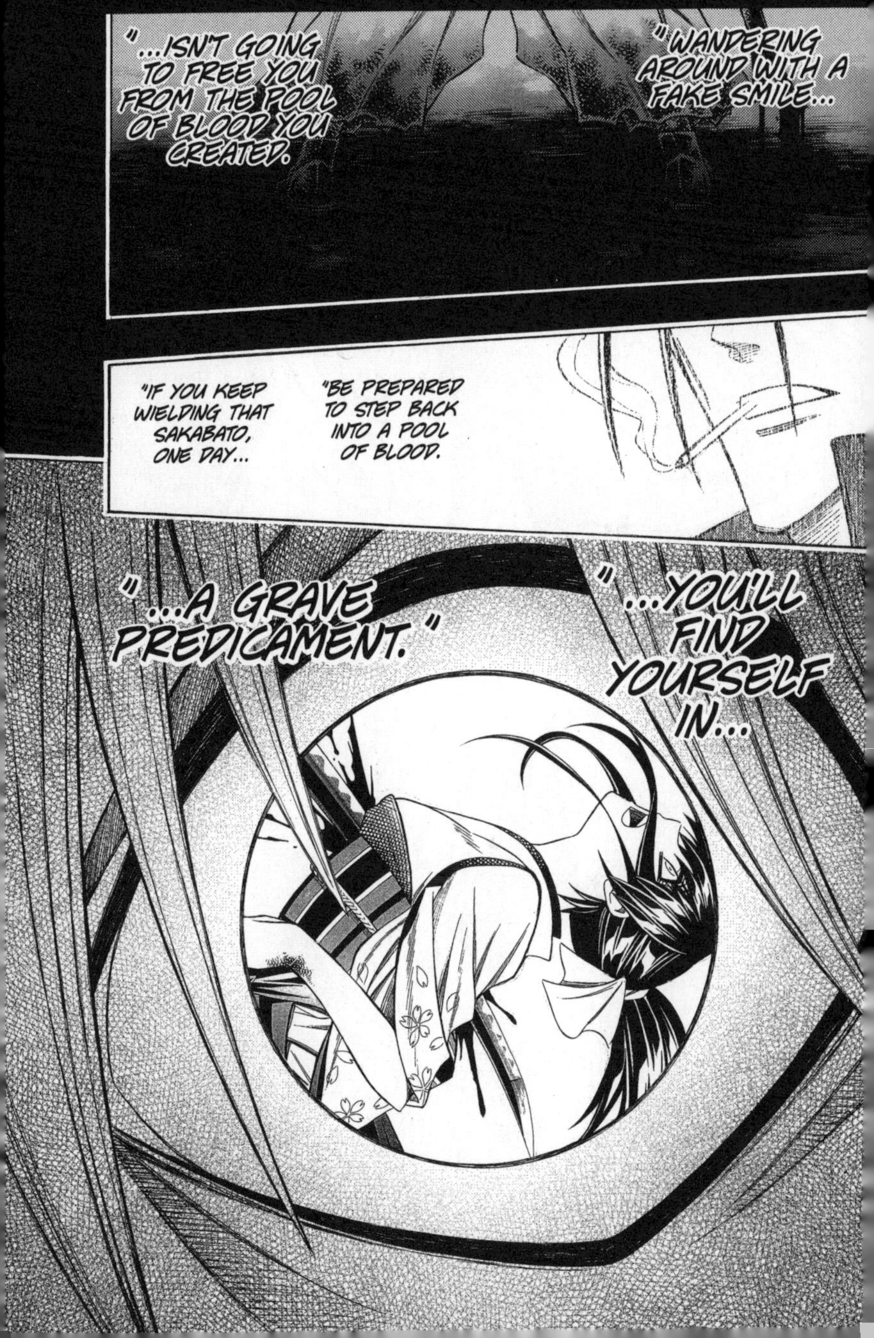
"WANDERING AROUND WITH A FAKE SMILE...
"...ISN'T GOING TO FREE YOU FROM THE POOL OF BLOOD YOU CREATED.
"BE PREPARED TO STEP BACK INTO A POOL OF BLOOD.
"IF YOU KEEP WIELDING THAT SAKABATO, ONE DAY...
"...YOU'LL FIND YOURSELF IN...
"...A GRAVE PREDICAMENT."

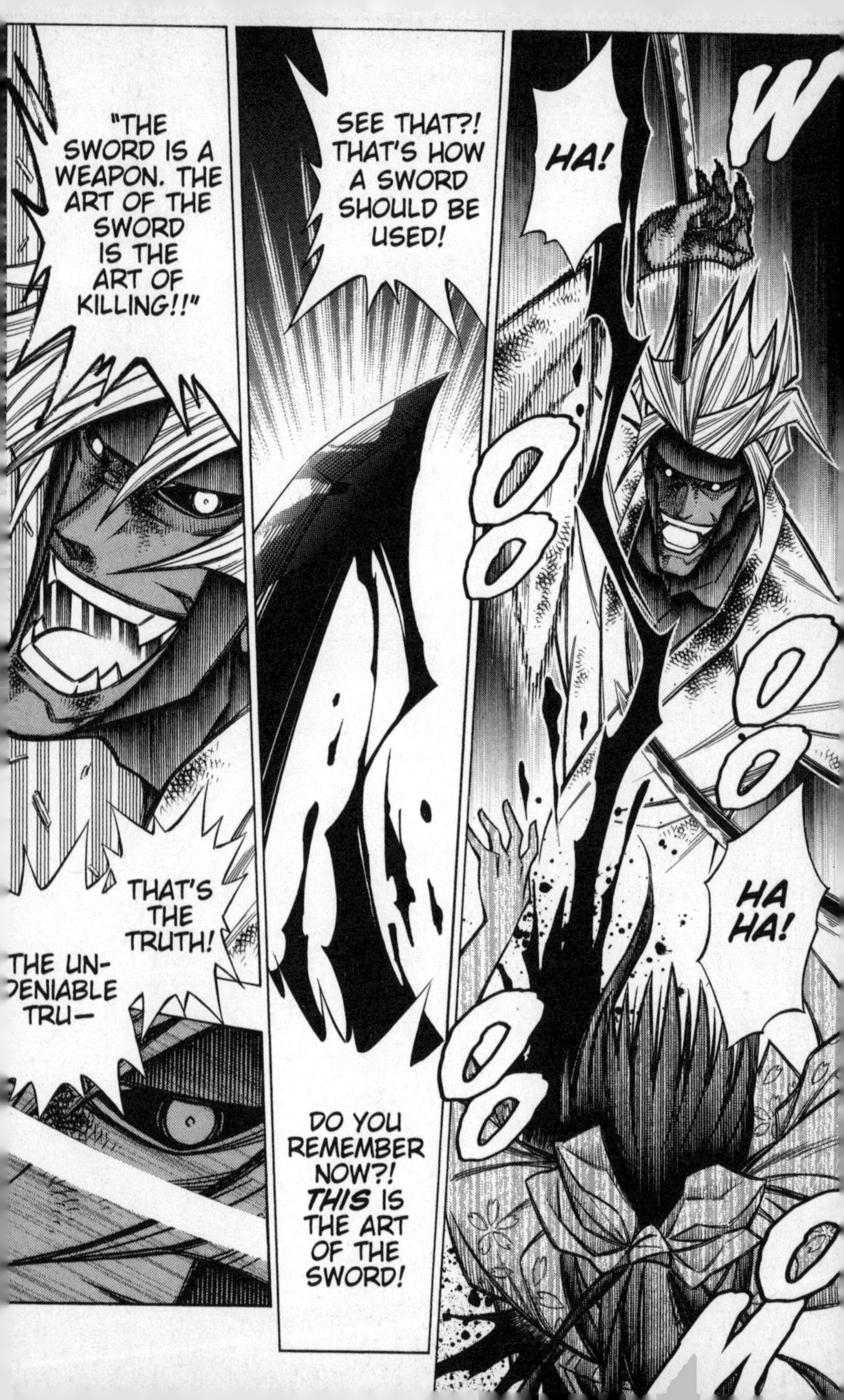
HA!
HA HA!
SEE THAT?! THAT'S HOW A SWORD SHOULD BE USED!
DO YOU REMEMBER NOW?! *THIS* IS THE ART OF THE SWORD!
"THE SWORD IS A WEAPON. THE ART OF THE SWORD IS THE ART OF KILLING!!"
THAT'S THE TRUTH!
THE UN-DENIABLE TRU—

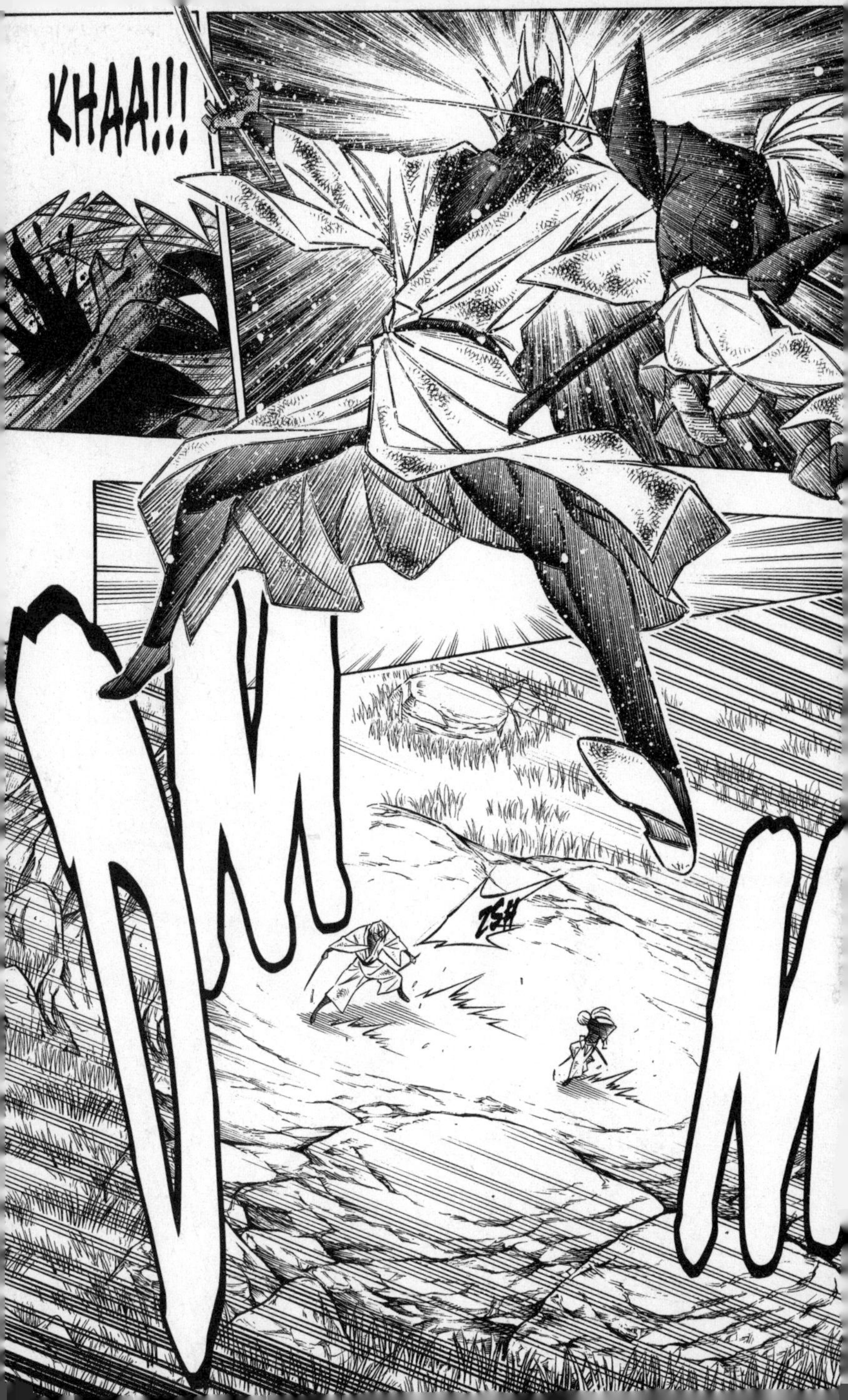
KHAA!!!
TSH

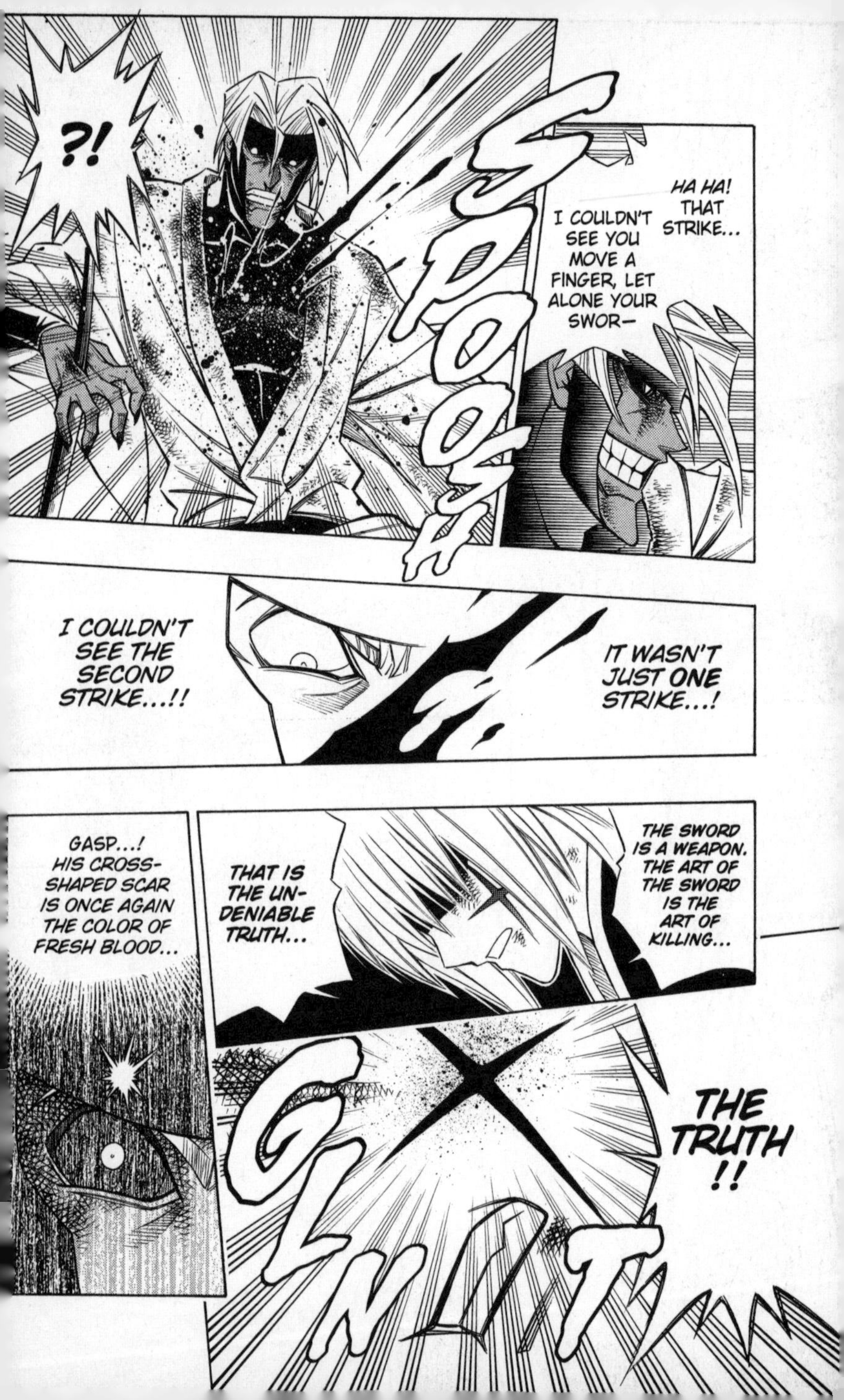
HA HA! THAT STRIKE...
I COULDN'T SEE YOU MOVE A FINGER, LET ALONE YOUR SWOR—
SPOOSH
?!
IT WASN'T JUST ONE STRIKE...!
I COULDN'T SEE THE SECOND STRIKE...!!
THE SWORD IS A WEAPON. THE ART OF THE SWORD IS THE ART OF KILLING...
THAT IS THE UN-DENIABLE TRUTH...
GASP...! HIS CROSS-SHAPED SCAR IS ONCE AGAIN THE COLOR OF FRESH BLOOD...
THE TRUTH !!

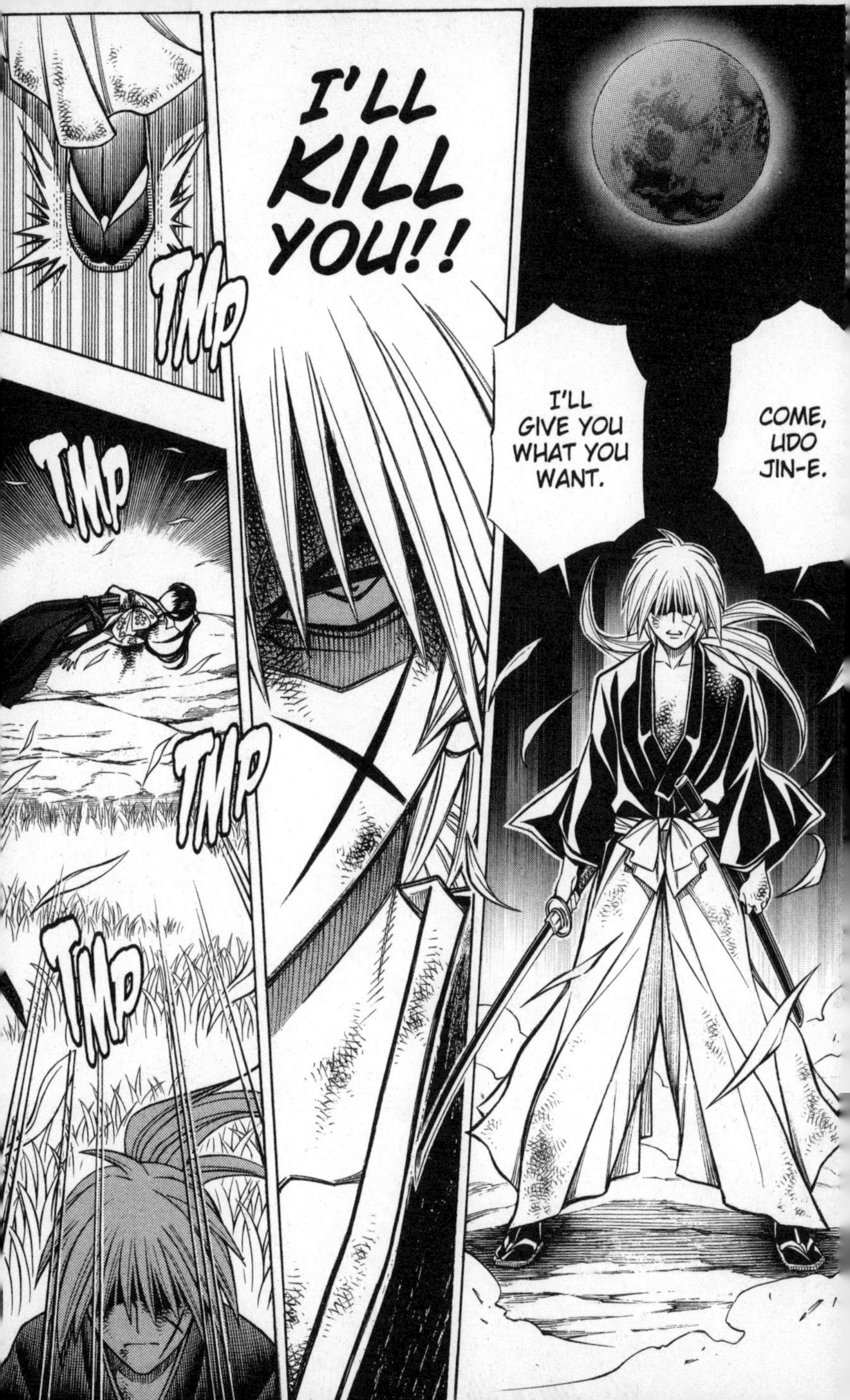
COME, UDO JIN-E.
I'LL GIVE YOU WHAT YOU WANT.
I'LL KILL YOU!!
TMP
TMP
TMP
TMP

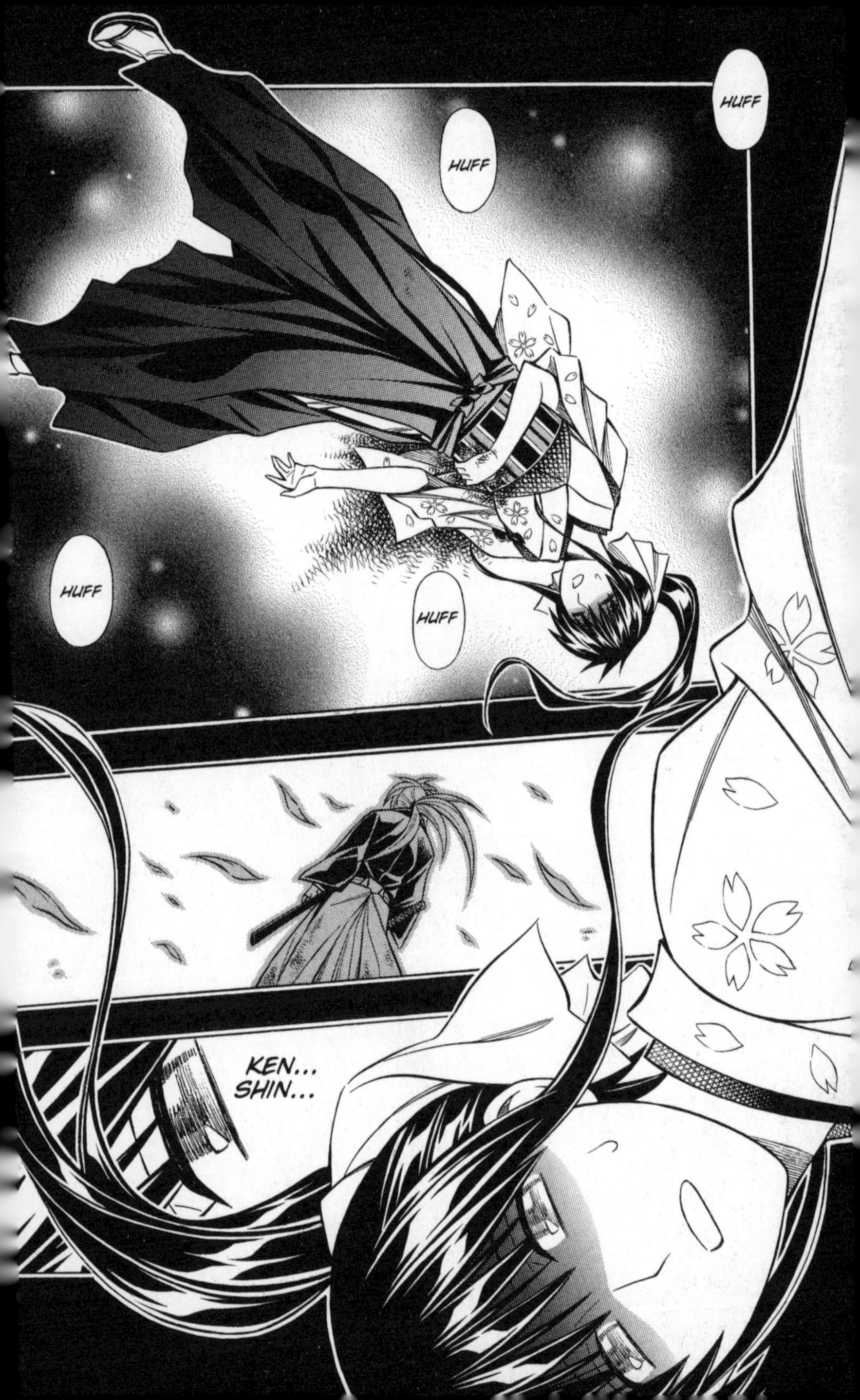
HUFF
HUFF
HUFF
HUFF
KEN... SHIN...

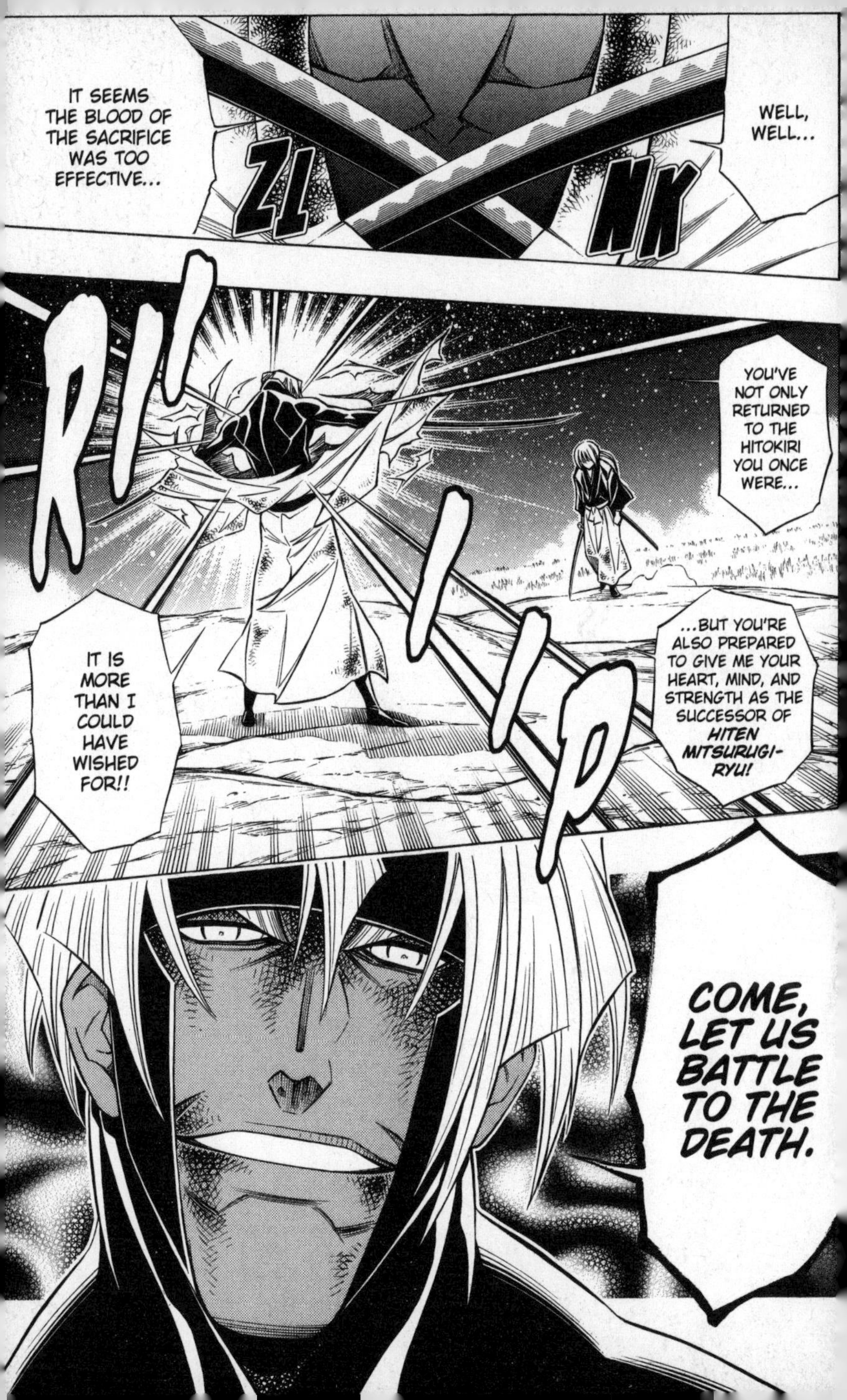
WELL, WELL...
IT SEEMS THE BLOOD OF THE SACRIFICE WAS TOO EFFECTIVE...
ZINK
YOU'VE NOT ONLY RETURNED TO THE HITOKIRI YOU ONCE WERE...
...BUT YOU'RE ALSO PREPARED TO GIVE ME YOUR HEART, MIND, AND STRENGTH AS THE SUCCESSOR OF *HITEN MITSURUGI-RYU!*
RIIIP
IT IS MORE THAN I COULD HAVE WISHED FOR!!
COME, LET US BATTLE TO THE DEATH.

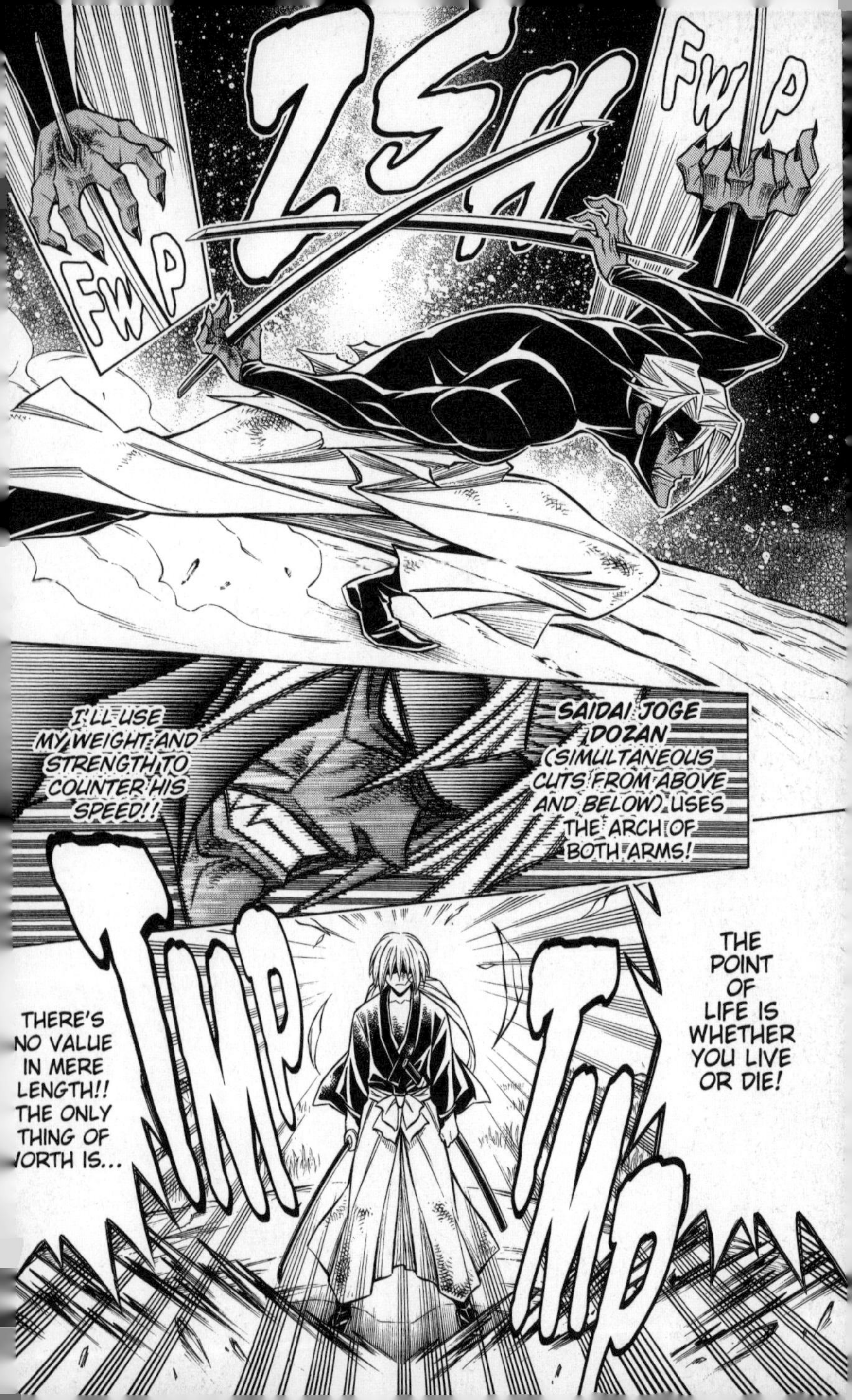
ZSA
FWP
FWP
SAIDAI JOGE DOZAN (SIMULTANEOUS CUTS FROM ABOVE AND BELOW) USES THE ARCH OF BOTH ARMS!
I'LL USE MY WEIGHT AND STRENGTH TO COUNTER HIS SPEED!!
THMP
THMP
THE POINT OF LIFE IS WHETHER YOU LIVE OR DIE!
THERE'S NO VALUE IN MERE LENGTH!! THE ONLY THING OF ORTH IS...

HITEN MITSURUGI-RYU OGI (ULTIMATE TECHNIQUE)

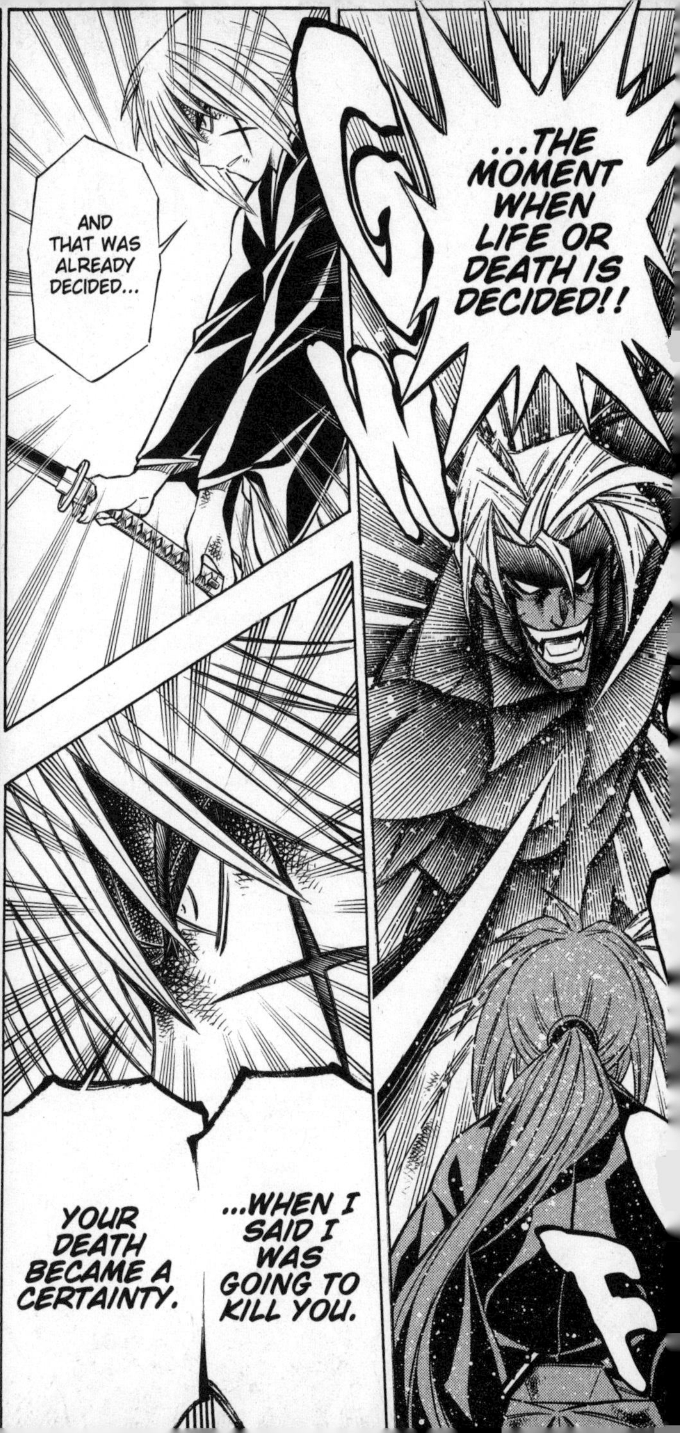
...THE MOMENT WHEN LIFE OR DEATH IS DECIDED!!
AND THAT WAS ALREADY DECIDED...
...WHEN I SAID I WAS GOING TO KILL YOU.
YOUR DEATH BECAME A CERTAINTY.

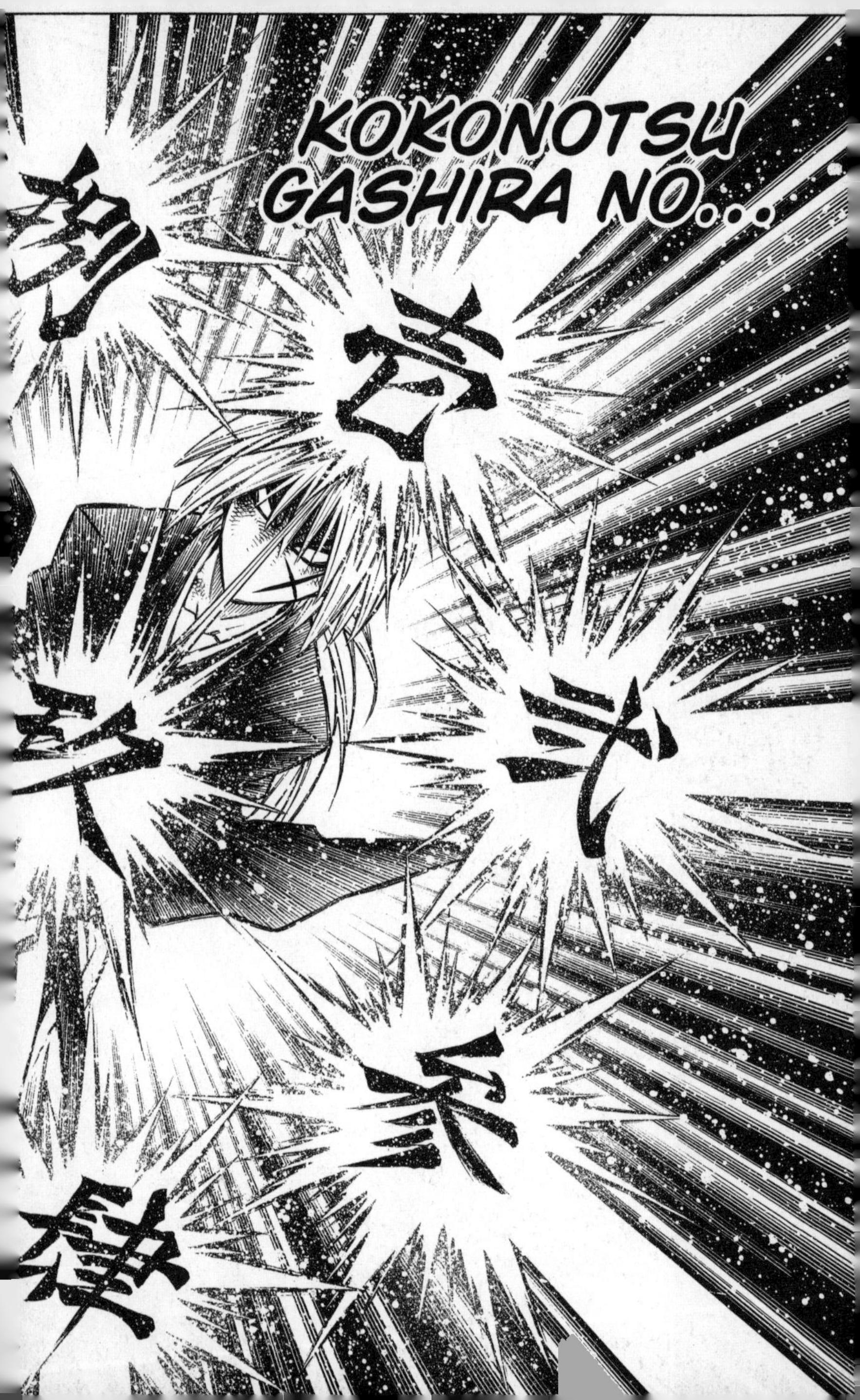
KOKONOTSU GASHIRA NO...

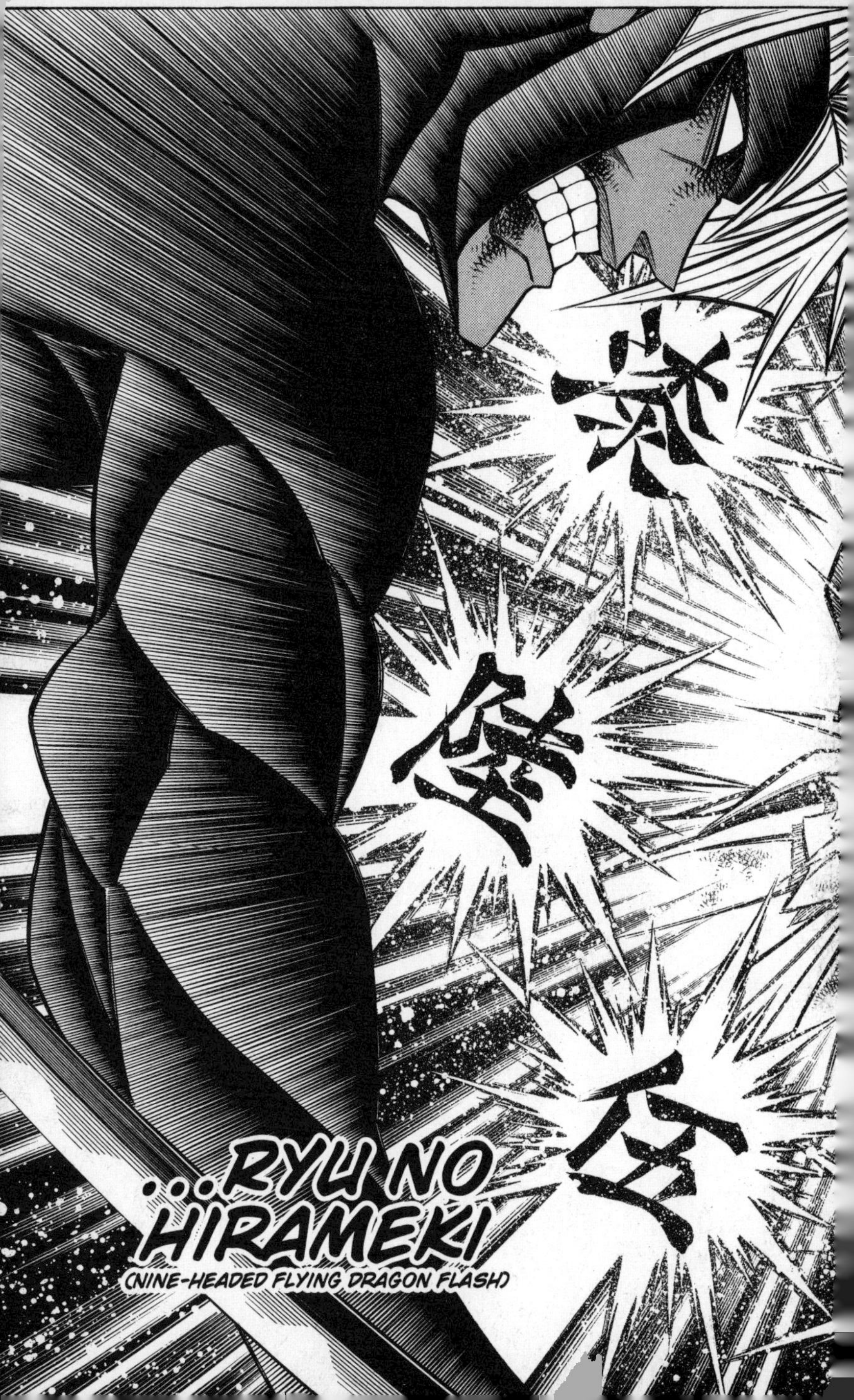
...RYU NO HIRAMEKI
(NINE-HEADED FLYING DRAGON FLASH)

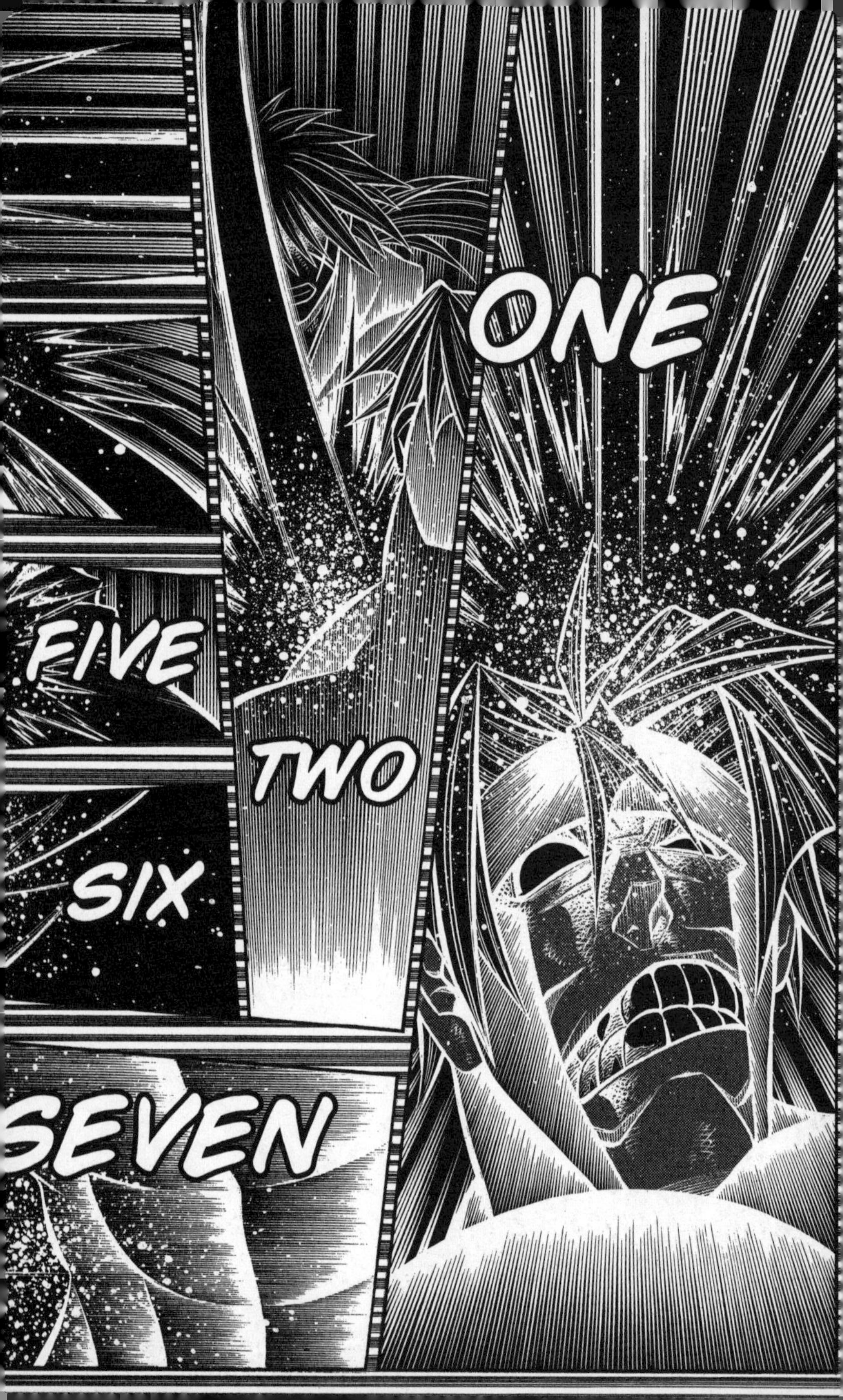
ONE
TWO
FIVE
SIX
SEVEN

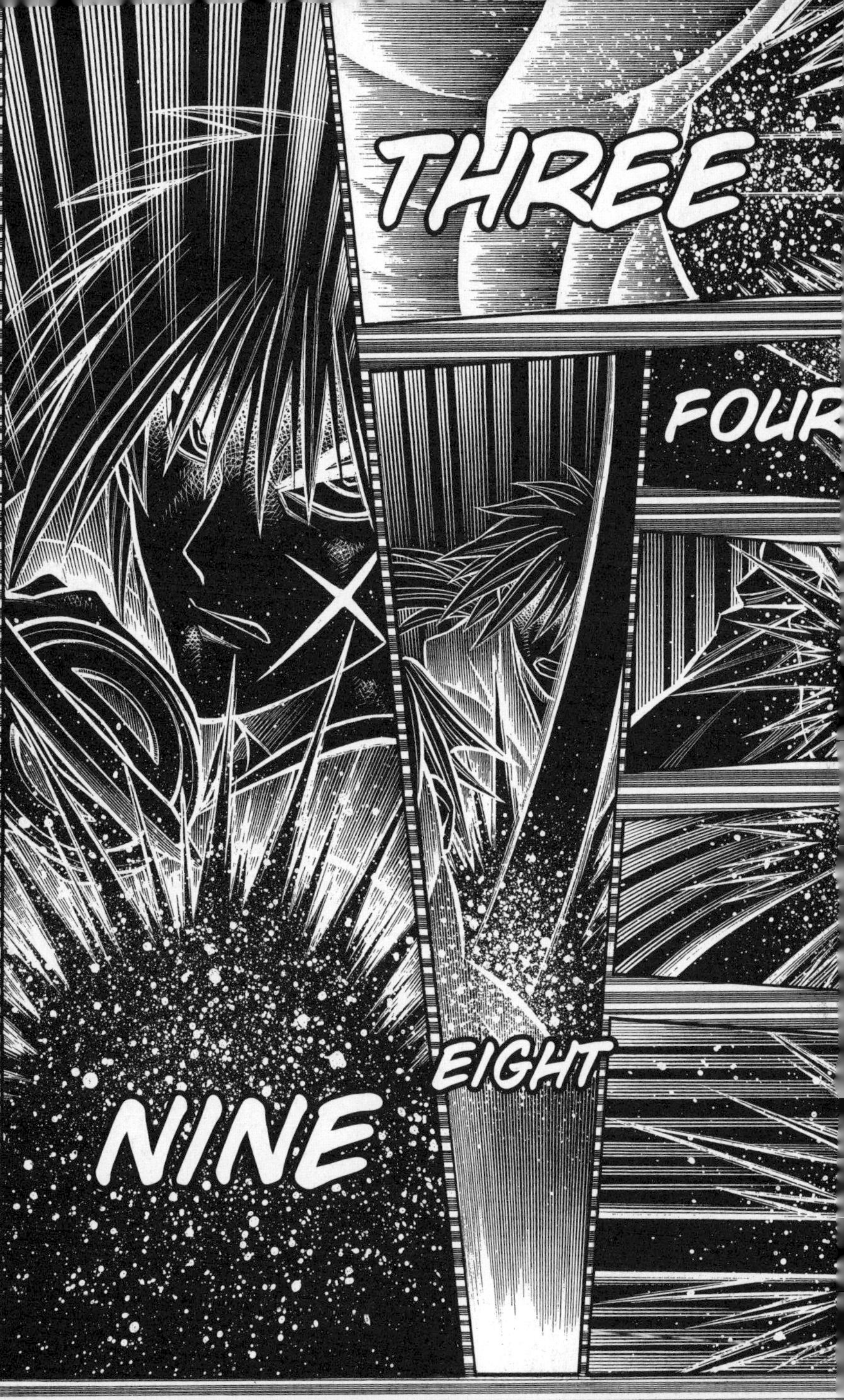
THREE
FOUR
EIGHT
NINE

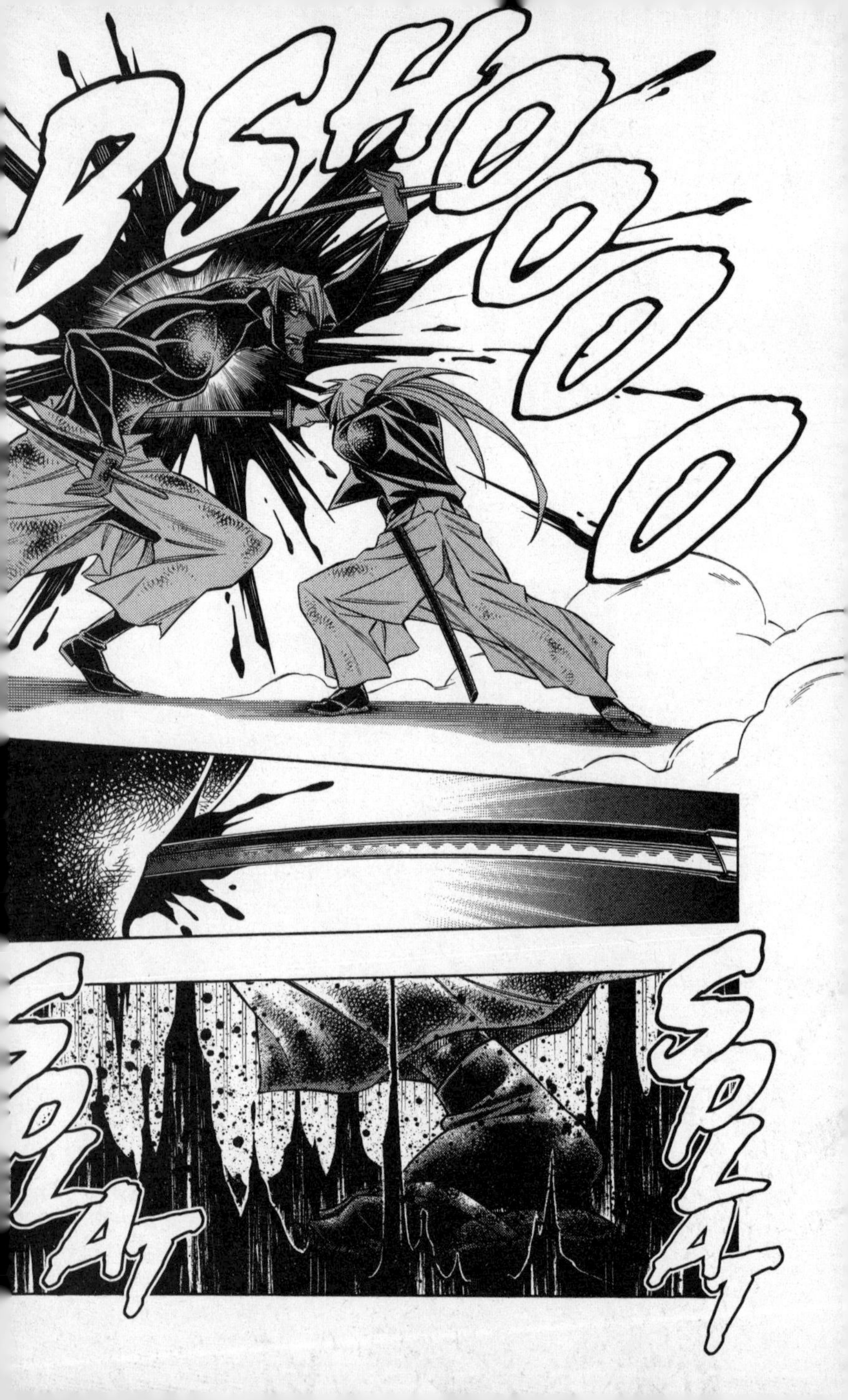
BSHOOOOO
SPLAT
SPLAT

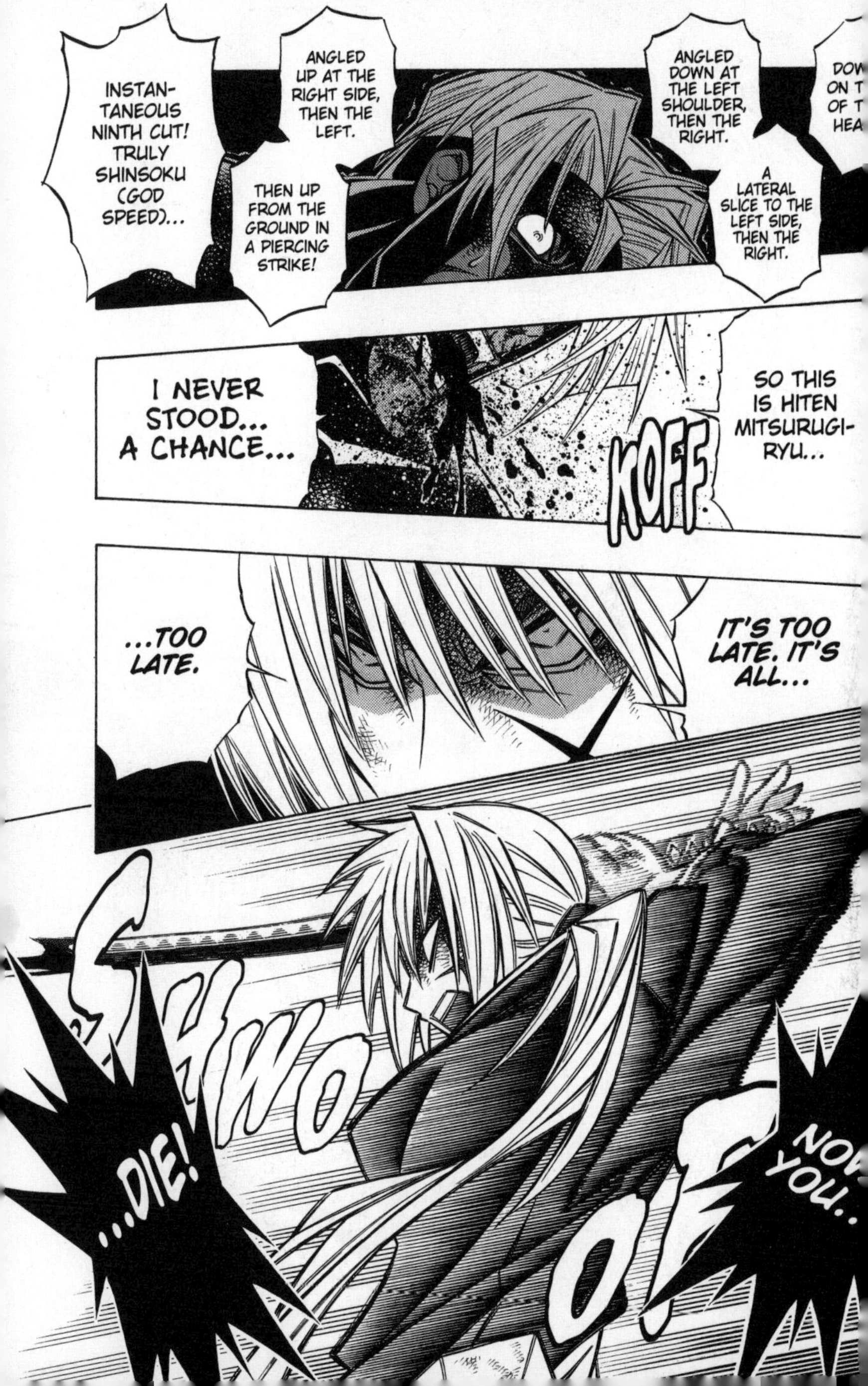
DOW ON T OF T HEA
ANGLED DOWN AT THE LEFT SHOULDER, THEN THE RIGHT.
A LATERAL SLICE TO THE LEFT SIDE, THEN THE RIGHT.
ANGLED UP AT THE RIGHT SIDE, THEN THE LEFT.
THEN UP FROM THE GROUND IN A PIERCING STRIKE!
INSTAN-TANEOUS NINTH CUT! TRULY SHINSOKU (GOD SPEED)...
SO THIS IS HITEN MITSURUGI-RYU...
KOFF
I NEVER STOOD... A CHANCE...
IT'S TOO LATE. IT'S ALL...
...TOO LATE.
NO YOU...
...DIE!

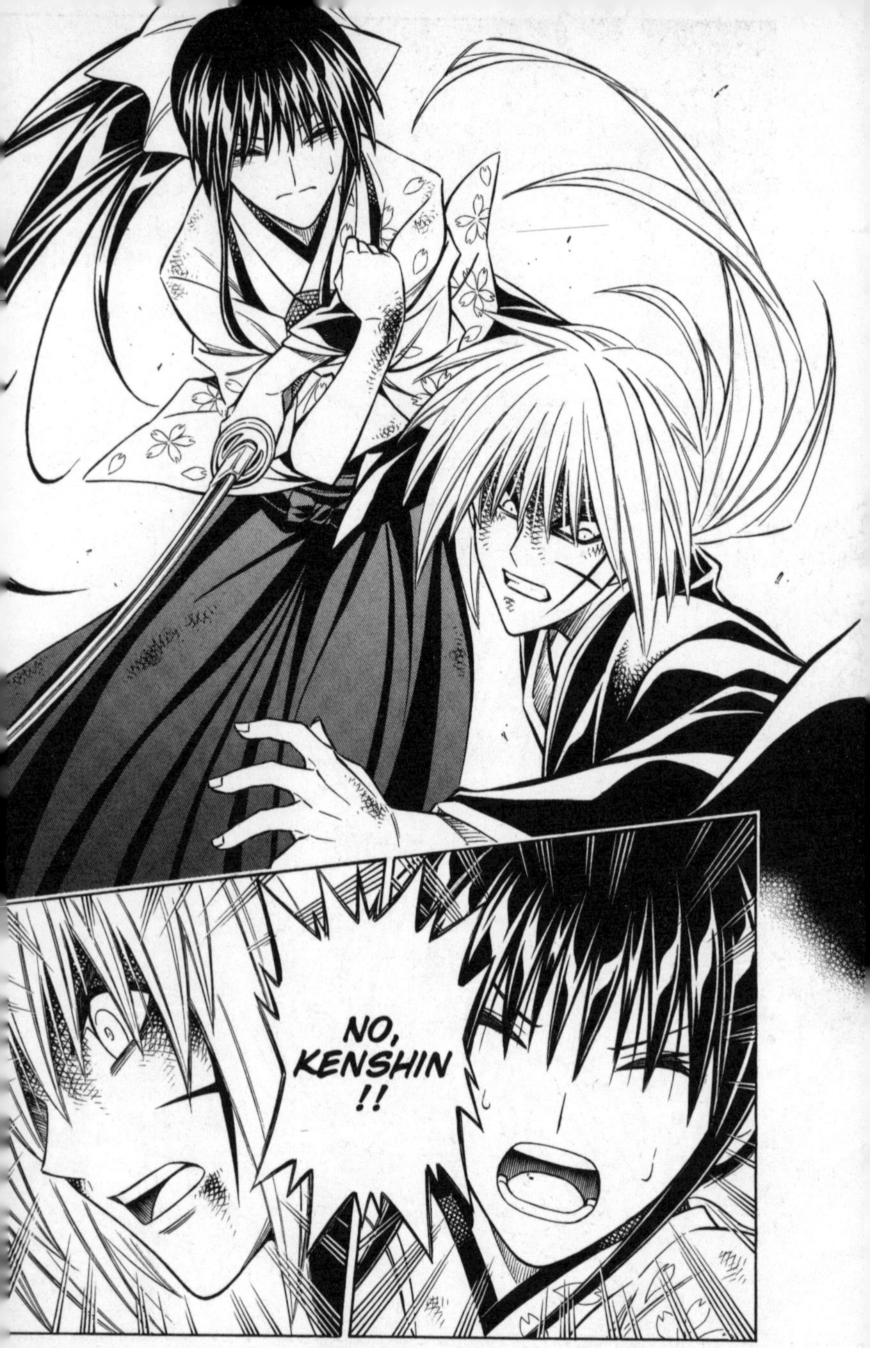
NO, KENSHIN!!

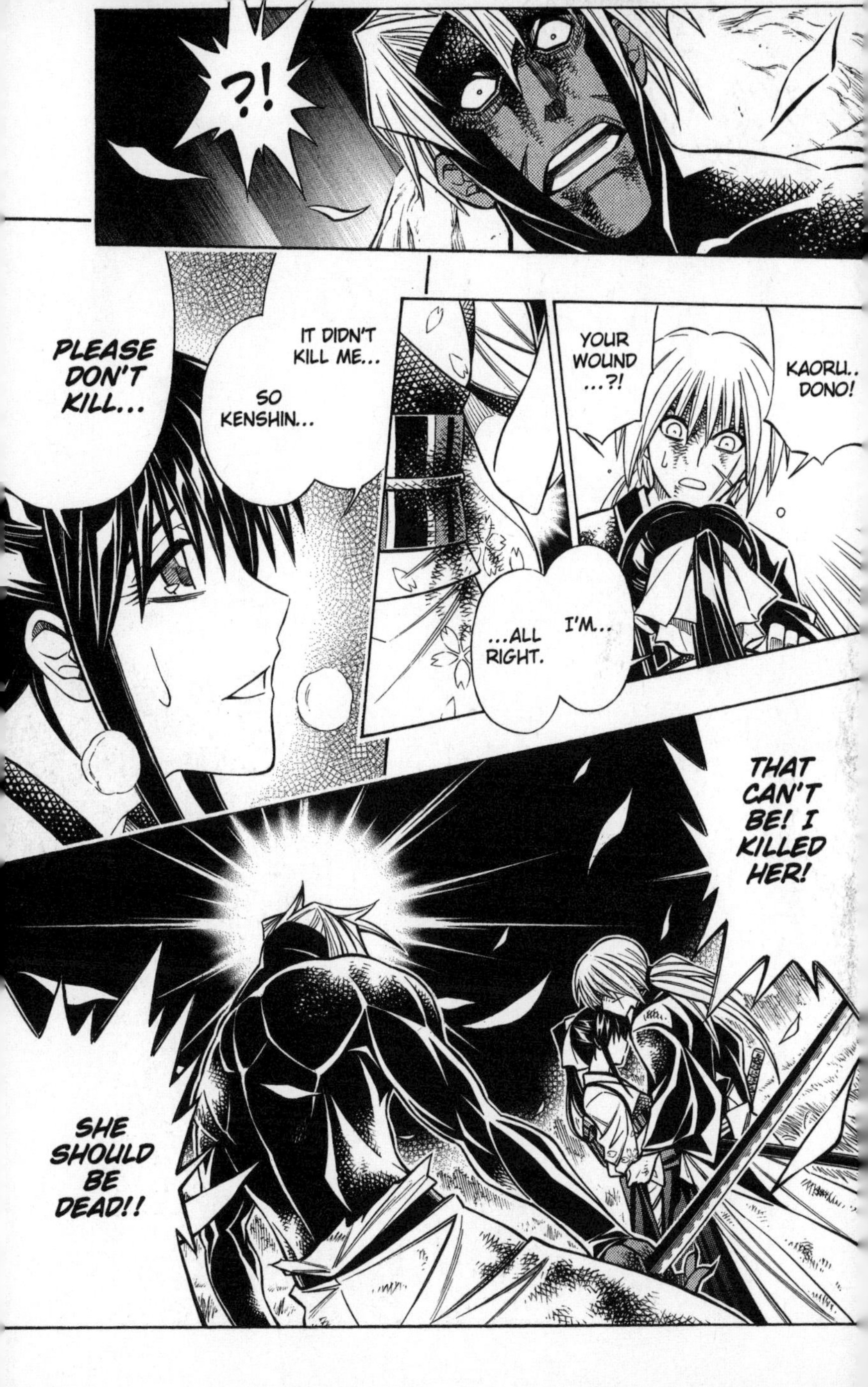
?!
KAORU.. DONO!
YOUR WOUND ...?!
I'M...
...ALL RIGHT.
IT DIDN'T KILL ME...
SO KENSHIN...
PLEASE DON'T KILL...
THAT CAN'T BE! I KILLED HER!
SHE SHOULD BE DEAD!!

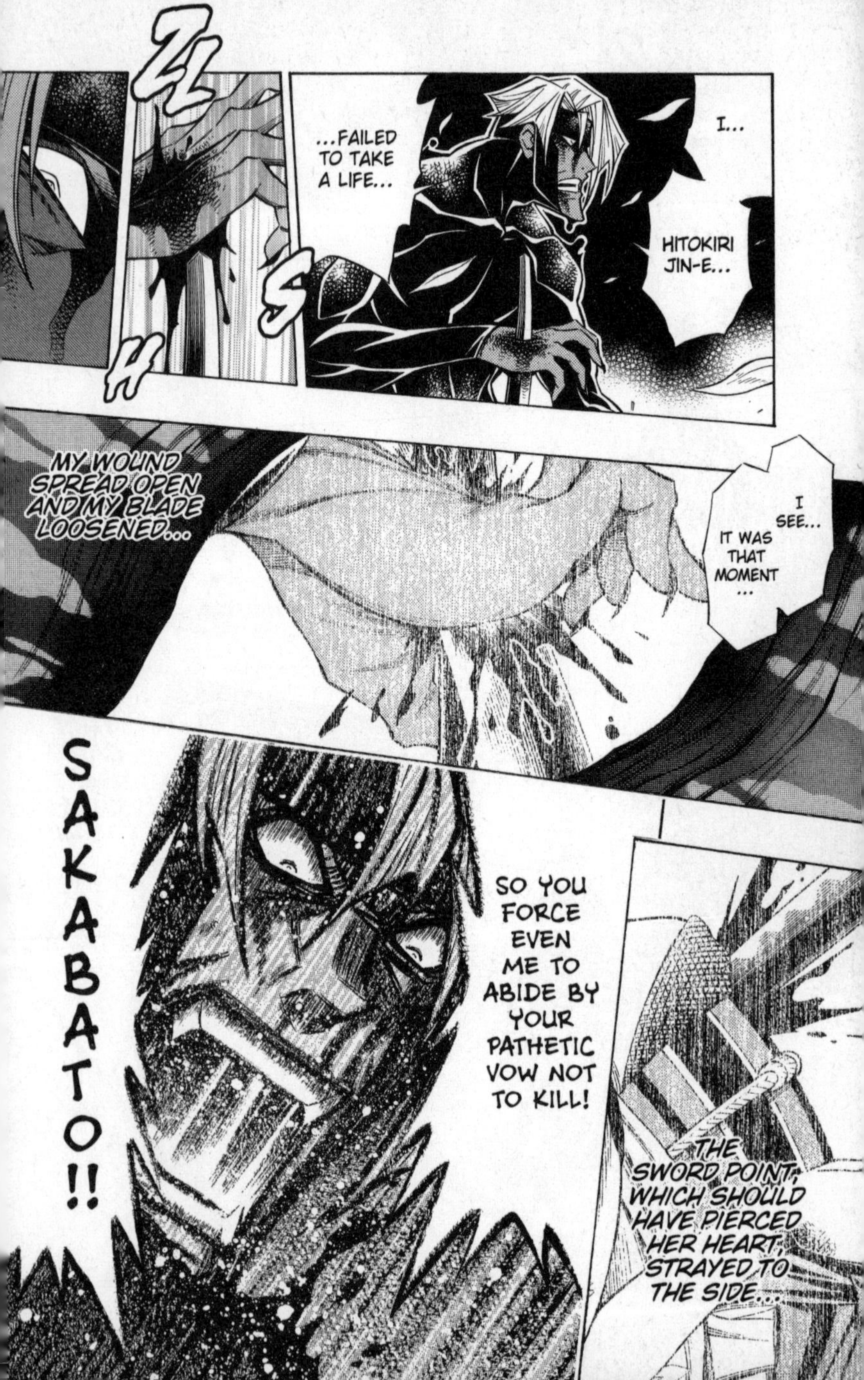
I...
HITOKIRI JIN-E...
...FAILED TO TAKE A LIFE...
ZZL
SH
I SEE... IT WAS THAT MOMENT...
MY WOUND SPREAD OPEN AND MY BLADE LOOSENED...
THE SWORD POINT, WHICH SHOULD HAVE PIERCED HER HEART, STRAYED TO THE SIDE...
SO YOU FORCE EVEN ME TO ABIDE BY YOUR PATHETIC VOW NOT TO KILL!
SAKABATO!!

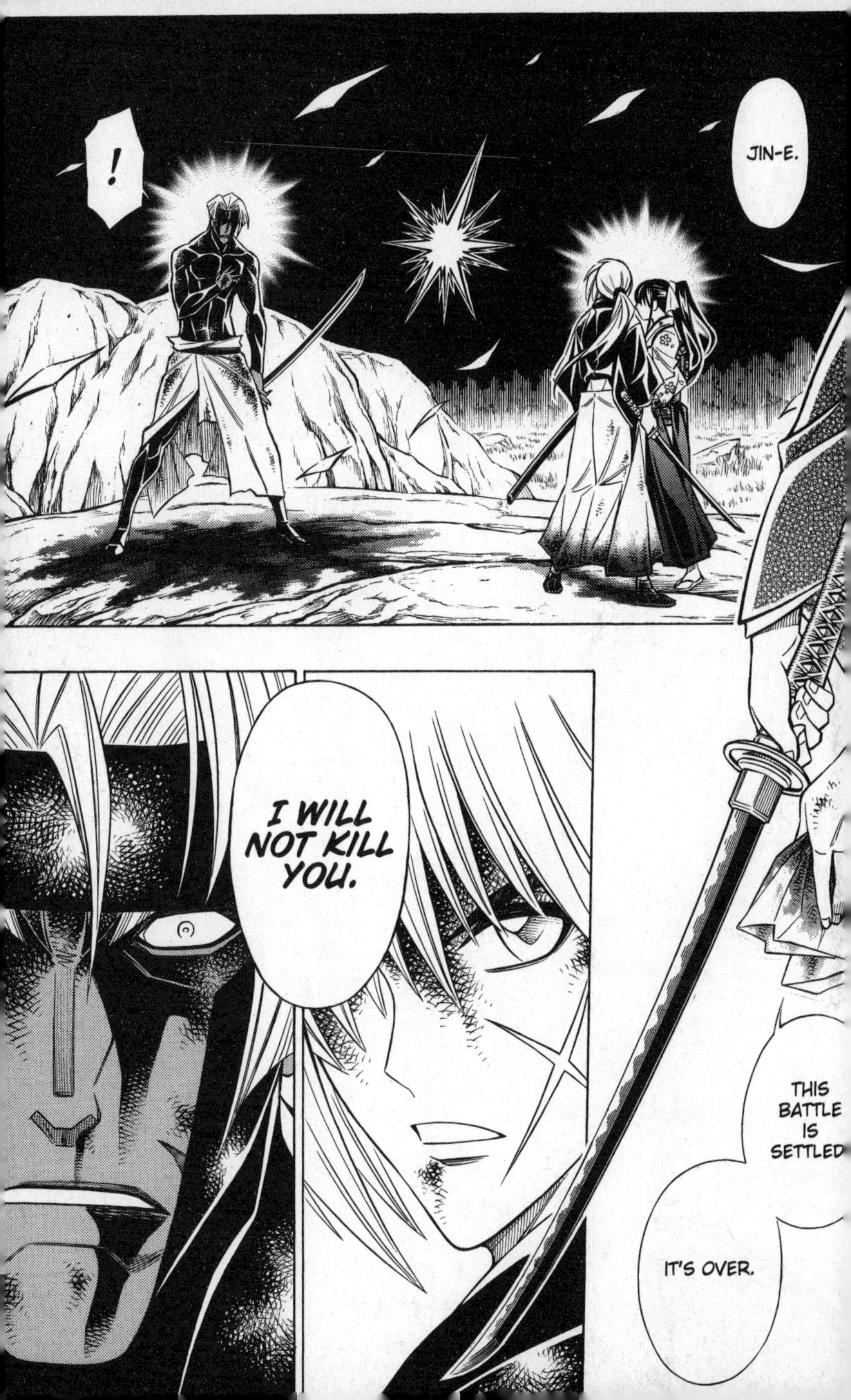
JIN-E.
!
THIS BATTLE IS SETTLED
IT'S OVER.
I WILL NOT KILL YOU.

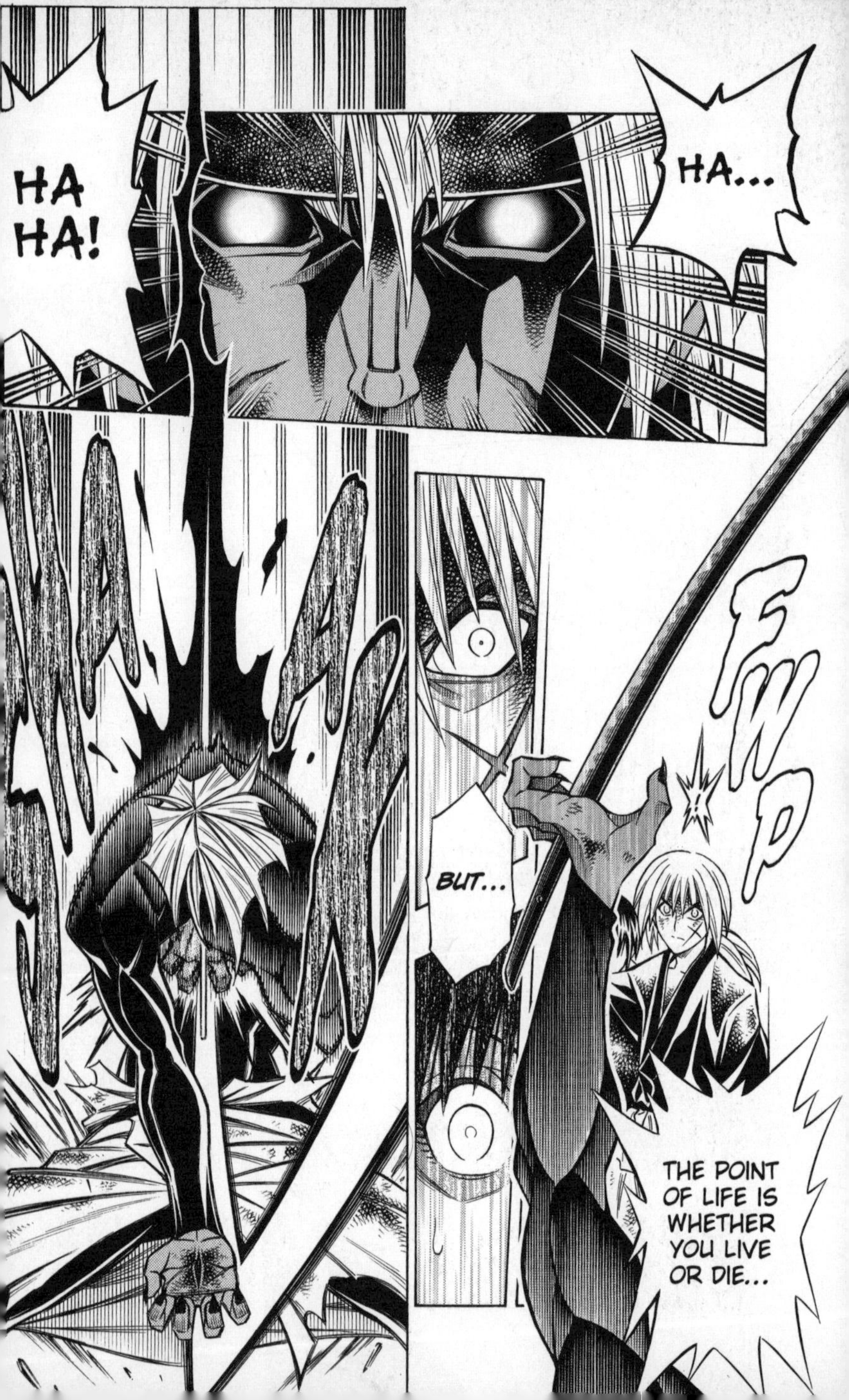
HA...
HA HA!
FWIP
THE POINT OF LIFE IS WHETHER YOU LIVE OR DIE...
BUT...

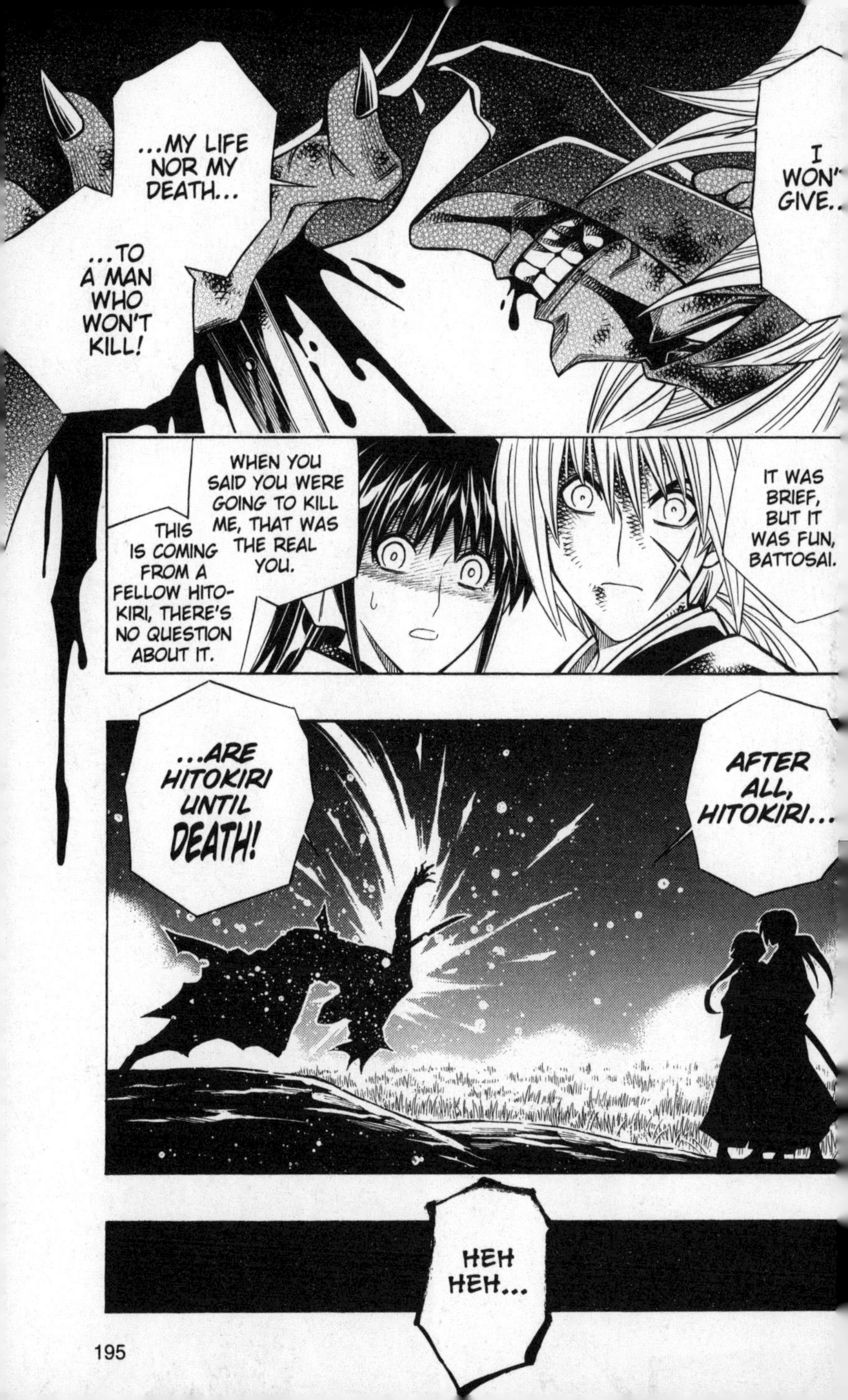
I WON' GIVE..
...MY LIFE NOR MY DEATH...
...TO A MAN WHO WON'T KILL!
IT WAS BRIEF, BUT IT WAS FUN, BATTOSAI.
WHEN YOU SAID YOU WERE GOING TO KILL ME, THAT WAS THE REAL YOU.
THIS IS COMING FROM A FELLOW HITO-KIRI, THERE'S NO QUESTION ABOUT IT.
AFTER ALL, HITOKIRI...
...ARE HITOKIRI UNTIL DEATH!
HEH HEH...

AFTER ALL,
HITOKIRI ARE
HITOKIRI UNTIL
DEATH...

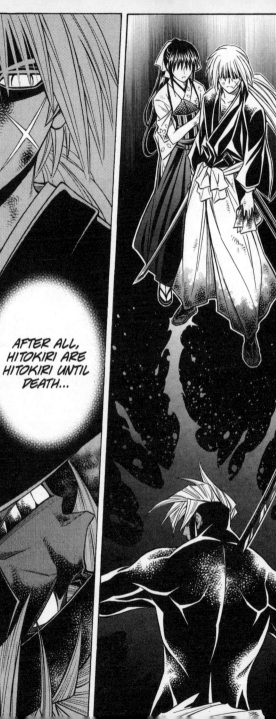

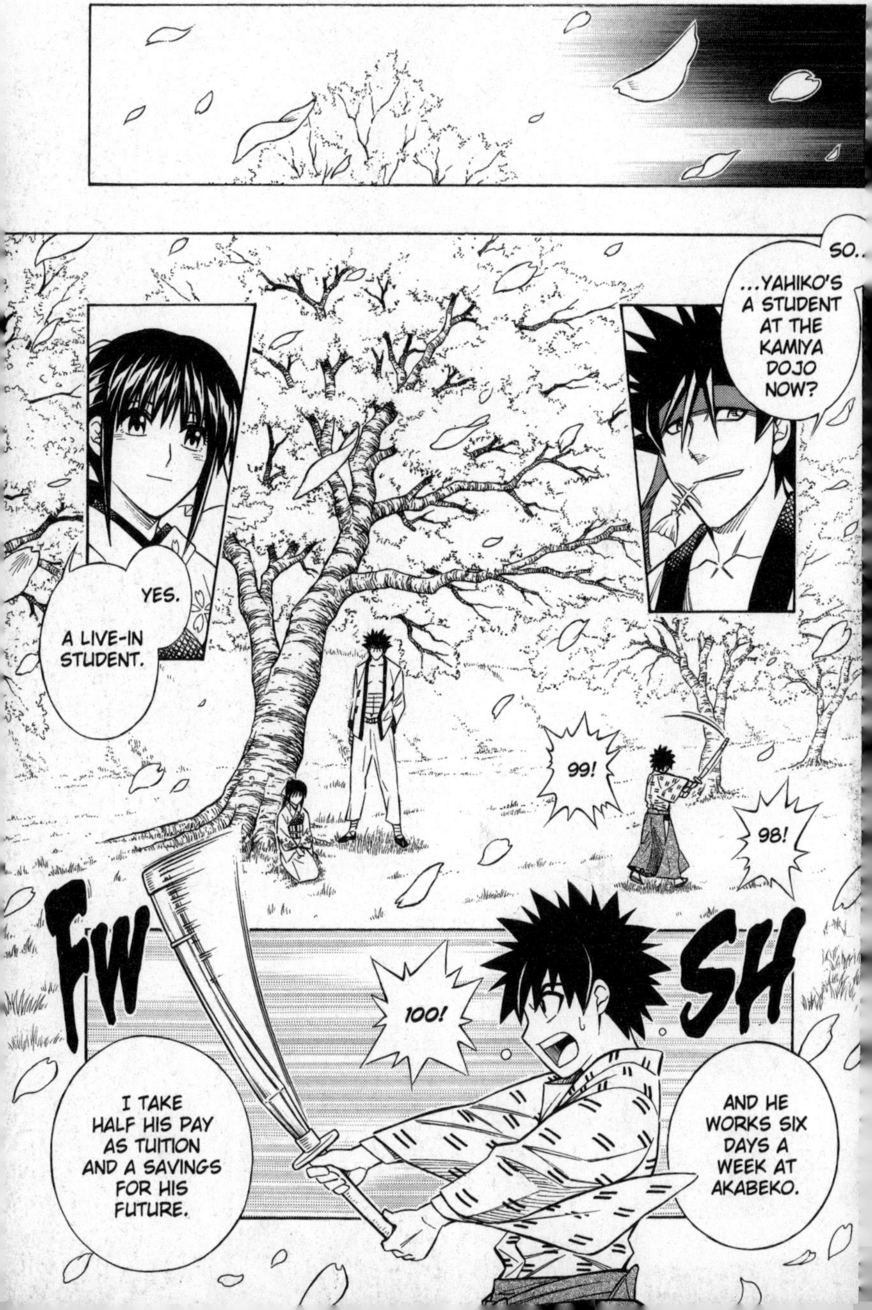

SO...
...YAHIKO'S A STUDENT AT THE KAMIYA DOJO NOW?
YES.
A LIVE-IN STUDENT.
98!
99!
FWSH
AND HE WORKS SIX DAYS A WEEK AT AKABEKO.
100!
I TAKE HALF HIS PAY AS TUITION AND A SAVINGS FOR HIS FUTURE.

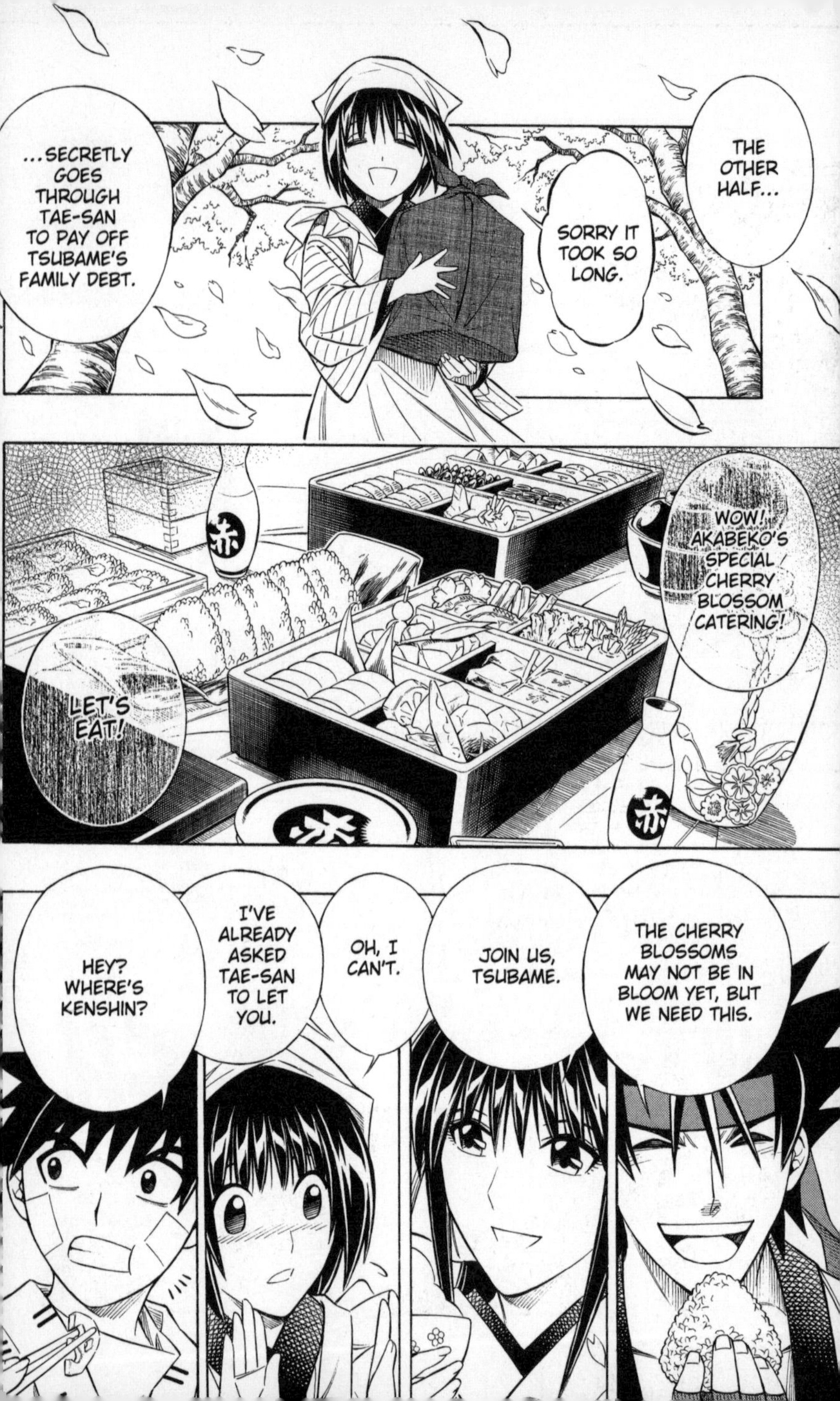
THE OTHER HALF...
SORRY IT TOOK SO LONG.
...SECRETLY GOES THROUGH TAE-SAN TO PAY OFF TSUBAME'S FAMILY DEBT.
WOW! AKABEKO'S SPECIAL CHERRY BLOSSOM CATERING!
LET'S EAT!
THE CHERRY BLOSSOMS MAY NOT BE IN BLOOM YET, BUT WE NEED THIS.
JOIN US, TSUBAME.
OH, I CAN'T.
I'VE ALREADY ASKED TAE-SAN TO LET YOU.
HEY? WHERE'S KENSHIN?

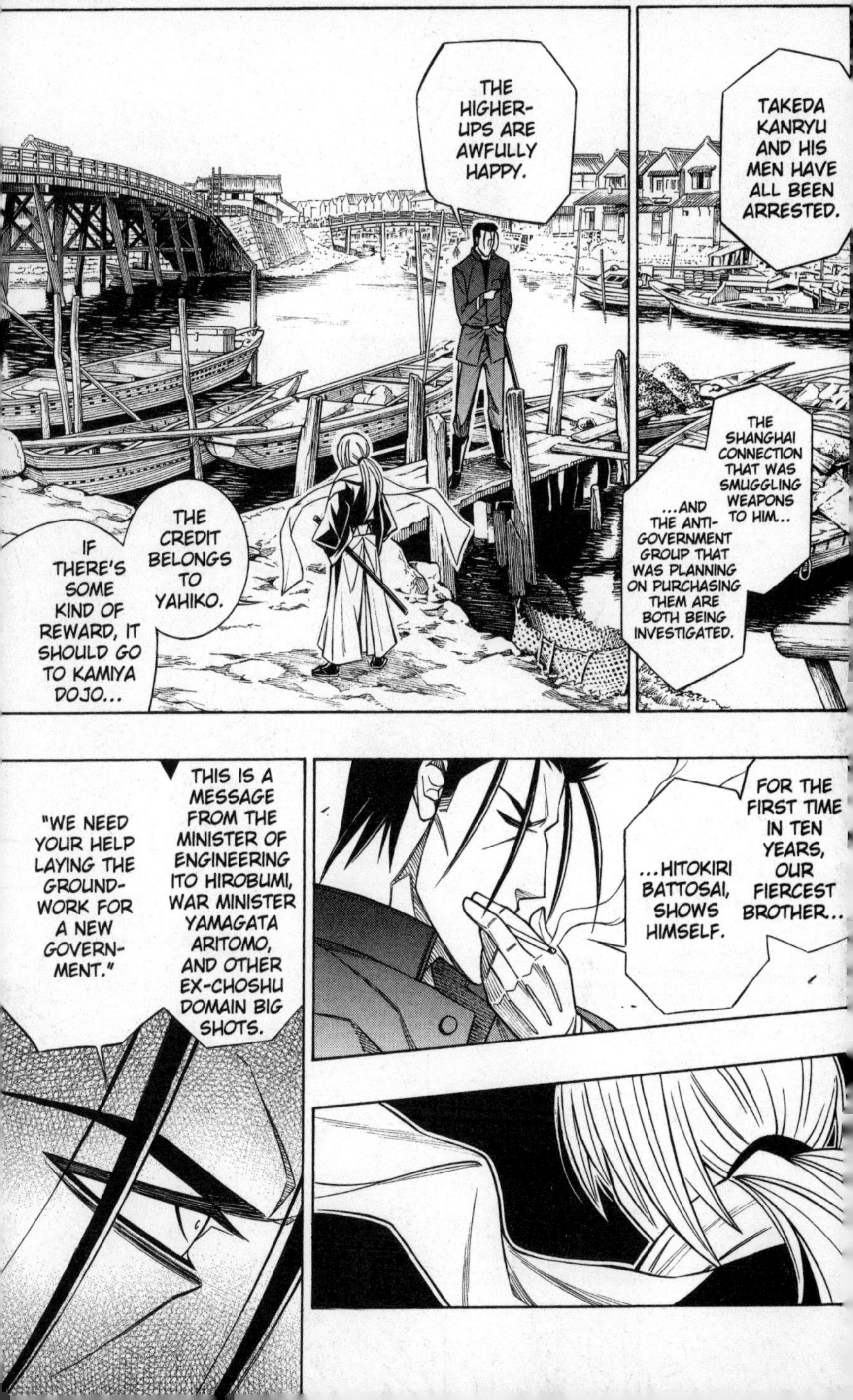
TAKEDA KANRYU AND HIS MEN HAVE ALL BEEN ARRESTED.
THE SHANGHAI CONNECTION THAT WAS SMUGGLING WEAPONS TO HIM...
...AND THE ANTI-GOVERNMENT GROUP THAT WAS PLANNING ON PURCHASING THEM ARE BOTH BEING INVESTIGATED.
THE HIGHER-UPS ARE AWFULLY HAPPY.
THE CREDIT BELONGS TO YAHIKO.
IF THERE'S SOME KIND OF REWARD, IT SHOULD GO TO KAMIYA DOJO...
FOR THE FIRST TIME IN TEN YEARS, OUR FIERCEST BROTHER...
...HITOKIRI BATTOSAI, SHOWS HIMSELF.
THIS IS A MESSAGE FROM THE MINISTER OF ENGINEERING ITO HIROBUMI, WAR MINISTER YAMAGATA ARITOMO, AND OTHER EX-CHOSHU DOMAIN BIG SHOTS.
"WE NEED YOUR HELP LAYING THE GROUNDWORK FOR A NEW GOVERNMENT."

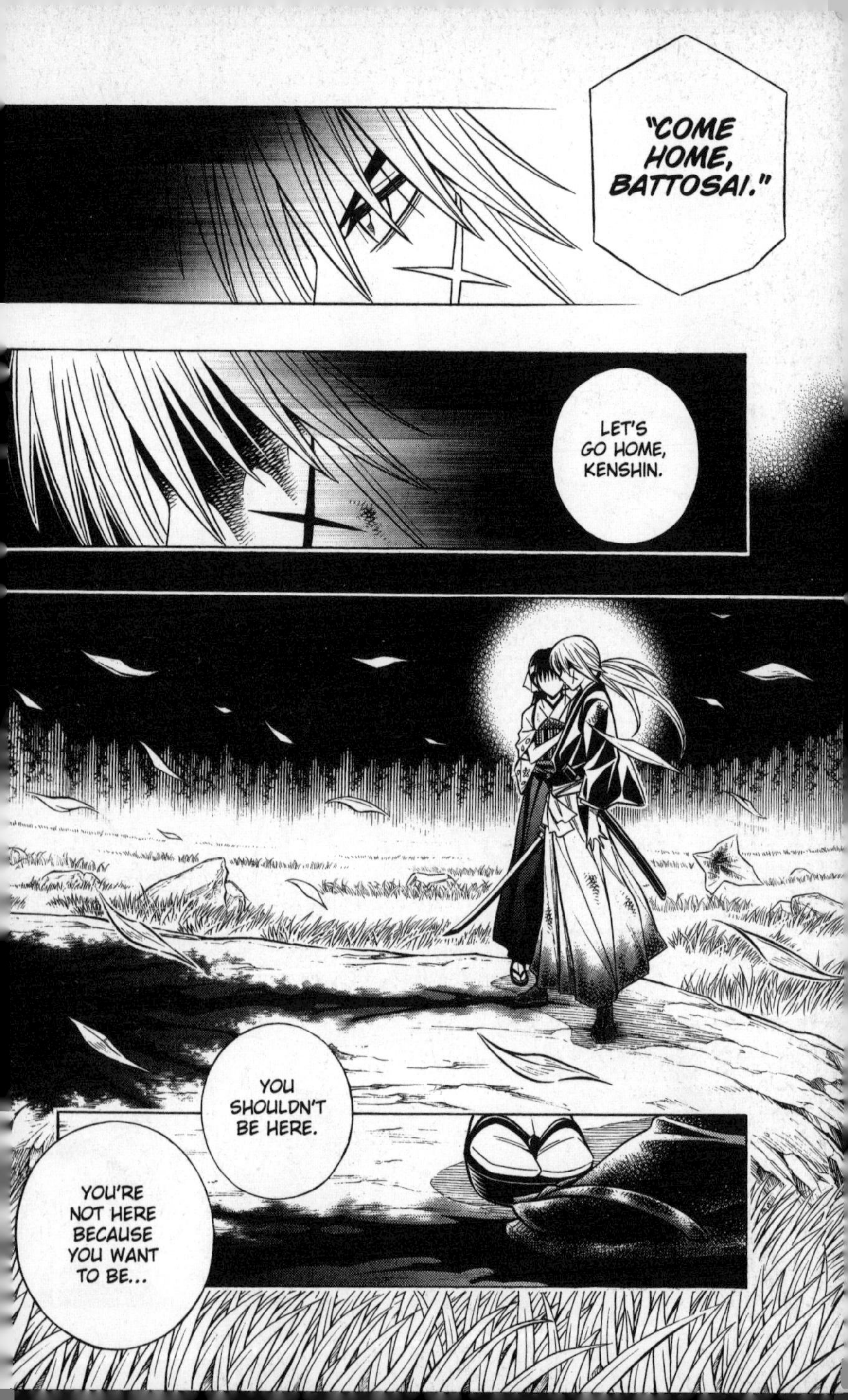
"COME HOME, BATTOSAI."
LET'S GO HOME, KENSHIN.
YOU SHOULDN'T BE HERE.
YOU'RE NOT HERE BECAUSE YOU WANT TO BE...

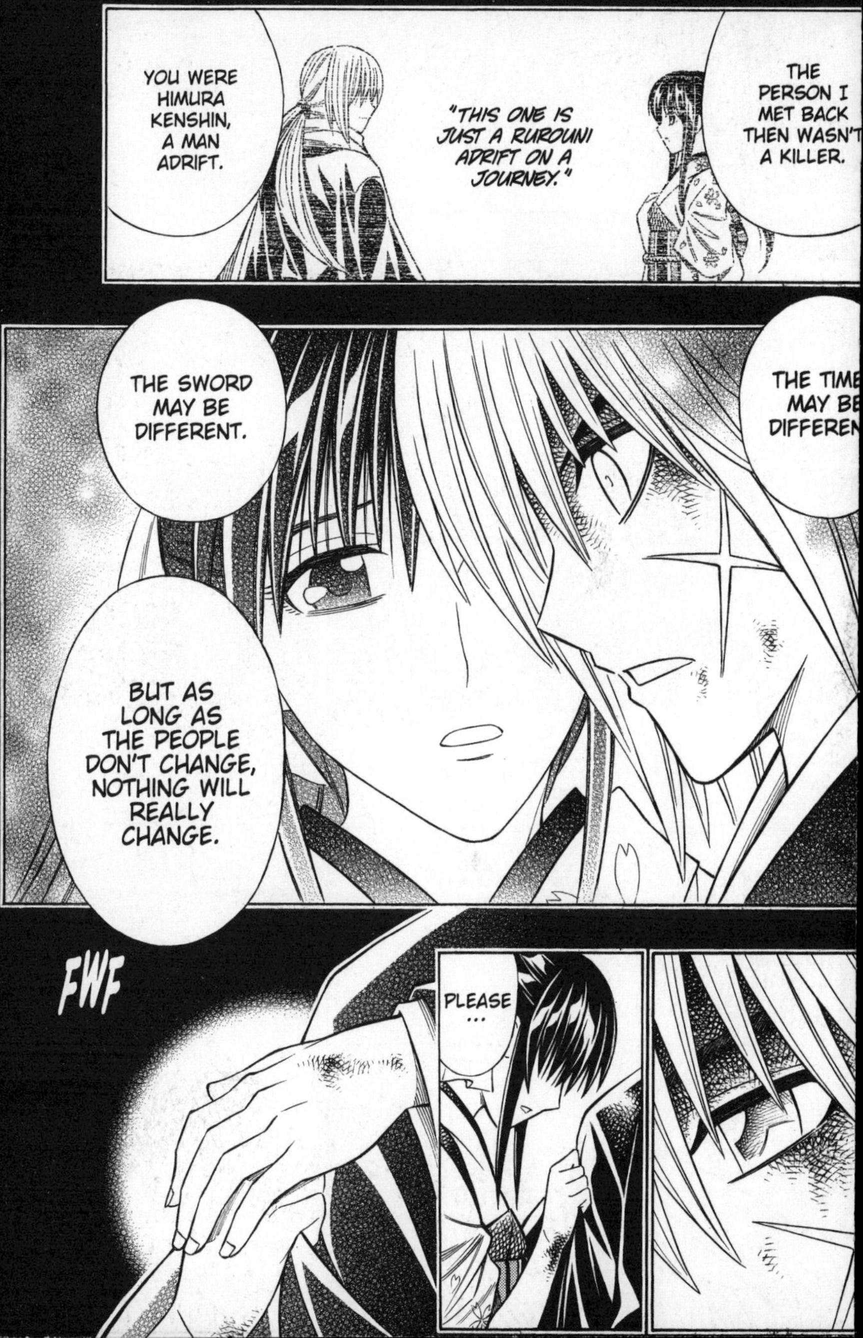
THE PERSON I MET BACK THEN WASN'T A KILLER.
"THIS ONE IS JUST A RUROUNI ADRIFT ON A JOURNEY."
YOU WERE HIMURA KENSHIN, A MAN ADRIFT.
THE TIME MAY BE DIFFEREN
THE SWORD MAY BE DIFFERENT.
BUT AS LONG AS THE PEOPLE DON'T CHANGE, NOTHING WILL REALLY CHANGE.
PLEASE ...
FWF

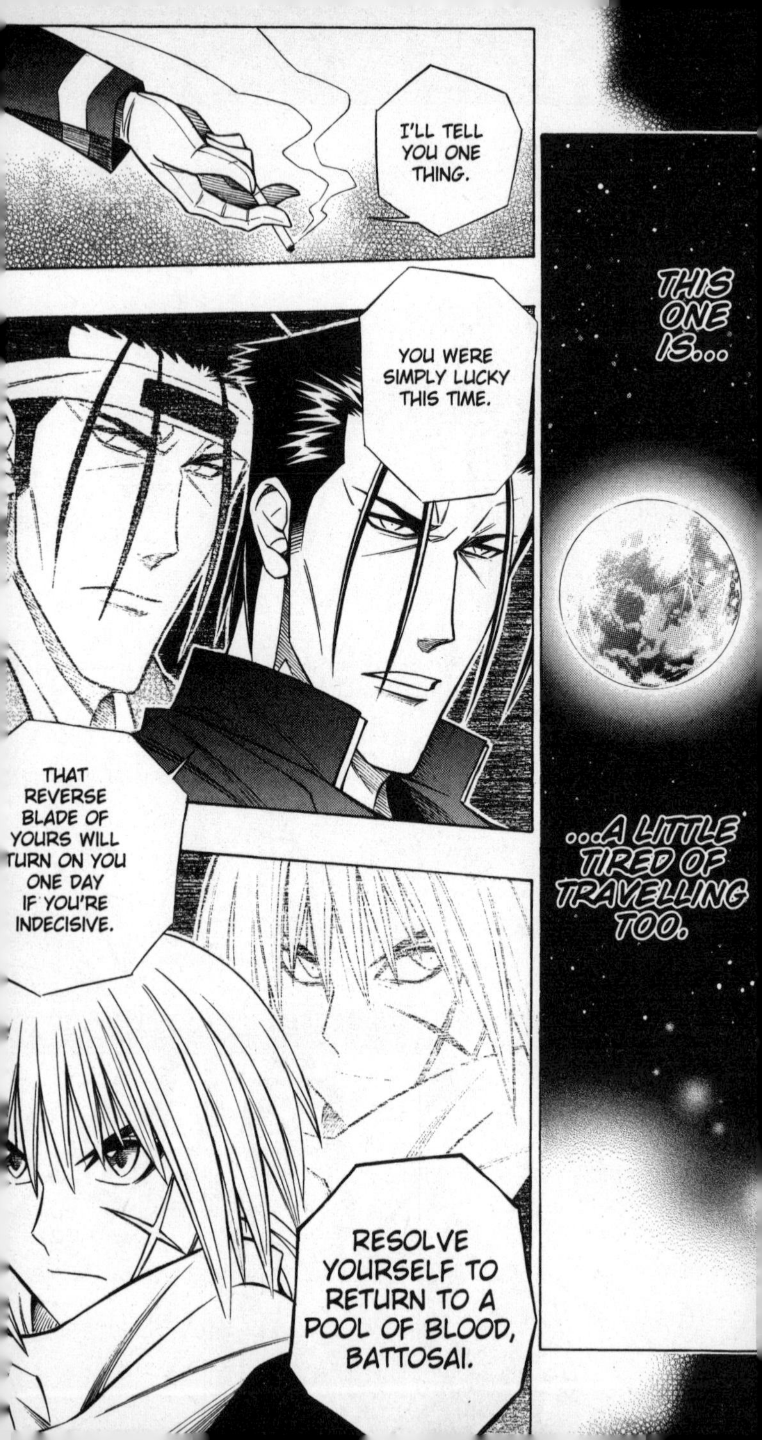
I'LL TELL YOU ONE THING.
YOU WERE SIMPLY LUCKY THIS TIME.
THAT REVERSE BLADE OF YOURS WILL TURN ON YOU ONE DAY IF YOU'RE INDECISIVE.
RESOLVE YOURSELF TO RETURN TO A POOL OF BLOOD, BATTOSAI.
THIS ONE IS...
...A LITTLE TIRED OF TRAVELLING TOO.

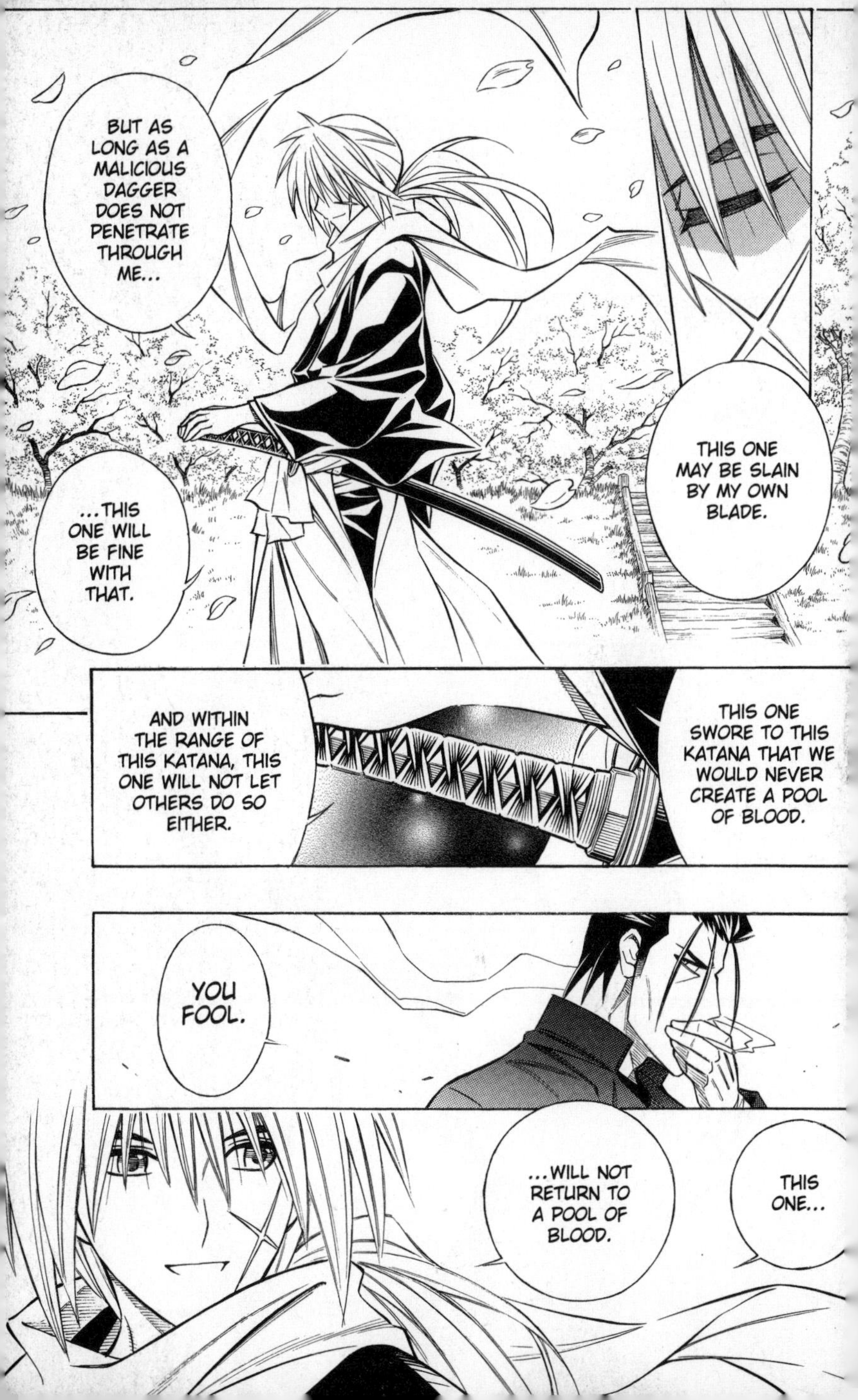
THIS ONE MAY BE SLAIN BY MY OWN BLADE.
BUT AS LONG AS A MALICIOUS DAGGER DOES NOT PENETRATE THROUGH ME...
...THIS ONE WILL BE FINE WITH THAT.
THIS ONE SWORE TO THIS KATANA THAT WE WOULD NEVER CREATE A POOL OF BLOOD.
AND WITHIN THE RANGE OF THIS KATANA, THIS ONE WILL NOT LET OTHERS DO SO EITHER.
YOU FOOL.
THIS ONE...
...WILL NOT RETURN TO A POOL OF BLOOD.

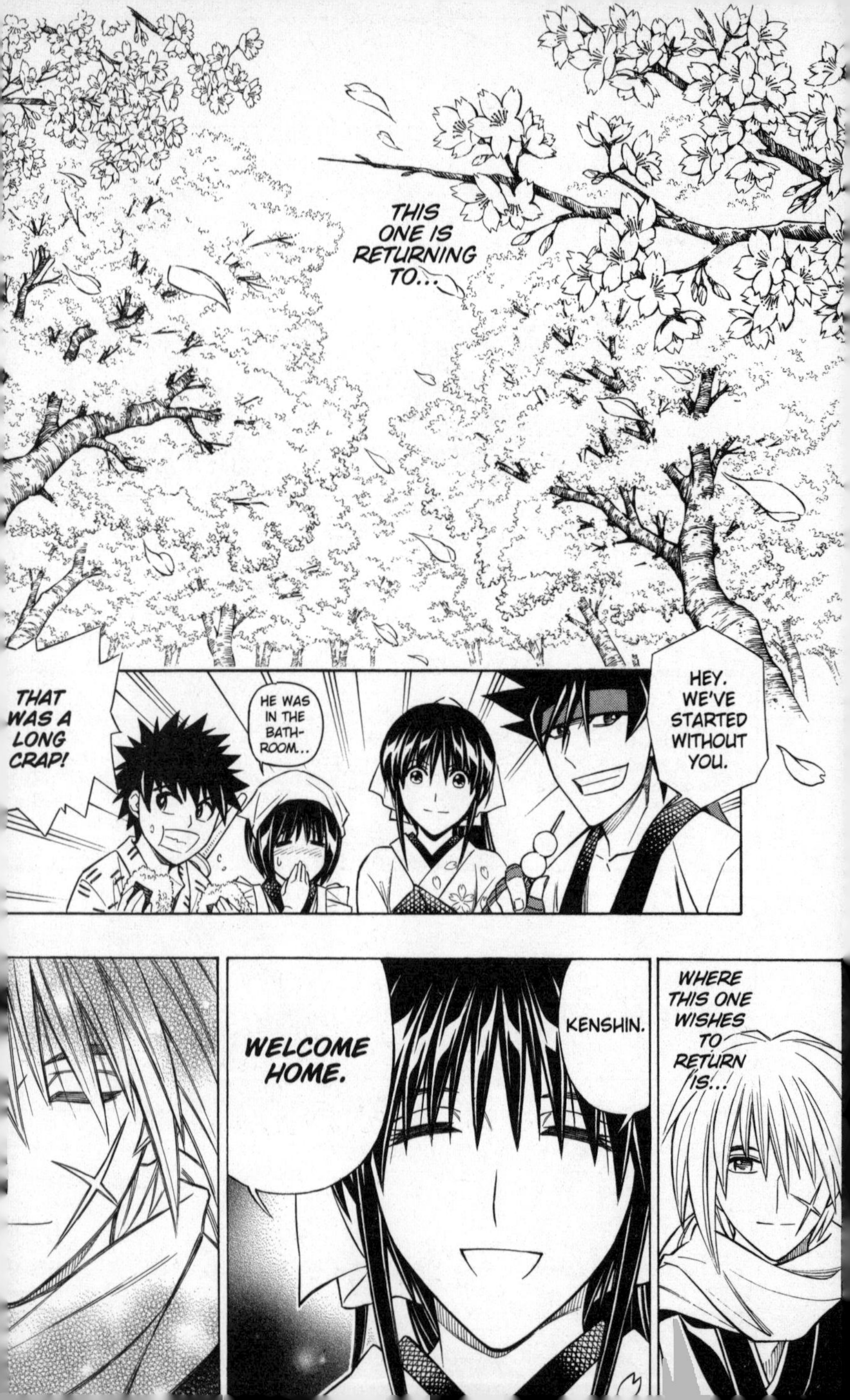
THIS ONE IS RETURNING TO...
HEY. WE'VE STARTED WITHOUT YOU.
HE WAS IN THE BATH-ROOM...
THAT WAS A LONG CRAP!
WHERE THIS ONE WISHES TO RETURN IS...
KENSHIN.
WELCOME HOME.

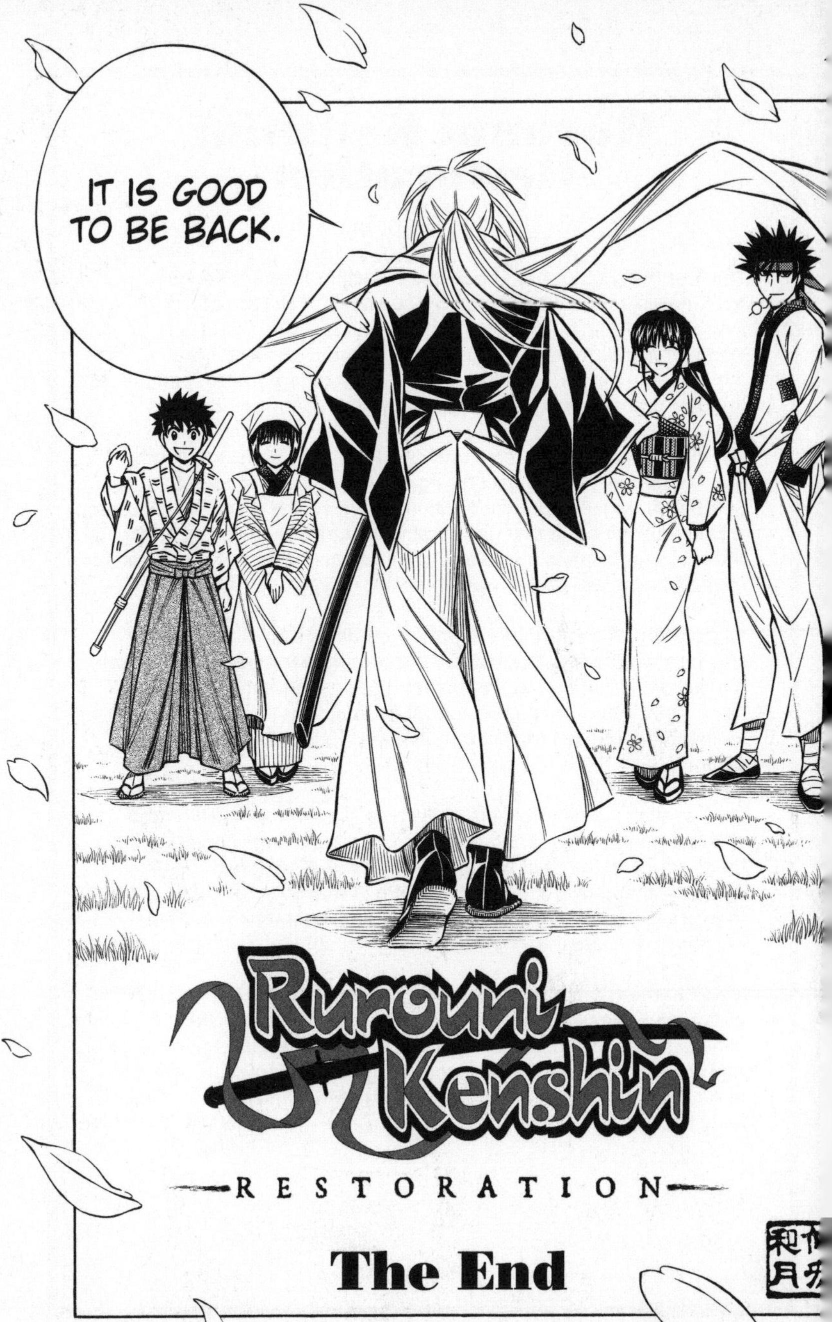
IT IS GOOD TO BE BACK.
Rurouni Kenshin
RESTORATION
The End

Rurouni Kenshin: Restoration

The first thing I thought about when starting *Rurouni Kenshin: Restoration* was what should I change besides the structure.

Writing a serial manga is like building a multi-layered three-dimensional puzzle. How do I put together differently shaped pieces to make it entertaining and worth reading every week or every month? It's an organic process, and even the author himself cannot envision its completed form until it's done. One-shots are similar to a flat puzzle. How to best fit together the pieces to turn a limited number of pages into an entertaining and worthy read. The process is like your left brain and right brain asking and answering Zen riddles to each other. If you don't have a clear vision of its completed form, it won't end up the way you want it.

Restoration was a monthly serial (three-dimensional puzzle), but since it's been built once before, the complete form was visible. In that sense, it's similar to a one-shot (flat puzzle) that can be seen from a bird's eye view. I had to first decide what to change and how to change it. I posed myself a challenge: "Express Kenshin's inner feelings."

Early in the original, Kenshin's role was like Komon in *Mito Komon* or Yoshimune in *Abarenbo Shogun*. The supporting characters built the drama and Kenshin was the hero who would defeat the villains. Drama = changes in the characters. So in that structure, it was easy to express the thoughts of the surrounding characters, but not Kenshin's. I decided to dig deeper into Kenshin for *Restoration*.

It was harder than I imagined once I started writing! The process of drawing it wasn't that difficult, but when I tried to make it entertaining, the story ended up getting gloomier due to Kenshin's regrets. I started getting worried during his conversation with Saito in Act 4 and figured it could be a repeat of the Jinchu Arc during his conversation with Kaoru on the bridge.

Honestly, that is when I gave up digging deeper into Kenshin's thoughts.

According to Kaoru Kurosaki, who was writing the novelization around the same time, "Kenshin was depicted more comically early in the original. There were noticeably more comedic elements than in *Buso Renkin*, which you intentionally tried to make comical. Maybe the comical side of Kenshin is a big part of his appeal."

That may be the case. I purposely made Act Zero comedic so it would be more accessible to first-time readers. Both myself and the editorial staff were surprised by how well it was received by readers and how high it ranked in reader surveys. We were told overseas readers wanted it translated as soon as possible. That really opened my eyes.

Honestly, Watsuki is not very good at writing jokes or comedy. I'm well aware that it's not in my arsenal as a manga artist. However, I don't give up on it or take it lightly, because contained in laughter are smiles and happiness, the greatest common denominators.

The opportunity to write two new versions of *Rurouni Kenshin* was truly a gift. Comparing them with the original made it clear to me "what I was writing," "what I am writing," and "what I want to write." The desire to write manga flowed out of me like lava.

I would like to thank the editorial staff, film crew, and mostly the readers who have continued to love *Kenshin* for the past 20 years for giving me such a great gift.

From my workplace in June 2013.

 Nobuhiro Watsuki

RUROUNI KENSHIN: RESTORATION VOL. 2

SHONEN JUMP Manga Edition

STORY AND ART BY
NOBUHIRO WATSUKI

Translation/Joe Yamazaki
Touch-up Art & Lettering/Steve Dutro
Design/Kam Li
Editor/Pancha Diaz

RUROUNI KENSHIN © 1994 by Nobuhiro Watsuki
All rights reserved.
First published in Japan in 1994 by SHUEISHA Inc., Tokyo.
English translation rights arranged by SHUEISHA Inc.

Printed in the U.S.A.

Published by VIZ Media, LLC
P.O. Box 77010
San Francisco, CA 94107

10 9 8 7 6 5 4 3 2 1
First printing, January 2014

www.viz.com

www.shonenjump.com